Reframing Visual Social Science

The burgeoning field of 'visual social science' is rooted in the idea that valid scientific insight into culture and society can be acquired by observing, analyzing and theorizing its visual manifestations: visible behavior of people and material products of culture. *Reframing Visual Social Science* provides a well-balanced, critical-constructive and systematic overview of existing and emerging modes of visual social and cultural research. The book includes integrated models and conceptual frameworks, analytical approaches to scrutinizing existing imagery and multimodal phenomena, a systematic presentation of more active ways and formats of visual scholarly production and communication, and a number of case studies which exemplify the broad fields of application. Finally, visual social research is situated within a wider perspective by addressing the issue of ethics; by presenting a generic approach to producing, selecting and using visual representations; and through discussing the specific challenges and opportunities of a 'more visual' social science.

Luc Pauwels is Professor of Visual Research Methods in the Faculty of Social Sciences (Department of Communication Studies) and Director of the Visual and Digital Cultures Research Center (ViDi) at the University of Antwerp.

Reframing Visual Social Science

Towards a More Visual Sociology and Anthropology

Luc Pauwels

CAMBRIDGE
UNIVERSITY PRESS

CAMBRIDGE
UNIVERSITY PRESS

University Printing House, Cambridge CB2 8BS, United Kingdom

Cambridge University Press is part of the University of Cambridge.

It furthers the University's mission by disseminating knowledge in the pursuit of education, learning and research at the highest international levels of excellence.

www.cambridge.org
Information on this title: www.cambridge.org/9781107008076

© Luc Pauwels 2015

First published 2015

A catalogue record for this publication is available from the British Library

ISBN 978-1-107-00807-6 Hardback

In memory of my father
(1926–1996)

Contents

List of figures   *page* ix

Part I Remodeling visual social science

1   Prologue and outline: (re)framing visual social science?   3

2   An integrated framework for conducting and assessing visual social research   16

Part II The visual researcher as collector and interpreter

3   Researching 'found' or 'pre-existing' visual materials   47

4   A visual and multimodal model for analyzing online environments   65

Part III The visual researcher as producer, facilitator and communicator

5   The mimetic mode: from exploratory to systematic visual data production   97

6   Visual elicitation techniques, respondent-generated image production and 'participatory' visual activism   117

7   The 'visual essay' as a scholarly format: art meets (social) science?   139

8   Social scientific filmmaking and multimedia production: key features and debates   167

Part IV Applications / case studies

9   Family photography as a social practice: from the analogue to the digital networked world   193

10   A visual study of corporate culture: the workplace as
       metaphor   220

11   Health communication in South Africa: a visual study
       of posters, billboards and grassroots media   236

Part V Visual research in a wider perspective

12   Ethics of visual research in the offline and online world   257

13   A meta-disciplinary framework for producing and
       assessing visual representations   280

14   Advancing visual research: pending issues and future
       directions   309

       Index   328

Figures

Cover photo, 'Life', © Luc Pauwels

In memoriam photograph, © Private collection
Luc Pauwels

2.1 Origin/production context, © Luc Pauwels   *page* 21
2.2 Referent/subject, © Luc Pauwels   23
2.3 Visual medium/technique, © Luc Pauwels   24
2.4 Analytical focus, © Luc Pauwels   27
2.5 Theoretical foundation, © Luc Pauwels   28
2.6 Visual competencies, © Luc Pauwels   30
2.7 Sampling issues and data production strategies,
    © Luc Pauwels   30
2.8 Controlling unintentional and intentional
    modifications, © Luc Pauwels   32
2.9 Degree of field involvement, © Luc Pauwels   33
2.10 Provision of necessary context, © Luc Pauwels   35
2.11 Ethical aspects, © Luc Pauwels   35
2.12 Output/presentational format, © Luc Pauwels   36
2.13 Status of the visual, © Luc Pauwels   37
2.14 Intended and secondary uses, © Luc Pauwels   38
2.15 An integrated framework for visual social research,
    © Luc Pauwels   39
3.1 Janard advertisement as published in a Belgian
    magazine, © Janard   58
4.1 Main phases of 'a multimodal framework for analyzing
    websites', © Luc Pauwels   75
4.2 A multimodal framework for analyzing websites, © Luc
    Pauwels   87
5.1 Southern Docks, Antwerp (undated/anonymous)   113
5.2 Southern Docks, Antwerp (April 2014), © Luc Pauwels   113
5.3 Billingsgate Fish Market, © Dawn Lyon   114
6.1 Wheelchair, © Kathleen Jaspers   122
6.2 Ramp and pole, © Kathleen Jaspers   122

6.3 Aagje 1, © Nathalie Claessens   126
6.4 Aagje 2, © Nathalie Claessens   126
6.5 Red Cloth, © Alina Dragan   131
6.6 Signage, © Alina Dragan   131
6.7 A basic taxonomy of participatory visual techniques,
     © Luc Pauwels   134
7.1 Home page of 'I Photograph to Remember',
     © Pedro Meyer   148
7.2 One of the inner pages of *The Burden of Existence*,
     © Marrie Bot   149
7.3 Eva's room, © Nannie Bronshoff   152
7.4 Zwier's room, © Nannie Bronshoff   152
7.5 Caressing Melissa's cheek, © Cathy Greenblat   154
7.6 Flower class, © Cathy Greenblat   155
7.7 Kevin and Carmella, © Cathy Greenblat   155
7.8 The Right Way, © Luc Pauwels   158
7.9 Cracked Window, © Luc Pauwels   159
7.10 Framing Race and Class, © Luc Pauwels   159
7.11 Upward Mobility, © Luc Pauwels   160
7.12 Urban Panopticon, © Luc Pauwels   160
7.13 Hitchcock Meets McDonald's, © Luc Pauwels   161
7.14 Uptown-Downtown, © Luc Pauwels   161
7.15 Heart of the Matter, © Luc Pauwels   162
7.16 Silent Metropolis, © Luc Pauwels   162
8.1 Still from *Tobelo Marriage*, © Asinoellah/Rioly   174
8.2 *Polka*: the Austrian's choice of framing, © Robert
     Boonzajer Flaes / Maarten Rens   179
8.3 *Polka*: the Chicano's preferred way of framing, © Robert
     Boonzajer Flaes / Maarten Rens   179
8.4 Still from *A Country Auction*, © Frances Cox   183
8.5 Screenshot from *Mise en images d'un rituel*, © Jean-Paul
     Terrenoire   185
8.6 Screenshot from *Mise en images d'un rituel*, © Jean-Paul
     Terrenoire   185
8.7 Screenshot from *Yanomamö Interactive*, © Peter Biella,
     Napoleon Chagnon and Gary Seaman   187
9.1 Soldiers in studio, private collection: Luc Pauwels   196
9.2 Promotional material from catalog, © Action Photo   196
9.3 Screenshot from web-based family album   198
9.4 Screenshot from web-based family album   199
9.5 Screenshot from web-based family album   203
9.6 Screenshot from web-based family album   204

9.7   Screenshot from web-based family album   206
9.8   Screenshot from web-based family album   207
9.9   Screenshot from web-based family album   208
9.10 Inherited and emerging functions of web-based family
      communications, © Luc Pauwels   209
9.11 Screenshot from web-based family album   213
9.12 Screenshot from web-based family album   214
9.13 Screenshot from web-based personal profile   216
10.1 Lobby and reception area 1, © Luc Pauwels   226
10.2 Lobby and reception area 2, © Luc Pauwels   226
10.3 Technical / drawing office, © Luc Pauwels   227
10.4 Chartering department 1, © Luc Pauwels   228
10.5 Chartering department 2, © Luc Pauwels   228
10.6 Purchasing Manager's office, © Luc Pauwels   229
10.7 Chartering department 3, © Luc Pauwels   230
10.8 Executive Secretary's Desk, © Luc Pauwels   231
10.9 Vice-President's office 1, © Luc Pauwels   232
10.10 Vice-President's office 2, © Luc Pauwels   232
10.11 President's office 1, © Luc Pauwels   233
10.12 President's office 2, © Luc Pauwels   234
10.13 Executive boardroom, © Luc Pauwels   235
11.1 'Tekens en Simptome' poster, © Department of Health,
      South Africa   239
11.2 'Patient-centered care' poster, © Department of Health,
      South Africa   241
11.3 'Prevent HIV/AIDS' poster, © Department of health,
      South Africa   243
11.4 Photo: 'AIDS Helpline' billboard, Bloemfontein, © Luc
      Pauwels   244
11.5 Bloemfontein's black township, © Luc Pauwels   245
11.6 Love Life billboard, Bloemfontein, © Luc Pauwels   245
11.7 'ABC of AIDS' billboard, Kingdom of Lesotho, © Luc
      Pauwels   246
11.8 Christian place of devotion, Kingdom of Lesotho, © Luc
      Pauwels   247
11.9 'AIDS does not forgive' billboard, Kingdom of Lesotho,
      © Luc Pauwels   247
11.10 Traditional healer's shack, Bloemfontein, © Luc
      Pauwels   247
11.11 AIDS-related 'grassroots' mural, © Luc Pauwels   248
11.12 South African funeral home, 'Now Open', © Luc
      Pauwels   249

11.13 Graveyard Bloemfontein, © Luc Pauwels   249
12.1 Emergency exit, © Luc Pauwels   258
13.1 Chess players, © Luc Pauwels   284
13.2 Microscopic image of dog parasite (source unknown)   284
13.3 X-ray image of elbow, © Private collection Luc Pauwels   284
13.4 Visualization of a Chopin Mazurka, © Martin
       Wattenberg   285
13.5 Histogram of average temperatures, © Luc Pauwels   286
13.6 Artist's impression of a 'black hole,' GNU Free
       Documentation License   287
13.7 Mind map (source unknown)   287
13.8 Mendeljev's periodic table of the elements (source
       unknown)   287
13.9 The divergent nature of the referent, © Luc Pauwels   288
13.10 Low-resolution flower (source unknown)   293
13.11 Brain scan (source unknown)   293
13.12 Photo of heron (source unknown)   294
13.13 Drawing of heron (source unknown)   294
13.14 Glass window drawing of heron (source unknown)   294
13.15 Determining aspects of the production and
       transformational processes, © Luc Pauwels   295
13.16 Line art drawing of porcupine (source unknown)   298
13.17 Line art drawing of porcupine, © Katherine Hocker   298
13.18 Inherited, medium-related and execution-specific
       characteristics, © Luc Pauwels   299
13.19 Representational status, context and use, © Luc Pauwels 303
13.20 A meta-disciplinary framework for producing and
       assessing visual representations, © Luc Pauwels   306
14.1 Key challenges and opportunities of visual social
       science, © Luc Pauwels   324

Part I

Remodeling visual social science

1   Prologue and outline: (re)framing visual social science?

1   Contours of a 'more visual' sociology and anthropology

While visual methods in sociology and anthropology today experience a growing number of supporters and active users, still many social scientists are completely unaware of their existence or unique research potential. 'Visual sociology' and 'visual anthropology,' the main venues where visual (production) methods and techniques tend to blossom, are grounded in the idea that valid scientific insight into society can be acquired by observing, analyzing and theorizing its visual manifestations: visible behavior of people and material products of culture. But a truly 'visual' social science also seeks to actively employ the visual and multi-modal in a broad sense to communicate its insights.

Visual social science today is not only about scrutinizing the visually observable aspects of society as a gateway to the deeper immaterial traits of culture, but also about using visual means to visualize the material, immaterial and conceptual for improved understanding. Therefore, visual social science is a study not just 'about' the visual, but also 'through' visuals and visualizations of a varied nature. More concretely, visual social research ranges from the study of existing visual data of a variety of sources ('found' visual materials) to the production of visual data – often photographs and film/video records, but also drawings – by the research team ('researcher-produced materials') or by the field ('respondent-generated production,' photovoice), and to using visual materials in interview situations to trigger partly unanticipated factual information and projective comments (visual elicitation, photo elicitation). The results of these methods and techniques can be presented in a variety of ways: conventional articles, with or without visual materials, up to fairly self-contained films or multimedia products (Pauwels, 2002, 2010). Obviously not all forms of visual research will – nor need to – result in a (partly) visual end product. Sometimes visual data collected or produced during a visual research project can indeed be transcribed and/ or summarized in numeric form or described in words.

The growing popularity of visual methods in the social sciences has given rise to a significant number of specialized social science journals: *Visual Studies* (formerly *Visual Sociology*), *Visual Anthropology* and *Visual Anthropology Review*, next to other well-established and highly regarded journals that originate from a broader humanities background, such as *Visual Communication* and the *Journal of Visual Culture*. Equally significant is the steady stream of dedicated handbooks (Ball and Smith, 1992; Chaplin, 1994; Pauwels, 1996; Emmison and Smith, 2000; Banks, 2001, 2007; Pink, 2001; Mitchell, 2011; Spencer, 2011; Harper, 2012), readers (Prosser, 2000; Grimshaw and Ravetz, 2004; Hamilton, 2007; Stanczac, 2007, Margolis and Pauwels, 2011), and a marked rise in membership of scholarly organizations devoted to the visual, for example the International Visual Sociology Association (IVSA), the Society for Visual Anthropology (SVA) of the American Anthropological Association, the Visual Sociology Working Group of the International Sociological Association (ISA), the Visual Communication Studies Division of the International Communication Association (ICA) and the International Visual Literacy Association (IVLA).

However, despite this increased interest in the visual domain, there is fairly little integration with respect to the findings and practices of visual methods, especially between the social sciences, the humanities and behavioral sciences. Visual methods seem to be reinvented over and over again without gaining much methodological depth and often without consideration of long-existing classics in the field (Mead and Bateson, 1985; Mead, 1963, 1975; Collier, [1967] 1986 with M. Collier; Hockings, [1975] 2003; Rouch, 1975; Heider, [1976] 2006; Curry and Clarke, [1977] 1983; Wagner, 1979; Becker, 1986; Ruby, 1986, 2000; De Heusch, 1988; MacDougall and Taylor, 1998). Often more effort seems to be expended in trying to 'appropriate' a burgeoning field – through renaming it, by relabeling its techniques, and by imposing particular theoretical perspectives and themes – rather than in developing a more cumulative and integrative stance. Yet it should be noted that, in fact, many of the early works of visual sociology and anthropology also paid relatively little attention to the development of a more explicit and systematic methodology for the collection, production, analysis and communication of visual aspects and insights. Nor did they seem to contribute very substantially to a more in-depth description and discussion of using the mimetic and expressive capabilities and intricacies of distinct visual media within a social science context. When reporting their research, visual scholars often tend to start with very general celebratory descriptions of the iconic and indexical powers of the visual and to then jump to the presentation of their found or self-produced visual data, without offering a detailed description of the many important intentionally or less deliberately made decisions in between. In a number of instances, it even remains unclear what the exact role or status of the visual materials is.

Visual sociology and visual anthropology tend to transcend the conventional subdivisions of the social sciences in that they are not confined to a particular theme or to any sector of societal activity (like law, sports, politics, medicine, urban context). Instead, they seek to take full advantage of a central sensory channel in our knowledge of the world – vision – and of evolving visual technologies to gather, process and communicate this knowledge. This involves a broader view of what constitutes social scientific 'data': not just easily quantifiable phenomena and verbal responses, but visual and multisensory inputs and responses as well. It also includes creatively rethinking the options to process and transfer data and insights into more advanced visual and multimodal ways.

This idea of a visual social science, which could complement and enrich sociology as a whole instead of just becoming yet another specialism, goes in fact back to Leonard Henny (1986), a seminal figure in the advent of the International Visual Sociology Association and the editor of its first journal (the *International Journal of Visual Sociology*). Henny indeed advocated a 'more visual' sociology instead of just more 'visual sociology,' and he also made an appeal to visual scholars to try to break out of their self-imposed ghetto (of isolated conferences and barely viable 'in-house' produced publications with restricted distribution).

Thus, the ultimate goal of a visual social science might lie beyond the (mere) ambition to become a well-established and legitimate way of doing social research, by striving to change social scientists' ways of looking at and thinking about society in a more profound way. In other words, visual methods and visual thinking could become an integral part of social science (education) per se, in its conceptualizing, capturing and dissemination of knowledge about human society.

2   About the title and themes

The slightly presumptuous title of this book *Reframing Visual Social Science* is more of a wake-up call for social scientists (oblivious to this field or locked in a narrow version of it), rather than yet another effort to (re)appropriate or (re)claim a territory. Given the wide application of visual methods in virtually all disciplines and fields of application, the chosen title also helps to shrink the vast territory somewhat and to develop a certain focus on visually researching social and cultural issues. Yet many of the discussed matters and approaches are applicable to the broader domain of the social sciences and the humanities and even to the – terribly misnomered – 'hard' or 'exact' sciences and life sciences. At the same time, it is recognition of the fact that visual sociology and visual anthropology represent rich traditions of visual research that tend to be forgotten in today's strive for novelty and first birth right.

Visual methods could also be reframed in the whole of social science methodology, not as an alien or quirky set of approaches, but as a legitimate and sometimes rather obvious series of options for doing social science research, for example when looking for more direct data of a holistic nature, when (material) context is important, when past events are only accessible via visual representation, or when field involvement and views of participants are sought. Without being too compulsive about the importance of visual aspects of society and visual methods to disclose them, and refraining from being too dismissive of established methods and techniques, it remains quite bewildering that social scientists put so much (and above all) almost exclusive efforts and belief in verbalized or reported behavior and opinions via surveys and interviews. They (and even more so the mass media when reporting about bizarre, juicy or unexpected findings) continue to confuse perceptions, reported views and recalled behavior with social realities, when much of social life is expressed and materialized in observable behavior and artifacts. In fact, much social research is very *indirect* in its interrogation of the social world, asking people to tick or fill in predefined answering categories or focusing on the emic perspective alone (what the respondents 'say' in a particular situation, not what they actually do in a real-life situation). Validity is often sacrificed to representativity, for which statistics then offer a false sense of security and reassurance.

The term 'reframing' also serves to highlight the explicit attention that is given to newer strands of visual research and to broadening its scope to include activities and themes which are being explored by other (sub) fields of enquiry: media and expressive modes other than film and photography, new technologies, more visually expressive forms of science, science practices, visual competency, science communications and so on. Visual social science, after a period characterized by a strong focus on photography as a data source and as a research tool, indeed began to develop an interest in other representational techniques (as data sources and data production tools) and in other referents (other than visible material culture and human behavior). So today this includes the more conceptual visual practices of sociology as a field of study (charts, maps, models, simulations) as well the great variety of visual practices and traditions of other sciences. This extension brings visual social science into closer contact with such fields as sociology of science, science and technology studies, and information design. It is important to recognize the contributions of other (visual) fields, while acknowledging the unique contributions of sociology and anthropology with regard to data *production* methods (as opposed to the development of visual theory and methods of image analysis, which have blossomed in other disciplines such as visual communication, linguistics, art history, etc.).

Finally, the term 'reframing' in the title of the book also refers to the explicit and specific emphasis that lies upon developing a more systematic and analytical approach to visual research practices and ideas. This explicit intention becomes most apparent in the different typological attempts (e.g., of types and modes of research as exemplified through the way the chapters have been structured), models or frameworks (Chapters 2, 4 and 13), and tables summarizing analytic distinctions (Chapters 6 and 9). Such categorical frameworks and distinctions may prove vulnerable to occasional rebuff as some may consider them too restrictive or failing to take into account other important dimensions of the matter at hand. Yet, they are not positioned as complete and definite statements on the current state of things in visual research, but merely as 'proposals' – or 'work in progress' – that hopefully may offer some guidance to scholars in need of it. In addition, it is hoped that a more analytical approach may generate further constructive discussion, aiming to gradually develop a more solid methodology for visual research.

Above all, this work aims to provide a balanced, critical-constructive and systematic overview of existing and emerging forms of visual research into society and culture, in a manner that is both respectful to its rich traditions and forward looking (new technologies, multisensory and multimodal research, modes of visual expression, information visualization). The book is not a loose collection of articles in which visual methods are being applied to various research fields, but an effort to more systematically address the different options, their issues and consequences of the visual study of society and culture. A monographic account may be better suited to perform this task than a collection of loosely related articles written from a variety of perspectives. However, this work will not venture to describe the advent and development of visual social science from a historical perspective by pointing out the key figures and key events. One could write histories of important institutions in the field like the IVSA or the SVA or study its influential outlets (journals and conferences), but this will never yield a complete picture of what visual approaches in the study of society and culture really encompass, how they evolved, or what or who influenced exactly what or who and in what way. Visual approaches are not limited to any one discipline, nor to geographic location, and so discipline-centric or nation-centric historical accounts of visual research provide at best a very partial picture of a much broader domain.

Some key themes will run across the different chapters. First of all, ample attention will go to *visual aesthetics*, a somewhat neglected but crucial aspect of visual communication, which tends to generate much misunderstanding. The formal characteristics of images indeed serve as prime but subtle vehicles of meaning. For, in addition to the information that can be directly derived from the depicted subject matter of (the 'what') as a record of what was before the camera (or before the drafts-man), the aesthetic choices made during the image production (the 'how') are an extra source of information about the makers and their culture. But the formal qualities of the image and the many post-production options, when used with deliberation and skill, also provide the researcher with an exciting set of opportunities to visually express that which cannot be put in words or numbers. Obviously this requires specific visual competencies to detect this layer of meaning in existing materials and even more advanced competencies to actively use these expressive means to construct a scholarly argument. Visual social science indeed involves trying to make the most of both the reproductive capabilities ('mimesis') and the predicative capabilities ('expression') of visual media and technologies.

As visual social science has always entertained an intricate relation with *technology* (and 'technology as culture') this is not surprisingly a second recurring topic of this book. But since technology is an integral part of most practices of data gathering, processing and presentation, it is not dealt with in a separate chapter but is a staple feature of most chapters in one way or another. Online culture and Web technologies in particular receive special attention from different angles: as research opportunities (data source and tools) and as important societal evolutions that pose particular challenges of an ethical, social and political nature.

3   Contents at a glance

The chapters in this book are grouped into five parts, offering consecutively:
1. a structured introduction to the field, which serves as the central framework of this work;
2. analytical approaches to analyzing existing imagery and multimodal phenomena in offline and online contexts;
3. a systematic presentation of more active ways and formats of visual scholarly production;
4. a collection of case studies involving visual social science approaches and visual analysis;

5. an effort to situate visual social research within a wider perspective by covering the issue of ethics, by offering a generic approach to producing, selecting and using visual representations, and through a concluding discussion of the current challenges and opportunities of visual social science.

Part I • *Remodeling visual social science*

Following the current Chapter 1, 'Prologue and outline,' Chapter 2, 'An integrated framework for conducting and assessing visual social research', immediately addresses the issue that visual research remains a rather dispersed and ill-defined domain within the social sciences, by proposing and systematically discussing an encompassing and refined analytical framework for visual methods of research. This 'integrated framework' tries to account for the great variety within each of the currently discerned types or methods, by moving in a very analytical way beyond the more or less arbitrary and often very hybridly defined modes and techniques, with a clear focus on what connects or transcends them. This chapter seeks to provide the backbone for most of the following chapters, which then further develop and illustrate the different modes, options and issues of visual research in the social sciences in a more elaborate way. While the framework serves as a signpost or roadmap for what is to follow, it needs to cover much ground in a rather condensed manner. Therefore, it might be advisable to revisit the framework when all the chapters have been read, to help draw all the pieces together.

Part II • *The visual researcher as collector and interpreter*

Chapter 3, 'Researching "found" or "pre-existing" visual materials,' then starts out with a form of visual research that does not involve primary data production but careful selection and analysis of previously existing visual materials as an entry to studying aspects of society. This chapter draws attention to the unique potential of this extremely rich and varied data source, which allows us to move back in time and to encounter cultures without leaving home. However, it also points out the specific intricacies of using visuals that have been produced outside a controlled research environment or for some unknown purpose. After conferring some key features of social scientific image analysis, the chapter very briefly discusses some of the characteristics of the prevalent theoretical and analytical frameworks for examining images and pleads for a better integration of these approaches. Moreover, these frameworks frequently tend to offer few methodological directions and in addition they often prove ill-equipped to disclose the complex layers of meaning (content, form, context) of visual artifacts from distinct visual media.

Chapter 4, 'A visual and multimodal model for analyzing online environments,' moves the research agenda to the Internet as a very timely field of enquiry. Departing from a broad conceptualization of culture and the need for a more adapted and sophisticated tool to disclose the Internet as a rich cultural data source, this chapter provides the foundations of a 'multimodal framework for analyzing websites,' from both a medium-specific and socio-cultural perspective. The six-phased framework contains a structured repository of potential cultural signifiers and a methodology for moving from salient aspects to more implicit meanings. While the framework may help researchers to make more and better use of the many layers of potential meaning that reside in the rich multimodal nature of websites, it does not provide a shortcut to determine the cultural meaning of these signifiers and their interrelated effects.

Part III • The visual researcher as producer, facilitator and communicator

Chapter 5, 'The mimetic mode: from exploratory to more systematic visual data production,' introduces well-established and varied ways to study society through forms of researcher-produced visual materials that typically seeks to exploit the reproductive (mimetic) qualities of the camera (while 'controlling' or downplaying its expressive capabilities). Such visual data production may vary from more exploratory recordings of events and artifacts as they are being encountered, right through to rigid sampling and scripted set-ups with a view to testing hypotheses. This chapter pays special attention to two related but distinct visual data production techniques that explicitly focus on sequentially researching social change and cultural expressions as they develop over time in a particular physical or cultural space: interval and time-lapse photography. While recognizing the important research potential of these mimetic recording techniques, the chapter critically examines the status of these products (as both partial reproductions and inevitably expressive constructions).

Chapter 6, 'Visual elicitation techniques, respondent-generated image production and "participatory" visual activism,' presents yet another source of (visual) data production. In addition to studying existing images or producing visuals themselves, visual scholars indeed may try to offer the research subjects a more active role in the production of visual data.

This chapter focuses on the wide variety of approaches currently presented under the umbrella of 'participatory' or 'collaborative' visual techniques. But rather than the customary celebratory and somewhat nebulous treatment of these promising methodologies, this chapter provides a critical-constructive view on their extensive ethical and epistemological potential as well as on their many unresolved issues. This chapter aims to clarify the specific strengths and weaknesses of the many different and similar, but differently labeled, options in 'respondent-generated image production' and other forms of 'participatory research' (e.g., photovoice, photo novella, community video, auto-driven photo elicitation) as well as interrogate their underlying goals and largely undisclosed assumptions.

Chapter 7, 'The "visual essay" as a scholarly format: art meets (social) science?,' discusses and exemplifies more visual and expressive ways of constructing and presenting sociological insight. It seeks to articulate the specific demands, traits and potentials of the 'visual essay' as a societal and sociological practice and format. In particular, it provides some observations, propositions and arguments that may further help to clarify what the visual sociological essay, as an unorthodox scholarly product, might entail and what place it should acquire in the broader scholarly discourse. This theoretical discussion is complemented with excerpts from concrete visual essays of both scholarly and non-scholarly origin. These examples help to explain some of the basic strengths of this format, which tries to play out the synergy of distinct, but combined, forms of expression: images, words, layout and design, adding up to a scientifically informed statement.

Chapter 8, 'Social scientific filmmaking and multimedia production: key features and debates,' offers a critical overview of the development and deployment of film in the scientific endeavors of social and cultural scientists. It addresses some of the key issues involved in the use of a rich medium such as film to document, analyze and communicate society and culture. While the extent to which filmic means should be applied is still a matter of concern, it is gradually being recognized that a more expressive approach is not only unavoidable, but also much more productive, if it goes hand in hand with a clear and duly communicated sense of purpose. The fact that film creates opportunities for the field to 'talk back' and be actively involved is increasingly recognized and indeed it is increasingly explored in practice, as this approach often yields unique and richer data. Finally, this chapter discusses 'reflexivity': the growing awareness among scientific filmmakers of the far-reaching consequences of their role, as humans who are studying other humans from different cultures.

Part IV • Applications / case studies

Chapter 9, 'Family photography as a social practice: from the analo-gue to the digital networked world,' as the first of three 'applied research' chapters, examines whether the shift from album-based private photography to the semi-public space of the Internet, which is unfolding in dialogue with ever-changing technologies, has rein-forced, expanded or radically changed the nature of family commu-nications and the very significant social and cultural functions this highly codified practice has fulfilled from the onset. From an explora-tory research study into online family websites (so a combination of 'found' imagery and texts), the chapter discusses examples, which illustrate the similarities and changes taking place, the possible cultural-propagandistic and emancipatory effects, and the wealth of cultural information that can be decoded. Also covered are the meth-odological aspects and implications of decoding these new and very vivid exponents of culture.

Chapter 10, 'A visual study of corporate culture: the workplace as metaphor,' provides an example of the 'mimetic mode' in visual research, as a systematic and standardized approach to record aspects of material culture and human behavior. It demonstrates how corpora-tions – and in this case a Norwegian multinational – visually commu-nicate their values and norms through the deliberate and/or less conscious construction of the material environment, which often seems to have a symbolic and metaphoric rather than a practical func-tion. Significant information about aspects of a corporation's culture, which otherwise often remain intangible or inaccessible, can be obtained by systematically studying these cultural products and other material traces.

Chapter 11, 'Health communication in South Africa: a visual study of posters, billboards and grassroots media,' combines different approaches of visual research: it uses 'found images,' researcher-produced images and at the end a 'visual essay' approach. This study examines TB- and HIV/AIDS-related health promotion materials cur-rently in use in the Free State (South Africa) and in the Kingdom of Lesotho. First, attention is paid to the cultural implications of employing divergent visual and verbal design elements in a health message. Next, a number of health promotion posters are analyzed on the basis of research findings and principles of message design in a multicultural context. Finally, a 'visual essay' approach is taken to comment on roadside media – billboards and alternative media – encountered in the Free State and Lesotho.

Part V • *Visual research in a wider perspective*

Chapter 12, 'Ethics of visual research in the offline and online world,' discusses ethical issues and dilemmas specific to visual research. It elucidates how visual researchers and research approval committees struggle with these issues in practice, to best protect the researched without introducing double standards or hindering visual research entirely. The chapter first deals with issues particularly relevant to ethics of visual research: the question of anonymity and privacy expectations in different contexts of society, the concept of harm to subjects, and the nature and methods of acquiring consent. It then considers ethics in an online environment, the unusual and emerging phenomena of ethics in society and in the academic world, to conclude with a number of suggestions on how best to develop ethical approaches for visual research.

Chapter 13, 'A meta-disciplinary framework for producing and assessing visual representations,' intends to broaden the scope of visual social science to the study of imaging and visualization techniques and issues in processes of knowledge building and dissemination at large. It contributes to a more systematic and fine-grained understanding of the complex processes and decisions that go into producing and using visual representations as prime vehicles of knowledge building and dissemination. To that aim, the chapter gradually develops an integrated conceptual model for disclosing the vast array of interrelated aspects in visual representational practices that affect the appearance and the uses that can be made of their end products. In developing the model, explicit attention is paid to the diverse nature of referents, the complex interplay across various types of 'transformational processes,' the imminent ambiguities and growing hybridity of visual representational methods and techniques, and the functions, which the visual end products need to serve.

Chapter 14, 'Advancing visual research: pending issues and future directions,' by way of conclusion, discusses some key issues that continue to challenge visual research (and 'visual studies' in a broader sense) as a practice. These issues – which can be turned into opportunities for advancement when dealt with appropriately – include the need to develop more specific and more integrated visual competencies to adequately deal with different aspects of the visual (mimetic and expressive properties), visual media types and languages, and the multimodal interplay of expressive systems (visual and non-visual); the need to gain more control over the whole process of meaning-making and to develop optimal working relations with other visual professionals; the need for a further theoretical and methodological grounding of visual enquiry, including the customization of existing frameworks; the broadening of the field in terms of referents, media and types of representation; the pivotal but complex role of visual technology in addressing different research opportunities and particularly in developing a more expressive and proficient visual scientific language; the need to continue to entertain an open and critical view on the different possibilities and approaches of visual research; and the need to deal more adequately with a number of external forces that continue to limit the execution and dissemination of visual research.

For the visual part of this book, I used predominantly my own pictures and those of students who have taken my visual sociology and anthropology or visual cultures class over the past decades. This was done in part to avoid copyright issues, but also because I am obviously more aware of the exact production contexts and intentions of these visual materials. In addition, using students' work is a tribute to their excellent efforts which otherwise probably would remain unseen.

4   References

Ball, M. and G. Smith (1992) *Analyzing Visual Data*. Newbury Park, CA/ London/New Delhi: Sage.

Banks, M. (2001) *Visual Methods in Social Research*. London: Sage.

Banks, M. (2007) *Using Visual Data in Qualitative Research*. Los Angeles: Sage.

Becker, H. S. (1986) *Doing Things Together: Selected Papers*. Evanston, IL: Northwestern University Press.

Chaplin, E. (1994) *Sociology and Visual Representation*. London: Routledge.

Collier, J. (1967) *Visual Anthropology: Photography as a Research Method*. New York/London: Holt, Rinehart and Winston. Revised and expanded edition with M. Collier (1986), Albuquerque: University of New Mexico Press.

Curry, T. and A. Clarke (1983) [1977] *Introducing Visual Sociology*. 2nd edn. Dubuque, IA: Kendall/Hunt.

De Heusch, L. (1988) 'The Cinema and Social Science: A Survey of Ethnographic and Sociological Films.' *Visual Anthropology* 1: 99–156.

Emmison, M. and P. Smith (2000) *Researching the Visual: Images, Objects, Contexts and Interactions in Social and Cultural Inquiry*. London/Thousand Oaks, CA/New Delhi: Sage.

Grimshaw, A. and A. Ravetz (eds.) (2004) *Visualizing Anthropology: Experimenting with Image-Based Ethnography*. Bristol: Intellect Books.

Hamilton, P. (ed.) (2007) *Visual Research Methods*. London: Sage.

Harper, D. (2012) *Visual Sociology*. New York: Routledge.

Heider, K. (2006) [1976] *Ethnographic Film*, revised edn. Austin: University of Texas Press.

Henny, L. (1986) 'Theory and Practice of Visual Sociology.' *Current Sociology* 34(3): 1–76.

Hockings, P. (ed.) (2003) [1975] *Principles of Visual Anthropology*, 3rd ed. The Hague: Mouton de Gruyter.

MacDougall, D. and L. Taylor (eds.) (1998) *Transcultural Cinema*. Princeton University Press.

Margolis, E. and L. Pauwels (2011) *SAGE Handbook of Visual Research Methods*, Beverly Hills, CA/London: Sage.

Mead, M. (1963) 'Anthropology and the Camera.' In: W. Morgan (ed.) *The Encyclopedia of Photography*, New York: Greystone Press, pp. 166–84.

Mead, M. (1975) 'Visual Anthropology in a Discipline of Words.' In: P. Hockings (ed.) (2003) *Principles of Visual Anthropology*, 3rd edn. The Hague: Mouton de Gruyter, pp. 3–10

Mead, M. and G. Bateson (1985) [1942] *Balinese Character: A Photographic Analysis*. New York Academy of Sciences.

Mitchell, C. (2011) *Doing Visual Research*. London/Thousand Oaks, CA/New Delhi/Singapore: Sage.

Pauwels, L. (1996) *De Verbeelde Samenleving: Camera, Kennisverwerving en Communicatie*. Leuven/Apeldoorn: Garant.

Pauwels, L. (2002) 'The Video- and Multimedia-Article as a Mode of Scholarly Communication: Toward Scientifically Informed Expression and Aesthetics.' *Visual Studies* 17: 150–9.

Pauwels, L. (2010) 'Visual Sociology Reframed: An Analytical Synthesis and Discussion of Visual Methods in Social and Cultural Research.' *Sociological Methods & Research*, 38(4): 545–81.

Pink, S. (2001) *Doing Visual Ethnography: Images, Media and Representation in Research*. London: Sage.

Prosser, J. (ed.) (2000) *Image-Based Research: A Sourcebook for Qualitative Researchers*. London: Routledge.

Rouch, J. (1975) 'The Camera and Man.' In: P. Hockings (2003) [1975] (ed.) *Principles of Visual Anthropology*, 3rd edn. The Hague: Mouton de Gruyter, pp. 83–102.

Ruby, J. (1986) 'The Future of Anthropological Cinema: A Modest Polemic.' *Visual Sociology Review* 1: 9–13.

Ruby, J. (2000) *Picturing Culture: Explorations of Film and Anthropology*. The University of Chicago Press.

Spencer, S. (2011) *Visual Research Methods in the Social Sciences: Awakening Visions*, London: Routledge.

Stanczak, G. (ed.) (2007) *Visual Research Methods: Image, Society and Representation*. Thousand Oaks, CA: Sage.

Wagner, J. (ed.) (1979) *Images of Information: Still Photography in the Social Sciences*. Beverly Hills, CA/London: Sage.

2 An integrated framework for conducting and assessing visual social research

The 'integrated framework for visual social research' as presented in this chapter is an attempt to offer a unified overview of the wide variety of interconnected options and opportunities researchers have when considering producing or using visual input and/or output in the study of society and culture. These options or choices are discussed systematically and are placed in perspective within the complete trajectory of a visual research project from its conception to the dissemination of the research findings or insights.

Such an integrated conceptual framework for visual research is hitherto lacking. Most authors in the field limit themselves to discussing some existing modes or techniques (for example photo elicitation, native image-making, systematic recording) or presentational formats (for example film, visual essay), often without trying to explain the existing diversity or variation within each mode, their distinct underlying claims or methodological caveats. While good examples and discussions of particular types of visual research do exist, few authors have ventured to provide an analytical and integrated approach to visual research as a whole. The purpose of this framework is not just to provide a synthesis of existing methods and techniques. It deliberately does not follow customary distinctions and labels to address the essential elements of visual research in their most meaningful and basic components. It aims to offer better insight into current possibilities and approaches and to stimulate new and more refined approaches to visual research. It does not in any way seek to restrict the vast potential of enquiry to a number of standardized techniques and approaches.

The chapters to follow address in more detail the different modes and issues of visual research but the framework serves as the backbone for the book, tying all discussed elements together in unifying whole. Because of its very condensed and somewhat 'meta-perspective' it may be useful to revisit this chapter after reading the whole book.

---

* Parts of this chapter first appeared in L. Pauwels (2010) Visual Sociology Reframed: An Analytical Synthesis and Discussion of Visual Methods in Social and Cultural Research', *Sociological Methods & Research*, 38(4) 545–581, Beverly Hills / London: Sage Publications.

The framework is built around three major themes:
1. origin and nature of visuals;
2. research focus and design;
3. format and purpose.

These themes correspond more or less with the interrelated aspects of the input, processing and output phases of a visual research project. Within each of these themes different options and aspects are presented and discussed in the context of the broader research project.

1   Origin and nature of visuals

1.1   *Origin/production context of visuals*

One of the most essential choices or options in visual research is whether to use (or restrict oneself to using) existing visual material ('found' visuals) as primary data for research, or to initiate as a researcher first-hand observations or visual products. This choice has many consequences with respect to important aspects such as the nature and amount of control over different aspects of the production of the visual materials, access to the field (less-more; direct-indirect), knowledge of the broader ethnographic context, acceptable uses of the visual outcome and ethical issues.

1.1.1   *Found materials as data source*

First and foremost, social scientists should take advantage of the wide sweep of visual data sources available in society. Societal images and visual artifacts are ubiquitous, and produced on a daily basis without any researcher effort (for example advertisements, news reels, CCTV images, website content, artworks, cartoons) resulting in huge data repositories of actual, historic and fictional(ized) worlds, which have become more accessible nowadays with network and database technologies. This huge offering of both contemporary and historic material has a highly divergent nature: it consists of naïve, utilitarian, mundane or very professional types of visuals (family photography, advertising, fiction and nonfiction film, drawings, maps, diagrams, etc.) spanning many sectors of society (commercial, governmental, educational, entertainment, science, etc.) and thus offering access to a wide variety of public and private worlds.

Studying these materials, sociologists may acquire insight into the social functions of the cultural product itself (for example family pictures or advertisements), but also gain access to broader and more profound aspects of society (the broader realm of values and norms of a given culture). Images often tend to offer a (not unproblematic) window to the depicted world, but at the same time they invariably constitute cultural artifacts in themselves, and may offer a gateway to the culture of the producer and that of the implied audience.

On the down side, when using found materials, sociologists as 'image collectors' often lack sufficient background knowledge or contextual information with respect to the exact origin, the production circumstances, and the representative character of the acquired visual data set. This applies a fortiori to 'anonymous' visual artifacts (for example family pictures found on a flea market) and to a varying degree to artifacts with known provenance. Researchers remain highly dependent on knowledgeable informants, to be able to contextualize the 'visual as presented' (the images or visual artifacts) through data from the past and/or outside their immediate frame of view.

Apart from a broad and specific cultural knowledge, researchers benefit from developing the expertise to analyze both content and form (style) of the visual product, which requires knowledge of both visual technologies and representational cultures over time and space. Moreover, researchers may encounter problems of quite another nature, such as copyright issues and censorship.

1.1.2   Researcher-initiated production of visual data and meanings

With the collection of existing imagery from society, the emphasis of research lies on the decoding of a 'secondary' (mediated) visual reality, which is often no longer directly accessible. However, a number of key modes of visual research (including image production) begin with the primary reality from which the social scientist selects events and phenomena to be visually recorded and processed as an intermediate phase in a research project, or as a proper scientific end product. Researcher-generated production of visuals in general allows more control over the data-gathering procedures (and ideally more reflexivity) so that more highly contextualized material can be produced. In theory, this should provide better insight into the limitations of the produced material (external influences, sample characteristics, etc.).

Some typical strands of visual research based on researcher-produced imagery include a variety of topics and issues, such as social change (Rieger, 1996, 2003; Page, 2001), urban processes (Suchar, 1988, 1992), education (Wagner, 1999; Prosser, 2007), corporate culture (Pauwels, 1996), burial rituals (Synnott, 1985; Chalfen, 2003), gender construction (Harper and Faccioli, 2000; Brown, 2001), pedestrian behavior (Zube, 1979; McPhail and Wohlstein, 1982), youth culture (Hethorn and Kaiser, 1999; Wagner, 1999), social activism (Schwartz,

2002; David, 2007) and migration and ethnicity (Krase, 1997; Gold, 2007).

1.1.3   Secondary research uses and respondent-generated material

The origin or provenance of visual materials is one of the more solid and basic distinctions in visual research. A clear distinction can be made between 'found materials' of no known origin and researcher-generated visuals. But these types of materials represent only the extremes of what can be thought of as a continuum that slides from 'anonymous artifacts,' 'collected artifacts with known provenance,' to 'other researchers' data,' 'respondent-generated data' and finally 'researcher-generated visuals.' Moreover, concrete examples of each of these categories may show a great deal of variation in terms of contextual background, production control and expertise, thus really expressing the idea of a continuum.

A discussion of two specific categories in between the two extremes of the continuum 'found imagery' versus 'researcher-generated' may further illuminate the diverse nature visual materials may take and point out their implications for research.

First, I will address the case of 'secondary research material' or 'other researchers' visual data.' Researchers may indeed choose to use materials that have been produced by other researchers for similar or different research purposes. This material may be used for comparison with new data or (as a historic source) be revisited by a new researcher for the same purposes or to answer different research questions, for example revisiting earlier anthropological and ethnographic pictures as cultural specific visualizations of the 'Other' (see for example Edwards, 1990; Geary, 1990; Pinney, 1990; Hammond, 1998). This form of visual research combines features from both sides of the continuum: it uses pre-existing material that has been produced for research purposes. The central issue here is how much information is available regarding the exact context of production. Knowledge of the context is often better documented for research material than for other types of found material, but may still be insufficient. As availability of such information may vary considerably, this type of research may lie somewhere along the continuum. For the purpose of classification, I have positioned this visual material with 'found' or 'pre-existing material,' since it is not specifically produced with the current research purpose in mind, and thus lacks full control or freedom over several crucial aspects of production. Visual materials produced for research purposes are not the only highly contextualized data sources on the continuum. There are many more pre-existing visual materials, which have been produced in a more or less systematic and documented way, for example private and state archives of all sorts, formal portraits and police photography.

A second distinctive instance along the line of the continuum is the now increasingly popular technique in the social sciences (and currently even in art practice and community development) called 'native image production' (Worth and Adair, 1975; Wagner, 1979: a term that cannot deny its anthropological roots), 'cultural self-portrayal' (Pauwels, 1996) or the use of 'respondent-generated imagery' (probably the broadest and most descriptive term). These materials differ from pre-existing or 'societal' imagery or artifacts in that they are clearly produced within a research context, although not by the researchers or their collaborators, but on their request and following their basic instructions. These materials therefore belong to the broader category of researcher-initiated (or prompted) materials. The respondents or culture under study produce their own cultural data in a visual form. The researcher's control over the production process is therefore more limited than with researcher-generated visuals, but usually higher than with found visual data. It is important to note that the respondent-generated material, while offering a unique (insider) perspective, is never an end product, but just an intermediate step in the research. Researchers still need to analyze and make sense of the visual output generated by the respondents; their cultural self-portrayal or vision needs to be verbally or visually framed within the research output.

One of the most telling and reputed examples of the power of respondent-generated imagery is still the 'Through Navajo Eyes' project, whereby Worth and Adair (1975) taught the Navajo the very basics of handling a camera. The films produced by the Navajo were at first somewhat puzzling as they did not meet the (Western) expectations of the anthropologists. On closer inspection, this very quality established the films as extremely relevant expressions of Navajo culture. Cameras (both still and moving image) or paper and pencil have subsequently been handed out to many different groups of respondents such as school children (Prosser, 2007), adolescents (Niesyto, 2000; Mizen, 2005), migrant children (Clark-Ibanez, 2007) and chronically ill patients (Rich and Chalfen, 1999) to depict aspects of their culture and experience for further scrutiny.

1.2   Referent/subject of research

Visual research in the social sciences predominantly has material culture and human behavior as its subject and – when visual representations are being produced – as its 'referent' (= that which is being depicted or visually referred to). Visual 'material culture' includes artifacts and objects (for example boardrooms, home settings, art objects) and larger visible structures (for example urban areas, cemeteries) that may provide useful information about both the material and the immaterial traits (in as much as they embody values and norms) of a given society.

- Pre-existing visuals or visual artifacts
  - Societal/'found' visuals
  - Secondary research material
- Researcher-instigated visuals
  - Provoked products (respondent-generated visuals)
  - Researcher-produced visuals (possibly in collaboration with professionals)

Figure 2.1 Origin/production context (1.1)

'Naturally occurring or spontaneous behavior' is another crucially important subject of visual social research. This type of behavior is often looked upon as one of the most valuable sources for visual data gathering. The main issue with this type of source is exactly its adjective, 'naturally occurring,' which seems to imply non-reactivity, a requirement that is hardly attainable when the researchers and their recording equipment are visible to the research subjects. Moreover, researchers and their recording equipment being invisible is often questioned from an ethical viewpoint. It is therefore useful to assess the amount and nature of reactivity for each individual situation and the impact on what exactly we need to study. The same applies to relevant ethical aspects.

Of course it is not only naturally occurring or non-reactive behavior that is a valid subject of research; 'elicited behavior of both a verbal or visual nature' may also yield valuable input for research. Researchers can prompt people to react (most often verbally) to visual stimuli (pictures, drawings, artifacts) and use these reactions as input or to correct their research (Collier, 1967; Wagner, 1979; Harper, 2002). Or researchers may even prompt people to produce their own imagery or visual representations as a response to a specific assignment (for example 'depict a typical day of your life'). The first technique is known as 'photo or film elicitation' (the term 'visual elicitation' may be better, since it does not limit this technique to photographic media, but also includes drawing, for example). The latter technique whereby the respondents themselves produce imagery or visual representations about aspects of their culture for further use by the researcher is (as stated earlier) best described by the broad category of 'respondent-generated imagery.'

Though less common in social science than in psychological research, visual social scientists may also opt to record behavior resulting from an experimental situation, which has been constructed solely for the purpose, for example an uncommon artifact is introduced or elements of a built-up environment are suddenly altered to study pedestrians' reactions. The recorded behavior in this situation is not (only) reactive to the research set-up, the camera and the crew (which are often concealed), but also to the new and artificial situation (assumed to be real by the passers-by). The stimulus is not provided in an acknowledged research situation (different, for instance, from using pictures in an interview). The behavior thus recorded is 'spontaneous' but not 'naturally occurring' in the sense that 'it would have occurred anyway' (for example without a researcher intervention).

'Rituals and other highly prescribed activities' in a society offer very condensed information on important aspects of human organization. Depicting these processes may also benefit from a visual approach, because of its ability to capture the richness and complexity of the event, its capacity to cope with the semiotic hybridity (different types of signs and orders of signification) of the depicted including its cultural specificity, and development over time and space (especially when using continuous visual recording techniques: film or video).

Social scientists may even opt for 'staged or re-enacted behavior' as the referent for their visual research, not just for educational purposes (to show others how something has happened or could have been in the past) but also to generate new data in much the same way as a 'reconstruction' of a crime may generate new insights into what really happened. Crucial points in reconstruction are the number and nature of reconstructed aspects versus aspects that have remained unchanged over time; the knowledge, skills and the exact briefing/training of the participants, the sources that are being used to guide the reconstruction, such as memory, writings, oral accounts, visual materials, artifacts and so on. When re-enacting behavior from the past (for example hunting or farming techniques), we often need to 'reconstruct accompanying aspects of material culture' (for example tools such as bows, ploughs, huts). It is important that the audience is kept informed of exactly how the information about the reconstruction was acquired and processed so that they know what they are looking at. This is important because whether behavioral and material reconstructions are based on memory, written accounts or earlier visual representations, and whether an event is re-enacted by survivors or mere actors both influence the outcome in numerous ways.

Finally, a more comprehensive and contemporary view on visual sociology and anthropology also includes the study and use of types of imagery and visual representations that do not necessarily have a (visual) referent in the material world, but rather embody relational and comparative constructs of 'non-visual data and conceptual representations of ideas' (see further Tufte, 1983, 1990, 1997; Lynch, 1985; Grady, 2006;

and Chapter 13). Hitherto these aspects have been more prominently studied in the sociology of science, or by scholars from educational technology, visual communication, and science and technology studies (Latour and Woolgar, 1979; Cambrosio et al., 1993; Knor-Cetina, 1981; Lynch, 1985; Goodwin, 1995; Gordin and Pea, 1995). This expansion of non-visual data and conceptual representations of ideas, and the gradual interest arising constitute a very important aspect of social science becoming 'more visual.'

- Material culture
  - Actual
  - Reconstructed
- Behavior
  - Naturally occurring
  - Elicited (visual/verbal)
  - Staged
  - Re-enacted
- Concepts

Figure 2.2 Referent/subject (1.2)

1.3 Visual medium/technique

Visual sociologists and anthropologists have primarily focused on camera-based imagery (both static and moving). The paramount importance of these kinds of imagery is beyond question, both because of their ubiquity in society, the ease with which they are produced, and because of their specific iconic and indexical qualities (mostly understood as their high level of 'resemblance' and the 'natural' or even 'causal' relation to the depicted object). However, researchers may also take advantage of non-(technically) mediated or directly observed aspects of visual culture (signage, architecture) and of studying and using non-photographic representations (such as drawings, paintings, murals, graffiti, maps, charts). In many cases 'fixing the shadows,' however, by producing a permanent (most often photographic) record is helpful or even necessary.

Any visual practice and its products embody a complex meeting of the cultures of the depicted and of the depicter along with the – again culturally influenced – intricacies of the representational techniques or the medium. Visuals produced with 'non-algorithmic techniques' (techniques that require many 'intentional' choices by the maker, such as drawings: Mitchell, 1992) are readily used as existing data sources (for example paintings, murals, graffiti, children's drawings). For 'researcher-generated' types of imagery, however, this category of

- (Direct observation transcribed in writing/counting/measuring = no permanent visual recording)
- Non-algorithmic/intentional techniques (drawings, sand paintings, graffiti)
- Algorithmic/'automated' techniques (photographs, film, medical-imaging techniques...)

Figure 2.3 Visual medium/technique (1.3)

imaging techniques is a far less obvious choice. Indeed, social scientists routinely turn to photography and film to record material cultural and human behavior in all of its complexity. Yet in some instances, non-algorithmic techniques (more intentional or less automated techniques) can be more suited or may even prove to be the only option (for example to depict concepts or relational constructs as these 'entities' cannot be photographed since they have no visual material referent, or in cases where photography is not allowed). Intentional techniques, moreover, may be chosen because they allow simplification and abstraction; photos can be too detailed and particularistic. Intentional techniques also allow the simultaneous application of many different representational codes, for example a map may combine many types of iconic and symbolic information: pictograms, arrows, colors, gradients, texts and so forth. The relation between a picture and its depicted content potentially becomes more problematic as more specialized (or non-canonic) techniques (special lenses, unusual vantage points, use of rays that are not visible to the naked eye) are used, or when the depicted cannot be observed directly and thus is only 'available' as a representation (see Chapter 13).

2   Research focus and design

2.1   Analytical foci and fields of application

The analytical focus of a visual research project may be quite varied. Whereas we may primarily think of a detailed analysis of the visual product, it may also involve the processes of making (production) these visual artifacts or entail uses (consumption, reception) the visual representations are being put to, and the focal point of interest may even lie on the verbal reactions to visuals (verbal feedback).

The analytical focus will always be determined by the particular research questions being addressed. These research questions may cover a vast number of possible areas of research as long the right visual angles to answer the questions are found.

2.1.1   *Product: the depicted and the depiction*

The content or that which is depicted is an important source of data, and for most researcher-generated visuals the focal point of analysis. Indeed, much research tries to produce images in a systematic way and thus relies explicitly or implicitly on the mimetic strengths of the camera image, thereby seeking to minimize the variations and expressive effects of style originating from dissimilar applications of filmic parameters (for example camera distance, angle, position). Essentially we then try to use images as 'windows' to the depicted world. This rather 'realist' approach is legitimate if we are primarily interested in the depicted matter for further scrutiny. However, researchers always need to be aware of the inevitable difference between the depicted (the referent) and the depiction (the visual representation), a difference that can seriously influence or even misinform their views on the depicted. This difference can also become a field of study in its own right: the study of style as a gateway to the norms and values and other immaterial traits of a culture.

Operationalizing research questions and foci from visually observable elements may involve deriving data from images in a fairly straightforward way (for example number of people, distances, cultural inventory of objects) or may require more interpretative decoding (emotional states, complex relations). Such operationalization may implicate the image or visual field as an integrated whole (the spatial organization of a town square, the global impression of a city as a cultural meeting place) or just small parts or aspects of it (clearly defined types of exchange between people, for example a handshake, eye contact, a nod).

Research of 'found' or pre-existing visuals (for example advertising, family pictures) in general will also have a primary focus on the depicted (for example changes in fashion, architecture, street art, events, poses and persons in a family snap or an advertisement). However, the researcher can also benefit from focusing on the depiction as a result of a representational practice (which involves cultural and technological normative systems) and thus scrutinize the ways in which particular objects or events are being represented visually by certain actors or institutions over time. Thus the focus of attention moves to researching form and style, and so to the world of the image producers rather than that of the depicted (unless these worlds largely coincide, as is often the case with family photography). Studies, for instance on the colonial gaze, have focused on how the Other is represented (staged, selected, stereotyped, made docile). This research involves both looking at what is depicted and how it is depicted on a pro-filmic (mise-en-scène) and filmic level (framing, editing, postproduction, etc.)

So an important focus of visual research is also the representational practices as cultural expressions in relation to what the visuals depict. The visual form is then problematized and the image no longer seen as an unproblematic window to the depicted world, but (also) as mirroring the social and cultural world of the image producer. This focus of analysis requires sufficient knowledge of the medium and its culture (for example the evolution of analogue/digital camera techniques, the cultural codes of picture-making and the depicted culture in a broad sense).

2.1.2   *Analyzing production processes and product uses*

Analyzing the processes of image-making and the subsequent uses and cultural practices surrounding the use of imagery and visual representations are not the most dominant foci in current visual research, but they too may yield unique data. Indeed, in some cases the process may be more revealing than the end product. Anthropologists may for instance look at how a large sand painting is being created by members of a tribe. The process of negotiating the different choices, the forms of collaboration, the required skills that are being made and displayed make up a research interest in themselves. Next to studying the visual end products, family researchers can also take an interest in the dynamics just *before* and *during* the production of a family snap (the directing, posing, negotiations, the technical choices and the implicit power relations) and the processes by which the snaps are *afterwards* selected, manipulated and combined with texts in an album or on a website; where, how and which photos are displayed in the home or distributed among friends and acquaintances, for which reasons and so on (Chalfen, 1987; and Chapter 9). Psychotherapists may ask children of families under severe strain to make a drawing of the members of their family and study the order in which family members are drawn, for example the mother before the father or vice versa, based on the belief that 'what is drawn' first may reveal what is most important for the drawer (Diem-Wille, 2001: 119). In a way, these examples, of course, involve (direct) observation of behavior (spontaneous, ritual or instigated), yet the interesting link between the behavior and its immediate result in material culture, and the fact that it involves behavior related to image-making and handling, make them an area of special relevance to the visual researcher.

2.1.3   *Analysis of feedback*

Some types of visual research (for example visual interviewing or photo elicitation) rely to a large part on the analysis of verbal reactions to visual stimuli (drawings, photos, film). Visual stimuli are provided by the researcher to gather factual information about the depicted cultural elements and – a very powerful and unique trait of the visual elicitation technique – to 'trigger' more projective information with the respondents (their deeper feelings, opinions). The method of 'respondent-generated images' also generates 'feedback,' but of a mainly visual nature and thus this feedback needs to be analyzed for both its content and its form. It is to be considered as a research 'input' not an end product, even if it takes the form of a completed film or video. Through detailed analysis, the researcher will try to make sense of it and situate it within the larger framework of the discipline.

In a more general sense, visual researchers today are routinely using the reactions of their subjects to correct and improve their visual account and interpretations, for example through regular screenings of the unfinished visual product in front of the culturally savvy audience.

In summary, the focus of analysis in visual research can lie: on the content of a visual representation (the depicted), on its form and style (most often in conjunction with the depicted), on the processes that are related with the production and use of visual representations, and finally on the verbal reactions to visual stimuli.

2.1.4   Fields of application

Possible fields and types of subject matter that can be studied with visual methods are virtually limitless so long as what is being researched has a significant visual dimension. Some questions about aspects and processes of the social world that have sizeable visual aspects (for example status (display), social class, enculturation) may be more suited for visual research than others (for example relative deprivation, fraudulent behavior), but it all comes down to finding the right visual entry points to disclose relevant aspects of social and cultural life. The inquisitive and visually literate mind may come up with many novel ways of looking at what (at first sight) might seem too abstract a subject.

- The visual product (content and form)
- The production process
- Respondents' verbal feedback
- Visual practices/uses

Figure 2.4 Analytical focus (2.1)

2.2   *Theoretical foundation*

As in most types of research, theory usually guides visual data production and analysis. So whether looking at existing visual representations or producing new visual data, both approaches require a solid and fully motivated theoretical grounding. Without theory, our seeing is blind or tends to rest on unexplained views and expectations (implicit theory), which we may even be unaware of. It is fairly naïve to expect that the camera will automatically collect large quantities of relevant data. Theory is needed to give scientific research some direction. It can focus attention on issues which at first sight are not expected to have much significance, but which from a specific stance, hypothesis or idea can yield relevant scientific information.

- Selection of theories related to visual analysis/production
- Theories related to the applied field and subject matter

Figure 2.5 Theoretical foundation (2.2)

Visual researchers can make use of several theoretical frameworks, which have been adapted over the course of the years to visual analysis (Smith et al., 2005; Rose, 2006), for example semiotics, socio-semiotics, rhetoric, several sociological paradigms, psychoanalysis, cultural studies, post-colonial theory, feminist theory. Others have been developed for that very purpose, for example iconology. Many embody already very particular interests in the image (from determining its subject and explaining its deeper meanings, to uncovering its signifying structure, revealing its power structure, gender biases or racial prejudices). Some of these frameworks offer concrete methodological tools, while others do not seem to suggest any method of investigation and leave it to the researcher to incorporate their views in a more or less systematic qualitative and/or quantitative type of content analysis. In fact, relatively few theories seem to offer handles for concrete in-depth analysis of both the depicted (or content) and the depiction (the stylistic choices at the level of the execution and the characteristics of the medium). Many visual studies, therefore, limit themselves to the analysis of the depicted, whereas the level of the depiction – which often proves much harder to investigate, since it falls outside the scope of expertise of most social scientists – may reveal particularly relevant data, for example about the norms and values of the image makers or their commissioning institutions. Such data at the level of depiction may prove highly complementary with the content-related data.

However, the theoretical grounding of a project not only involves the visual analytical side (how to deal with the form and content of the visual products) but also includes the main subject matter or the thematic focus of the project. Researchers who, for instance, study gentrification processes or poverty issues start by selecting particular definitions and aspects of gentrification or poverty theories and research, and combine those in a solid framework that is compatible with the goals of the research and with the particular combination of research methods and techniques.

2.3   Methodological issues

2.3.1   Visual competencies: aspects and implementation options

Working towards a more visual scientific discourse implies the development of a particular sort of visual competence. When collecting pre-existing imagery ('societal imagery'), researchers preferably need at least a passive knowledge of the technical and expressive aspects of imagery and representational techniques, to be able to read and make use of them adequately. In analyzing such found imagery, most often special attention is paid to the historical and cultural context of production and consumption. When researchers produce imagery themselves ('researcher-generated imagery') or are using visual elements in one or more stages of their research and scholarly communication, a more active visual knowledge and skill is required, since all technical or medium-related decisions have epistemological consequences. Thus not only do competent visual researchers not only have a sufficient degree of technical knowledge, allowing them to produce images or other types of visual representations with the required amount of visual detail (data richness), but they are also aware of the cultural conventions regarding the medium they are using, and consequently of the perceptual cultures of the academic or non-academic audience they intend to address.

Visual scientific competence thus implies a thorough insight into the specific characteristics of visual media along with the skill to translate scientific insights into partly visual constructs. Ultimately, visual scientific literacy manifests itself as a form of visual thinking and doing throughout the complete research process. This starts with the conception of a problem, and continues through the phase of data gathering or production of visual material, the phase of analysis or further preparation and handling, up to the presentation of the data and findings.

- Appropriate operationalization and visual translation of theory
- Choice of recording devices with respect to their epistemological consequences
- Active knowledge of the dynamic language and conventions of visual media in their cultural context
- Collaboration / expertise issues / skills: technical, normative, creative aspects

Figure 2.6 Visual competencies (2.3.1)

2.3.2   Sampling and data production strategies

Different questions and research methods necessitate different sampling strategies and data collection/production (shooting) techniques. Hypothesis-testing visual research may require systematic recording techniques, and often include random or stratified sampling (for example every tenth house in a street), while more explorative research may benefit from more 'opportunistic sampling' (Sorenson and Jablonko, 1975). The latter is used for recording things which attract the researcher's attention or which can only be collected on an ad hoc – 'when it occurs' or 'comes into view' – basis. Examples are the reactions of bystanders at the site of a car accident, illegal street sellers, and unanticipated or remarkable aspects of visual culture. As always, the sampling technique co-determines the inferences possible from the visual data in a later stage.

Standardized research designs often benefit from the use of 'shooting scripts' (Suchar, 1997) detailing the exact positions, subject matter and time, enabling comparison. A longitudinal variant of systematic observation, known as 'repeat photography,' is very much focused on keeping the recording parameters (angle of view, camera distance, framing) constant over time to record (social) change (Rieger, 1996).

- Explorative/opportunistic/randomized
- Systematic (snapshot, time series or longitudinal/repeat)

Figure 2.7 Sampling issues and data production strategies (2.3.2)

Thus a clearly theory-driven or systematically conceptualized research project does not rule out more exploratory and intuitive approaches (Collier, 1967). These latter approaches may be particularly suited to getting acquainted with a new field (a new city, settlement, culture, kind of behavior) and its products may stimulate going back and forth to the field, as suggested by the 'grounded theory' approach. Often it is very rewarding for research to remain open to the unexpected and the unanticipated events. Stochastic or conversely more exploratory and opportunistic approaches do therefore have a place in the process, as they can lead to new insights and sometimes even succeed in reaching the heart of the matter. Visual research in particular benefits from the continued fertilization between theory and practice, thinking and doing. Non-systematically acquired data can often serve as a test for more systematically acquired data.

2.3.3   Controlling intentional and unintentional influences and modifications

Visual researchers usually have a keen eye for unintended and uncontrolled influences on the researched situation, which could be attributed to their and/or their camera's presence (or to some other 'limiting' or 'disturbing' instances, for example forms of censorship before, during or after the shooting). It is their task then to evaluate how and to what extent these influences and instances affect what is considered 'normal,' or at least what could be considered acceptable within the context of their research. They are expected to be knowledgeable of techniques to reduce the occurrence of various forms of 'obtrusiveness' (Grimshaw, 1982) or other kinds of unintentional influence, or find ways to creatively take advantage of them (for example by making them part of the focus of the research).

Undesired influences may be reduced first of all by a thorough investigation and preparation of the field of research ('prior ethnography'; see Corsaro, 1982), including a gradual introduction of both the set-up and the instrument of the research (the camera), and by providing information about the possible consequences for the people involved. 'Monitored' behavior (self-conscious reactions to being observed) often stems from an understandable fear on the part of the observed of being harmed by the way they are being represented visually (see Chapter 12).

Data are likely to be more representative when people have been given time to grow accustomed to the special situation and have sufficient information regarding the purpose of the research. Whether behavior is representative is also influenced by the varying degrees of freedom subjects have to respond to the camera (Becker, 1986). Recordings of rituals and other strictly prescribed activities are far less problematic in this regard than trying to record spontaneous behavior (for example an informal conversation), where a certain degree of reactivity is unavoidable. The relation and interaction between the researchers and the observed before, during and after the recording session may also prove to be important factors. In some cases interaction may be desirable, while in others keeping a distance is preferable to obtain valid data. Effects of 'monitoring' not only relate to behavior, but may also occur when recording material aspects of culture: thus researchers could try to find out to what extent the setting has been modified (for example what objects have been moved, removed or added) in anticipation of the recordings.

Sometimes 'reality' needs to be brought back to life via re-enactments or 'adapted' for technical or other reasons to be 'revealed' (for example filming a sacred ritual, which is normally performed at night, during daylight). Obviously these rather radical types of interventions need to be well thought through, and, above all, well-motivated and explained so that the spectators know what they are looking at and what inferences can be drawn from the interplay of the depicted elements. The visual end product needs to be critically examined more than ever as a particular construction (a series of transformations and choices), not just as an unproblematic reflection of an unproblematic or pristine reality.

Next to reconstructing parts of the culture under study, for example Asen Balikci's film on the life of the Netsilik before the introduction of the rifle in 1919 (Balikci, 1975), social scientists may even go as far as to construct an experimental situation, which may never happen spontaneously in real life, but which may help to reveal some deeper aspects of a culture. For example, the anthropologist Rob Boonzajer Flaes once confronted Tibetan monks with Alp horns to see how they responded to something alien to their culture.

2.3.4   Nature and degree of field involvement

Exploring society with visual media requires thorough preparation and consideration with regard to the field and the subjects treated. Involving the field of research (the subjects or otherwise related or concerned parties) in a more active, less passive ('object') role in the visual research

---

- Proper assessment of the influences of the research conditions on the researched situation
- Preliminary investigation of the specific features of the field and the chances of using visual media
- Apply techniques and create favorable circumstances to diminish undesirable influences to an acceptable minimum
- Recognize and justify intentional interventions

Figure 2.8 Controlling unintentional and intentional modifications (2.3.3)

set-up and execution (production, decoding, revising) may take many forms. Such involvement may be chosen for a variety of reasons, both scientific (to acquire more in-depth knowledge from the 'inside') and for moral grounds (to pursue a more egalitarian relationship, with a willingness to share the benefits).

In a 'zero-state of involvement,' people may be 'totally unaware' of being the subject of research before, during and after the research has been completed. This may be the case when using pre-existing material (for example taken from archives) that is centrally stored and often relating to the past, or when hidden cameras are being used, or when fairly overt camera recording remains unnoticed due to the density of the public or the intensity of an event.

A further case may be that 'people are aware that they are being recorded' (for example at tourist sites where almost everybody is running around with digital still and moving cameras) but do not know the particular purpose (and erroneously assume it to be, for example, for private family pictures, or for journalistic purposes).

People may, however, react to being recorded whether or not they know its exact purpose: they may try to hide away, or to perform in front of the camera in less or more explicit ways. When people know they are being recorded they most often display a degree of reactivity. Looking in the camera is the most noticeable but not necessarily the most significant reaction. This reactivity may even be or become the very subject matter of the research.

Many visual researchers have experienced the value of involving the field in a more active and encompassing way (not just during the recording, but before and afterwards), which can lead to more 'participatory and joint forms of production' (Rouch, 1975). In fact, sometimes this participation of the community under study may be the main objective of the project, which then, rather than having a scientific purpose, seeks to promote community empowerment or activism. In this case the researcher helps the community realize its goals rather than vice versa, which is normally the case.

- No awareness
- Unacknowledged
- Reactive
- Interactive
- Participatory
- Joint production

Figure 2.9 Degree of field involvement (2.3.4)

2.3.5   *Provision of the necessary (internal and external) context*

It is important that visual researchers make every effort to situate the subject of their research and their specific take on it, in its broader context, both visually and verbally. Researchers need to pay special attention to the scientific consequences of all the choices and decisions which have been made during research. Consequently, there must be a preparedness to make all these issues public, for example to consider them as an integral part of the final research report. This is a particularly heavy and sizeable obligation, even more so than with other types of research. Limiting reporting to general descriptions of the steps taken is very seldom sufficient.

First of all significant contextual information should, whenever possible, be part of the visual record or product itself (which may or may not consist of verbal and auditory types of information). To some extent 'part to whole' relationships are automatically provided by algorithmic visual recording devices such as a camera. Examples are an artifact pictured in its context of use, or moving images of an event as it chronologically unfolds itself. Hence many ethnographers prefer using wide-angle lenses, although the issue is far more complex than this. Providing image-internal contexts requires a very active and careful effort on the part of the researcher; it is not something that is automatically – at least not in full – achieved by the camera, even though some cameras automatically record potentially useful information such as exposure data (aperture and shutter speed), date of exposure and geographic coordinates (GPS).

Secondly, the relative meaning of the visual product (which may or may not contain verbal types of information) also needs to be related to, and contrasted against information obtained through other sources and techniques. Complex visual productions usually require an extensive verbal documentation addressing the methodology followed, the choices made (technical, ethical, etc.) and the problems and uncertainties encountered from the concept to the end result. Also some additional information should be provided about the broader context (cultural, historical) in which the visual product needs to be considered.

These basic requirements today form part and parcel of a broader call for *reflexivity* in science which entails a clear recognition that all knowledge is 'work in progress,' incomplete and 'positioned' (see more with Rosaldo, 1989; Ruby, 2000; and Chapter 8). With respect to visual research, reflexivity in particular involves giving a concrete shape to the idea that research is a complex 'meeting of cultures' (MacDougall, 1975: 119): to start with the cultures of the researchers (personal beliefs, preferences, experiences, characteristics, cultural backgrounds) and those of

- Provide image-internal context
- Provide image-external context
- Reflexivity Issues

Figure 2.10 Provision of necessary context (2.3.5)

the researched, and at a later stage with the cultural stance of the viewers or users of the resulting visual product.

2.3.6 Ethical and legal aspects of visual research

The most important question here is how visual researchers can use visual media to collect data or communicate insights about human behavior and material culture in a way that will not harm subjects. The relatively irrefutable nature of (camera) images used in end reporting is likely to breach anonymity and thus raise rightful concerns with subjects. Both researchers and subjects are often unable to anticipate all the possible risks of being 'exposed' in such a way. Complex consideration of all contextual issues relevant to the particular research is required, including aspects such as how recognizable subjects are in images, the acceptability of possible negative consequences, the conditions for access to the data, and the extent of participation on the part of those involved (see Chapter 12).

- Informed consent
- Fair use
- Ownership

Figure 2.11 Ethical aspects (2.3.6)

While protection of subjects' rights is a paramount issue in visual research, issues such as authorship and copyright also require special attention. Image producers have the right to benefit from their creations, and researchers should observe these rights when conducting visual research on the basis of pre-existing materials (for example advertisements, documentary film, art). In particular, this includes using visual material from the Internet (see Chapter 4). On the other hand, many visual researchers experience an urgent need for a more widely adopted and ratified 'fair use' policy. This would avoid being constantly slowed down (seeking permissions) or prevented (by pecuniary demands, absence of reactions, or negative responses) from using the materials for their study or from performing their customary 'intertextual' practice of citing and critiquing for strictly academic purposes.

3   Format and purpose of end product

3.1   Output/presentational format

The output or end result of visual social science can take different forms ranging from the standard article or research report (words only, or scant tables and graphs) to highly illustrated articles, added CD-ROMs, self-contained films, multimedia programs on DVD, or websites. Posters and exhibitions may also be used as a more temporary and space-bound outlet for visual research. The number of pictures or visualization elements (color, animation, design features) is not a valid indicator of the quality of research. The appropriate use of visuals and their interplay with other design elements is what counts most.

For some types of research it may be the right decision to limit the visuals to the bare minimum, to put them aside altogether, or to transform them into more manageable representations. This could be the solution for some forms of systematic camera recording whereby the significant data can easily be reduced to simpler types of data that still bear the essence: for example numbers of people on a square at a given time, distances between actors, or vectors and so on. On the other hand, visual reporting approaches such as the 'visual essay' (Grady, 1991; Pauwels, 1993) rest to a large part on thoughtfully using most of the parameters of visual and verbal communication. Both the individual visuals and their interplay with the verbal may express insights that cannot be produced as effectively as in another, more traditional (at least for the sciences) form.

3.2   Status of the visual

The visual can take different roles in the end product. In principle, visuals should only be used in the end product if they fulfill a definite and unique role; they should not just be included as illustrations that have little or no added (informational or expressive) value. So it is conceivable that some visual research may have no visuals in the end product, for example if the

---

> Article without visuals
> Article with graphical or conceptual representations
> Pictures/visuals and words (illustrated article; poster; lecture; visual essay)
> Self-contained linear film/video
> Interactive multimedia product
> Exhibition/performance

Figure 2.12 Output/presentational format (3.1)

relevant aspects of photographs or direct observations can be transcribed into numbers or a verbal description for ease of use. But often the creation of a new visual representation (for example a graphic representation of the summarized data) adds clarity to the insights conveyed.

- Indispensable output with varying roles: illustration / example / exception / synthesis / conceptual construct
- Use and recognition as mimetic and expressive tools
- Relations/interplay with other expressive systems

Figure 2.13 Status of the visual (3.2)

While visuals can play just an intermediate role in the research process (often the case with systematic and mimetic types of research), the collected or researcher-produced visuals more often play a very varied role in communicating what has come out of the study. Visuals can illustrate 'typical' settings and processes, give examples or describe deviant or exceptional cases, and in doing so provide a 'holistic' account of elements in their often very meaningful spatial and relational surroundings.

As visuals may communicate a great variety of things and thus come to embody a particularly varied 'status,' the problem is to adequately communicate this status. Users and audiences have a right to know what exactly they are looking at and to understand what current and potential purposes the depictions can serve.

3.3   *Intended and secondary uses*

Visual representations often have no 'intrinsic' or fixed value for research. Their research value is the combined result of a valid and representative data set for a given purpose, a particular research question and a sound process of going from visual facts or indications to a reasoned and substantiated set of inferences. As with any type of research, visual research is purpose driven and yields its particular design for a large part from this purpose. Purposes can be manifold and sometimes they can be combined. They not only determine the look of the end product, but also determine the choices that should have been made in many of the previous steps. Images and visual representations to a large extent derive their significance from the process and the context from which they emerge.

'Found images' by definition have not been produced with the researchers' particular purposes in mind. However, to the extent that they have been purposefully selected and insight has been acquired into the specific context from which they originate, they become capable of providing valid answers to particular research questions. The potential usefulness of a particular visual data set for particular purposes depends largely on the amount of contextual data which can be obtained.

The visual data or visual end product of visual research (for example an anthropological film) or the intermediate visual data (systematic recordings of pedestrian activity on a square) may be used for new purposes, for example as new input data or for other audiences (for example lay audiences instead of students, or fieldworkers). Often, however, there will be at least some (minor or essential) reframing (or revisualization) and contextualization required for this to be successful. Some purposes are hard to combine (for example highly specialized knowledge transfer with broad appeal) while others have much more leeway.

> Fundamental research output
> Specialist (peer) communications
> Educate students and general audiences
> Institutional support (policy development)
> Community empowerment / induce social change

Figure 2.14 Intended and secondary uses (3.3)

Sometimes the 'raw data' of a research product (for example unedited film footage) can be packaged right away to suit various needs: for example to produce a specialized visual report, to be included in a training module, to be edited into a product that can convince policy makers to try to remedy an unwanted situation, or help to empower a community in its struggle for a better life. But combining purposes or re-using materials for other purposes obviously always requires specific expertise and extra effort (time and money). Without proper care, the end result can easily become invalid, misleading or at least less effective.

4   Conclusion

Acknowledging the stark contrast between the current surge of interest in exploring visual aspects of society by scholars from the humanities and the social and behavioral sciences, and the relatively weak conceptual and methodical basis for realizing this interest in a more widely accepted manner, I have argued for a more integrated and analytical approach to visual research. This serves as a basis for the construction of more explicit, appropriate and refined visual methodologies. Therefore, this chapter was devoted to the systematic presentation and clarification of an 'integrated framework for visual social research' as represented in Figure 2.15. In addition to providing a synthesis of current research practices in an analytical manner, I sought to offer with this framework a broader and

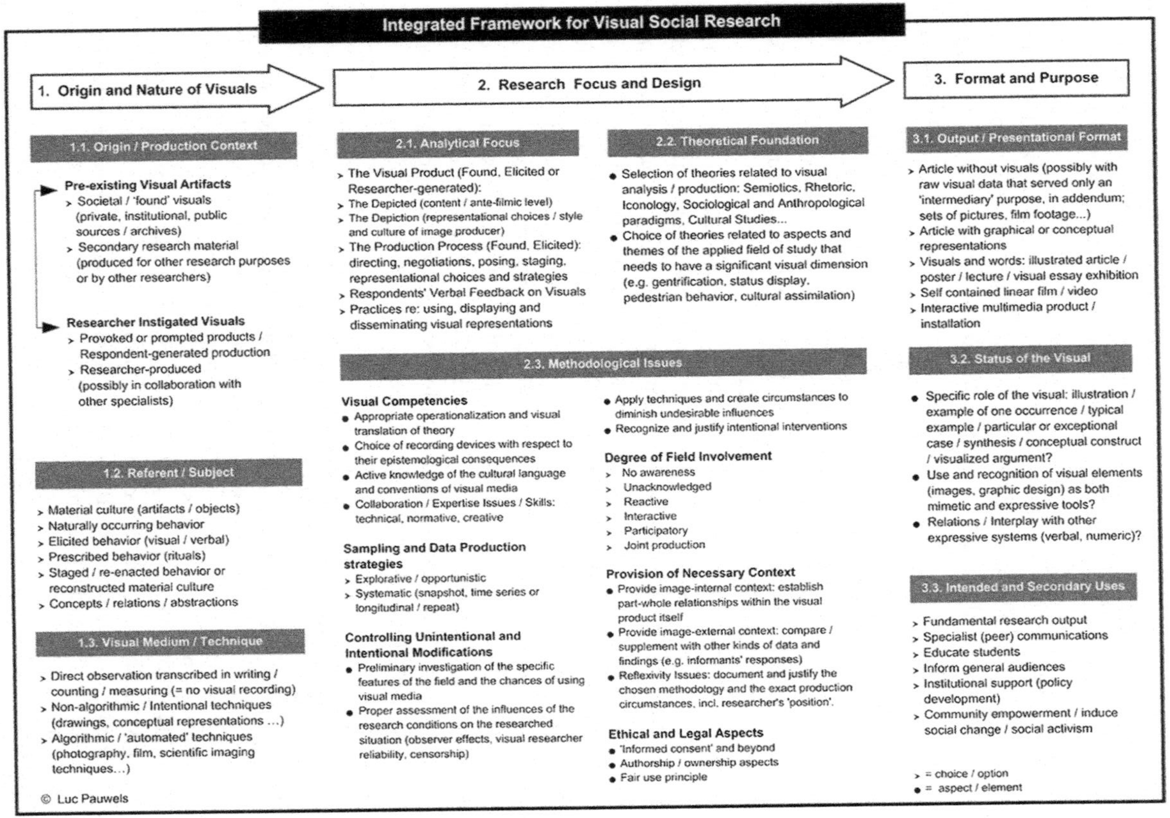

Integrated Framework for Visual Social Research

1. Origin and Nature of Visuals

2. Research Focus and Design

3. Format and Purpose

1.1. Origin / Production Context

Pre-existing Visual Artifacts

➢ Societal / 'found' visuals (private, institutional, public sources / archives)
➢ Secondary research material (produced for other research purposes or by other researchers)

Researcher Instigated Visuals

➢ Provoked or prompted products / Respondent-generated production
➢ Researcher-produced (possibly in collaboration with other specialists)

1.2. Referent / Subject

➢ Material culture (artifacts / objects)
➢ Naturally occurring behavior
➢ Elicited behavior (visual / verbal)
➢ Prescribed behavior (rituals)
➢ Staged / re-enacted behavior or reconstructed material culture
➢ Concepts / relations / abstractions

1.3. Visual Medium / Technique

➢ Direct observation transcribed in writing / counting / measuring (= no visual recording)
➢ Non-algorithmic / Intentional techniques (drawings, conceptual representations ....)
➢ Algorithmic / 'automated' techniques (photography, film, scientific imaging techniques...)

© Luc Pauwels

2.1. Analytical Focus

➢ The Visual Product (Found, Elicited or Researcher-generated):
  ➢ The Depicted (content / ante-filmic level)
  ➢ The Depiction (representational choices / style and culture of image producer)
➢ The Production Process (Found, Elicited): directing, negotiations, posing, staging, representational choices and strategies
➢ Respondents' Verbal Feedback on Visuals
➢ Practices re: using, displaying and disseminating visual representations

2.2. Theoretical Foundation

➢ Selection of theories related to visual analysis / production: Semiotics, Rhetoric, Iconology, Sociological and Anthropological paradigms, Cultural Studies...
➢ Choice of theories related to aspects and themes of the applied field of study that needs to have a significant visual dimension (e.g. gentrification, status display, pedestrian behavior, cultural assimilation)

2.3. Methodological Issues

● Apply techniques and create circumstances to diminish undesirable influences
● Recognize and justify intentional interventions

Degree of Field Involvement
➢ No awareness
➢ Unacknowledged
➢ Reactive
➢ Interactive
➢ Participatory
➢ Joint production

Provision of Necessary Context
● Provide image-internal context: establish part-whole relationships within the visual product itself
● Provide image-external context: compare / supplement with other kinds of data and findings (e.g. informants' responses)
● Reflexivity Issues: document and justify the chosen methodology and the exact production circumstances, incl. researcher's 'position'.

Ethical and Legal Aspects
● 'Informed consent' and beyond
● Authorship / ownership aspects
● Fair use principle

Visual Competencies
● Appropriate operationalization and visual translation of theory
● Choice of recording devices with respect to their epistemological consequences
● Active knowledge of the cultural language and conventions of visual media
● Collaboration / Expertise Issues / Skills: technical, normative, creative

Sampling and Data Production strategies
➢ Explorative / opportunistic
➢ Systematic (snapshot, time series or longitudinal / repeat)

Controlling Unintentional and Intentional Modifications
● Preliminary investigation of the specific features of the field and the chances of using visual media
● Proper assessment of the influences of the research conditions on the researched situation (observer effects, visual researcher reliability, censoring)

3.1. Output / Presentational Format

➢ Article without visuals (possibly with raw visual data that served only an 'intermediary' purpose, in addendum: sets of pictures, film footage...)
➢ Article with graphical or conceptual representations
➢ Visuals and words: illustrated article / poster / lecture / visual essay exhibition
➢ Self contained linear film / video
➢ Interactive multimedia product / installation

3.2. Status of the Visual

● Specific role of the visual: illustration / example of one occurrence / typical example / particular or exceptional case / synthesis / conceptual construct / visualized argument?
● Use and recognition of visual elements (images, graphic design) as both mimetic and expressive tools?
● Relations / Interplay with other expressive systems (verbal, numeric)?

3.3. Intended and Secondary Uses

➢ Fundamental research output
➢ Specialist (peer) communications
➢ Educate students
➢ Inform general audiences
➢ Institutional support (policy development)
➢ Community empowerment / induce social change / social activism

➢ = choice / option
● = aspect / element

Figure 2.15 An integrated framework for visual social research

better understanding of the visual production, processing and communication/dissemination stages of visual research and of the related methodological issues and research design concerns. As such it may serve as a checklist for starting new research, for assessing current research, or for offering insight into the many options in visual research, assumptions and consequences.

So the framework is not just an analytical synthesis of existing options and issues, but also embodies a broader, future-directed program for a more visual social science, aimed at inspiring further and more targeted methodological development. This framework – dense as it may already look – can be made even more detailed (for example by linking specific ethical issues to specific approaches and techniques, and strategies to deal with these). However, this is exactly what is meant by the assertion that an overall framework may further feed and inspire more detailed and methodological expounding, focused on particular combinations of approaches, both visual and non-visual.

The use of the visual as a data source, or as a medium for capturing, processing and expressing social scientific knowledge continues to challenge current scholarship as it is both a demanding and rewarding – but hitherto still rather uncommon (non-mainstream) and largely unchartered – territory. Both visual researchers and their diverse audiences should be prepared and educated to move further along this road. More explicit and transparent methodologies and exemplary visual studies may help visual research to gradually enter the realm of widely accepted options in the study of society. The remainder of this book is set up to contribute to this call for a more systematic, explicit and specific methodology for a visual social science.

5   References

Balikci, A. (1975) 'Reconstructing Cultures on Film.' In: P. Hockings (ed.) *Principles of Visual Anthropology*. The Hague/Paris: Mouton Publishers, pp. 191–200.

Becker, H. S. (1986) *Doing Things Together: Selected Papers*. Evanston, IL: Northwestern University Press.

Brown, B. (2001) 'Doing Drag: A Visual Case Study of Gender Performance and Gay Masculinities.' *Visual Sociology*, 16: 37–54.

Cambrosio, A., D. Jacobi and P. Keating (1993) 'Ehrlich's "Beautiful Pictures" and the Controversial Beginnings of Immunological Imagery.' *ISIS* 1993, 84: 662–99.

Chalfen, R. (1987) *Snapshot Versions of Life*. Bowling Green State University Popular Press.

Chalfen, R. (2003) 'Celebrating Life after Death: The Appearance of Snapshots in Japanese Pet Gravesites.' *Visual Studies*, 18: 144–56.

Clark-Ibanez, M. (2007) 'Inner-City Children in Sharper Focus: Sociology of Childhood and Photo Elicitation Interviews.' In: G. Stanczak (ed.) *Visual Research Methods*. Thousand Oaks, CA: Sage, pp. 167–98.

Collier, J. (1967) *Visual Anthropology: Photography as a Research Method*. New York/London: Holt, Rinehart and Winston. (Revised and expanded edition with M. Collier (1986). Albuquerque: University of New Mexico Press.)

Corsaro, W. (1982) 'Something Old and Something New: The Importance of Prior Ethnography in the Collection and Analysis of Audiovisual Data.' *Sociological Methods & Research* ('Special Issue on Sound-Image Records in Social Interaction Research'), 11: 145–66.

David, E. (2007) 'Signs of Resistance: Marking Public Space Through a Renewed Cultural Activism.' In: G. Stanczak (ed.) *Visual Research Methods*. Thousand Oaks, CA: Sage, pp. 225–54.

Diem-Wille, Gertrude (2001) 'A Therapeutic Perspective: The Use of Drawings in Child Psychoanalysis and Social Science.' In: T. Van Leeuwen and C. Jewitt (eds.), *Handbook of Visual Analysis*. London/Thousand Oaks, CA/New Delhi: Sage, pp. 157–82.

Edwards, E. (1990) 'Photographic "Types": The Pursuit of Method.' *Visual Anthropology*, 3: 235–58.

Geary, C. M. (1990) 'Impressions of the African Past: Interpreting Ethnographic Photographs from Cameroon.' *Visual Anthropology*, 3: 289–315.

Gold, S. J. (2007) 'Using Photography in Studies of Immigrant Communities: Reflecting across Projects and Populations.' In: G. Stanczak (ed.), *Visual Research Methods*, Thousand Oaks, CA: Sage, pp. 141–66.

Goodwin, C. (1995) 'Seeing in Depth.' *Social Studies of Science* 25: 237–74.

Gordin, D. N. and R. D. Pea (1995) 'Prospects for Scientific Visualization as an Educational Technology.' *The Journal of the Learning Sciences* 4: 249–79.

Grady, J. (1991) 'The Visual Essay and Sociology.' *Visual Sociology*, 6: 23–38.

Grady, J. (2006) 'Edward Tufte and the Promise of a Visual Social Science.' In: L. Pauwels (ed.) *Visual Cultures of Science: Rethinking Representational Practices in Knowledge Building and Science Communication*. Hanover, NH/London: Dartmouth College Press – University Press of New England, pp. 222–65.

Grimshaw, A. (ed.) (1982) 'Special Issue on Sound-Image Records in Social Interaction Research.' *Sociological Methods & Research*, 11: 115–255.

Hammond, J. D. (1998) 'Photography and the "Natives": Examining the Hidden Curriculum of Photographs in Introductory Anthropology Texts.' *Visual Sociology*, 13(2): 57–73.

Harper, D. (2002) 'Talking about Pictures: A Case for Photo Elicitation.' *Visual Studies*, 17: 13–26.

Harper, D. and P. Faccioli (2000) 'Small, Silly Insults: Mutual Seduction and Misogyny: The Interpretation of Italian Advertising Signs.' *Visual Sociology*, 15: 23–49.

Hethorn, J. and S. Kaiser (1999) 'Youth Style: Articulating Cultural Anxiety.' *Visual Sociology*, 14: 109–25.

Knor-Cetina, K. (1981) *The Manufacture of Knowledge: An Essay on the Constructivist and Contextual Nature of Science*. New York: Pergamon.

Krase, J. (1997) 'Polish and Italian Vernacular Landscapes in Brooklyn.' *Polish American Studies*, 54: 9–31.

Latour, B. and S. Woolgar (1979) *Laboratory Life: The Social Construction of Scientific Facts*. London: Sage.

Lynch, M. (1985) 'Discipline and the Material Form of Images: An Analysis of Scientific Visibility.' *Social Studies of Science*, 15: 37–66.

MacDougall, D. (1975) 'Beyond Observational Cinema.' In: P. Hockings (ed.) *Principles of Visual Anthropology*. The Hague/Paris: Mouton de Gruyter, pp. 109–24.

McPhail, C. and R. T. Wohlstein (1982) 'Using Film to Analyze Pedestrian Behavior,' *Sociological Methods & Research*, 10: 347–75.

Mitchell, W. J. (1992) *The Reconfigured Eye: Visual Truth in the Post-Photographic Era*. Cambridge, MA: The MIT Press.

Mizen, P. (2005) 'A Little "Light Work"? Children's Images of Their Labor.' *Visual Studies*, 20: 124–58.

Niesyto, H. (2000) 'Youth Research on Video Self-Productions: Reflections on a Social Aesthetic Approach.' *Visual Sociology*, 15: 135–53.

Page, E. R. (2001) 'Social Change at Bike Week.' *Visual Sociology*, 16: 7–35.

Pauwels, L. (1993) 'The Visual Essay: Affinities and Divergences between the Social Scientific and the Social Documentary Modes.' *Visual Anthropology*, 6: 199–210.

Pauwels, L. (1996) *De Verbeelde Samenleving: Camera, Kennisverwerving en Communicatie*. Leuven/Apeldoorn: Garant.

Pinney, C. (1990) 'Classification and Fantasy in the Photographic Construction of Caste and Tribe.' *Visual Anthropology*, 3: 259–88.

Prosser, J. (2007) 'Visual Methods and the Visual Culture of Schools.' *Visual Studies*, 22: 13–30.

Rich, M. and R. Chalfen (1999) 'Showing and Telling Asthma: Children Teaching Physicians with Visual Narrative.' *Visual Sociology*, 14: 51–71.

Rieger, J. H. (1996) 'Photographing Social Change.' *Visual Sociology*, 11: 5–49.

Rieger, J. H. (2003) 'A Retrospective Visual Study of Social Change: The Pulp-Logging Industry in an Upper Peninsula Michigan County.' *Visual Studies*, 18: 157–78.

Rosaldo, R. (1989) 'Grief and the Headhunter's Rage.' In: *Culture and Truth*. London/New York: Routledge, 1–21.

Rose, G. (2006) *Visual Methodologies: An Introduction to the Interpretation of Visual Methods*, 2nd edn. London: Sage.

Rouch, J. (1975) 'The Camera and Man.' In: P. Hockings (ed.) *Principles in Visual Anthropology*. Chicago, IL: Aldine, pp. 83–102.

Ruby, J. (2000) *Picturing Culture: Explorations of Film and Anthropology*. The University of Chicago Press.

Schwartz, D. (2002) 'Pictures at a Demonstration.' *Visual Studies*, 17: 27–36.

Smith, K. L., S. Moriarty, G. Barbatsis and K. Kenney (eds.) (2005) *Handbook of Visual Communication: Theory, Methods, and Media*. Mahwah, NJ: Lawrence Erlbaum Associates.

Sorenson, E. R. and A. Jablonko (1975) 'Research Filming of Naturally Occurring Phenomena: Basic Strategies.' In: P. Hockings (ed.) *Principles in Visual Anthropology*. Chicago, IL: Aldine, pp. 151–63.

Suchar, C. (1988) 'Photographing the Changing Material Culture of a Gentrified Community.' *Visual Sociology Review*, 3: 17–22.

Suchar, C. (1992) 'Icons and Images of Gentrification: The Changed Material Culture of an Urban Community.' In: R. Hutchinson (ed.) *Gentrification and Urban Change: Research in Urban Sociology*. Greenwich, CT: JAI Press, pp. 33–55.

Suchar, C. (1997) 'Grounding Visual Sociology Research in Shooting Scripts.' *Qualitative Research*, 20(1): 33–22

Synnott, A. (1985) 'Symbolic Replica: A Sociology of Cemeteries.' *International Journal of Visual Sociology*, 2: 46–56.

Tufte, E. (1983) *The Visual Display of Quantitative Information*. Cheshire, CT: Graphics Press.

Tufte, E. (1990) *Envisioning Information*. Cheshire, CT: Graphics Press.

Tufte, E. (1997) *Visual Explanations*. Cheshire, CT: Graphics Press.

Wagner, J. (ed.) (1979) *Images of Information: Still Photography in the Social Sciences*. Beverly Hills, CA/London: Sage.

Wagner, J. (1999) 'Beyond the Body in a Box: Visualizing Contexts of Children's Action.' *Visual Sociology*, 14: 143–60.

Worth, S. and J. Adair (1975) *Through Navajo Eyes: An Exploration in Film Communication and Anthropology*. Bloomington: Indiana University Press.

Zube, E. (1979) 'Pedestrians and Wind.' In: J. W. Wagner (ed.) *Images of Information: Still Photography in the Social Sciences*. Beverly Hills, CA/London: Sage, pp. 69–83.

Part II

The visual researcher as collector and interpreter

3   Researching 'found' or 'pre-existing' visual materials

One of the most obvious ways to study visual aspects of society is to collect and analyze images, visual representations and artifacts that already exist. It is not uncommon for visual sociologists and anthropologists to take this road, yet scholars from other disciplines also regularly examine pre-existing imagery from multiple sources for a variety of reasons and from a myriad of perspectives. Thus looking at 'found imagery' (and the ways they are used) is in no way restricted to visual social science, though sociologists and anthropologists will obviously study these artifacts from their specific disciplinary angles and interests.

Visuals produced in a given culture can be looked upon both as cultural artifacts in their own right (with specific social and cultural functions) and as rich – though not unproblematic – gateways or windows to aspects of the depicted culture. They can also to some extent provide access to the culture of the image makers (by 'mirroring' their culturally specific points of views). Family pictures or picture advertisements can be scrutinized for learning more about photographic practices at a particular time and place, or for focusing on changes in gender or family relations, or even as a point of access for studying social and cultural change with a more encompassing perspective.

1   Benefits and challenges of using found visuals

The potential *benefits* of using existing images or visualizations of society are manifold. First of all, these 'found' visuals or visual artifacts are truly ubiquitous and their offer is constantly growing. Not only is the amount of imagery produced on a daily basis still growing exponentially, but also there is an almost constant influx of new media and visual tools to produce, disseminate, access and store huge quantities of visuals (e.g. phone cam images stored on the Internet). Likewise the social and cultural functions that these visual artifacts perform are in constant flux, and opening up new opportunities for researching visual culture. Not only is the constant supply of societal imagery and visual artifacts immense, but their nature is highly varied and the purposes for which they are employed very divergent. They in fact span the whole range from naïve (e.g., children's drawings, family photographs), utilitarian (ID card pictures, school photography, CCTV recordings) to very professional and sophisticated – both popular and high-brow – visual products (such as advertising, art, fiction and nonfiction film, Web sites, games . . .) originating from many segments of society (private, commercial, governmental, education, entertainment . . .). Moreover, these huge repositories are becoming better organized as well as more widely accessible in today's networked society. As such, they provide access to a wide variety of public and private worlds, possibly across different cultures, from times long past to the almost immediate present. Often they provide a unique 'inside view' (in homes, institutions . . .). As they have not been made for the particular research use for which they later serve, they are at least in that respect 'non-reactive' records (though of course they should often be considered as performances of some kind and for some purpose).

However, using visual materials that have not originated from an explicit research context does pose a number of *challenges*. 'Found' images almost as a rule lack contextual information to some degree, as the researcher typically had no control over, nor complete knowledge about, the exact production circumstances (historical, technical, cultural), or the intended goals and uses. The abyss of time, space and culture that lies between the world of the depicted and the world of the researcher may prove quite arduous to overcome. There are many ways by which researchers may try to improve their knowledge about the causes and explanations of particular appearances – for example through well-placed informants and a variety of other sources of cultural, historical and technical information – but it is seldom an easy task. The absence of sufficient contextual information may easily lead to misinterpretation, for example by reading too much or too little in the visual representation and its societal impact. Lacking crucial information can invalidate or jeopardize the usability of these visual records.

Whereas the access to many visual data sources steadily improves, researchers should still be aware of unaccounted-for selectivity, either on their own part or contributed from the archival source. Moreover, certain sources (e.g., Web-based sources) are hard to sample because it is often unclear what the total population is and content may prove to be highly dynamic or volatile. But even if access to a source is easy and transparent (e.g., non-protected web-based sources), that does not imply that any kind of use can be made of the source. The rights of the subjects ('informed consent') and owners (e.g., copyright) should be observed at all times, and thus publishing pre-existing visuals may still prove cumbersome in the absence of a world-wide consensus about 'fair use' (see Chapter 12).

Found visuals obviously represent a hybrid category, and every source has its own characteristics and thus its specific opportunities and methodological issues. So while it is difficult to speak about this in general terms, the difference between (more) controlled versus uncontrolled (or less controlled) production is probably the most important distinction between 'for explicit research purposes produced' and 'found' visual materials (see Chapter 2). A particular image may thus end up in either category according to who uses it (the author/researcher or someone else) and for what purpose exactly (the initial research purpose or another one). Using pre-existing images is also the only option if the researchers want to go back in time.

2   The breadth and wealth of pre-existing visual data sources

Discussing all the possible visual data sources within society is an impractical task, because no image is completely predestined or excluded in advance from being used as a resource for research. To date, many types of 'societal' imagery (for example family pictures, advertisements, post cards, paintings, news reels, feature and documentary film, various picture archives, maps and charts) have been used by social, cultural and behavioral scientists to study a variety of subjects and issues, such as labor (Margolis, 1994), school culture (Margolis, 2004; Burke and Grosvenor, 2007), family dynamics (Musello, 1979; Chalfen, 1987; Pauwels, 2008), traumatic experiences (McAllister, 2006; Gödel, 2007), youth culture (Larson, 1999), stereotyping (Hagaman, 1993), migration (Wright, 2001), nature versus culture (Papson, 1991; Suonpää, 2000; Bousé, 2003), deviance (Lackey, 2001), race and ethnicity (Mellinger, 1992; Tomaselli and Shepperson, 2002; Grady, 2007), health (Bogdan and Marshall, 1997), gender and identity (Goffman, 1979; Edge, 1998) and globalization (Barndt, 1997). However, many areas of enquiry and many types of visual materials are still waiting to be explored, for social science has not even scratched the surface of opportunities in this regard.

To gain insight into the past or current norms and values of societies, one should not neglect or rule out fictional and artistic genres (feature film, art, comic books, games) and focus uniquely on so-called nonfiction genres (e.g., documentary, press photography). For visual materials explicitly labeled as fictional can often be seen as forms of condensed and abstracted social reality. John Weakland in an early reader on visual anthropology points at the striking analogy concerning the nature and cultural meaning (world views, forms of social interaction) between the fictional film productions in modern society and the myths and rituals in primitive society, which have already been studied for a long time by anthropologists as significant reflections of structure and culture (Weakland, 1975: 240). According to Weakland, therefore, the study of fictional images as cultural documents has specific advantages:

compared to daily life a fictional work represents a more highly ordered and defined unity, whose premises and patterns can be more readily studied. For the case of large, complex, modern societies, where fieldwork could cover an extremely limited fraction of actual behaviour, some such simplification appears an essential starting point. (Weakland, 1975: 246)

3   Key features of social scientific image analysis

The primary purpose of social scientific image analysis is to discover significant patterns in the depicted and in the way of depicting, in order to subsequently develop plausible interpretations, which link observations to past or current social processes and normative structures. Image analysis thus in general concerns the study of the observable elements in the image: people, attributes, physical circumstances, their organization and multiple interrelations. The main endeavor here is to analyze diverse socially and culturally relevant indications in direct and indirect ways (e.g., dress code, objects or circumstances which can indicate status, profession). But as any image creation process definitely produces additional potentially socially relevant information, attention must be paid to visual language and camera technique, in other words to the 'remodeling' of the referent by the diverse actors and stages of the image production process. It must be established to what degree certain choices – for example point of view, framing, composition, the moment – are sparked by technical, physical or other circumstances, or intentionally or unintentionally generated by the image producer(s).

So a thorough analysis of found images should not limit itself to analyzing the level of the depicted (often referred to as the content or the subject), but also interrogate the more subtle layer or level of the depiction process. It is imperative that both layers are taken into account as they both produce meaning, and moreover the significance of an image often resides in the combined effect of these two layers.

Unexpected issues which repeatedly return in the image material collected can direct the analysis in a unforeseen direction. Also, what may seem at first sight to be marginal image information – unintended by the image producer or person who commissioned the work – could also be researched. In addition, it may be worthwhile to develop an awareness for things which *never* appear in the collected images. Issues or situations which are never depicted in the image can potentially be just as meaningful as those which are continually captured, as they may point to fundamental but less manifest values and norms. This applies mostly to certain situations or topics around which a taboo exists (e.g., death, sickness, misfortune, sex, religion).

Although the depicted reality and its particular formal transformation often constitute the main focus of analysis, the broader context of the referent beyond the image frame is also worth considering. Many elements of an image indicate aspects of the phenomena being depicted that are not directly visible or present within the frame: the broader culture within which the image originated, background information about the image producer and about the primary audiences and uses of the images, specific political, social or physical circumstances and so forth. Many valuable facets also remain completely outside the frame, and can be brought in through meticulous research of the production and reception context of the visual materials.

Basic information external to the image may include the following.

• Concise verbal references in the periphery of the image revealing part of its 'provenance' (a caption, some writing on the back or an imprint, which can indicate time and place of the picture, the referent, the author, who commissioned the image, the event, the printer or the photographic studio, the agency, etc.); digital images may have useful information stored in their file properties or through 'tagging.'

• Information that resides in the material layer of the image, for example the type of printing paper (texture, color characteristics, weight) and traces of use and handling (unfortunately the material aspect of the analogue image is largely lost once it gets digitized and stored in a digital archive, which eradicates these many subtle markers of time and space and use).

• Information concerning the technical and social production methods (knowledge of the technical possibilities and limitations of the material used and of particular social practices at the time; information about who made the images, who directed the event and who selected and post-produced the end product).

• Data generated by applying other research materials and techniques, for example interviews with those directly involved, or with informants (these can possibly provide some factual data – who is photographed, relationships, places, events, year, etc. – but often certain details in the image also invoke respondents to describe certain feelings and opinions, so new data concerning the broader context of the referent are thus acquired: see further visual interviewing in Chapter 7).

- Comparing results of similar research; statistical materials (e.g., numerical data gathered by producers of image technology and consumables, market research and sales trends).

Finally, the separate observations and findings from the diverse detailed analyses and sources can be combined to obtain a plausible answer to the research questions.

The value of images from society for social science research remains to an important degree dependent on the correct interpretation of the codes transferred or constructed consciously or unconsciously by the maker, both at the level of the referent (gestures, mimicry, clothing, spatial set-up) and at the level of the image creation process (style, image connotations, conventions). Decoding, therefore, is not a simple task, especially when it concerns visual products which were produced a long time ago, or which originated within a (sub)culture with which the researcher is unfamiliar.

4   Some prevalent theoretical and analytical frameworks for examining images

Content, form and context (including both production and use/reception) are the three basic foci of image analysis. These aspects are covered in varying degrees and with a different disciplinary or thematic emphasis by different analytical or theoretical frameworks. As different ways to analyze images have been covered fairly extensively in several recent works (see Van Leeuwen and Jewitt, 2001; Margolis and Pauwels, 2011; Rose, 2012), just a few observations with respect to the specific strengths and limitations of some of the most widespread approaches are offered here.

4.1   Content analysis and 'formal' analysis

Content analysis is still one of the basic, most widely known, applied and accepted methods for systematically looking at larger quantities of images (and written texts) primarily. In general, it offers more guarantees (than most other methods) for representativeness and generalization, and it comprises the most straightforward and explicit methodology. But one major limitation of this approach already becomes clear through its name: only (manifest) 'content' at the level of the 'depicted' is being looked at, and often in a fragmented, disconnected and decontextualized way. In addition, a strictly 'quantitative' focus (counting occurrences of something) may not succeed in bringing out the most important features and meaning of a 'text,' for elements that are abundantly present are not necessarily the most significant ones. For this latter reason Bell considers content analysis a 'necessary but not sufficient methodology for answering questions about what the media depicts or represents' (Bell, 2001: 13), and he further states that it is 'seldom able to support statements about significance, effects or interpreted meaning of a domain of representation.'

Content analysis is mostly used to count and measure the 'pro-filmic' elements of the depicted scene (physical features of people, objects and elements within the depicted setting). But this basic method for visual analysis could be further developed to look in a more subtle or refined way at *formal* or stylistic features of the depiction process, which serve as sources of consciously or unintentionally constructed (by the sender) and/or afterwards ascribed (by the receiver) meaning. The often made distinction between content and form is misleading as images in particular tend to get their meaning or effect from the intricate relation of the depicted (the presented subject matter) and the depiction process. The 'form' in other words is part of the content, as the subject or referent of an image is molded (recreated) through the form. A formal analysis is a necessary step to take an image more seriously, as *form* is not just an add-on or artistic bonus of an image, but a primary source of potential meaning and effects. Historian Hayden White (1987) astutely phrased this idea, speaking about the 'content of the form,' when referring to his (somewhat contested) view that linguistic form (e.g., narrative conventions) is an important carrier of content in the description of historical facts and events by historians. Thus 'content analysis' should in fact always be a 'content + form' analysis and develop more sophisticated approaches to deal with the variety of (visual) media and styles of execution.

To date, when visual form is taken into account in studies using content analysis (or even when using other analytic approaches!) it often comprises an oversimplified and reductionist categorization of only some of the many visual traits and parameters of an image. In addition this approach typically implies a fragmentation of the formal whole (the syntagmatic structure), which in the case of the visual will often be particularly detrimental. However, the numerous choices made during the shooting and printing processes involve much more than taking 'camera angle' and 'camera distance' into account. Every analysis necessitates a good knowledge of the particular formal parameters, the building blocks of the medium and the many ways in which they can be applied and combined (styles, traditions). What Rose (2012: 51) calls 'compositional interpretation' is a kind of formal analysis of an image, but one that can hardly deny its roots in art history; its focus is on assessing compositional splendor rather than using composition to unveil social and political realities (of the maker, the depicted or the audience).

4.2   *(Socio-)semiotics and rhetorical analysis*

Semiotics – and its visual variant in particular – offers a useful theoretical frame and vocabulary to analyze how meaning is constructed by discerning different types of signs (e.g., icons, indexes, symbols), orders of signification (denotation and connotation) and by making clear that meaning arises from particular choices from a series of para-digms (e.g., choosing a wide-angle lens out of all possible focal lengths, or opting for a close-up instead of a medium or long shot) (Nöth, 2011). The *combination* of these *choices* in a syntagmatic structure results in a parti-cular effect (e.g., a distorted face or a dramatic landscape). These syntag-matic structures occur at the level of the static image, the diachronic shot, the edited sequence or a whole film, and are formed by particular combi-nations of 'signifiers' at the level of the depicted (e.g., events, mise-en-scène) and the depiction (e.g., photographic choices).

In response to the critique that semiotics tends to neglect the specific social contexts of use of signs, a 'socio-semiotic' variant was developed which tried to address this problem by focusing on the variable and context dependent nature of the 'rules' (and 'use' of them) that govern the signification process. Socio-semiotics also tends to devote more explicit attention to the interactions between different communication modes ('multimodality': see Jewitt, 2009; Kress, 2010; and Van Leeuwen, 2005). Obviously, questioning the subjective and constructed nature of imagery is not a unique feature of social semiotics. Issues of visual representation have a firm tradition in film theory (most notably in documentary theory) and visual communication science, and so have questions about power, ideology and so on. More tedious to apply on a larger scale than content analysis, (socio-)semiotic analysis, in contrast, does have an eye for relations between elements and is better suited for uncovering more hidden (e.g., symbolic or connotative) meanings as opposed to just manifest and quantifiable elements of an image.

Visual rhetoric shares with semiotics the quest to reveal how meaning is being constructed through different persuasive devices and techniques. In particular, this method seeks to uncover the persuasive strategies of visual texts, by looking at distinct functions of parts of the text and how they work together to achieve a certain goal. Rhetorical analysis benefits from the rich tradition of the classical Greek rhetoricians, focusing also on the many figures of speech and the four fundamental rhetorical operations which lie at the root of all figures of speech: addition, omission, transfer-ence and substitution. These figures of speech, which also have their 'visual' counterpart, are often divided into main categories of 'schemes' (changing the expected pattern of words or image elements: e.g., ellipse, tautology) and 'tropes' (changing the general meaning: e.g., irony, metaphor, metonym, paradox).

Rhetorical analysis can not only be used for explicitly persuasive forms of communication such as advertising or propaganda images, but can equally be applied to study the communicative structure of, for example, documentary images, family snaps or press photographs, as they all tend to employ rhetorical techniques and devices to make an impression on the viewer (Durand, 1987; Berger, 1998).

Roman Jakobson's linguistic model of communicative functions (1960) is also helpful to analyze the ways that images (or visual environments like cities) operate to communicate specific messages or desired outcomes. Getting a (visual) message across generally constitutes different acts: 'showing' something in particular (the referential function), adding a certain appreciative view to it (the expressive or emotive function), trying to capture the attention of the receiver (phatic function), trying to obtain the willingness or support of the receiver (conative function), seeking to present things in an attractive way (aesthetic or poetic function) and ensuring that all codes are being understood (meta-lingual function). Keeping those functions in mind while creating (persuasive) images may also help to increase their effectiveness.

4.3   Discourse analysis

'Discourse analysis' presents itself as a critical methodology for exploring 'how images construct specific views of the social world.' Gillian Rose (2012) proposes a distinction between two forms of discourse analysis. The first 'tends to pay rather more attention to the notion of discourses articulated through various kinds of visual images and verbal texts than it does to the practices entailed by the specific discourses' and the second form 'tends to pay more attention to the material practices of institutions than it does to the visual images and verbal texts. Its methodology is usually left implicit. It tends to be more explicitly concerned with issues of power, regimes of truth and technologies' (Rose, 2012: 195). To some extent, it is fair to say that discourse analysis (and 'hegemonic analysis') is primarily characterized by a very focused concern with disclosing power relations and ideology in 'texts' (in a broad sense, also including images) rather than by any distinct methodological or analytic contribution. The task of discourse analysts and scholars performing 'hegemonic analysis' will typically involve finding expressions of hierarchy, dominance/submissiveness or inequality through scrutinizing both the content (e.g., use of certain words, roles, activities and positions of depicted subjects) and the form (e.g., camera angle, shot types, point of view, use of metaphors).

However, the term 'discourse analysis' is being applied today in a rather loose way to very different and hybrid approaches of image and text analysis (borrowing and combining aspects from semiotics, content analysis, rhetoric, etc.) and for investigating a wide variety of themes, issues and practices, not all of which are centered on revealing power relations.

4.4   Cultural studies

While several scholars have tried to build a case for a specific *cultural studies approach* to analyzing the visual by discussing a number of essential aspects of visual analysis from a certain theoretical angle, what they are putting forward as typical traits of a 'visual cultural studies' approach (analysis of contexts of production and consumption, cultural codes, etc.) is fairly common in the works of many sociologists and communication scientists, who have for many decades been working independently from this paradigm. However, the literary scholarship that lies at the root of this approach did contribute some theoretical vitality to image analysis and to the study of material culture – a somewhat neglected area in traditional sociology. But to date, this school of thought still seems to offer not much more than what Van Leeuwen and Jewitt call 'not . . . a specific methodology, but an agenda of questions and issues for addressing specific images' (Van Leeuwen and Jewitt, 2001: 2). Such an extended agenda of questions and themes (preferably not limited to race, gender and identity) may be very valuable and lead to valuable applications and insight.

4.5   Iconology

Iconography as a preoccupation to reveal the meaning of depictions goes back to the ancient Greeks, and blossomed in the seventeenth and eighteenth centuries, but its current theoretical base rests to an important extent on the work of Aby Warburg (1866–1929) and Erwin Panofsky (1892–1968). Iconography, according to Panofsky (1955), is that branch of art history which focuses on the subject matter or meaning of works of art rather than on their form (or artistic merit). His influential three-step methodology seeks to uncover the natural (pre-iconographical description), conventional (iconographical analysis) and symbolic meanings (iconographical interpretation (1939) later: iconological analysis (1955)) of a visual representation. This method is concerned with both detailed image analysis and intertextual relations (other visual and verbal sources) moving from the primary meaning or the most basic understanding of what is depicted ('thirteen men around a table') to the secondary meaning or the conventional understanding (in this example based on knowledge from the Bible: 'The Last Supper of Christ'), to the tertiary or deeper meaning (why was the 'Last Supper' chosen as a subject in a certain historical and cultural context?) (Bialostocki, 1973; Van Straten, 1994; Müller, 2011).

4.6   Ethnomethodology

Finally, an ethnomethodological perspective may provide another essential complement to the study of imagery that seeks to go beyond textual borders and into the broader contexts of production and uses. A recent and very insightful account of ethnomethodology in visual research is provided by Ball and Smith (2011). These authors characterize ethnomethodology as 'a sustained commitment to study empirically the characteristics of actual social practices' (Ball and Smith, 2011: 392), with much attention to the participant's point of view and 'the contextual particulars of talk and action as a source of the understandings and orientations that guide participants' actions' (2011: 396). The focus of an ethnomethodological approach with respect to visuals is, according to Goodwin, another key figure of this tradition, 'not thus representations or vision per se, but instead the part played by visual phenomena in the production of meaningful action,' which he evidenced by drawing on several fields of expertise and modes of practice (various practices in scientific image-making, practices of map-making by archaeologists, the use of videotape as evidence in court, etc.) (Goodwin, 2001: 157).

Analyzing picture advertisements

Picture advertisements rank among the most vivid and hybrid expressions of society. They are becoming ever more sophisticated constructions that also present distinct societal and cultural views in forthright or more subtle and indirect ways. Advertisements often contain behavioral prescriptions and role models, which consumers are persuaded to adopt. While most often focused on stimulating consumption of particular goods or services, advertisements – in a myriad of purposeful and inadvertent ways – also refer to the broader material and immaterial achievements of a given culture at a given time. As complex multimodal constructions – both in form and content – picture advertisements tend to borrow 'indiscriminately from the aesthetic reservoirs of our culture, incorporating diverse fictional devices, genres, styles and modes' (Schrøder, 1987: 89). Therefore, researching picture advertisements as indicators of social and cultural change requires a high degree of visual/ multimodal competency and a broad cultural literacy to adequately decode and attribute such complicated, 'multi-authored' (advertiser, account executive, copywriter, art-director, photographer, etc.) messages, which are imbued with norms and values.

The advertisement by Janard (Figure 3.1) was published several decades ago in Belgian magazines, and marked a significant change in the way women had typically been depicted until then in advertisements, which had previously been in rather subservient and passive roles (as persuasively described and illustrated in Goffman's *Gender Advertisements*, 1979). The well-composed black-and-white photograph in combination with the textual parts: the headline 'The Decision' (*De Beslissing*) and the pay-off or baseline 'Fashion for women who make their own decisions' (*Mode voor vrouwen die zelf beslissen*), cleverly constructs a remarkable reversal of the traditional gender roles. Depicted is a young, well-dressed woman, who apparently took advantage of the anonymous (interchangeable) man to satisfy one of her needs, and who is now ready to move on to other business or pleasures. This fashion advertisement clearly uses a 'lifestyle approach' (as opposed to a more product-centered strategy), and in doing so touches upon aspects of gender, class, ethnicity and sexuality.

Figure 3.1 Janard advertisement as published in a Belgian magazine (*Knack*)

Visual social scientists would typically address research questions such as: to what extent does this advertisement represent a genuine change in sexual mores and gender roles or rather constitute a (class-bound) exception, a projection of an ideal, or a fiction fostered by the media? How do these depictions relate to fashion advertisements of a decade earlier within the same culture or to those of other cultures (American, Japanese, Indian, etc.) in the same period and do they correspond to otherwise documented evolutions in those societies?

To investigate advertisements as agents or indicators of change in society, the analyst can choose among or – even better – combine different theoretical and analytical frameworks. Answers to the above mentioned and similar research questions may not only be found in the images themselves, but may also involve a study of the broader contexts of their production, application and reception.

A *content analysis* of this image and a larger set of fashion advertisements of the same cultural context would aim to categorize and quantify elements of the depicted scene – age, sex, skin and hair color, attire, class, situation, place (hotel room, bedroom), words – in order to detect trends related to what types of situations, environments, props and actors were being used and what this could possibly convey about societal evolutions.

A *rhetorical analysis* could then help to reveal the specific communicative functions of the different image elements and how they together strategically build the message(s): the brand name Janard clearly refers to the sender, and the women's dress is most probably a Janard product (= referential function); the receiver's attention is drawn by the beautiful young woman, who very prominently fills the frame (= phatic function). The baseline appeals to the female reader by creating the desire to belong to this group of women, who take their own decisions (= conative function). The sender tries to put the product – though very indirectly (see lifestyle approach) – in a positive light (= expressive function), by linking the product to beautiful, successful women. The whole picture has an aesthetic quality that may seem attractive to the receiver (= poetic function). No verbal or visual elements (like specialized terms or unknown objects) need to be 'explained' (there is, therefore, no meta-linguistic function).

A *semiotic approach* offers a rich set of concepts to scrutinize this advertisement in terms of the different types of signs (icons, indexes and symbols), the choice of particular elements out of series of possibilities (paradigms) and their specific combination (syntagmatic structure), both at the level of the mise-en-scène and through the photographic choices. Different signifiers at the level of the depicted (the bed, the looks of the depicted persons, the woman's dress) connote class and good taste. The man is in a passive role and completely unaware of the women's intentions, whereas she is depicted upright, engaged in an activity and looking outside the frame towards her next move. Camera position and framing clearly connote the primacy of the female person. The black bar over the eyes of the man (a code and practice borrowed from news reporting to secure anonymity for victims) further diminishes his role in this story.

Looking at this advertisement from a *discourse analysis perspective* could move the attention to power relations as they reside in different aspects of the image (and outside of it). One would first of all note the apparent gender role reversal, but then also try to go deeper into this superficial layer and ask: who is really being used here for what purposes? Stepping beyond the mere image to an institutional critique may expose this advertisement as a fake construction, whereby an illusory connection is being made between wearing a particular clothing brand and obtaining a certain way of life, and thus luring women into buying a particular brand of clothing through fake pretenses.

An *iconographic/iconological approach* to this advertisement would first concentrate on trying to recognize the depicted situation ('a bed with two persons'), comparing this 'motive' to other literary, visual (a love scene from a feature film, a painting?), mythical or religious sources to next uncover its conventional meaning (who are the persons compared to: Romeo and Juliet, Judith and Holofernes? What is really going on here: an affair, sexual liberation?) and finally its deeper meaning (why would a young woman be depicted with reference to this or that historic or mythical figure or event, in a particular cultural context?).

Most of these approaches will imply knowledge of the formal aspects of visual images as a source of expressive information.

5   Concluding observations

Whereas the offer of analytical tools and theoretical frameworks to analyze visuals to date seems very broad, most of those approaches provide only a narrow view of the matter, and very few scholars engage in the effort to integrate these valuable views into a more encompassing model for analysis. Moreover, many of these approaches offer hardly any clear methodological directions and often prove ill-equipped to disclose the complex layers of meaning of visual artifacts from distinct visual media. Some approaches in actual fact offer little more than a thematic focus, and their proponents often tend to be more concerned with re-appropriating long-existing texts and authors and relabeling pre-existing concepts and ideas. The indistinctness/overlap of and idiosyncratic variations within these different approaches may at least in part account for the fact that visual research projects are often not very explicit about the frameworks and theories they use to disclose the information that is within the resulting images or that are being used to support interpretations.

When analyzing images both naïve realists, who treat images as unproblematic windows to the world, as well as extreme relativists or constructivists, who deny almost completely the practicability of the depicted 'reality' as 'data' of sorts (while obviously not to be considered 'truth' or 'reality') are on the wrong foot when trying to understand the complex role and impact of imagery in cultures. Van Leeuwen and Jewitt (2001: 5), editors of the *Handbook of Visual Analysis*, also refer to the persistent – though not always very illuminating – debate on 'reality' versus 'construction' of images, and they propose not to polarize the issue, as is commonly the case:

the choice of an appropriate method of analysis is dependent on the nature of the project in which it is to be used, on the visual material that is being investigated, and on the goals of the research project. . . . The issue of 'record' versus 'construct' exists because many images have an element of both and so require a mode of analysis which is sensitive to both. (Van Leeuwen and Jewitt, 2001: 5)

Malcolm Collier takes a similar stance with respect to this highly debated issue:

Much has been said regarding the 'constructed' character of photographs, video and film, heightening our awareness of the influences of individual, cultural, political and other variables on the making, viewing and analysis of visual records. While this discourse has enriched our understanding of images it can also create an illusion that they contain nothing beyond their constructed content. (Collier, 2001: 35)

Van Leeuwen and Jewitt (2001) also take a thoughtful approach in presenting and discussing the different perspectives on text (the visual 'product'), context and social practices, thereby stressing the need to include the producers' and viewers' side in an encompassing analysis. They do acknowledge, however, that for specific research questions and angles one may have good reasons to narrow the focus down to just one or several of those aspects.

Though visual social scientists often favor an empirical approach which involves – to a higher or lesser degree – meticulously looking at images as visual records of society, they do not necessarily perform these analyses from a naïve realist stance (seeking for 'truth'). However, it should be admitted that often the representational or stylistic features of the found or researcher-produced records could have been brought more to the fore. The layer of the depiction is paradoxically far too often neglected by visual social scientists as well as by other 'visual' scholars (visual communication, cultural studies . . .). Many studies indeed are limited to analyzing only 'what' is depicted and only scantily looking at 'how' something is depicted, as if images are mere windows to reality.

One possible reason for this neglect is the lack of expertise to analyze the formal aspects of the visual in terms of meaning, since that requires a very specific knowledge of the transformational processes, the technologies and the representational traditions of a particular visual medium. Fortunately, there are studies that do look explicitly at the representational features of imagery as data in their own right, as well as examples where social scientists try to deliberately use aesthetics to visually communicate with peers and the general audience. Visual researchers should at all times have an eye for the politics of representation, while not neglecting the wealth of data that resides in all layers of the images they are using.

A more integrated and explicit methodology focused on both form and content would ideally form the basis of different theoretical and conceptual frameworks of image analysis, whether geared towards quantifiable and manifestly present elements or characterized by more qualitative/ interpretative approaches. Although many analytical frameworks seek to go further than quantifying a limited set of visual elements, they are and will remain cumbersome to apply to large sets of data (a trait or dilemma that applies to most qualitative approaches).

As every medium has its particular transmission codes and expressive capabilities, researchers can only take full advantage of the rich offer of varied data when they know the technical and cultural particulars of the specific products of each medium they choose to analyze. Knowledge of drawing and painting, for example, does not suffice to disclose the full informative and expressive potential of camera-based media (photography, video, film), and vice versa.

A social scientific study of existing imagery (as well as 'researcher-initiated' visuals; see Part III) will benefit from a broad and intimate knowledge of the different analytical tools and an ability to construct a workable and customized approach, which dares to be somewhat eclectic at times and which is geared towards providing specific answers to pertinent research questions. Images should not (only) be used to illustrate or prove previously held conceptions or expectations, but be allowed through meticulous empirical research to challenge and enrich current insights and convictions.

6   References

Ball, M. and G. Smith (2011) 'Ethnomethodology and the Visual: Practices of Looking, Visualization, and Embodied Action.' In: E. Margolis and L. Pauwels (eds.) *SAGE Handbook of Visual Research Methods*. London/New Delhi: Sage, pp. 392–413.

Barndt, D. (1997) 'Zooming out/Zooming in: Visualizing Globalization.' *Visual Sociology*, 12: 5–32.

Bell, P. (2001) 'Content Analysis of Visual Images. ' In: T. Van Leeuwen and C. Jewitt (eds.) *Handbook of Visual Analysis*. London: Sage, pp. 10–34.

Berger, A. A. (1998) *Media Research Techniques*. Thousand Oaks, CA/London/ New Delhi: Sage.

Bialostocki, J. (1973) 'Iconography.' In: P. Wiener (ed.) *Dictionary of the History of Ideas*. New York: Charles Scribner's Sons, Vol. 2, pp. 524–42.

Bogdan, R. and A. Marshall (1997) 'Views of the Asylum: Picture Postcard Depictions of Institutions for People with Mental Disorders in the Early 20th Century.' *Visual Sociology*, 12: 4–27.

Bousé, D. (2003) 'False Intimacy: Close-Ups and Viewer Involvement in Wildlife Films.' *Visual Studies*, 18: 123–32.

Burke, C. and I. Grosvenor (2007) 'The Progressive Image in the History of Education: Stories of Two Schools.' *Visual Studies* 22: 155–68.

Chalfen, R. (1987) *Snapshot Versions of Life*. Bowling Green State University Popular Press.

Collier, M. (2001) 'Approaches to Analysis in Visual Anthropology.' In: T. Van Leeuwen and C. Jewitt (eds.) *The Handbook of Visual Analysis*. London/ Thousand Oaks, CA/New Delhi: Sage, pp. 35–60

Durand, J. (1987) 'Rhetorical Figures in the Advertising Image.' In: J. Umiker-Sebeok (ed.) *Marketing and Semiotics: New Directions in the Study of Signs for Sale*. Berlin: Mouton de Gruyter, pp. 295–318.

Edge, S. (1998) 'The Power to Fix the Gaze: Gender and Class in Victorian Photographs of Pit-Brown Women.' *Visual Sociology*, 13: 37–56.

Gödel, M. (2007) 'Images of Stillbirth: Memory, Mourning and Memorial.' *Visual Studies*, 22: 253–69.

Goffman, E. (1979) *Gender Advertisements*. New York/London: Harper & Row.

Goodwin, C. (2001) 'Practices of Seeing Visual Analysis: An Ethnomethodological Approach.' In: T. Van Leeuwen and C. Jewitt (eds.) *Handbook of Visual Analysis*. London: Sage, pp. 157–82.

Grady, J. (2007) 'Advertising Images as Social Indicators: Depictions of Blacks in LIFE Magazine, 1936–2000.' *Visual Studies*, 22: 211–39.

Hagaman, D. (1993) 'The Joy of Victory, the Agony of Defeat: Stereotypes in Newspaper Sports Feature Photographs.' *Visual Sociology*, 8: 48–66.

Jakobson, R. (1960) 'Closing Statements: Linguistics and Poetics.' In: T. A. Sebeok, *Style In Language*. Cambridge, MA: The MIT Press, pp. 350–77.

Jewitt, C. (2009) *The Routledge Handbook of Multimodal Analysis*. London: Routledge.

Kress, G. (2010) *Multimodality: A Social Semiotic Approach to Contemporary Communication*. London: Routledge.

Lackey, C. (2001) 'Visualizing White-Collar Crime: Generic Imagery in Popular Film.' *Visual Sociology*, 16: 75–94.

Larson, H. (1999) 'Voices of Pacific Youth: Video Research as a Tool for Youth Expression.' *Visual Sociology*, 14: 163–72.

Margolis, E. (1994) 'Images in Struggle: Photographs of Colorado Coal Camps.' *Visual Sociology*, 9: 4–26.

Margolis, E. (2004) 'Looking at Discipline, Looking at Labor: Photographic Representations of Indian Boarding Schools.' *Visual Studies*, 19: 72–96.

Margolis, E. and L. Pauwels (eds.) (2011) *SAGE Handbook of Visual Research Methods*. London/New Delhi: Sage.

McAllister, K. (2006) 'Photographs of a Japanese Canadian Internment Camp: Mourning Loss and Invoking a Future.' *Visual Studies*, 21: 133–56.

Mellinger, W. M. (1992) 'Representing Blackness in the White Imagination: Images of "Happy Darkeys" in Popular Culture, 1893–1917.' *Visual Sociology*, 7: 3–21.

Müller, M. (2011) 'Iconography and Iconology as a Visual Method and Approach.' In: E. Margolis and L. Pauwels (eds.) *SAGE Handbook of Visual Research Methods*. London/New Delhi: Sage, pp. 283–97.

Musello, C. (1979) 'Family Photography.' In: J. Wagner (ed.) *Images of Information*. Los Angeles: Sage, pp. 101–18

Nöth, W. (2011) 'Visual Semiotics: Key Features and an Application to Picture Ads.' In: E. Margolis and L. Pauwels (eds.) *SAGE Handbook of Visual Research Methods*. London/New Delhi: Sage, pp. 298–316.

Panofsky, E. (1939) *Studies in Iconology: Humanistic Themes in the Art of the Renaissance*. New York: Oxford University Press.

Panofsky, E. (1955) 'Iconography and Iconology: An Introduction to the Study of Renaissance Art.' In: E. Panofsky, *Meaning in the Visual Arts*. University of Chicago Press, pp. 26–41.

Papson, S. (1991) 'Looking at Nature: The Politics of Landscape Photography.' *Visual Sociology*, 6: 4–12.

Pauwels, L. (2008) 'A Private Visual Practice Going Public? Social Functions and Sociological Research Opportunities of Web-Based Family Photography.' *Visual Studies*, 23: 34–49.

Rose, G. (2012) *Visual Methodologies: An Introduction to Researching with Visual Materials*, 3rd edn. London: Sage.

Schröder, K. (1987) 'Snapshot Fables: The True Nature of Magazine Advertisements.' In: L. Henny (ed.) *Semiotics of Advertisements*, International Studies in Visual Sociology and Anthropology, vol. 1. Aachen: Edition Herodot, Rader Verlag, pp. 78–93.

Suonpää, J. (2000) 'Taming Predators Through Photograph.' *Visual Sociology*, 15: 51–64.

Tomaselli, K. G. and A. Shepperson (2002) 'Where's Shaka Zulu?: Shaka Zulu as an Intervention in Contemporary Political Discourse.' *Visual Studies*, 17: 129–140.

Van Leeuwen, T. (2005) *Introducing Social Semiotics*. London: Routledge.

Van Leeuwen, T. and C. Jewitt (eds.) (2001) *The Handbook of Visual Analysis*. London: Sage.

Van Straten, R. (1994) *An Introduction to Iconography*. Abingdon/New York: Taylor and Francis.

Weakland, J. (1975) 'Feature Films as Cultural Documents.' In: P. Hockings (ed.) *Principles of Visual Anthropology*. The Hague: Mouton de Gruyter, pp. 231–52.

White, H. (1987) *The Content of the Form: Narrative Discourse and Historical Representation*. Baltimore, MD/London: The Johns Hopkins University Press.

Wright, T. (2001) 'Reflections on "The Looking Glass War": Photography, Espionage and the Cold War.' *Visual Sociology*, 16: 75–88.

4   A visual and multimodal model for analyzing online environments

1   Disclosing 'culture' in websites

The Internet is a rich resource for researchers in many respects: as a field of study, a research tool and a means for scholarly communication. This chapter will focus on the online environment as a contemporary and highly productive field of research. Internet phenomena, and websites in particular, are indeed unique expressions of present-day culture, and as such they constitute a huge repository of potential data about contemporary ways of doing and thinking of large groups of people across ethnic and national boundaries.

Several authors have dealt with the implications of using established research methods (survey, focus groups, content analysis, interviewing) in an online mode, scrutinized the specific opportunities and impediments of the Web both as a source and a tool of research or examined the question of how to take advantage of new practices of Web users (for example chatting, social networking) for studying culture (Paccagnella, 1997; Jones, 1999; Hine, 2000, 2006; Mann and Stewart, 2000; Wakeford, 2000; Weare and Lin, 2000; Lievrouw and Livingstone, 2002; Rossler, 2002; Andrews et al., 2003; Lister et al., 2003; Carter, 2005; Stewart and Williams, 2005).

However, to date the appeal of this rich resource has largely been limited to those aspects that can be addressed with more or less established, verbally oriented, methods. Therefore – and quite paradoxically – several of the more basic characteristics of the Web have been neglected. Most notably, this applies to the exploration of the visual and multimedia features of the Web (as opposed to mainly verbal utterances and practices), both as a very significant source of cultural information and as an opportunity for improving the nature and depth of scholarly communications. So there is still a need for a more adapted and sophisticated tool or methodology to disclose this cultural data source in all of its apparent and less apparent modalities and to adequately address the interplay between these different expressive aspects as the prime generators of meaning.

This chapter seeks to provide the foundations for such an integrated tool by way of a multimodal framework for analyzing Web phenomena from both a medium-specific and socio-cultural perspective.

2   Real and perceived issues of web-based research

It took some time before social scientists looked at cyberspace as an integral part of contemporary society and not as a strange refuge for some of its members or a sort of 'parallel' virtual universe. But since then the insight gained currency that there are many complex interactions and highly significant connections between offline and online worlds, and that both are part of the contemporary social life of an increasing number of people (Dutton et al., 2009: 5).

2.1   'Reliable' constructs?

Deliberate constructs and mediated forms of communication such as websites are not necessarily less significant for studying culture and social life. Some studies even provide evidence for the fact that, in computer-mediated communications, the absence of real-life cues – which are so intrinsic a part of face-to-face interaction – tends to help more profound aspects of identity to emerge. Thus people may reveal more of their identities and provide more valid information than in face-to-face situations, where their anonymity cannot be secured and where their conduct may be challenged directly (though asynchronous online communication also occasionally produces flame wars and specific forms of 'cyber-bullying'). Cyber-psychologists have coined the remarkable 'openness' and freedom of reserve of people on the semi-public space of the Internet, the 'Online Disinhibition Effect' (Suler, 2004). Therefore a 'disembodied environment' (Mann and Stewart, 2000: 210) like the Internet may have at least as much 'significance' for getting to someone's personal and cultural identity or self as meeting in person. All forms of communication and interaction have their techniques for identity construction, impression management and conscious self-presentation. None should be taken for granted or dismissed, and all – including the mediated ones – are valid for cultural research.

When researching websites, clearly one is looking at contemporary forms of 'material culture' rather than at human behavior as it unfolds in interaction (unless there are webcams to provide more fleeting and possibly unplanned visual accounts of behavior, or chat-room interaction, which provides another more or less dynamic version of (verbal) behavior). But even as relatively 'static' cultural products they provide much potentially significant material, a large part of which, in turn, is not available in 'real-life' (better: offline) situations.

Furthermore, studying online phenomena should not be seen as an alternative to more direct forms of fieldwork, but as a contemporary complement to them. Whereas modes of computer-mediated communication in general may be chosen because they are felt to be 'safer' than a direct confrontation with a possibly judgmental audience, this 'advantage' applies even more to websites than it does to other electronically mediated, but still more or less 'confrontational' environments, like online discussion groups. 'Identity play' (adopting another 'persona' or altering parts of one's persona by pretending to be of a another sex, age, culture or profession) is much less a practical option in (private or institutional) websites than it is in purely verbal online forms of communication (multi-user dungeon environments or discussion lists) where the participants enjoy (visual) anonymity.

Deliberate identity construction – trying to present a particular, most often polished, image of oneself, not by telling blatant lies but by offering a selective amount of information – is a standard practice in most forms of human exchange, only the means and degree may differ according to medium, purpose and circumstance. Furthermore, these 'constructions' are themselves very significant online phenomena that belong to social and cultural life in the broader sense, and for that reason are worthy of much (more) academic attention. They do not necessarily need to be fully validated by present 'real-life realities' but sometimes should be considered as reflections of the aspirations or desires of their creators (Pauwels, 2002). In general they are not to be regarded as smokescreens or obstacles, obscuring insight into the social and cultural world of their producers.

2.2   Sampling and representativity

When using the Web to gain insight into cultures at large, obtaining a representative sample is an important issue. Some of the more optimistic authors believe that the Web population is no longer predominantly male, highly educated and based in the more affluent parts of the world. Kehoe and Pitkow (1996), for example, observed many years ago that the age of web users was becoming more diverse, that the gender imbalance of the early days was gradually diminishing, and that the web really was coming within the reach of a growing audience world-wide (Lee, 2000: 118). Others still believe that using the Internet as a 'window' on the world continues to be problematic. However, even the more modest estimates of coverage (distribution and growth rate) note that the Internet is becoming a part of many aspects of different sorts of people's lives (see: www.internetworldstats.com/stats.htm and www.worldinternetproject. net; Mesch and Talmud, 2006; Dutton et al., 2009), and that its technology offers many unique opportunities for research, even in its present phase of development. Obviously the issue of the representativeness of the population under study is closely tied with the type of research undertaken and the aims of the research project. When research is confined to web-related phenomena – for example, corporate websites – or targets populations that are known to have an important web presence (academics, multinational companies, government agencies) there are – at least theoretically – very few problems. Nonetheless, obtaining a 'representative sample' of web-active populations or phenomena (for example certain types of websites) is often not easy because the Internet is, for the most part, and despite sophisticated search engines and efforts to add some structure and control to it, an uncharted domain: we do not conclusively know who or what is 'out there.' Moreover, changes occur at an exceptional rate: new or radically overhauled sites constantly appear while existing websites migrate or 'die' while not being eradicated from cyberspace. The Internet is a huge data repository, but not necessarily a very permanent or predictable one. As Lee comments: 'The diffuse and democratic character of the Internet, the very attributes that make it such a valuable source for information, also make the finding of available information difficult' (2000: 119). Despite all of these difficulties, web-based research does allow types of cross-national research that before were only feasible for affluent research institutions because of the high costs of travel and the time-consuming nature of such an enterprise

3   Previous research on 'culture' in websites

The interest in cultural aspects of the web is shared with other scholars, yet it has a distinct focus. The core concern here is not how to develop or design culturally 'appropriate' and/or 'effective' web sites (in a commercial or persuasive sense) but how to decode/disclose the cultural information that resides both in the form and content (and the content of the form; see White, 1987) of web sites. Both strands of research ('cultural effectiveness' versus 'cultural expressiveness' in a broad sense) can inform one another to some extent, as designing and decoding are flip sides of the same coin.

The bulk of research on cultural aspects of web phenomena to date takes Hall's 'high' versus 'low context' model for analyzing interpersonal communication (1966, 1976) and/or Hofstede's key dimensions of culture (1980, 2001) as its prime conceptual framework. Moreover, these mainly business- and management-oriented studies predominantly adopt a cultural comparative stance focused on producing 'culturally aware' and 'effective' web communication. Hofstede's popular cultural framework comprises five key dimensions (high/low power distance, individualism/collectivism, masculinity/femininity, high/low uncertainty avoidance, long/short-term orientation), which originally were used to identify and explain differences in conduct between members of different nationalities. Most culturally oriented website research either tested or replicated parts of Hofstede's framework (see Sondergaard, 1994, for an extensive study of reviews, citations and replications of Hofstede up to 1994, and see Kirkman et al., 2006, for a further overview).

However, over the years Hofstede's approach has received some fierce criticism (as most elaborately and dismissively phrased by McSweeney (2002), but also by Kim (2007)) that focused on different epistemological and methodological aspects: for example measuring culture uniquely through surveys; equating/reducing culture to the idea of a monolithic (so with no internal variation) national culture; using (old) data of employees of one multinational (IBM) to extrapolate to national culture; focusing on only four, later five (ethnocentrically defined) dimensions. But in fact studies that fairly unproblematically adopt (with minor adaptations) Hall and Hofstede's concepts to the Internet by far outweigh those that are more critical or downright dismissive (see Marcus and Gould, 2000; Triandis, 2004; Ess and Sudweeks, 2005; Callahan, 2006; Würtz, 2005; Gevorgyan and Manucharova, 2009).

More fundamental than disputing the data that were at the basis of the development of the dimensions is challenging the idea that culture can be framed in four or five dimensions and that typifying aspects of culture should take the form of binary oppositions or polarizing scales. Kim (2007) rightly questions the use of polar opposites as exemplified in Hofstede's five binary dimensions (a practice continued by others), which she connects with a 'prevailing ideology of unidimensional model of cultural identity' (Kim, 2007: 27), and she goes on to contend 'there is nothing illogical about the coexistence of apparently contrasting cultural orientations' while 'elements of seemingly opposite worldviews may exist at the cultural and individual levels' (2007: 28). The use of a limited set of 'passe-partout' cultural dimensions also tends to predefine or at the least pre-mold the outcomes and focus the researcher's attention on just a limited set of aspects. If we are, for instance, interested in finding out how the cultural practice of family photography changed in and across different cultures once it became web-based (Pauwels, 2008a), then the application of Hofstede's dimensions will not lead us much further as the cultural shifts in this domain of social and cultural practices involve issues like the moving boundaries of private versus public space, the change of a private audience of family and friends to an unknown global audience and the opportunities/intricacies that this creates (e.g., for voicing political and religious views or for pursuing commercial goals). Nor will this or a similar framework (e.g., Kluckhohn and Strodtbeck, 1961; Trompenaars, 1994) help us to disclose relevant information as expressed by the different multimodal features of a website. Focusing on preconceived cultural differences does not warrant that the most specific or intriguing aspects of particular sites are picked up. And it does not seem to stimulate a broader, more encompassing approach to studying aspects of culture. To be clear, cultural conceptualizations such as that by Hofstede do not need to be rejected as such, as focused choices will have to be made, but the fact that one such conceptualization tends to be taken for granted and rather routinely and unsophisticatedly applied to different contexts, irrespective of the research interest or cultural setting, may be considered problematic.

While the criticism mostly focused on the reductionist (limited aspects of (corporate) culture and a dichotomous approach) and ethnocentric definition (a 'Western' perspective) of culture, another major flaw/ challenge of culture on the Internet has been largely overlooked: the often very partial and questionable operationalization of the cultural aspects into observable aspects of the hybrid medium. To illustrate this point, one could refer to a table created by Callahan summarizing a selection of the literature on the use of Hofstede's framework for the interpretation of differences in what she calls 'graphical design.' This table (Table 1. 'Web site characteristics in relation to Hofstede's dimensions of culture,' Callahan, 2006: 248) reveals rather coarse operationalizations of Hofstede's initial four dimensions. Images, for instance (implicitly classified by Callahan as 'graphical design features' and not as prime sources of information in both direct and metaphoric ways!), are treated as mere windows to the depicted and only operationalized with respect to 'what' they depict (leaders or buildings or emblems to signify 'high power distance', or the everyday activities of students, both genders, to signify 'low power distance'). No attention is paid to the meaning that for instance resides in the formal qualities of the pictures ('how' the subject matter is being depicted). Clearly, image analysis should involve more than counting the number of images and their immediate content categories (people, building, event . . .) or categorizing the depicted in crude categories as types of people, events and so on.

The fact that Hofstede's conceptualization of culture (in multinational organizations) continues to be popular probably has to do with the fact that it provides a shortcut to complex issues of culture and that researchers thus can rely or build on previous research. Hofstede's conceptualization of culture is not only too limited for framing culture in a broader way (as in sociology and anthropology), but also for studying a complex phenomenon such as the Internet where culture resides in many aspects and increasingly is becoming multi-authored and hybrid. However, Hofstede cannot be held responsible for this latter flaw, which is two-fold: the questionable operationalization of the dimensions to observable traits of the Internet and the inadequate knowledge of the expressive means of the Internet. Indeed, his conceptual framework was taken by others from the interpersonal level (getting along with colleagues and customers from other cultures) to mediated environments (e.g. advertising campaigns) and finally to extremely complex techno-cultural environments, such as the Internet. The framework thus acquired an 'almost paradigmatic status outside its initial context' (Sondergaard, 1994: 453).

The above discussed criticisms, though fairly fundamental in some instances, have not yet resulted in elaborate or fundamental revisions or the development of alternatives, to encompass a broader conceptualization both of culture and of the specifics of the culture of the Internet which is highly hybrid on all counts. In fact, Hofstede's framework continues to be taken as the basis for new research, and dichotomous thinking about culture(s) continues to characterize many contemporary research efforts.

The focus on cultural expressiveness requires a broader sociological/anthropological view on society through analyzing human behavior and material culture, and consequently a more encompassing conception of culture, that includes both inter- and intra-cultural differences and expressions of norms and values, expectations, roles, goals and so forth. The hereafter presented framework will therefore be relevant for researching cultural differences between countries or ethnicities but will equally be suited to track differences and specificities in organizational cultures (departmental or professional cultures) or small groups from a diachronic (longitudinal) or synchronic (comparative) perspective. Finally the presented analytical framework here is very much focused on taking into account the medium-specific modes and sub-modes, their multimodal interplay and their origin and purpose.

4   'Multimodal' cultural analysis defined

As the previous section tried to argue, a substantial part of cultural research of the Internet is characterized by a triple form of problematic reductionism: firstly with respect to the definition of culture (monolithic national cultures, 'culturability'), secondly in the way these cultural dimensions are operationalized (often a limited set of cross-cultural dimensions, and an exclusive focus on 'differences') and thirdly with respect to taking the aspects of the different expressive systems into account (most of the time only a very limited number of cultural signifiers and a bias towards the verbal mode). This chapter strives to deal with these problems with an emphasis on the latter by proposing a multimodal tool to address cultural aspects of websites.

4.1   The concept of multimodality

The detailed and multifaceted analysis of the Internet and websites with all of their constituting parts requires what today would be called in a somewhat trendy way a 'multimodal' analysis. Modality, and by extension multimodality, lacks a succinct and acknowledged definition (see Kress and Van Leeuwen, 2001, and O'Halloran 2005, both working in a systemic functional framework but with important differences in theoretical underpinning and definition of modality). The term 'mode' (or 'modality'), as distinct aspects of a communicative utterance or a medium is sometimes used in connection with physiological or sensory channels or capacities such as seeing (the visual mode), hearing (auditory mode), touching (tactile mode or the 'haptic' mode when considered as aspects of a device), tasting (gustatory mode) and smelling (the olfactory mode). Modalities quite often are also defined from the medium side, thus one speaks for instance about images and texts, music and vocal and non-vocal sounds, though they all belong to the visual or auditory channel or mode. Even the most hybrid and advanced (multi)media still only succeed (as do most other media) in addressing two out of our five senses (sight and hearing), as we either look at or hear texts, and almost all media fail to transmit tactile, olfactory or gustatory experiences. Thus the multimodal nature of the Internet too is in fact limited to two (super) modes: the 'visual' and the 'auditory,' ruling out all modes that address the tactile, olfactory and taste sense. However, the visual mode in a broad sense includes a wide variety of expressive systems that are often not readily considered as 'visual': the textual parts (have to be viewed or heard), typography, layout and design features. Likewise the auditory mode (spoken or sung texts, music, noises) exhibits a growing diversity of aspects and applications and a corresponding importance in website communications.

Returning to the earlier mentioned terminological confusion, written texts, images and gestures – while all 'visual' – are according to some definitions only sub-modes but are referred to by others as separate modes. And some scholars even use the term mode to indicate, for example, different genres of texts or different genres of photographic images (a documentary versus an artistic mode). But to cut this discussion short, whenever at least two input (senses) or output (medium/device) modes (or sub-modes) are involved, one could speak about multimodality. Multimodal analysis not only takes different modes into account but also has a strong focus on the effects of their interplay. The older concept, multimedia, has a far more restricted meaning, as it refers mainly to the capabilities of a technical device or to a technology (not to a communicative act or to the perceptual processing of data by people). Multimodal research is an ambitious venture given the fact that even most forms of mono-modal or single mode analysis (for example, the analysis of static photographs) are still underdeveloped – in other words, not able to tap into the full expressive potential of this medium.

4.2   The cultural decoding of hybrid media

Few choices and options in websites and the broader infrastructure of the Internet are culturally neutral. Cultural research of the Internet, therefore, could be focused on uncovering explicit and implicit statements on a broad range of issues such as values, norms and opinions regarding gender, class, race, religion, state and so forth as they are intentionally or unintentionally expressed and materialized in the many features of this highly hybrid medium (Pauwels, 2005). Consequently, one of the pillars of such a broad interest in mediated culture is a thorough knowledge of the medium's building blocks and of the effects of their advertent or inadvertent selection and combination.

Cultural website analysis, as with any type of media research, may take a snapshot approach (focusing on a static slice of a dynamic medium at a certain point in time) or opt for a diachronic approach in the form of a longitudinal study that consists of different snapshot data at certain time intervals, or for a more dynamic diachronic approach, focused on examining changes (actions and reactions) in a shorter period of time (key transitions, events). It goes without saying that cross-cultural research (synchronic and a fortiori diachronic) poses extra challenges to the researchers involved and that one of the major challenges is the hybridity of the required expertise that needs to be integrated.

The breadth of knowledge with regard to these building blocks is pretty daunting. And the size limit of this chapter only allows a very concise introduction to the most important parameters.

The presented research approach does not seek to take a predetermined (based on standard or 'universal' cultural indicators), predictive ('what works best') or normative ('how should it be done') stand, but advocates a rather explorative, descriptive ('what is there to be found') and interpretative ('what could it possibly tell us about aspects of culture') approach. Thus, rather than departing from a rather reductionist view on (national) culture that is subsequently operationalized in only a few preconceived aspects of websites, this method tries to gain insight into the complex paradigmatic choices and signifiers of websites. The approach addresses in a more sophisticated and integrated way how specific combinations of these paradigmatic choices may inadvertently or advertently construct cultural statements. However, it does not provide a ready-made tool to 'read' or 'decode' culture in each of those aspects, for reasons that will be explained later.

This approach highlights some of the differences between the dominant focus on 'cultural usability' and a research approach that seeks to uncover 'cultural expressiveness' in a broad sense. Such an 'open' attitude towards cultural analysis should not conceal or exclude a theoretical focus, a clear methodological framework and a set of expectations, as an unfocused and under-theorized observation would largely remain blind or impressionistic.

The framework as presented in the next section contains both a structured repository of potential cultural signifiers and a plan of attack, a methodology for moving from the general/salient/quantitative to the specific/implicit/qualitative and from mono-modal to multimodal analysis.

While it may very well be that some cultural interpretations of certain paradigmatic choices and their combination into larger syntagms are relatively 'fixed' and 'universal' (or cross-cultural to some extent) – as the very valuable work of Kress and Van Leeuwen (1996) on paradigmatic meanings of certain options in images and the design of pages seems to suggest and illustrate – one should at all times remain very cautious about adopting rather undifferentiated views on cultural expressions.

5   The multimodal framework for analyzing websites

The model for analyzing websites as social and cultural data sources consists of six phases which correspond to a certain logic of discovery: from looking at rather immediately manifest features and performing straightforward measurements (phase 2) to more in-depth interpretations of the constituting elements and their intricate relations. The research thus migrates from data that are fairly easy to quantify and code, to more interpretative analysis focused on discovering the metaphorical and symbolic dimensions of websites or to unraveling their intended and even unintended meanings. My discussion briefly explores each of these phases of analysis of websites, with examples of their potential to express aspects

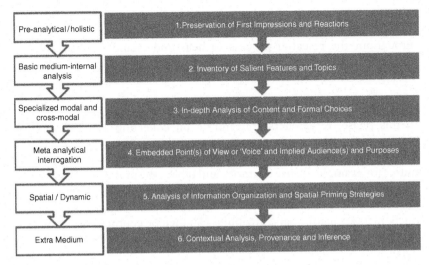

Figure 4.1 Main phases of 'a multimodal framework for analyzing websites' (Pauwels, 2011). The first column of this graph provides a further indication of the shifting focus within each of the phases: from noting down a holistic impression, to basic and more detailed analyses of each of the groups of signifiers of a Web environment, to an investigation of the interplay between those signifiers and its resulting meta-discourse, to the very medium-specific spatial and dynamic nature of websites and finally to broader analysis of the context of website production and use, thus going beyond the physical confines of the medium.

of culture. The references provided are only listed as sources for further reading.

5.1 Preservation of first impressions and reactions

This first phase precedes in fact the actual analysis. It is aimed at retaining the first general impression of the website before the researcher's initial reactions are possibly eradicated or supplanted by further, more in-depth research insights. In this initial phase, researchers will try to make an instant assessment of the website in terms of 'look and feel,' their first impression with respect to genre and purpose. They should also note down their affective reactions: whether they are attracted to the Web presentation, or intrigued by some features, what they immediately do not seem to like about it, what puzzles them and so forth. These first reflections need to be recorded while they remain spontaneous and they are important to feed a reflexive attitude, which implies the conscious reception of a website as a 'meeting of cultures' between producers, intended audiences and researchers. Such reflexivity is also required throughout the research process to help understand the reactions of other people, who have not studied the website as a focus of research.

5.2   Inventory of salient features and topics

In this phase, researchers concentrate on collecting and categorizing present and absent features and topics of the websites in their chosen sample. This involves making an inventory of website features and attributes (for example the use of graphs and tables, the presence of web cams, feedback areas) that are present, and an inventory of main content categories and topics (for example 'news,' 'about us,' 'photo gallery,' 'products'). These features and attributes can then be counted (or measured) and put into significant categories steered by theoretical insights or a hypothesis.

In addition to listing, counting and clustering the salient elements that are present, it is also useful to perform a 'negative' analysis – that is, to pay attention to those items, aspects or events that are 'meaningfully absent' (that is, in a way 'expected' or forming part and parcel of the cultural reality the website refers to, or the genre to which the website seems to subscribe). Absent topics and features or 'omissions' may be as culturally significant as the present ones in that they may point to cultural taboos, or implicit values and norms.

What is significant or not in this regard may require both deliberation and specific knowledge of the genre and the broader culture under study. Also, this assessment will be guided by the specific research interest. But, all in all, this phase entails a rather straightforward and fairly easy-to-quantify approach yielding a first basic set of indications regarding functions, purposes, genre conformity, affiliations, and opinions expressed in the selected websites. This phase is well adapted for large-scale research using standardized coding sheets by different coders, since it requires minimal interpretation and is limited to a primarily denotative reading of the content and form. Automated data collection may even be possible in some cases, for example the automated searching for certain words in content analysis of a text corpus (Bauer and Scharl, 2000; Bell, 2001).

5.3   In-depth analysis of content and stylistic features

While the preceding phases yield some basic insights, the central and no doubt most encompassing third phase proposes to first look at the potential information that resides in the separate modes (intra-modal analysis) and then to look at the complex forms of interplay between the different modes (cross-modal analysis). In an actual research project these phases may be combined at some points, as meaning is often produced by the interplay of expressive systems, yet it remains useful to devote separate attention to the specific signifiers within each of the modes and sub-modes with respect to their cultural connotations.

5.3.1   Intra-modal analysis (fixed/static and moving/dynamic elements)

5.3.1.1   Verbal/written signifiers   In this sub-phase, research is focused on analyzing potential culturally specific meanings that reside in the explicit and implicit content of the written utterances (for example opinions, propositions, descriptions) as well as in the stylistic features of the written language parts and their possible meaning/effect in a broad sense (syntactic, semantic and pragmatic aspects). The content can be analyzed in terms of topics and issues that are being dealt with and the expressed positions vis-à-vis these issues and topics: opinions, value statements (for example politically, corporate- or family-oriented), forms and degree of self-disclosure and so on. With respect to style, the analyst may look at such things as: word register/lexicon, forms of address, use of first person singular or plural or impersonal, temporal orientation, gendered statements, use of metaphors, rhetoric and narrative strategies, humor, connotative meanings, use of abbreviations, redundancy, use of paralanguage (emoticons) and numerous other language variations and choices that may potentially reveal useful information about the sender(s): social background, position, preferences, intended audience, purpose, beliefs and so forth (Wierzbicka, 1991; Foley, 1997; Crystal, 2001)

5.3.1.2   Typographic signifiers   This sub-phase focuses on analyzing the potential culturally specific meanings that reside in the visual properties of the written texts such as: font choice (font 'families' and their 'character': formal, informal, authoritative, elegant, playful, etc.); font size (importance, 'shouting' versus 'whispering'); font style and effects: bold (for emphasis, respect, phatic function, etc.); font direction (left to right, top to bottom, etc.) and curvature (straight or dancing); font color (cultural connotations, iconic and symbolic properties); combinations of different fonts (multiple 'voices'?); character and line spacing, legibility (font shape and size in combination with color and background); para-iconic qualities (type as image: 'bloody' characters); text animations (text in motion); intertextuality (reference to a specific type or logo, for example Coca Cola) (Brumberger, 2003; Stöckl, 2005; Van Leeuwen, 2005a, 2006; Cahalan, 2007).

5.3.1.3 Visual representational types and ignifiers   This sub-phase is a very complex one. This is, first, because visual representations come in many different types and shapes: graphical/conceptual representations (for example charts); algorithmic representations (for example photographs, scans); non-algorithmic representations (for example drawings, paintings); abstract or non-representational forms; symbols and icons, numerical representations (tables), each involving a different analytical stance because of their very diverse referents, and production processes and uses (see Pauwels, 2008b). Second, visual representations have to be analyzed meticulously both for 'what they depict' ('referent' or 'content') and 'how they depict or represent' (style). The latter aspect requires very specific knowledge of each of the distinct representational processes and therefore is often overlooked (many visual studies indeed limit themselves erroneously to the depicted content). In looking at the characteristics of the depicted, the analyst should be well aware of the nature of the referent (imaginary, material, conceptual; visible/invisible, etc.?). The mode of depiction is also important (Carroll, 1996: 241); the mode may be 'nominal,' representing a class or general example, or 'physical,' depicting a particular person, thing or event. Due to space restrictions, I will limit the discussion of concrete characteristics of visual representations that might bear some cultural meaning to the ubiquitous 'photographic' image in websites.

To analyze the 'level of the depicted' in the case of photographs or films means consideration of the 'pre-photographic' or 'ante-filmic' level. This requires analyzing, for example, the depicted event, visual 'motives,' characteristics of persons (the age, gender, acted character or natural behavior, type of behavior, etc.), background, lighting and use of visual rhetorical figures (such as metaphors, metonyms, etc.).

The analysis of the 'level of depiction' then addresses the style, medium-specific characteristics and post-production processes. This includes careful study of:

a) the *'material characteristics of the image'*: these characteristics are limited in this specific case, namely websites, to 'images projected on a computer screen.' They include: texture, resolution, sharpness, color spectrum, image ratio (square, panoramic, etc.), image form, image borders;

b) the *'signifiers and codes of the static image'*: these include: composition (prominent elements, balance, planes, light contrasts, color, direction, shapes and forms); use of superimposition, reflections or double exposures; nature of lighting (intensity, direction, diffusion); camera distance (extreme close-up to very long shot); focus (deep focus/ selective focus, soft-focus, center focus, etc.); depth of field: broad (deep focus photography) versus narrow (shallow focus); camera angle (high/low, canted angle, etc.); focal length (wide-angle to telephoto); shutter speed (frozen to blurred effect); exposure (correct or over/underexposure); special effects (filters, digital effects, etc.);

c) the *'signifiers and codes of the shot'* (moving image): camera movements (panning, tilting, rolling, travelling, crane, handheld, steady cam, zooming, follow focus, rack focus); shutter speed (slow motion, fast motion, time-lapse, freeze-frame);

d) *editing choices*: shot length (short, long duration); image transitions (dissolve, fade to black, etc.); editing style (continuity editing, propositional, dialectic, etc.);

e) *post-production*: digital effects, (relative) size of visuals, position on screen, sequenced or randomly changing images, live Web cam images (Web cam).

Each of these parameters and signifiers may express a particular culturally significant view of the depicted (for example respect or superstition by avoiding a close-up, high and low camera angles to express domination or subordination, shallow focus to help steer (direct or obscure) the visitor's look) (Boggs, 1991; Monaco, 2000; Giannetti, 2007).

5.3.1.4 Sonic types and signifiers Websites are increasingly including sonic or auditory aspects, which in turn are becoming increasingly varied:

a) 'spoken words or sung lyrics': these have syntactic, semantic and pragmatic features similar to written texts. However, in addition, they have a set of potentially significant phonetic characteristics, which also need to be studied, such as tone, accent, intonation, articulation, pauses, volume and so on;

b) vocal sound which is nonverbal (e.g., laughter, screams, sighs);

c) non-vocal sound/noise (e.g., car breaks, train whistles, ticking clocks);

d) music (instrumental or vocal).

In particular, the iconic, indexical and symbolic qualities of music can provide strong cultural indicators of such things as genre, ethnic origin, ritual function and sub-cultural affiliation. Indeed, all the types of auditory signifiers listed above can be analyzed in terms of 'content,' mainly through their iconic and indexical properties as well as through symbolic /metaphorical features.

5.3.1.5 Layout and design signifiers The proverb 'design is thinking made visual' (credited to the American graphic designer Saul Bass) also applies to websites. Website design and layout features are essentially tools used to attract, direct and invoke the desired effect on, or response from, website visitors. However, through these choices, they also convey producer-related ideas, opinions and aspirations. Particular combinations of choices may, for instance, express more conservative or nostalgic feelings or conversely embody a more experimental, daring or 'avant-garde' attitude. Layout and design features will work to guide potential visitors through a web page by the use of dominant elements, iterative features and compositional choices: themes, templates, color schemes, use of columns and frames, backgrounds, white space, spatial balance (symmetry/asymmetry, horizontal, vertical or diagonal structure,) left-right, top-bottom relations and expectations, relative size and position of texts and visual representations and so on (Kress and Van Leeuwen, 2002).

These choices may result in a very rigid structure (predefined categories and spaces and pathways) or embody a more open space to wander around. They may seem to blend to a recognizable 'genre' (newsletter, family album, institutional) or exhibit a very hybrid and eclectic appearance. Again explicit attention should be paid to cultural connotations/ metaphor and intertextual references (for example a politicians' website adopting the form of a family album).

It is important to note that the design and layout will be more revealing about the culture of the immediate sender(s) the more they are responsible for each of the constituting choices. When prefabricated templates are being used (which include content categories, for example commercially operated companies offering family website templates), researchers may be learning more about the culture (ideas, preferences) of the developers of templates and browsers and the hosting services than about their users, though the choice by the user for a particular ready-made template, graphic theme, browser also remains significant.

5.3.2   Analysis of cross-modal interplay

This sub-phase pays explicit attention to the forms of interplay between linguistic, visual, auditory, spatial and time-based elements. Very often meaning is constructed by an interplay of two or more elements and while the constituting parts may express a specific idea, this idea may be completely reversed in combination with other elements.

More concretely, research here could focus on:
- Relations between written parts (captions, titles, body copy) and visuals, which can be characterized by a tightly bound or a loose relation: a mere illustrative, redundant or highly complementary one (Garner et al., 2003; Hocks and Kendrick, 2003; Martinec and Salway, 2005; Hagan, 2007).
- Relations between sound and visuals (for example use of off-screen comments, on-screen speakers, musical score, synchronous sound),

which may be characterized by a balanced/complementary, or hierarchic (dominant/subservient), or contradictory-contrapuntist (for example irony) stance. Sound can be used, for example, to enhance realism of the images or conversely serve a primarily expressive-symbolic function (Chion, 1994; Van Leeuwen, 2007).

- And, further, all possible interactions between typography: layout and design elements versus textual content, visual representations and sound, which may for instance contribute to a unified view or position or reveal many incongruent ideas (for example a retro design combined with avant-garde opinions). This includes even relations between different elements within the same mode and is the meaning that resides in the juxtaposition of images, or a specific combination of music or writing styles (Kress and Van Leeuwen, 1996; Van Leeuwen, 2005b; Knox, 2007).

5.3.3   In-depth 'inverted' analysis: significantly missing or incomplete content, arguments and formal choices

This sub-phase in a way reprises phase 2, but now it involves a much more in-depth analysis of aspects, issues and arguments that are not covered and which exactly by their absence seem to become significant (for example no use of close-ups, no people in images, or no old people in images, absence of ethnic diversity in an ethnic diverse context, no external links, no information about a certain family member or aspects). Observing Watzlawick et al.'s (1967: 48) maxim 'one cannot not communicate' it may further help to uncover cultural taboos or highly sensitive issues through much 'reading between the lines.' It is important to note that negative analysis can in fact be applied to all phases of the framework including the study of points of view, implied audiences and purposes, information organization and priming strategies, up to the analysis of the broader technological and cultural context.

5.4   Embedded point(s) of view or 'voice' and implied audience(s) and purposes

As the previous phase involved a detailed analysis of what is being said or expressed through form and content, this next phase tries to further complement the inquiry into the cultural meaning of web utterances with the question: who is really saying (the earlier captured and analyzed) what to whom with what purpose? This complex question is addressed in a meta-analytical way combining different expressive elements that have been identified before (for example modes of address, camera angles, and personal and possessive pronouns).

The point(s) of view (POV) and/or 'voice(s)' of a website are the result of a combination of many features; they can be manifold and even contradictory (for example pictures and texts originating from different people) or very consistent and unified. Obviously POVs reside in many aspects of the website (visuals, textual, design elements like templates, etc.) and they do not easily 'add up' to one dominant or unified POV, since many websites contain materials from very different sources (for example archive pictures, templates, journalistic texts). Yet the purpose of this phase is mainly to uncover what the dominant points of view (or 'master narratives') are as expressed in the website as a 'grand syntagm.' So a website may, for example, present itself at first sight as a family website where different family members have their say, but after closer scrutiny it may become clear that one family member is really pulling the strings and using the website as a vehicle to propagate his or her political views to an outside audience. The POVs can be very manifest (using first person singular or plural, or a third person voice in text or adopting subjective, half-subjective and objective camera positions in images), but often it remains difficult to determine whose point of view in a metaphorical way is being expressed. The picture taker typically remains invisible and the expressed (or literal) standpoint is not necessarily a 'position' in a more metaphorical sense. POVs and personae as described or depicted in texts and images may even be fictitious or false (for example in family websites parents often 'voice' the ideas and feelings of the younger children; in corporate and commercial websites copywriters often put some words into the mouth of some real or fictitious employee or customer). The nature and variety of the POVs may add a sub-textual meaning to the content (embody indicators of democracy, multi-vocality or openness, or conversely reveal autocratic traits). A meaning that is not always easy to determine, such as for instance the presence of multiple voices, can be interpreted as a sign of democracy or conversely a token of disorganization.

Paired to the analysis of POVs is the effort to derive/determine the intended/implied primary (for example children) and secondary (for example their parents) audience(s) and connected to that the embedded goals and purposes, only some of which are explicitly stated (and true). This analysis will further add to an understanding of whose goals are served, whose values are propagated and who is to benefit from expressing them.

Again, purposes and audiences can be explicitly stated, but they can also more indirectly be derived from 'expected visitor/user behavior.' Website offerings, particular features (feedback areas, polls) types of address, expressed POVs and so forth may hold indications of expected behaviors such as subscribing to views, buying a product or service, or being converted. Thus implied audiences can be identified/constructed in terms of economic status or class (for example 'well to do' consumers), conviction (non-believers/believers), specific age groups (young children, elderly persons), other characteristics (same name bearers, nationality, hobby, health condition) and so forth.

This phase thus interrogates and complements 'first impressions' (phase 1) with a more in-depth analysis of manifest and latent aims. It also implies comparing explicitly stated purposes/audiences with latent/secondary ones. For example, family websites today are not limited to celebrating family events and values, but often include as secondary (or primary) goals: showing off technical or creative skills, selling products or oneself (for example by including a résumé), or voicing political and religious opinions (Pauwels, 2008a). As this research phase, like the preceding one, usually involves a rather 'sub-textual' reading of all elements and their interplay, it consequently may involve much interpretation.

5.5   Analysis of dynamic information organization and spatial priming strategies

This phase focuses on analyzing the structural and navigational options and constraints (the 'dynamic' organization as opposed to static layout and design features) of websites, as well as their priming strategies and outer-directed features with respect to steering preferred readings and conduct, and exercising control. Navigational structures tend to embody thought patterns, such as 'linear' and explicitly guided patterns often associated with low context cultures, as opposed to 'more subtle or obscure' ways in high-context cultures (Würtz, 2005: 23).

Researchers should look both at the overall information architecture/organization and to the place or position of different bits of information in that structure. The structure (menus, internal links, navigational tools) may allow for free roaming of the website or exhibit a tight order and set of rules that visitors should follow. The content as linked with its spatial hierarchy/rhetoric (for example items with more or less space occupied in the website, items on the homepage or buried deeper into the website, the order and flow of elements, pathways and vectors) may express a social or cultural hierarchy as well. For example, if in a family website the father's interests (hobbies, past, opinions) occupy more space and need fewer 'clicks' to find, this may be interpreted as a reflection of more traditional (less equal) gender roles. The numbers of layers one has to pass may sometimes be indicative of the importance or sensitivity of the item ('burying' as the counter-strategy to 'priming'). And even search engines (their options and undisclosed algorithms) may be considered potentially significant in terms of control and materialized cultural preferences (for example when going first for commercial links, or most popular links, or blocking certain content).

Contemporary websites often use (or are being flooded by) a gamut of priming tools and strategies ('most viewed videos,' 'news,' 'eye catchers,' banners, pop-ups, internal links) of a very different nature and origin. They may also make use of numerous control mechanisms: passwords, counters, rules of conduct, forms of censorship, copyright disclaimers, change, copying or printing blocking, privacy-invading practices (cookies, or tools that capture part of the identity of the visitor). The use of each of these items can potentially tell us something about the value and belief system of its originator (trust/distrust, respect/disrespect, generous/self-serving). Other outer-directed features may include: chat rooms, bulletin boards, email contacts, wikis, blogs, guest books, forms, YouTube video links, ads, dynamic links/updates (for example weather updates, financial info, web cam images). It may be important to study the nature and sought degree of 'interactivity' carefully. What exactly is the visitor or user of the website allowed to do, or expected to do: just select content (menus), place an order, post a reply, add content, change content or engage in one-to-one, one-to-many, or many-to-many communication? Are they allowed to leave the website at any point? Or are connections with the rest of the Internet highly constrained?

The study of external hyperlinks in particular is often very rewarding, as these virtual 'affiliations' are further and clear indicators and expressions of particular interests, preferences, value systems, and aspirations (political, religious, commercial, educational, etc.).

The control over the look, functionality and contents of the website may be exercised by one person or distributed over several persons and groups (as with, for example, social networking sites: SNSs).

5.6   Contextual analysis, provenance and inference

When researching websites it is key not only to identify the most significant cultural indicators, but furthermore to attribute these traits to cultural actors (culture of software producers, community of users, peer group or sub-cultures, personal preferences) and to find out how this all amalgamates in extremely complex multi-authored cultural expressions. Indeed, all inferences with respect to possible cultural significance and meaning need to be based on a solid insight into the origin and circumstances of the different constituting elements. However, the issue of 'authorship' and 'origin,' and in this case the question of who to attribute certain choices to, is an increasingly complex matter with websites, not only because of the multi-authored nature of many sites (especially SNSs), but also because of the supporting technologies of multiple sources (which are themselves forms of materialized culture) and the strongly intertextual and globalizing aspects of contemporary media.

Design and infrastructure may be political in their consequences (and even in their inception), to the extent that they preclude certain uses or users (e.g., because a certain expensive tool is needed or when a particular knowledge or skill is required) or stimulate a certain conduct or choice. Thus technologies and platforms in and by themselves (templates, browsers, programming languages, database structures, graphic tools), with (and without) certain functionalities already embody certain cultural norms. And the same goes for the specific application of these technologies and their interaction with the set-up and purpose of the website (enable or constrain). These culturally significant aspects of infrastructure to a large extent remain invisible as they are very much embedded in other structures, social arrangements and technologies, and in their routine application. As Star (1999: 382) observed, it is only when infrastructure breaks down or malfunctions that its presence and impact is noticed.

The ability to construe useful information from the embedded cultural signifiers of websites rests for an important part on the assumption that one knows who or what exactly is responsible for choices and how these different choices combine to deliver intended and unintended effects. When sources are mentioned or detected one should further investigate their authority and trustworthiness, and whether they are up to date (the 'last updated on' clause referring to the whole website provides a first yardstick). Clearly one cannot assume that website creators are fully aware of or knowledgeable about all aspects and effects of combining different communication elements (e.g., texts and images, font types, layout templates). In that respect the overall meaning of the resulting website may transcend the conscious intentions of the (different) creator(s).

Essentially the proposed analytical framework provides a structured overview of the many website aspects that may potentially carry culturally specific meanings in a broad sense. As such it should only be considered as a starting point for further investigation of how values, norms and expectations are inscribed into technical systems (the 'politics of artifacts'; see Winner, 1986) and the ways they are put to use.

6   Operationalizing and decoding culture

The crucial part of researching websites as cultural expressions remains the valid operationalization ('material translation') of a particular research interest (e.g., status display, gender roles) or of a predefined cultural frame-work (like Hofstede's five dimensions) or theory into the most indicative and duly observable/measurable aspects of a website.

If one is interested, for example, in researching changing power dynamics in the family setting (gender roles, or changing relations between children, parents and grandparents), one needs to operationalize this concept or phenomenon in terms of concrete paradigmatic choices and syntagmatic effects of the website based on knowledge of cultural manifestations of this phenomenon or concept. Thus one might benefit from looking more closely at who is talking in what manner for whom, what personal space (both in a literal and metaphorical sense) every member is entitled to, what view resides in the overall design and struc-ture of the website, who is depicted in what way and under what circum-stances and so forth. When researching larger samples of websites, many of such 'cultural markers' need to be translated into codebooks that stipulate the different options for each indicator. A broad cultural and multimodal literacy is required to succeed with this task.

The presented framework of website signifiers in the previous section may help researchers to make more and better use of the many layers of potential meaning that reside in the rich multimodal nature of websites. However, it cannot help them to automatically identify the most signifi-cant parameters that will then serve as a set of 'cultural markers' for a specific research question. Nor does it provide a shortcut to cultural interpretations of the paradigmatic choices and their specific intra-modal and cross-modal combinations.

The visual, verbal and auditory parameters of websites are in principle finite in number – though not necessarily fixed or static in nature – as new features or options of existing parameters may be added (paradigmatic aspect), while on the other hand the combination of choices that can be made within each of the parameters is virtually limitless (the syntagmatic aspect). Thus the already extensive list of possibly significant parameters of websites needs to be regularly updated. Also it is important to under-stand that paradigmatic choices do not necessarily add up or work together to compose a well-balanced and consistent syntagm. Websites may well contain very hybrid and even contradictory cultural expressions. Analyses of websites as cultural constructs need to involve both the mono-modal and the multimodal meanings as a result of both deliberate and inadvertent multi-authored choices and combinations.

Consequently each research project using this framework will benefit from the development of a more customized model for selecting and codifying the most significant parameters for a specific research question or interest. For, indeed, not all dimensions of the model will yield

1. **Preservation of first impressions and reactions**
   - Categorization of 'look and feel' at a glance
   - Recording of affective reactions
2. **Inventory of salient features and topics**
   - Inventory of present website features and attributes
   - Inventory of main content categories and topics
   - Categorization and quantification of features and topics
   - Performance of 'negative' analysis: significantly absent topics and features
3. **In-depth analysis of content and formal choices**
   3.1 **Intra-modal analysis (fixed/static and moving/dynamic elements)**
      - Verbal/written signifiers
      - Typographic signifiers
      - Visual representational signifiers
      - Sonic signifiers
      - Layout and design signifiers
   3.2 **Analysis of cross-modal interplay**
      - Image / written text relations and typography-written text relations
      - Sound/image relations
      - Overall design / linguistic, visual and auditory interplay
   3.3 **In-depth 'negative' analysis**
4. **Embedded point(s) of view or 'voice,' and implied audience(s) and purposes**
   - Analysis of POVs and constructed personae
   - Analysis of intended/implied primary and secondary audience(s)
   - Analysis of embedded goals and purposes
5. **Analysis of information organization and spatial priming strategies**
   - Structural and navigational options and constraints (dynamic organization)
   - Analysis of priming strategies and gate-keeping tools
   - Analysis of outer-directed and/or interactive features
   - Analysis of external hyperlinks
6. **Contextual analysis, provenance and inference**
   - Identification of sender(s) and sources
   - Technological platforms and their constraints/implications
   - Attribution of cultural hybridity

Figure 4.2 A multimodal framework for analyzing websites (Pauwels, 2011)

sufficiently important data for every possible research question, and some questions will need a more refined approach to certain signifiers.

To avoid being forced to look at all of the possible signifiers of a website or, in other words, to reduce the efforts to more manageable proportions, new research can at times be based on choices made in previous research or depart from a set of parameters selected at face value that seems to be most indicative of a given cultural issue. Further research on specific cultural (off- and online) settings as well as pretests may gradually help to identify the most salient and expressive aspects of websites (in some cultures or for some cultural aspects) and generate/inspire appropriate hypotheses or advance more plausible interpretations.

Specific input from the culture under study (the 'emic' viewpoint) as well as a multidisciplinary scholarly knowledge (the 'etic' viewpoint) will always be needed throughout the research design and in particular when trying to attribute cultural meanings to the findings. Otherwise, findings risk being funneled by certain static preconceptions of culture and as a result possibly the most unique aspects may not be recorded as they typically tend to escape the other culture's concepts.

Extreme caution needs to be observed for ready-made cultural interpretation schemes. To give just one example: color (background color, color of type, colored pictures. . .) often is an important cultural indicator (in a symbolic, iconic or indexical sense) but the existing cultural classifications linking 'this color' with 'that (universal) meaning' have very limited use. Using simple lists of meanings of color (as, for example, do Badre, 2001, and Fletcher, 2006) for different cultures is not recommended because those colors' meanings are dependent on the precise context of their use. For instance, in the table that Badre (2001: 3) is using in his study, the color 'red' signifies 'danger,' or 'stop,' while Fletcher's table (2006: 268) lists as possible cultural connotations for the same color 'love,' 'adventurous,' 'happy,' 'inexpensive' and so on. It is clear that even in the same culture the same color may have widely different meanings according to the context (traffic, religion, fashion, entertainment, health, politics) and to a certain extent even to different members (based on past experiences, preferences, specific expertise and interests, affiliations, etc.).

A type of 'grounded theory' approach (Glaser and Strauss, 1967) is recommended, as cultural knowledge (etic and emic) should inform the construction of categories/concepts, and empirical observations should be used to revisit those categories/concepts. This approach is slower and more demanding than research that starts from preconceived cultural dimensions and operationalizations, but it may prove to be more culturally 'thick' and better suited to uncover more specific and possibly unexpected aspects of culture. So in conclusion, a broad cultural and multimodal literacy or competency will be required to succeed.

7   Conclusion: challenges and rewards

The Internet is, apart from an impressive technological achievement, also a vast cultural accomplishment, a set of practices and options that reflects the culture of its production and that continues to exert an impact on subsequent uses by and within different cultures. The Internet is not considered here simply as a data repository that merely reflects distinct offline cultures or a venue that embodies a confined world of experiences and expressions. It is a highly hybrid multi-authored cultural meeting place, connecting offline and online practices of different cultures in transition. To some extent it can be considered a cultural agent in its own right, exemplifying processes of globalization and glocalization in an unparalleled manner.

More than a decade ago Weare and Lin noted with respect to websites that 'the newness of this multimedia genre and the continued evolution of design standards have outstripped our understanding of the syntax, semantics, and logic of multimedia messages, complicating the development of valid categorization schemes for Web-based messages' (2000: 289), and to a large extent this observation still stands.

The emphasis in this chapter was not on how to produce culturally appropriate or sensitive websites in a global economy to construct 'happy customers' (as Marcus and Gould, 2000, and many others are pursuing based on Hofstede's dimensions of culture). Departing from a very broad conceptualization of culture and a very broad and detailed look at the different multimodal elements that constitute web-based communicative utterances, the main idea was to contribute to the development of a more refined and elaborate analytical tool for disclosing cultural aspects.

As the framework only proposes a checklist and a multimodal methodology for discerning cultural indicators, analyzing websites with all of their cultural aspects will remain a very arduous and specialized task, which will involve in-depth and specific cultural knowledge, and a host of technical and arts-based competencies.

While one can never be equally competent in all of the discussed aspects, a basic understanding of the constituting multimodal elements of websites and their respective disciplinary frames of reference may help scholars to further disclose the Internet as a rich cultural data source.

Ultimately, what researchers can get out of websites also depends on what they bring to it in terms of specialized and integrated knowledge and skills. An anthropological linguist, for instance, will be able to derive much more information from the textual parts than the average social scientist and, likewise, visually literate scholars will discover many layers of meaning in the visuals that will go largely unnoticed by the majority of website researchers.

But it is also clear that every researcher, and every research, is limited in scope and culturally positioned (e.g., regarding research focus, chosen methods, selection of samples, etc.). One way to reduce potential ethnocentric biases in conceptualizing and researching culture is to be more self-reflexive and thus to be more critical and explicit about one's choices and the reasons that might feed them. But of course this self-critical introspection and communication will always be limited by one's cultural background and experiences and thus they will necessitate a critical examination and confrontation with thinkers and representatives of different cultural legacies.

On a final note it could be argued that the very demanding nature of website research is well compensated by the unmatched data richness and availability of websites, which can be regarded true multicultural vaults of largely untapped data. Moreover, the cultural and multimodal competencies gradually acquired while trying to disclose these sumptuous repositories can also be employed in scholarly communications and media uses, so that social and cultural sciences themselves can become more multimodal, interdisciplinary and technologically savvy.

8   References

Andrews, D., B. Nonnecke and J. Preece (2003) 'Electronic Survey Methodology: A Case Study in Reaching Hard-to-Involve Internet Users.' *International Journal of Human-Computer Interaction*, 16: 185–210.

Badre, A. (2001) *The Effects of Cross Cultural Interface Design Orientation on World Wide Web User Performance*, GVU Technical Report; GIT-GVU-01-03 [Online]. Available from: http://hdl.handle.net/1853/3315 [accessed January 21, 2011].

Bauer, C. and A. Scharl (2000) 'Quantitative Evaluation of Web Site Content and Structure.' *Internet Research*, 10(1): 31–43.

Bell, P. (2001) 'Content Analysis of Visual Images.' In: T. Van Leeuwen and C. Jewitt (eds.) *Handbook of Visual Analysis*. London: Sage, pp. 10–34.

Boggs, J. M. (1991) *The Art of Watching Films*. Mountain View, CA/London/Toronto: Mayfield Publishing Company.

Brumberger, E. R. (2003) 'The Rhetoric of Typography: The Persona of Typeface and Text.' *Technical Communication*, 50(2): 206–23.

Cahalan, A. (2007) 'Multitudes of Interpretations: Intentions, Connotations and Associations of Typeface Designs.' *Research Journal of the Australian Graphic Design Association*, 3(1): 9–18.

Callahan, E. (2006) 'Cultural Similarities and Differences in the Design of University Web Sites.' *Journal of Computer-Mediated Communication*, 11: 239–73.

Carroll, N. (1996) 'From Real to Reel: Entangled in Nonfiction Film.' In: N. Carroll *Theorizing the Moving Image*. New York: Cambridge University Press, pp. 224–51.

Carter, D. (2005) 'Living in Virtual Communities: An Ethnography of Human Relationships in Cyberspace.' *Information, Communication & Society*, 8(2): 148–67.

Chion, M. (1994) *Audio-Vision: Sound on Screen*, edited and translated by Claudia Gorbman, with foreword by Walter Murch. New York: Columbia University Press.

Crystal, D. (2001) *Language and the Internet*. Cambridge University Press.

Dutton, W. H., E. J. Helsper and M. M. Gerber (2009) *The Internet in Britain: 2009, Oxford Internet Surveys*. Oxford Internet Institute, University of Oxford.

Ess, C. and F. Sudweeks (2005) 'Culture and Computer-Mediated Communication: Toward New Understandings.' *Journal of Computer-Mediated Communication*, 11(1): article 9. [Online]. Available from: http://jcmc.indiana.edu/vol11/issue1/ess.html [accessed January 27, 2011].

Fletcher, R. (2006) 'The Impact of Culture on Web Site Content, Design and Structure: An International and Multicultural Perspective.' *Journal of Communication Management*, 10(3): 259–73.

Foley, W. A. (1997) *Anthropological Linguistics: An Introduction*. Oxford: Blackwell.

Garner, R., M. Gillingham and Y. Zhao (2003) 'Writing Photo Captions for the Web.' *First Monday*, 8(9)[Online]. Available from: http://firstmonday.org/htbin/cgiwrap/bin/ojs/index.php/fm/article/view/1078/998 [accessed October 12, 2010].

Gevorgyan, G. and N. Manucharova (2009) 'Does Culturally Adapted Online Communication Work? A Study of American and Chinese Internet Users' Attitudes and Preferences Toward Culturally Customized Web Design Elements.' *Journal of Computer Mediated Communication*, 14 (2): 393–413.

Giannetti, L. (2007) *Understanding Movies*, 11th edn. Englewood Cliffs, NJ: Prentice-Hall.

Glaser, B. G. and A. L. Strauss (1967) *The Discovery of Grounded Theory: Strategies for Qualitative Research*. Chicago, IL: Aldine.

Hagan, S. M. (2007) 'Visual/Verbal Collaboration in Print: Complementary Differences, Necessary Ties, and an Untapped Rhetorical Opportunity.' *Written Communication*, 24(1): 49–73.

Hall, E. T. (1966) *The Hidden Dimension*. New York: Doubleday.

Hall, E. T. (1976) *Beyond Culture*. New York: Random House.

Hine, C. (2000) *Virtual Ethnography*. London/Thousand Oaks, CA/New Delhi: Sage.

Hine, C. (ed.) (2006) *Virtual Methods: Issues in Social Research on the Internet*. Oxford: Berg.

Hocks, M. E. and M. R. Kendrick (2003) *Eloquent Images: Word and Image in the Age of New Media*. Cambridge, MA: The MIT Press.

Hofstede, G. (1980) *Culture's Consequences: International Differences in Work-Related Values*. Newbury Park, CA: Sage.

Hofstede, G. (2001) *Culture's Consequences: Comparing Values, Behaviours, Institutions, and Organizations Across Nations*, 2nd edn. Thousand Oaks, CA: Sage.

Jones, S. (1999) *Doing Internet Research: Critical Issues and Methods for Examining the Net*. London/Thousand Oaks, CA/New Delhi: Sage.

Kehoe, C. and J. Pitkow (1996) 'Emerging Trends in the WWW User Population.' *Communications of the ACM*, 39(6): 106–8.

Kim, M. S. (2007) 'Commentary: Our Culture, Their Culture and Beyond: Further Thoughts on Ethnocentrism in Hofstede's Discourse.' *Journal on Multicultural Discourses*, 2(1): 26–31.

Kirkman, B., K. B. Lowe and C. B. Gibson (2006) 'A Quarter Century of Culture's Consequences: A Review of Empirical Research Incorporating Hofstede's Cultural Values Framework.' *Journal of International Business*, 37: 285–320.

Kluckhohn F. R and F. L. Strodtbeck (1961) *Variations in Value Orientations*. Westport, CT: Greenwood Press.

Knox, J. (2007) 'Visual-Verbal Communication on Online Newspaper Home Pages.' *Visual Communication*, 6(1): 19–53.

Kress, G. and T. Van Leeuwen (1996) *Reading Images: The Grammar of Visual Design*. London: Routledge.

Kress, G. and T. Van Leeuwen (2001) *Multimodal Discourse: The Modes and Media of Contemporary Communication*. London: Hodder Arnold.

Kress, G. and T. Van Leeuwen (2002) 'Colour as a Semiotic Mode: Notes for a Grammar of Colour.' *Visual Communication*, 1(3): 343–68.

Lee, R. M. (2000) *Unobtrusive Methods in Social Research*. Buckingham/ Philadelphia, PA: Open University Press.

Lievrouw, L. and S. Livingstone (2002) *The Handbook of New Media*. London/ Thousand Oaks, CA/New Delhi: Sage.

Lister, M., J. Dovey, S. Giddings, I. Grant and K. Kelly (2003) *New Media: A Critical Introduction*. Abingdon/New York: Routledge.

Mann, C. and F. Stewart (2000) *Internet Communication and Qualitative Research: A Handbook for Researching Online*. London/Thousand Oaks, CA/New Delhi: Sage.

Marcus, A. and E. W. Gould (2000) *Cultural Dimensions and Global Web User-Interface-Design: What? So what? Now what?* 6th Conference on Human Factors and the Web. [Online] Available from: www.amanda.com/resources/ hfweb200/hfweb00.marcus.html [accessed September 20, 2007].

Martinec, R. and A. Salway (2005) 'A System for Image-Text Relations in New (and OldM media.' *Visual Communication*, 4(3): 337–70.

McSweeney, B. (2002) 'Hofstede's Model of National Cultural Differences and Their Consequences: A Triumph of Faith – a Failure of Analysis.' *Human Relations*, 55(1): 89–118.

Mesch, G. and I. Talmud (2006) 'The Quality of Online and Offline Relationships: The Role of Multiplexity and Duration.' *The Information Society*, 22(3): 137–48.

Monaco, James (2000) *How to Read a Film. The World of Movies, Media, and Multimedia: Language, History, Theory*, 3rd edn. Oxford University Press.

O'Halloran, K. L. (2005) *Mathematical Discourse: Language, Symbolism and Visual Images*. London: Continuum.

Paccagnella, L. (1997) 'Getting the Seats of Your Pants Dirty: Strategies for Ethnographic Research on Virtual Communities.' *Journal of Computer Mediated Communication*, 3(1) [Online]. Available from: http://jcmc.indiana. edu/vol3/issue1/paccagnella.html [accessed September 13, 2010].

Pauwels, L. (2002) 'Communicating Desired Pasts: On the Digital Construction of Private Histories: What Is Really at Stake?' *Journal of Visual Literacy*, 22(2): 161–74.

Pauwels, L. (2005) 'Websites as Visual and Multimodal Cultural Expressions: Opportunities and Issues of Online Hybrid Media Research.' *Media, Culture & Society*, (27)4: 604–13.

Pauwels, L. (2008a) 'A Private Visual Practice Going Public? Social Functions and Sociological Research Opportunities of Web-based Family Photography.' *Visual Studies*, 23(1): 34–49.

Pauwels, L. (2008b) 'An Integrated Model for Conceptualizing Visual Competence in Scientific Research and Communications.' *Visual Studies*, 23 (2): 147–61.

Pauwels, L. (2011) 'Researching Websites as Social and Cultural Expressions: Methodological Predicaments and a Multimodal Model for Analysis.' In: E. Margolis and L. Pauwels (eds.) *SAGE Handbook of Visual Research Methods*, London/New Delhi: Sage, pp. 571–90.

Rossler, P. (2002) 'Content Analysis in Online Communication: A Challenge for Traditional Methodology.' In: B. Batinic, U. D. Reips and M. Bosnjak (eds.) *Online Social Sciences*. Seattle, WA: Hofgrefe & Huber Publishers, pp. 291–307.

Sondergaard, M. (1994). 'Research Note: Hofstede Consequences – a Study of Reviews, Citations and Replications.' *Organization Studies*, 15(3): 447–56.

Star, S. L. (1999) 'The Ethnography of Infrastructure.' *American Behavioral Scientist*, 43(3): 377–91.

Stewart, K. and M. Williams (2005) 'Researching Online Populations: The Use of Online Focus Groups for Social Research.' *Qualitative Research*, 5(4): 395–416.

Stöckl, H. (2005) 'Typography: Body and Dress of a Text – A Signing Mode Between Language and Image.' *Visual Communication*, 4(2): 204–14.

Suler, J. (2004) 'The Online Disinhibition Effect.' *Cyberpsychology and Behavior*, 7: 321–26.

Triandis, H. C. (2004) 'The Many Dimensions of Culture: Academic Commentary by Harry C. Triandis.' *Academy of Management Executive*, 18(1): 88–93.

Trompenaars, F. (1994) *Riding the Waves of Culture: Understanding Diversity in Global Business*. New York: Professional Publishing.

Van Leeuwen, T. (2005a) *Introducing Social Semiotics*. London: Routledge.

Van Leeuwen, T. (2005b) 'Typographic Meaning.' *Visual Communication*, 4: 137–43.

Van Leeuwen, T. (2006) 'Towards a Semiotics of Typography.' *Information Design Journal*, 14(2): 139–55.

Van Leeuwen, T. (2007) 'Sound and Vision.' *Visual Communication*, 6(2): 136–45.

Wakeford, Nina (2000) 'New Methodologies: Studying the Web.' In: D. Gauntlett (ed.) *Web Studies: Rewiring Media Studies for the Digital Age*. London: Arnold, pp. 31–41.

Watzlawick, P., J. Beavin-Bavelas and D. D. Jackson (1967) *Pragmatics of Human Communication: A Study of Interactional Patterns, Pathologies, and Paradoxes*. New York: W. W. Norton.

Weare, C. and W. Y. Lin (2000) 'Content Analysis of the World Wide Web: Opportunities and Challenges.' *Social Science Computer Review*, 18(3): 272–92.

White, H. (1987) *The Content of the Form: Narrative Discourse and Historical Representation*. Baltimore, MD/London: The Johns Hopkins University Press.

Wierzbicka, A. (1991) *Cross-Cultural Pragmatics: The Semantics of Human Interaction*. Berlin/New York: Mouton de Gruyter.

Winner, L. (1986) 'Do Artifacts Have Politics?' In: J. Wacjman and D. Mackenzie (eds.) *The Social Shaping of Technology: How the Refrigerator Got Its Hum*. Milton Keynes: Open University Press, pp. 26–37.

Würtz, E. (2005) 'Intercultural Communication on Web Sites: A Cross-Cultural Analysis of Websites from High-Context Cultures and Low-Context Cultures.' *Journal of Computer-Mediated Communication*, 11(1): 274–99.

Part III

The visual researcher as producer, facilitator and communicator

5   The mimetic mode: from exploratory to systematic visual data production

1   Employing the 'reproductive' potential of (camera) images to study society

A first and very dominant and varied way to more actively study society through its visual manifestations (in comparison to using existing images) could be placed under the broad concept of the 'mimetic mode.' While direct (eye) observation (without mechanical registration and/or immediate transcription of the observed in words) remains a viable option, and in some sensitive environments the only acceptable option (e.g., a courtroom or very intimate situations), the 'mimetic' approach comprises primarily all of the applications in which a visual recording device (mainly, though not exclusively, a camera) is used by the researcher for documenting meaningful aspects of visual reality, which then can become newly created visual 'data.' The mimetic mode typically seeks to exploit the reproductive qualities of the camera in those circumstances where the human eye is inadequate to capture the full richness of complex or fleeting events. In addition, the permanent and predictable character of the camera image and the ability to retain aspects of behavior or material culture more or less in their original context are powerful traits of this approach.

The 'mimetic approach' involves determining and capturing visual indicators for sociologically relevant concepts, phenomena and processes (such as social interaction, status display, structure, etc.) and producing visual records of them for further scrutiny. Direct observation is not usually capable of capturing the complexities of the visual environment and, moreover, does not yield a permanent record, which can be revisited afterwards and shared with others.

Whereas researching 'existing images' usually implies scrutinizing both form and content of the depictions, producing (raw) visual 'data', on the other hand, primarily seeks to yield records that offer as much as possible a 'mimetic' (aimed at pure 'reproduction') as opposed to an 'expressive' view on the depicted subject. The mimetic 'ideal' is for the researcher to produce visual records that correspond as closely as possible to the focal phenomena (so to elements of the 'pro-filmic' as opposed to the 'filmic') of the research at hand.

John Collier, a pioneer of the use of photography in anthropology, very strongly emphasizes the instrumental research potential of the camera as a mimetic tool:

It is important to recognize that the research opportunity afforded by the camera record has allowed us to consider, often for the first time, materials either too complex or too baffling in relationships for the human mind-eye to encompass, or circumstances too baffling in motion to track and analyze. (Collier, 1975: 211)

Collier (1975: 213) also states that the ability to count occurrences, measure distances, make inventories of the things we see in the pictures and so forth (as archaeologists have always done) still epitomizes the most fundamental research abilities of the camera image.

However, the other side of photography, its vast expressive capability, remains largely unmentioned by Collier. He argues, for example, that 'unless we are able to process, organize, and compute these data, nothing much happens for research or human understanding (1975: 223), and further 'The photographic record can remain wholly impressionistic unless it undergoes disciplined computing' (1975: 224). While Collier rightly underscores the importance of meticulous analysis of mimetic imagery – pictures usually are not self-explanatory – he sets aside too quickly the use of images as holistic and expressive tools for scientific communication. These more expressive modes or formats of visual research (such as anthropological film and the visual essay; see Chapters 8 and 7) can draw on the varied and rich expressive potential of visual representational techniques – 'visual form' – to communicate 'unwordable' scientific insight.

For most social scientists, the 'basic' or instrumental use of cameras and other image-recording devices is the least controversial mode of visual research. By emphasizing mimetic representations, few if any changes are necessary in the established forms and norms of research methodology – particularly for occasions when the visual representation fulfills no more than an intermediary role in the research project. Mimetic modes of visual data production often start with a distinct theoretical insight or research interest (operationalized in visual indicators), or aim towards answering particular research questions. However, this approach is also used to record and preserve aspects of culture that would otherwise disappear from view. When records of this kind are made systematically, they can be used afterwards to answer research questions that were not part of the data production process.

An early, powerful example of a visual study using the reproductive capabilities of the photographic record is Collier's photographic inventory of twenty-two homes of Native American families who moved to the San Francisco Bay area in search of employment. Collier photographed all visible properties in their living rooms, kitchens and bedrooms to investigate the dynamics of adjustment to or failure of their relocation. These pictures revealed a strong relation between the 'look of things' in those households and the degree to which they succeeded or failed to adapt to their new cultural setting. Corroborated by other outcomes (e.g., statistics with respect to families with issues), the visual data also proved to have a 'predictive' potential.

> How the home was organised, the nature of order and disorder, and the treatment of cultural symbols: all spoke of why they succeeded, and at other times how they failed. Their possessions and the use of space also spoke of the acculturation process, what they could afford to leave behind, and what was important to re-employ in the urban setting. (Collier, 1975: 217)

The mimetic recording of material culture can be fairly straightforward and provide a feasible approach for novice photographers and researchers. Expert image-production skills may be useful, but not necessary to move a project forward – unless records with very fine detail and tonal nuance are required, or lighting conditions are problematic. However, the recording of small-scale behaviors and social interaction usually proves more technically difficult, ethically challenging, and vulnerable to reactive behavior. But recording even material dimensions of culture can sometimes be embarrassing or problematic due to perceived intimacy – e.g. personal items in the home.

Mimetic forms of visual recording are not limited to pre-existing aspects of material culture or naturally occurring events. They can also involve more experimental set-ups where respondents react to an unexpected stimulus (e.g., a 'strange' object put in the middle of a square to prompt pedestrian reactions).

The choice between still (photographs, drawings) and continuous (film, video) records depends primarily on the phenomenon under study (material cultural, snapshots or timeframes versus fleeting phenomena in their context of cause and effect) and the information one wants to extract from them.

2   Exploratory, randomized and systematic aspects of visual data production

Visual data production may vary from more exploratory recordings of events and artifacts as they are being encountered, right through to rigid sampling and scripted set-ups with a view to testing hypotheses.

The first phase of visual field work often benefits from an orientation phase in which numerous types of existing data sources[1] (visual and non-visual) are explored, and the researchers start to engage in responsible and ethical rapport building and occasional image-making. The initial visual exploration of the research site with a camera may involve the pursuit of a particular interest or theme – or be open to whatever captures the attention of the researcher at a given moment.[2] During such visual explorations (e.g., of an urban area in a foreign land), quite unexpected things may happen. Researchers may be alert for or even focused on particular events or phenomena that cannot be (fully) predicted or planned, let alone sampled (e.g., riots or accidents). In news photography, these events are called 'spot news.' Much like journalists, social researchers may acquire valuable data by being at the right place at the right time and recording an unplanned event. These 'spot' data may potentially enrich the project as a complement to more systematically acquired data (or even take a more central role).

However, what makes a 'worthwhile subject' is not an objective 'fact.' One should be aware that exploratory data collection to an important extent epitomizes the cultural encounter of the explorer and the explored. Naïve photographers and other image producers are likely to focus on what seems different, noteworthy, unexpected, deviant, interesting, but always as perceived from their perspective and cultural position. Nevertheless, exploring and making explicit this 'bias' may yield interesting cross-cultural data and introduce a valuable outsider's look as a starting point, to interrogate the everyday of local community in more in-depth and culturally diverse positions.

Though exploring an environment in an unplanned way with a camera or through direct observation (and note taking) may generate interesting first insights, it provides only a limited and partial view of an area or setting which is almost always more complex and subtle.

---

[1] Today, Google Earth images may be used as an additional tool to 'map and survey' an area and identify areas that are worth a ground-level visit by the researcher. And in some cases a street view may also be available. However, in many cases there may be a considerable time lag between the recorded image and the present state of the depicted site.

[2] Surrealists in the 1920s had already devised strategies to explore and experience the city in a random or subconscious fashion by using arbitrary techniques to 'get lost' in the city (like jump on the third train, get off at the fourth stop and take the fifth street on the right). Forty years later, the Situationist avant-garde also promoted 'walking the city' in an unplanned manner to experience the city in another way by using the technique of drifting (dérive). Yet as the most prominent theorist of the Situationists, Guy Debord, contended, such a journey is never completely driven by chance as the environment tends to exert psycho-geographic effects (through several attractions along the way), which draw people to subconsciously follow certain routes (Debord, 1956).

To mitigate or minimize bias (preconceptions and predispositions) from the researchers' side, several techniques have been employed to introduce a 'randomizing' perspective within the data production process. The concept of 'randomness' may mean different things in different fields and contexts of use, but in a statistical sense it basically means that research subjects or units have the same 'probability' or chance of being selected, or in this case 'to enter the picture.' Techniques that point in this direction can be useful in avoiding the problem of recording only what seems interesting at first sight (or preconceptions about what it takes to 'cover the field' in a somewhat representative way). However, a useful selection process in visual research involves choices not only of 'what' (e.g., determining and selecting the units of research), but also of 'how' (the exact manner in which the objects/subjects of research will be 'framed': viewpoint, instance, interval, etc.).

Techniques for randomizing or performing random samples may vary and each have their advantages and limitations. Moreover, what *may seem* random to one observer may not appear random to another, who, for example, has more in-depth knowledge of the field or phenomenon. There are no definite ways to ensure representative visual data or to make sure that all data that are of significance for a specific research interest are generated by a particular approach.

'Sampling' in visual research may occur both *before* and *during* the data production. A researcher could, for instance, use a sampling method (probability, selective or convenience methods) to select research units (e.g., houses or households in a neighborhood) that will be studied from a database, or draw a grid on a map to select the sites that will be photographed. Alternatively, one could decide to record every tenth house in a street, and so on. These are all examples of sampling decisions that are made prior to the shooting for which a degree of 'representativity' of the data to be collected is pursued.

Researchers operating within the mimetic mode and geared towards performing micro analysis of image content often try to standardize the way visual data are recorded, which in a certain way could be understood as a form of sampling of data *during* the shooting. To ensure that the research units are being treated in the same way during the data collection, mimetically oriented visual research often uses 'shooting scripts' (Suchar, 1997), which meticulously describe exactly what should be included in the picture, from what position and at what time. This approach may help to increase the informational value of the record and ensure a certain formal uniformity among the visual records so that they can be compared and processed more easily. Shooting scripts may bring out the choices that are being made more into the open and are a great help to the ones who actually need to produce the records. However, to a certain extent this technique is also limited to what is preconceived to be important. So preferably, shooting scripts should be based on an extensive pre-study (see 'prior ethnography': Corsaro, 1982).

An alternative to the preconceived nature of the standardized shooting scripts is Krase and Shortell's (2011) notion of a 'photographic survey.' This is a sampling technique, which is performed *during* the shooting, whereby the researchers try to eliminate their own particular interests and biases through inserting a form of randomness in the way the images are produced. Their technique seeks to record visual information (more in particular about ethnic neighborhoods) by 'systematically photographing public places without regard to particular content or aesthetics' (2011: 372), but in formally non-standardized ways, including 'shooting from the hip.' This approach requires multiple iterations to be able to cover a certain spatial and temporal setting and it also exemplifies that the notions 'sampling,' 'explorative' and 'systematic' may come to mean many different things that do not necessarily contradict or exclude one another.

Yet another option to introduce a certain randomness in the visual data gathering is the 'ten-step approach' – or 'X-step approach,' as the number of steps can be adjusted to the informational density of the environment. As explored by Douglas Harper (2012), this involved a form of structured observation in which he makes a picture every ten steps while walking a specific trajectory in a city – a tactic that could force a researcher to look at and register sights that would otherwise go unnoticed. Though they cannot ensure a usefully representative sample of a research site, similar structuring approaches can mitigate the tendency for image makers to be guided primarily by pre-existing interests that distract them from noticing or recording some aspects and sights that are potentially significant to a study. In assessing different approaches to visual data production for mimetic research purposes, it is useful to consider the treatment of 'visual sampling strategies' in a text on visual anthropology from forty years ago. Authors Richard Sorenson and Alison Jablonko (1975: 152) propose a 'tripartite strategy' to produce visual records of naturally occurring phenomena, and they also introduce useful terms to name these three approaches. A first strategy put forward by Sorenson and Jablonko to produce visual data is 'opportunistic sampling,' which they describe as 'a freewheeling yet indispensable approach to visual documentation' that 'takes advantage of events as they develop in unfamiliar settings.' Basically, this involves the creed 'when something interesting happens, pick up the camera and shoot' (1975: 152). Yet it is clear that 'seizing the opportunity' or documenting 'unanticipated and poorly understood phenomena as they occur' also brings the personality and the personal 'interests, inclinations and style' of the researcher into play. Footage or visual records obtained using this approach 'may not always be directly relevant to a predetermined scientific study, but ... can be a powerful resource in the quest for knowledge' (Sorenson and Jablonko, 1975: 153).

'Programmed sampling,' the second strategy they propose, then involves visual data production 'according to a predetermined plan – deciding in advance what, where, and when to film' (Sorenson and Jablonko, 1975: 153). The programmed approach does not rule out human interests and preconceived ideas, but unlike the unstated nature of these inclinations in the 'opportunistic' approach, an explicitly 'formulated statement' steers the visual data production, and choices are based on 'accumulated, systematized and articulated knowledge' of a discipline and of a broader cultural heritage (1975: 154).

To mitigate both the egocentric and ethnocentric traits of the previous approaches, Sorenson and Jablonko discuss a third approach which they deliberately call 'digressive (or semi-randomized) search' for documenting aspects of the phenomenon under study 'beyond the constraints of either personal intuition or sophisticated program, to document ahead of understanding and awareness' (Sorenson and Jablonko, 1975: 157). The idea is to introduce a kind of randomness or semi-randomness aimed at penetrating 'areas and situations peripheral to our attention, beyond our range of awareness or comprehension, and interstitial to our points of view and predilections' (1975: 155). This sampling strategy requires that we 'be purposefully digressive, in both space and subject matter turning our gaze from the familiar and "important" to events that appear incoherent and insignificant' (1975: 155).

Unfortunately, the authors provide little concrete guidance for 'looking into the unknown,' but they do succeed in making clear the specific advantages and disadvantages of each of these strategies and the way they tend to balance each other. The basic ideas expressed in this threefold approach are recapitulated in more recent efforts to develop visual data production strategies as discussed above (to be open to the unexpected, the unplanned, the at first sight insignificant, as well as to bring more method and structure to the visual data production).

3   Sequential and longitudinal production methods: 'interval/time-lapse' recordings and 're-photography'

Time, space, scale and movement are often essential aspects of visual data production. Some subject matter and research interests can be recorded with a single static record (e.g., aspects of contemporary material culture or snapshots of human behavior), but some phenomena and research interests may require a continuous record (e.g., a micro-analytical study of interactions during a meeting, or the detailed visual documentation of a complex ritual) and others may benefit from a discontinuous series of time slices or steps in time. Significant changes can indeed transpire in just a few minutes, hours or days, or span several years or decades. For example, a diachronic study of an urban environment could concentrate on the repetitive patterns of a number of activities and phenomena that occur during a day from the early morning till late in the evening, or focus on changes in the urban environment that span much larger periods of time.

Two related but distinct visual data production techniques that explicitly focus on sequentially researching social change and cultural expressions as they develop – rapidly or gradually – over time in a particular physical or cultural space will be discussed here.

3.1   Interval and time-lapse photography

Interval photography essentially involves making a series of images from the same vantage point with a set time span in between, resulting in a sequence of pictures that documents any visible changes that have occurred in the depicted scene. As a research technique, this combines the analytic convenience of the static visual record with a sequential development of the subject of research. Apart from the careful placement of the camera(s) (to allow the most suitable view of the depicted phenomenon), the challenge is to define the right length of the interval so that no crucial information is lost in between (if the intervals are too long) and no excess records are produced (if the intervals are too short and successive pictures fail to produce new information).

Time-lapse photography is a form of interval photography whereby the sequentially produced photographs can be shown in succession, giving the impression of a continuous record (a sort of film in 'fast motion'), so that very slowly progressing changes become visible. High-end digital cameras today have become powerful instruments for interval and time-lapse photography as well as for producing continuous records (filming). Using 'time-lapse mode,' modern digital single lens reflex cameras (DSLRs) often automatically produce a 'time-lapse movie' or video rather than a series of distinct frames that can be viewed and analyzed separately, as is the case when selecting the 'interval' option.

An early example of the power of interval photography for visual social research is Arthur Rothman's time-and-motion sociometric study of hospital culture (reported in a Southwest Anthropological Association conference paper in 1964), as discussed in Collier and Collier (1986: 87). The aim was to disclose the social structure of a hospital and in particular any interracial relations in a manner that was deemed less sensitive and disturbing than the usual techniques (e.g., interviews). Rothman observed the hospital staff during lunchtime by positioning nine cameras, each of which produced an image every fifteen minutes. This way he could clearly document the flow of interaction and the exact seating of every individual member of staff. The physical traits of the individuals as well as the costumes and attributes worn by the distinct professional categories (e.g., stethoscopes, emblems, white or green coats) proved very reliable and obvious visual indicators for the identification of professional position and race/ethnicity.

A detailed analysis revealed that the social structure in that American hospital mainly rested on professional status and specialization, and that racial and ethnic aspects did not seem to exert an (observable) influence. In other words, doctors sat with doctors, and nurses with nurses, whether they were black or white (Collier, 1967: 37–8). However, the analysis also showed an imbalance in the racial/ethnic proportion in different professions and specialties, clearly reflecting the lower opportunities for advancement in society at large for non-Caucasian groups (Collier and Collier, 1986: 87). Presenting – hypothetically – Rothman's interval images as a 'time-lapse movie' instead of a series of pictures might be helpful to visualize the flows of interaction during the lunch time (probably with peaks and quieter moments), but careful analysis of the professional and racial/ethnic composition of the individuals at the tables is better served by a detailed series of static images (which can be used for identification and counting).

In a way, interval photography and time-lapse photography are forms of 'repeat photography,' which will next be discussed. However, interval photography usually does not involve revisiting the site and 'retracing' and reproducing the initial framing and conditions of the scene, as data are being collected at a given (fairly limited) period of time, (most often) without removing the camera(s) from their position (tripod).

3.2   Repeat photography

The technique known as 'repeat photography' or 're-photography' is a special strand of visual research with a strictly mimetic orientation. Jon Rieger – a pioneer in visual sociology and most notably in re-photography as a longitudinal visual technique tool for sociological enquiry – defines it as 'a process by which we create a temporally ordered, that is, longitudinal, photographic record of a particular place, social group, or other phenomenon.' The thus acquired series is then scrutinized for 'evidence of change' (Rieger, 2011: 133).

Whether or not observable differences between sets of records made at different times have any (social or sociological) significance depends on the theory and insight one brings to them (as competently translated into specific 'visual indicators' of social change) and further on the acquisition of contextual information (e.g. statistical data, input from key informants, historic evidence, etc.).

3.2.1   Retrospective versus prospective studies

Re-photography projects can start from pictures made by the researcher or depart from existing pictures, often produced outside a research context (drawn from archives, illustrated books or family albums). Rieger (2011: 140) uses the terms *retrospective study* for re-photography projects that depart from found or existing pictures as the baseline (the initial or Time 1 pictures) – and possibly also at subsequent points in the past – which are then re-photographed at set time intervals in a research context, as opposed to *prospective studies*, which depart from an initial set of pictures produced by the researcher and repeated afterwards at set intervals. In fact, one could even conceive of studies that totally rely on found images (e.g., a municipal image archive which covers the same sites over several decades) and set-ups that combine a retrospective and prospective approach.

Both approaches have their distinct advantages and setbacks, largely resonating the earlier discussed traits of 'found' versus 'researcher-produced' imagery (see Chapters 2 and 3).

A retrospective approach allows going further back in time (to periods that pre-date the researcher's conception of the project) and may benefit from a wide variety of online image collections, which are becoming larger and more accessible. After collecting these existing 'Time 1' pictures, researchers can then immediately proceed to produce a set of 'Time 2' pictures, and start to analyze the two series of images for indications of social change. However, this approach gives less control to researchers over what they can focus on as they have to rely on the available views of a given place or phenomenon. Studying cities or communities, for example based on archive pictures, one will often have to rely on numerous pictures of only a limited number of places and events (tourist attractions, official events), while the majority of (back)streets or more mundane activities (including work processes!) are documented less frequently or extensively. A prospective approach, on the other hand, enables much more control by the researcher over the places, events and people that are visually recorded, as well as when and how exactly they are depicted. Researchers can then produce time series (including the all-important baseline series) according to a preconceived plan. As not all visual emanations of change can be foreseen, producing an extensive and multifaceted set of baseline pictures, covering as many aspects as possible of the phenomenon under study, is generally advisable. Working prospectively implies, however, that one cannot re-photograph subject matter that pre-dates the research project, and that covering a significant span of time (as some things tend to develop or change very slowly) demands a prolonged and sustained effort and commitment from the researchers (and their sources of funding), often without a solid warrant about the outcome.

3.2.2   Sites, events and people

Though the 'continuity' or longitudinal aspect of re-photography is often understood (and practiced) as making pictures of the same place and from the same position, the technique has a much broader range of applications in social research. Rieger points out that 'Continuity may reside in the fact that the photographs were of the same scene, or because they trace the experience of the same or similar participants, or because they follow the development of a particular function, activity, or process over time' (Rieger, 2011: 133).

Consequently, longitudinal visual research may involve re-photographing 'sites' (exteriors and interiors: e.g., streets, gardens, homes, factories, residential areas) and re-photographing 'events, activities and processes' (changes in rituals, work processes or activities of a varied nature), as well as re-photographing 'people' (their changing physical appearances, belongings and doings). Thus re-photography projects are not limited to revisiting environments from the same vantage point but they may, for example, also include the visual documentation of marriage or burial rituals over time, whether or not they take place at the same venue. Re-photography may even involve visually retracing a journey (e.g., an expedition) that was visually documented many years before.

Such long-term projects often experience obstacles of some sort, resulting in incomplete documentation. Rieger (2011: 141) also expounds on the possibilities of using *re-enactment* as a strategy for filling in missing pieces of visual documentation, as well as resorting to 'cross sectional designs' that seek to construct an evolution on the basis of different instances or cases that represent different stages in a presumed development process. For example, one could synchronically depict a diachronic evolution, for example selecting and depicting farms that represent different phases of modernization.

3.2.3   Analyzing the changing content while replicating the form

Re-photography research requires a very detailed analysis of the depicted subject matter from edge to edge. As Rieger contends: 'We have to examine every part of the image, not only the nominal subject of the photograph, but also the details in the background and near the edges of the picture for clues pertinent to our analysis' (2011: 132). For, indeed, every tiny detail may contain or embody a potentially significant indicator of the phenomenon under scrutiny. This should be stressed here, as too often visual researchers hastily reduce the rich content (and form) of a picture to the dominant or obvious subject matter or do not even bother to discuss or analyze the pictures they are using at any length or depth.

Analysis in repeat photography typically focuses on the level of the depicted (the subject matter) and not on the formal qualities of the depictions (e.g., the stylistic features of the photograph). To facilitate that kind of analysis, re-photographers try to keep these image variables (frame, focal length, camera position) as well as physical circumstances (time of day, season, weather conditions) constant as much as possible. This may not always be feasible because of tight recording schedules, unpredictable weather conditions, physical obstructions and changing technologies.

Re-photography can be considered a 'mimetic approach' in a dual sense: first, because re-photographers are focused on the level of the depicted (and in particular to changes that have occurred over time) and second, because they try to meticulously imitate or replicate the initial 'form of the depiction' by reproducing all the initial choices of material and recording conditions, some of which may have an 'expressive' load (i.e., embody a certain outlook of the author of the original image through specific formal choices like camera position of framing).

The mimetic emphasis on the depicted subject matter is facilitated in re-photography by 'controlling' the parameters of the depiction (the numerous formal choices) so that any observed changes between two pictures can (mainly) be attributed to changes in the depicted reality.

Obviously, the initial formal choices (for 'Time 1') can also provide interesting sociological information about the perspectives, technology and culture of the initial photographer – such as 'why did the producer of image T1 choose this particular instance, position etc.?' – but that tends towards another type of research. Re-photographers must remember that they are working with highly 'mediated' aspects of a presumed social reality and that, to some extent, they are reproducing 'representations' tied to initial choices made in the past. They cannot reveal changes other than those framed by a specific point in time and place and presented in an existing visual form.

3.2.4   Problems and solutions

Re-photography as a mimetic mode of visual research is obviously subject to the typical limitations and demands of visual research: the fact that not all social phenomena have a significant visual counterpart or dimension, and the strict reliance on sufficient contextual information to be able to make sense of the pictorial. In addition, longitudinal techniques pose a number of more specific challenges. Rieger (2011) points to an often observed time lag between 'visual' and 'social' change (one can precede or lag behind the other), to the varying strength of the relationship between the visual and social change (some visual changes have little social significance), as well as to the possibility that predetermined points in time may miss out on some changes that occurred and disappeared in between. Change processes are often unpredictable and do not always happen in a linear fashion, at the same rate or in the same direction. Therefore, being too strictly bound to a preset time interval for creating a time series can be problematic. A particular change process may suddenly accelerate so that intermediate phases may represent data worth collecting at intermediate intervals (Rieger, 2011: 144).

As noted above, while the retrospective approach has a clear time advantage over the prospective approach (by allowing enquiry to go further back in time and by providing comparative data much sooner), it is dependent on existing images, which may be biased to the spectacular/stereotypical (e.g., monuments, main streets, squares or events) and ill-suited to depicting specific details pertinent to the research. Moreover, as technology for producing pictures changes dramatically, special expertise is required of the researcher who wants to reproduce the formal choices of the baseline pictures (not only the exact position and framing, but also the same 'relative proportions' of the depicted subject matter, which is also determined by a particular combination of negative size and focal length). Visual technologies are in constant flux, but fortunately recent developments have included tools that can digitally mimic the 'look' created by past technologies and also replicate the exact positions and perspective (e.g., using overlay techniques; see Klett, 2011: 127) of old photographs.

Another challenge for re-photography as a long-term endeavor is that research subjects may disappear or become inaccessible or invisible.

Structures may become broken down or hidden from view by a newly erected structure, events may cease to exist, participants may die, move away or refuse to cooperate any further, sites may have shifted from public to private ownership, vantage points may be inaccessible because of changed traffic situations, and so on. Rieger refers to this as a form of 'subject mortality,' a well-known phenomenon in panel studies or longitudinal research in general (Rieger, 2011: 146).

When the original vantage point or research subject is no longer accessible or available, the researcher may have to improvise strategies for gathering the kind of documentation needed to proceed with a study. Using other vantage points or participants, and combining different pictures that together provide sufficient information for a comparison can both be useful in this process.

While replicating initial conditions (technical and physical) as much as possible can facilitate rephotographic analysis considerably, that should not become a dogma or an end in itself. One should not forget that ultimately the goal is to detect indications of social change. The extreme rigor needed to measure, for example, geological changes in landscapes (e.g., to measure the changing water levels in mountain lakes, or the erosion of mountains; see Klett, 2011) may not be necessary. At times the researcher may indeed be compelled to change (deflect, divert or redirect) the initial set-up to cope with unexpected situations and (re)focus on what is really important.

The longitudinal approach to producing visual records of people, places or events is not necessarily confined to the static image. Film can also be used to systematically 'revisit' aspects of society (although the term 're-filming' or repeat filming has not yet gained currency). A powerful example is Michael Apted's *Up* series of documentary films. Starting with the documentary *Seven Up* (1964), which explored the dreams and aspirations of fourteen British children aged 7, sequels were made featuring the same participants every seven years (the latest being *56 Up* (2012)). This extraordinary endeavor has been celebrated as one of the greatest documentary series of all time. However, it has also been challenged (by ethnographers and the subjects themselves) because of its basic assumptions (social class predetermines the outcome of life) and its editing style (which suggest links between a character's past and present, for which there is little evidence).

Regardless of the many restrictions and challenges, re-photography (and re-filming) as a technique has its unique merits when executed with much care during the production and analysis phase and when researchers succeed in developing in-depth knowledge of the sites and events, and a good rapport with any groups of people involved.

4   Analysis, processing and presentation of mimetic data

Meticulous analysis and processing of visual data are as central for self-produced visual data in the mimetic mode as they are for 'found' materials. To some extent researchers can use existing theoretical frameworks and tools for visual analysis, but they will invariably have to customize the tools to make them suitable for their particular research focus. Though images produced in a research context are usually more standardized and better documented/contextualized, researchers still have to rely on their own disciplinary and cultural knowledge and experience to be able to transcend the level of mere description or simple quantification of the depicted and start to detect significant patterns in and possible explanations for the noted visual differences.

The images resulting from a mimetic approach are routinely treated as sets of 'raw data' that whenever possible are transformed into more 'convenient' (most often 'quantitative') information. However, when reorganizing and in particular when transcribing visual representations in a non-visual form (words or numbers), there is a constant danger that the holistic nature (and possibly with it the very essence of the data) is being 'lost in translation.' Some qualitative research software applications allow the linking of images to verbal descriptions to limit this potential hazard. Often it is also advisable to integrate at least some of the visuals in the end report or the end product. When handling vast amounts of data in efficient and effective ways, semi-automated instruments to extract specific data from the visual records are required. Apart from using ever more sophisticated digital technologies, clearly identified visual indicators and well-trained coders are key in this demanding task.

By taking advantage of the iconic and indexical properties of camera images, mimetic recording can serve quantitative and qualitative research designs, in the first instance by reducing image content to measurable or countable categories, and in the second by keeping the holistic character of the image intact and examining elements of the picture in the image's internal and external contexts.

Many decades ago, researchers (like Scherer, 1975; Zube, 1979; McPhail and Wohlstein, 1982) had already developed photogrammetric techniques to perform relatively reliable measurements of variables such as distance (proximity) and movement (velocity and direction). Ervin Zube's multidisciplinary research on pedestrian behavior (in Wagner's influential reader *Images of Information*, 1979) offers an early textbook example of how camera images can be effectively processed into purely quantitative data and from there on re-emerge as a visual representation in the form of a graph.

Zube (1979: 69) chose a time-lapse photography approach (using an 8 mm film camera at 1.4 frames/second) to study the negative effects of wind turbulence created by high-rise buildings on pedestrian behavior (their ability to talk, sit, eat, shop and walk) in an effort to influence urban policy makers to take these observation into account when deciding on the location and design of structures in cities. To that aim, perspective grids were prepared for each site of observation (taking height, angle and filming distance into account) and 'pedestrian paths were analyzed by plotting frame by frame, the movements of selected subjects' by recording their coordinates on the grid (Zube, 1979: 74). These efforts resulted among others in charts representing typical or 'high probability' paths for pedestrians in both winter and summer, clearly marking out the adverse effects of wind on pedestrians' activities. The study is also exemplary with respect to applying a multi-method approach by skillfully combining the visual data with questionnaire and sales receipt data.

Retrospective re-photography of Antwerp's 'Southern Docks'

The Southern Docks in Antwerp were completed in 1881 for inland waterway navigation, while the larger maritime transport vessels were mainly located in the northern parts of the city. The central two-towered building is the Southern Hydraulic Power Plant (1883), which provided this part of the harbor with the energy to operate cranes, sluice-gates, swing bridges and windlasses. However, as ships became larger, these docks soon became too narrow. They became defunct in 1967 and were filled up with soil two years later, creating a large rectangular square, which serves today as a giant parking lot and a place for occasional events (fairs, concerts, circuses, theatre, cultural markets and student events). The industrial chimneys have disappeared, but the main building structures are still there, though they now fulfill completely different functions.

From a thriving industrial and commercial area focused on expediting goods (mainly coal, stones, sand and mussels), which required harsh and dangerous labor by men, women and children, this neighborhood developed through a period of destitution and neglect after the closing down of the harbor activities (1970s and 1980s), to its present status of a highly gentrified neighborhood with museums, art galleries, luxury lofts (in former warehouses), restaurants and cafés. Since 1993, the Hydraulic Power Plant (Zuiderpershuis) has accommodated the World Cultures Center, which organizes artistic events to foster a positive multicultural climate. The low building to the left of the Power Plant was originally a first aid facility for injured dock workers. It currently hosts a creative writing workshop. There is still some discussion over whether the Southern Docks area should continue to serve as a parking lot / events space (and what events should be allowed), whether it should become a park (its official status!) or whether the docks should be reinstalled to create a yachting harbor.

The exact position and focal length of the Figure 5.1 baseline image could not be replicated in Figure 5.2 due to a row of trees that now blocks the sight (a similar row of trees blocks the view of the houses on the opposite side).

Figure 5.1 and 5.2 (L) Southern Docks, Antwerp (undated, first half of the twentieth century). (R) Southern Docks, Antwerp (April 2014, L. Pauwels).

5   A final note

The mimetic mode periodically becomes a favorite target for self-proclaimed 'critical' visual researchers, who tend to call these approaches 'naïve realist' and '(post)positivist' (while paradoxically using images in much the same way!). But completely denying the important reproductive capabilities of camera images (both iconic and indexical) is unwise. Rather, the transformational processes and choices that go into the act of producing visual records of this kind should be further scrutinized and understood. Most researchers who use the camera as a recording tool are duly aware of the transformational traits and limitations of cameras, as well as of the expressive attributes (values, biases, preferences, points of views) inadvertently introduced through human interventions prior, during and following the act of photographing. Most audiences are partly aware of these mediations as well. Moreover, most 'mimetically oriented' researchers rely on other data and informants to make sense of these records and do not think of them as 'truth' or 'complete records.' They

Time-lapse photography project on London's Billingsgate Fish Market

The difficulty of apprehending the sensory environment of London's Billingsgate Fish Market through observation in real time prompted Dawn Lyon to explore the potential of time-lapse photography as an analytical tool for researching the elusive quality of market space and the work that takes place within it. Inspired by Lefebvre's project in rhythm-analysis, and with the help of filmmaker Kevin Reynolds (www.verymovingpictures.co. uk), Dawn made a film based on time-lapse photography of a day's work at the market (Figure 5.3), speeded up so one hour is presented in 30 seconds, and combined with sound corresponding to the same hour in which the images were made. This approach can generate insights into temporal and spatial rhythms, patterns and interconnections of work and consumption, and the ways in which embodied labor, interaction and mobility produce market space.

Figure 5.3 Frame from the start of the Billingsgate Fish Market at 4 o'clock (D. Lyon)

are just potential visual data that are open to multiple interpretations and that need sufficient contextual information to become useful.

In some ways, many mimetic approaches tend to take the visual as a unique source of information more seriously than approaches that use visual objects merely for contemplation, projection or critique. Most researchers operating in this paradigm are aware that 'looking at images' is not the same as looking at visual aspects of culture and society in a direct, multisensory way, and realize that every act of 'representation' has cultural, and not just mechanical, dimensions. Educated audiences realize this as well when watching a film or series of pictures. However, researchers operating in this paradigm should also realize that they limit themselves to exploring and employing only one (albeit powerful) aspect of visual mediation. The other potent aspect of image-making, its vast expressive capabilities, is tentatively being explored (as a data source or a communication tool) in other visual production methods (studies of the style of found images, respondent-generated image production) and/or more visual formats of reporting (visual essay, film).

6   References

Collier, J. (1967) *Visual Anthropology: Photography as a Research Method.* New York/London: Holt, Rinehart and Winston.

Collier, J. (1975) 'Photography and Visual Anthropology.' In: P. Hockings (ed.) *Principles of Visual Anthropology.* The Hague/Paris: Mouton.

Collier, J. and M. Collier (1986) *Visual Anthropology: Photography as a Research Method,* revised and expanded edition. Albuquerque: University of New Mexico Press.

Corsaro, W. (1982) 'Something Old and Something New: The Importance of Prior Ethnography in the Collection and Analysis of Audiovisual Data.' *Sociological Methods & Research* 11: 145–66.

Debord, G. (1956) 'Theory of the Dérive,' *Les Lèvres Nues* 9 (November); reprinted in *Internationale Situationniste* 2 (December 1958), translated by Ken Knabb.

Harper, D. (2012) 'A Ten Step Methodology,' presentation at the IVSA conference in Brooklyn.

Klett, M. (2011) 'Repeat Photography in Landscape Research.' In: E. Margolis and L. Pauwels (eds.) *SAGE Handbook of Visual Research Methods.* London/New Delhi: Sage, pp. 114–31.

Krase, J. and T. Shortell (2011) 'On the Spatial Semiotics of Vernacular Landscapes in Global Cities.' *Visual Communication,* 10 (3): 367–400.

McPhail, C. and R. Wohlstein (1982) 'Using Film to Analyze Pedestrian Behavior.' *Sociological Methods & Research,* 10 (3): 347–75.

Rieger, J. (2011) 'Rephotography for Documenting Social Change.' In: E. Margolis and L. Pauwels (eds.) *SAGE Handbook of Visual Research Methods.* London/New Delhi: Sage, pp. 132–49.

Rothman, A. (1964) 'The Value of Photographic Technique in Plotting Sociometric Interaction.' Paper presented at the Annual Meeting of the Southwest Anthropological Association, San Francisco.

Scherer, S. (1975) 'A Photographic Method for Recording and Evaluation of Cross-Cultural Proxemic Interaction Patterns.' In: P. Hockings (ed.) *Principles of Visual Anthropology.* The Hague/Paris: Mouton, pp. 365–72.

Sorenson, E. and A. Jablonko (1975) 'Research Filming of Naturally Occurring Phenomena: Basic Strategies.' In: P. Hockings (ed.) *Principles of Visual Anthropology*, The Hague/Paris: Mouton, pp. 151–63.

Suchar, C. (1997) 'Grounding Visual Sociology Research in Shooting Scripts.' *Qualitative Research*, 20(1): 33–55.

Wagner, J. (ed.) (1979) *Images of Information: Still Photography in the Social Sciences*. Beverly Hills/London: Sage.

Zube, E. (1979) 'Pedestrians and Wind.' In: J. Wagner (ed.) *Images of Information: Still Photography in the Social Sciences*. Beverly Hills/London: Sage, pp. 69–83.

6 Visual elicitation techniques, respondent-generated image production and 'participatory' visual activism

1 Introduction: collaborative and participatory visual research

Participatory techniques in visual research are quite popular these days, partly because of the idea that research should also benefit those who are subjected to it and more specifically that researchers should engage themselves in helping to solve problems of communities without thinking primarily about their own professional gains (the 'ethical' motive). But these visual research practices are also firmly grounded in the view that involving respondents or community members more actively may generate unique types of data (the 'scientific' motive). As such, participatory techniques seem to embody special opportunities to include the 'emic' view in research as a necessary complement to the dominant etic view, in an almost literal sense. Both are needed, as giving 'voice' to people is not adequate on its own merits, while the absence of subjects' points of view leads to incomplete depictions and interpretations by scholars despite their sophisticated theoretical and methodological frameworks.

What today are often presented as participatory or collaborative techniques and approaches in visual research merit separate attention not only because they are currently very popular but also because they present a great variety of approaches and implicit assumptions which may generate some confusion. The wide variety of approaches presented under the umbrella of participatory or collaborative visual research techniques reflect two distinct approaches, each with a long history – the use of visual stimuli in an interview situation, and the idea of stimulating participants from the field to produce its own imagery with respect to a certain issue. These two techniques are associated with two distinct groups of outcomes, scholarly knowledge production and social action (which may of course also produce new insights for the participants), and to a number of presentational options and uses. In actual practice, these two techniques and outcomes may be combined in many ways, generating numerous

117

opportunities for both knowledge production (in many ways and for different audiences) and social action.

This chapter will first introduce and elaborate on the two research techniques and then further discuss how they have stimulated a proliferation of related approaches and terms. I will also try to clarify specific strengths and weaknesses of participatory research options and to examine their underlying assumptions. To illustrate and explore the main techniques discussed in this chapter, it also includes excerpts and a brief discussion of several inspiring student projects from the class I teach in 'visual sociology and anthropology.'

2   Visual elicitation: verbal responses to images as interview stimuli

The technique whereby images are used as a stimulus in the context of an interview was originally applied in psychological research. It was subsequently adopted by a number of social scientists and is now primarily known as 'photo elicitation,' though in fact many types of images can be used (still and moving, paintings or drawings, etc.) and thus 'image elicitation' or 'visual elicitation' would be a more appropriate term. The visual materials used as 'stimuli' to obtain unique kinds of information from respondents and informants may include pre-existing 'societal imagery' (historic or archive pictures of cities, advertisements, etc.), as well as researcher- or respondent-generated materials.

The confrontation of the interviewee (or multiple respondents in a focus group situation) with the reality of (camera) images can provide two kinds of information for the researcher. First and foremost, the interview with visual materials can offer the researcher a fairly simple and quick way of *acquiring information about whatever is visible in the image*. A properly informed respondent (e.g., in the case of a visual report on a ceremonial or festive event) can often tell very accurately who or what has or has not been captured by the images, which actions are being performed, and what the significance is of certain signs and symbols. The purpose of the interview with photo or film elicitation is, however, not restricted to the collection/explanation of a series of concrete facts about whatever has been recorded. The technique also allows one to *elicit or trigger deeper, more abstract perceptions and values* of respondents as individuals who are involved in the depicted world. Carefully chosen visual material of a photographic or non-photographic nature (prints, drawings) combined with a good interview technique can broaden the interview from an information round about what has been recorded to a data collection session about the significance of the recorded material to the respondent. Thus, the focus of attention shifts from external manifestations to an 'experience,' to an 'interior' perspective, as it were. Using visuals as interview stimuli can yield 'verbal' feedback or data that needs to be further analyzed in much the same way as responses captured during open (verbal) interviews and focus groups.

The possibility to elicit crucial information (emotions, conceptions) in interviews through camera images has already been valued and employed by researchers many decades ago. Krebs (1975: 284) asserts that 'if the film elicitation technique is employed skilfully, the researcher may obtain some of the most exciting data of anthropology – how members conceptualise and structure the world in which they live.' Collier (1967: 49) goes even further, by claiming that 'methodologically, the only way we can use the full record of the camera is through the projective interpretation by the native.' Making sense of images will indeed necessitate involving different parties and perspectives (emic and etic).

In comparison to the purely verbal interview, the visual interview certainly offers a number of *specific benefits*. While researchers often find it difficult to convince their respondents to participate in interviews, visual material – especially if it concerns the immediate environment of or field of interest to the interviewee – can often serve as a door opener. Visual material can provide a kind of structure for the interview that is not usually considered irritating or confrontational by the respondent, so that it rarely forces the latter into a defensive or artificial position. It always provides a concrete talking point, while the stimulus provision that is characteristic for interview situations is experienced as less direct. The visual material often evokes spontaneous and unpredictable answers from respondents.

While the verbal interview is often characterized by a typical role differentiation between interviewer and interviewee (Segers, 1983: 216), this relationship can assume an entirely different form in the visual interview. Rather than being pushed into the role of the person who is being questioned, the respondents take on the role of an expert. This encourages them to speak more freely. When commenting on images, interviewees tend to feel much less as if they are talking about things they should not be talking about. Instead, they feel as if they are simply explaining things that have already been captured by the recording.

Collier (1967) found that purely verbal interviews tend to become unproductive much more quickly than interviews with visual stimuli. If new images are constantly made available, then the respondent's attention and interest can be retained for long periods of time. Irrelevant digressions on the part of the respondent can be elegantly prevented by providing a new image that focuses attention on a new fact. Visual material thus jolts the memory of the respondents who will tend to become more easily irritated during a purely verbal interview because of the lack of interesting new stimuli from the researcher and through the confrontation with the failure of their own memory (Collier, 1967: 48).

The attraction of visual interviewing for both researcher and researched can be explained by the poly-semic character and engaging nature of the stimulus (visuals tend to trigger quite vivid, varied and unanticipated reactions), and the mitigation or even reversal of the researcher/ researched hierarchy whereby the respondent gets to fulfill the role of 'knowledgeable' informant or even expert rather than a mere 'object of interrogation.' However, as a unique tool to obtain both factual information about what is depicted and to trigger more projective comments through elements in the picture that prove to be meaningful in some way to the respondent, the success of the visual interview or image elicitation process is contingent on resolving methodological issues tied to conducting the interview and selecting the materials. Visual materials can disrupt or distort the research process by being irrelevant to the issue studied, by being ill-adapted to the respondent or by creating an all too suggestive, one-sided or incomplete picture of the phenomenon or event considered. While the technique may seem simple and straightforward, special expertise is required for effective visual interviewers. They are expected to be familiar with the visual material used, the manner in which it was obtained, the research possibilities and interpretations. A solid knowledge of the respondents' culture and their particular cultural sensitivities are needed. Even if the visual material used by the interviewers has been collected and produced with the greatest possible care, interviewers need to avoid suggesting interpretations that ignore the conceptual frameworks of the respondents. Both Krebs (1975: 297) and Wagner (1979: 91) believe that this specific problem can be resolved by avoiding naming (or interpreting) depicted phenomena and by posing open questions ('What's happening here?,' 'What's that?,' 'Tell me about ...'). Also, researchers should be well versed in conducting these kinds of less directive interviews and be attentive to unexpected but meaningful verbal and nonverbal cues from the respondent. The information and significance that respondents find in the image cannot be approached in a strictly standardized manner. By always remaining alert for respondents' reactions to the visual material, and by adopting a flexible attitude towards unpredictable turns, one can often collect the most significant information. Preferably, the interviewer will try to retain control over the pace at which the images are shown, so that the respondents do not just skip images that are potentially important, or elaborate and linger on aspects of minor importance.

Many types of visuals (in terms of origin or nature) can be used as interview stimuli, but not every set of visuals will 'work' to trigger the desired reactions. Researchers should be able to assemble a set (based on prior testing) that prompts reactions to the pursued focus (the subject or theme at hand), and avoid eliciting responses that are completely off-topic. Attention should be paid to both content and style (the 'what' and 'how': what is the effect of particular formal choices such as color, framing or angle of view with respect to the depicting of the subject matter; I have yet to read a study that elaborates on this aspect). The visual material selected as interview prompts should be able to raise and retain the respondents' interest and cooperation, but if these are too explicit or obvious this will lower their projective potential. Not all material will have the same 'elicitation' potential for all respondents and the outcome will often remain fairly unpredictable.

As part of a focus group setting, using visuals can also yield specific strengths and weaknesses of these techniques in terms of the willingness of the respondents to disclose their reactions in a less secluded session and the ability to build on other people's reactions. People may be more inhibited to disclose very personal responses to a visual stimulus in a group, but the interactions in the group may stimulate and feed group members to provide richer responses. Visual researchers should be able to assess which approach (one-to-one interviews or focus groups) is preferable to obtain the desired outcome.

Douglas Harper, a sociologist who has frequently used the photo-elicitation method, has reviewed a wide variety of studies that have used this technique, primarily in sub-fields such as social class research, family studies, identity research, community research, historical ethnography projects and various culture-related topics (Harper, 2002: 16). However, potential application is much broader, and the types of imagery and visual media that can be employed are manifold. Today, different technologies

---

Example 1: Wheelchair users in the city / Kathleen Jaspers (2002)

Inspired by her friend in a wheelchair, Kathleen Jaspers produced a set of 'researcher-generated images,' which contained both images that refer to (sometimes problematic) material facilities and circumstances, as well as to behavioral/affective aspects of being physically challenged (with a focus on wheelchair users). These pictures were used in a regular photo-elicitation set-up, which revealed the widely divergent perspectives and experiences of wheelchair users, regular pedestrians and policy makers. Non-wheelchair users in general were not aware of the many challenges that the city presented to wheelchair users (like cobble-stone streets, small foot paths, treacherous street car tracks, high thresholds, ill-adapted public transportation) and moreover did not notice how many well-intended wheelchair facilities were in fact inadequate (e.g., ramps and entrances that are too steep or too narrow). Important to note here is that what makes a 'good' image for visual elicitation may differ considerably from what is expected in general from a 'successful' picture, such as a pleasing or dramatic composition. Even rather chaotic pictures, which may be 'poor' in an aesthetic sense (see Figures 6.1 and 6.2), may prove to have a significant 'projective' potential. Pictures used for photo elicitation should not be too explicit, but conversely should try to play out as much possible their poly-semic character.

Figures 6.1 and 6.2 (K. Jaspers)

A wheelchair-based respondent was touched by the picture showing a couple where only one person was in a wheelchair (Figure 6.1) and this triggered an emotional reaction about the chances to develop a relationship with non-wheelchair users (interestingly an effect the image producer did not anticipate). Stairs and a ramp at the entrance of a restaurant (Figure 6.2): to respondents who do not need a wheelchair, this is considered a 'solution' and a token that our city is quite accessible for everyone; for wheelchair users this is immediately identified as a problematic situation because of the steepness of the ramp and the striped pole blocking part of the passage.

(e.g., tablets, smartphones, netbooks) can be used to present the visual stimuli to the respondent in a manner that yields the best conditions for a hassle-free interview.

3   Respondent-generated image production: visual feedback from the field

The interview using visual stimuli can offer a wide range of relevant information about how respondents perceive their world (as verbalized on the basis of visual stimuli), but genuine *visual* feedback can be obtained by allowing the members of the group or culture studied to produce their *own* images in response to a researcher-initiated assignment. It is important to note that 'respondent-generated images' may also include images that were actually made with the help of (or by) another person, for instance when the respondent is part of the picture (see Example 3). The respondent then 'directs' the image production while someone else actually takes the picture.

The underlying premise of this approach is that significant patterns of the respondent's culture (norms, values, expectations, etc.) can be expressed in the images that respondents make (both in what they depict and how things are depicted) and thus revealed to researchers and other respondents. A comparable presupposition provides the basis for sociological research on static or dynamic familial images (photos, home video, family website, etc.). These are, in a sense, also forms of 'native image production' (the older somewhat outdated term of respondent-generated imagery, with clear roots in anthropology: Chalfen, 1987; Pauwels, 1996). An essential difference between the two, however, is that in the case of elicited self-portrayal, the image production occurs in a research context rather than in a naturally occurring social setting. Unlike the family photo album, elicited image production is not part of normal social life. After all, the researcher initiates and steers the production of (camera) images in places and at times that possibly are uncommon for the groups studied. Research subjects are prompted to 'respond in visuals' to a researcher's request or assignment.

This form of visual feedback typically has little structure: in large part because the researcher has only limited control over the manner in which certain aspects are portrayed (which makes it more difficult to compare). The fact that the influence of the researcher should be restricted to a minimum is after all the basic assumption in this approach (though the amount and nature of the guidance may vary according to the pursued research question and the specific assignment). Still, the question remains to what extent one can prevent, even in the teaching of the most elementary techniques for the production of camera images, that the cultural outlook (or, in this case, 'bias') of the researcher affects or disrupts the visual practice of the group studied. This bias may manifest itself in specific choices with regard to filmic parameters (framing, duration and structure of recordings, selection of topics, etc.). Although this issue does not necessarily compromise the applicability of the technique, researchers clearly must be wary of moments when they might inadvertently influence the research process, and try to assess their exact scope and effects. The visual outcome of a respondent-generated imagery project – even when resulting in a complete film or photo series – is not a scientific end product (while just 'data'), and researchers who work with such materials are left with the difficult task of meticulously analyzing the images for both significant content and style (as cultural patterns may reside in both).

One of the early and best-known studies in which the visual feedback technique is applied is *Through Navajo Eyes* by Sol Worth and John Adair (1972). These two researchers taught a number of Navajo Indians to operate a 16 mm camera. In an amazingly brief period of time, they succeeded in making a series of short films about their culture. This convinced Worth and Adair that teaching basic filmmaking techniques to members of other cultures could provide insight into typical cultural and mental patterns among such groups:

A working hypothesis for our study was that motion picture film, conceived, photographed, and sequentially arranged by a people such as the Navajo, would reveal aspects of coding, cognition and values that may be inhibited, not observable, or not analyzable when the investigator is totally dependent on verbal exchange – especially when such research must be done in the language of the investigator. We were interested not only in studying the general nature of the cognitive processes involved in this visual mode of communication itself, but were searching for specific pattern, code, and rules for visual communication within a cultural context. It was the interdependence between a mode of communication and its context as expressed in patterned, interrelated behavior that was sought. (Worth and Adair, 1972: 27–8)

The researchers noticed, for example, that the Navajo filmmakers used a significant amount of footage to record people who were moving from one place to another (e.g., in order to find the right wood for making a fire in a film on the activities of a silversmith). Later, they found that being 'under way' also plays an important role in Navajo songs, poems and everyday language. Moving from one place to another is considered a significant event in itself, and not just as a means to an end (Worth and Adair, 1972: 146). They noted, in contrast, that Western filmmakers tend to work more 'elliptically': they usually try to shorten the process by leaving out any moments that are perceived to be unimportant, such as a shot of a man who walks out of frame, possibly a number of short shots of someone picking up some twigs and then moving out of the picture again, and finally a shot of him back home with a load of wood.

Today, visual feedback techniques in various forms have become favored approaches for many visual sociologists and visual anthropologists, though the methodological tenets of this approach are considerable. The major challenge is how to instruct the field and educate participants about producing visuals for a particular aim without inadvertently transferring to the participant values and norms of the researcher's culture, which would thwart the outcome. In comparison with other visual techniques, however, researchers working with respondent image-making typically have limited control over the production process. And afterwards they need to be well versed in the broader culture of the respondents to be able to adequately decode the meanings of the depicted objects and situations, as well as the way they have been visualized and organized.

Respondent-generated image productions may put aspects of the broader culture of the respondent into the spotlight, keeping the image maker literally 'out of sight,' or take a more autobiographical stance. When respondents choose to depict aspects of their own intimate life they sometimes have to rely on another person (from their environment) to take pictures which they figure in themselves, but most often this is done according explicit instructions by the respondent and therefore still qualifies as 'respondent-generated image-making.'

Example 2: Nursing home views / Nathalie Claessens (2009)

Nathalie Claessens used the 'respondent-generated imagery' approach to investigate what elderly residents of a nursing home valued most in their environment. In particular, she was keen to find out to what extent the views – in terms of needs and facilities – as expressed in scholarly literature, government policies and regulations, matched those held by the residents. All residents who were considered by the nursing staff to be able to take photographs (a minority with ages varying between 82 and 93) were given a small digital camera for one day and asked to make pictures of what they found important in their current lives (Figures 6.3 and 6.4). The pictures were then used in an interview with the producer to elicit more information about what exactly the pictures (were meant to) depict and why they had been taken.

Figures 6.3 and 6.4 (courtesy of N. Claessens)
Religious subjects clearly dominate the series of pictures that Aagje (aged 93) made (Figure 6.3). The only site of which three pictures were made was the grotto with the statues of Bernadette and the Virgin Mary. Aagje's pictures also reveal how important opportunities to have social contacts in the communal spaces are to her (Figure 6.4), which she also confirmed in the subsequent interview. Significantly, none of her pictures included the personnel of her nursing home.

4   Reassessing contemporary 'participatory' visual research

The two dominant approaches described above have become fashionable in many areas of research and social work and are often called 'participatory' visual methods. Many new terms created or acquired by the researcher also have been invented to distinguish options within broadly defined participatory set-ups ('auto-driven photo elicitation,' 'photovoice,' 'photo novella,' 'community video') can be traced back to the two approaches described above: using visual materials to prompt verbal reactions or asking the respondents or participants to produce their own visual material (and subsequently comment on it). However, some options within this range are worth a closer look.

4.1   Auto-driven photo elicitation

Using images as visual stimuli in an interview and asking respondents to portray aspects of their life are distinct research techniques, but these often have been combined with good results. Images produced by respondents mostly need verbal clarification by the respondents, and such verbal clarifications may elucidate aspects that even the image makers were not aware of during the image capture. Today this combination of respondent-produced and subsequently commented upon imagery is often called 'auto-driven photo elicitation.'

This popular approach is somewhat under-theorized and rather unspecified in a methodological sense. 'Auto-driven photo elicitation,' contrary to what the term seems to suggest, is in fact more a variant of 'respondent-generated image production' than of 'photo elicitation.' It is a form of photo elicitation, to the extent that (respondent-generated) images are used to generate verbal feedback. But then most if not all respondent-generated image production projects necessitate the verbal input of respondents, to help make sense of the visual outcome. However, the fact that in this case people are asked to respond to images that they themselves produced (instead of reacting to pictures they may never have seen before or might never take themselves such as historical pictures or researched produced images) and that have been carefully selected by the researcher to address a certain problematic, warrants further scrutiny. For it is clear that the respondent will perform a somewhat different 'expert role' when commenting on self-made images, compared to talking about unexpected images created or acquired by the researcher. Other (largely undocumented) peculiarities of auto-driven photo elicitation are the scopic limitation of the images, as they have typically been produced in a short period of time in a particular place (whereas images selected by the researcher can cover many decades and geographic locations), and the fact that the researcher has less control over the visual stimuli that are provided to the respondent: because these are created by the latter they may not include details central to questions of interest to the researcher. Finally, researchers choosing this approach should not neglect to perform a detailed analysis of the respondent-produced visuals above and beyond the interpretations and rationalizations of their producers. The auto-driven photo-elicitation approach – unlike the regular photo-elicitation approach – clearly yields two types of data: verbal and visual, and an opportunity to merge or confront the emic and the etic perspective.

4.2   Respondent-generated production as social action: photovoice and community video

'Respondent-generated image approaches' come in many forms and guises, but the most popular terms are 'photovoice' (Wang, 1999), 'community video' or 'participatory video.' Indeed, the basic technique of the approaches is similar to what is described above: handing out (still or moving) picture-making devices to people and giving them a limited number of guidelines to depict aspects and events of their world.

Whereas the purpose of respondent-generated image production in a research project is primarily to acquire unique data about the respondents' world (their visualized experiences and environment as an entry point to their culture) and thus to generate scientific knowledge, the primary aim of many photovoice and community video projects is to initiate a positive change in the world of the participants, ideally by raising awareness of a problem in a community, empowering community members or marginalized individuals or by trying to exert influence on authorities or policy makers to improve a problematic situation.

The role of the 'project instigator' in photovoice or community video activities is mainly to organize/facilitate, provide the means (expertise and materials) and make sure that the social activist message is brought across though publications, exhibitions, public meetings and any combination of these. The end product (a book, exhibition, or video program) is often not a social scientific contribution, though it might very well provide valuable data for further study (as it potentially generates new 'local' or practice-based knowledge and insights).

A number of projects that explicitly use the term photovoice to characterize their approach do so in a way that fully complies with 'respondent-generated production' as a research method (e.g., Lorenz's work on patients with brain injuries, 2010: 210–23). However, more often the main goal of photovoice projects is social action rather than (strictly scientific) knowledge production, though these distinct options need not exclude one another. Often participatory action projects also provide a rich and unique (and largely untapped) source of data on community development and on grassroots expression.

For photovoice activities to be considered a research method (or as a contemporary variant of 'respondent-generated image production' or 'native image production') they would need to be grounded and guided by one or more research disciplines (sociology, health science, education, etc.). These perspectives would similarly require careful analysis of the visual (or multimodal) data as expressions of particular views and experiences of the participants. Visual products should not be taken at face value or considered self-evident. These principles would also apply to action-research approaches, for which the intended and presumed effect cannot be assumed, a priori – in other words, producing visual accounts and statements does not automatically produce effects or, more particularly, desired outcomes for the participants. Unfortunately, photovoice and other participatory approaches are often characterized and advocated by their intended outcome, and lack both empirical evidence and methodologies for arriving at that outcome, including criteria and indicators to evaluate whether ambitious claims and intentions have been realized.

As one example, the www.photovoiceworldwide.com website boldly asserts that photovoice:

- Strengthens writing and communications skills.
- Empowers people, families, and communities.
- Awakens appreciation for different points of view.
- Strengthens positive relations (between e.g. young adolescents, parents, community, etc.).
- Increases civic involvement.
- Fosters family and community dialog.
- Develops teamwork.
- Gives participants a voice in their community.
- Raises awareness of resources and problems.
- Creates powerful visual facts for fundraising and sponsorship.
- Has wide impact for low cost.
- Establishes partnerships for community change.

These are well-intentioned and laudable claims, but they refer to *possible* outcomes and *desired* effects, not essential 'features' or 'natural' results that appear automatically from handing out cameras to people, facilitating group processes and disseminating the results. Making pictures may be a valuable part of a process to improve the situation of under-represented or marginalized people, but there is nothing intrinsically or automatically empowering in using pictures. It is certainly one way to get a message across and a process that can yield new experiences with the participants, but so can writing stories or organizing debates or protests. The literature on participatory visual methods is replete with similar idealistic and celebratory accounts of photovoice and related participatory approaches, and most often little guidance is offered on to how to realize these distinct aspects. The growing number of scholars and professionals interested in learning how and when to apply this technique or format with good results would be better served with more critical and detailed accounts. The product and the internal (in-group) and external effects be scrutinized, documented and critically examined.

A distinction needs to be made between offering participants/respondents a 'voice' in the research process (for ethical or scientific reasons) while retaining the basic researcher's commitment to knowledge production (of fundamental or more 'applied' nature), and helping groups to have an immediate and tangible impact on their environment. Projects should try to be clear about this and adopt a reflexive and self-critical attitude: what are the real benefits/outcomes of this project and who ultimately stands to gain? Moreover, 'giving voice through visuals' only to some people on some topics and in some ways or formats does not ensure adequate coverage of the 'emic' perspective (for research purposes) or to the variety of views and concerns that may exist in the selected communities' (in a social activist perspective).

Some scholars and practitioners have begun to question the assumption that providing visual media opportunities (cameras, editing tools, exhibition space) to groups of people automatically gives them a 'voice' that will be heard and acted upon. They are also challenging the related assumption that pictures are self-evident and need no further elaboration, framing or analysis. Indeed, according to Chalfen, Sherman and Rich (2010: 201) the term 'photovoice,' albeit 'a noble calling' at times, appears to have paternalistic traits and has been 'more often than not, abused':

In truth, careful attention to what is 'said' is often a missing component in light of other harmful clichés – namely, 'the pictures speak for themselves' or even, 'every picture tells a story'. Thus the preferential attention to 'voice' might not be matched with attentive looking and listening to what first-time image-makers might be saying. (Chalfen, Sherman and Rich, 2010: 201)

Whether photographic projects really help individuals, groups or communities to obtain a 'voice' are empirical questions that need to be asked and answered on a case-by-case basis. A critical evaluation of the real effects or impact is overdue, both for the people involved and to fine-tune the method for future use.

4.3   Photo novella: method or format?

Though the 'photo novella' is often ascribed emancipatory powers, similar to photovoice (for which it is sometimes used as a synonym), there is nothing intrinsically liberating or special about it in its form or content. It is, in fact, just one of the possible presentational formats of photovoice projects, not a distinct participatory method, nor an 'alternative to classic photo-elicitation' (contrary to what Lapenta, 2011: 205, based on Hurworth, 2003, seems to suggest).

Typically, a photo novella combines photographs with words (text balloons, captions, or larger chunks of text) in paper or electronic form, and as such it is the more or less static counterpart of community videos. Some proponents, like Wang and Burris (1994: 171) try to limit it to a practice for a specific group of people (marginalized, less powerful) stating that this 'method': 'does not entrust cameras to health specialists, policymakers, or professional photographers, but puts them in the hands of children, rural women, grassroots workers, and other constituents with little access to those who make decisions over their lives.' This claim confounds presentational format with particular goals, target groups and applications. Photo novellas can be produced with media and formats that have a low threshold for expertise and cost and are therefore more accessible for all layers of society. However, there is no reason why people in less marginalized positions could not produce these types of output and with equal benefits for society or parts thereof.

In much the same way that photovoice can be considered socially and politically inspired projects involving respondent-generated image

---

Example 3: Living with acquired brain injury (ABI) / Alina Dragan (2009)

Alina Dragan, who prior to taking the visual sociology and anthropology course worked as a psychologist in a day-care center for people with a disability, used the 'respondent-generated image-making' method in her project as a means to help people with an acquired brain injury (ABI: e.g., victims of strokes, car accidents, tumors) to communicate how they see themselves and what the impact of their handicap is on their daily functioning (Figures 6.5 and 6.6). Looking at the results of this experiment, she discovered that persons suffering from ABI often express themselves in a very literal way and have difficulty with figurative meanings and irony.

Figures 6.5 and 6.6. (courtesy of A. Dragan)
Person A struggled trying to show that half of his brain is damaged and then came up with a red piece of cloth with which he covered half of his head (Figure 6.5). He commented on the resulting picture: 'I see myself as a sick person, who gets worse and worse. My brain is damaged at one side.' Other people had themselves pictured before signage (Figure 6.6) or bent over maps to indicate their difficulty in orienting themselves.

production, photo novella projects could more productively be considered as a respondent- or participant-produced counterpart of the scholarly 'visual essay' (Pauwels, 2012), which is also essentially a presentational format using visuals, text and design to get a message or story across.

5   Nature and degrees of participation/collaboration

As Jon Wagner duly noted, the term 'participatory research' does not really point to a separate form of research, as almost every research method (even the standard survey or structured interview), is to some extent participatory or cooperative in explicit or more implicit ways (Wagner, 1997: 13). Most human studies involve some kind of interaction between the researcher and the researched. Yet the approaches and techniques covered in this chapter do involve the respondents or participants more actively than most established social science methods and techniques. So, while there may not be an essential difference from other types of research, there may be at least one in degree.

However, while there is considerable overlap, 'respondent-generated image production' does not necessarily coincide with 'participatory visual research' (nor with a 'research' perspective per se), since the former presupposes that the respondents handle or direct the cameras themselves and thus visualize their views and experiences with minimal interference. The visual outcomes of this active involvement of the respondents constitute the prime data for the researchers. Participatory techniques go back to Rouch (1975) and even Flaherty (*Nanook of the North*, 1922), but do not necessarily imply that the respondents get 'behind the camera.' Participation is a very broad concept; participants may be involved in many different aspects of the production.

It is also important to make this distinction with respect to the end product as well as the process: respondent-generated visual materials cannot constitute, as such, a scientific end product. They need to be analyzed and framed within disciplinary methods and theory. Joint productions ('shared anthropology'; see Rouch, 1975) in contrast may take the form of a scholarly end-product character, as the expertise of researchers and field representatives have been skillfully combined during the process. Moreover, a well-balanced combination of etic and emic views may prove much more valuable than either on its own.

While some practitioners and scholars distinguish between collaboration and participation ('collaborative' versus 'participatory' video; see Mitchell and de Lange, 2011: 171), with the latter involving only minimal assistance from the researcher or community worker, this distinction has not gained currency. As a result, it is not self-explanatory in terms of what exactly these forms of participation or collaboration might entail. Rather, one should look more closely at the different types and phases of the collaboration or participatory processes. It should also be noted that the use of the term 'collaborative' as a synonym or further specification of 'participatory' in this regard only applies to forms of interaction with the field and not to collaboration of the researchers with other professionals like professional filmmakers or photographers.

In a recent publication, Chalfen (2011: 188), a pioneer and leading scholar in participatory research, gives some useful, although not mutually exclusive, examples of what collaboration or participation may entail:

- Asking for help from local people by having them appear on camera for a pre-planned theme, storyline, etc.
- Asking different members of the community to say what they want included and why they want certain subject matter filmed; more often than not, community members propose a selection of subject matter for purposes of local improvement in physical, social or political conditions.
- Asking for local people to collaborate in editing or otherwise organizing a film; this may also entail asking for preferred meanings of particular visual sequences and overall meaning of a film.

Clearly there is a need to better define 'participation' and degrees or levels within it, and look more closely at the wide variety of aims and beneficiaries of such participating or collaborative forms of visual research that figure today under various labels.

Moreover, the roles of respondents and researchers/facilitators are not always so straightforward and distinct in visual participatory projects. In truly 'joint' visual productions researchers and researched may act as 'partners' which constantly shift or share roles. In 'auto-ethnographic' accounts such as 'visual diaries' kept by researchers (see Chaplin, 2011) they may even become completely mixed up because the researcher combines two roles, that of a visual analyst and that of subject/participant.

6   Discussion and a proposal for further research

The participatory approaches covered in this chapter represent an important strand of visual research with a growing number of practitioners from a diversity of disciplines and professional fields. These 'participatory visual techniques,' in their many current forms and guises, have rediscovered and partly reinvented long-standing traditions of 'visual interviewing' (photo elicitation) and 'respondent-generated

A basic taxonomy of participatory visual techniques				
	Visual elicitation	'Auto-driven' visual elicitation	Respondent-generated image production	Participant-generated image production
Related terms and practices	• Photo elicitation / film elicitation; visual interview	• 'Auto-driven' photo elicitation / 'Visual elicitation' using 'respondent-generated visuals'	• 'Native image production' (and possibly terms listed to the right, i.e. Photovoice)	• Community video; Participatory video; visual voice; visible voice
Set-up and purpose	• Use 'found' and/or 'researcher-produced' *visuals as interview stimuli to generate verbal reactions* (factual and projective responses/meanings) as data for further analysis	• Instigate *respondents to produce visuals* and have them to *comment on them.* Both the images and the verbal elucidation serve as data for further analysis	• Instigate *respondents to produce images* as visual or multimodal expressions of aspects of their culture and life conditions as data for further analysis	• Help individuals and communities to '*voice*' *their views through self-produced visual materials* (and texts) aimed at *promoting social change* (empowerment, awareness, citizenship, political action to improve an undesired situation)
Output / format	• *Verbal* feedback from respondents analyzed and processed in research reports, journal articles and book chapters, or multimedia products	• *Visual and verbal* feedback from respondents analyzed and processed in research reports, journal articles and book chapters, or multimedia products	• *Visual* feedback from respondent analyzed and processed in research reports, journal articles and book chapters, or multimedia products	• Images and texts - usually not studied as 'data' - in various formats for public dissemination: printed matter, exhibitions, multimedia products (e.g. 'photo novella', 'digital storytelling'.)
Core issues	• Select and pre-test the visual interview materials on their projective potential and adequacy to trigger 'on topic' comments. • Conduct the visual interview in a non-directive and responsive manner	• Taking advantage of both types of data (visual and verbal) and thus not limit the approach to 'visual elicitation'. Researchers need to analyze the visual beyond the meaning given by the respondent / image producer	• Instruct the respondents to produce visual materials without inadvertently transferring researchers' cultural views. • In depth knowledge needed to decode cultural meanings of both visual form and content	• Measure instead of merely 'presume' effects. • Follow up and ethically manage immediate and long-term expectations of communities and participants

Figure 6.7 A basic taxonomy of participatory visual techniques (L. Pauwels)

This table summarizes some key distinctions of participatory visual (research) techniques, but projects may very well combine several of these traits (modes, purposes, perspectives, etc.) in even more hybrid approaches, whereby the roles of researchers and respondents or participants may become conflated. Also note that some projects which have explicit scientific aims may also use the term photovoice, visual voice or participatory video; these latter terms do not necessarily imply an exclusively social activist perspective.

image production' (native image production). These approaches also contribute to redefining the human subjects of research from objects of enquiry to more active agents of knowledge building and social change.

However, as Chalfen has noted, 'the observed lack of cross-referencing or continuity' has so far inhibited 'any comprehensive sense of accumulated knowledge and tradition' (Chalfen, 2011: 187–8) about participatory visual techniques. To correct that shortcoming, it is important to stand back from the customary celebratory and somewhat nebulous treatment of this promising approach, and adopt instead the kind of critical-constructive stance necessary to realize the extensive ethical and epistemological potential of participatory visual research.

A crucial step in this direction is the recognition that a significant distinction needs be made between involving the members of field communities in the production of visual materials for scientific purposes, on the one hand, and, on the other, helping members produce images to better an unwanted or disadvantaged situation. It is also important to acknowledge that respondent-generated imagery may serve two distinct purposes: scholarly knowledge production and social action (and awareness). These goals are not necessarily mutually exclusive goals (though in actual practice one seems to take precedence), but their different methodological implications do require separate and explicit attention. A more transparent and well-reasoned methodology is not just important for research purposes but also for non-academic projects, where some other criteria may apply but where generating some sort of knowledge, awareness or insight among the community members and other stakeholders is also of vital importance. Responsibly executed participatory visual research involves managing the expectations of the respondents/participants by providing precise and realistic information about the process and the possible outcomes. As an action-research or activist approach it also involves following up the process and making some serious efforts to measure the intended and unintended social effects (both the internal or 'in-group' and external upshots) with the actual and future well-being of those involved in mind.

In general, it seems at times that more effort has been expended in inventing new terms for existing practices, and claiming ownership or superiority of quite similar practices, than in explaining what these 'new' or revised techniques really involve. In particular, the terms photovoice, photo novella and photo elicitation are used (sometimes even interchangeably) for a wide variety of research set-ups and outcomes. Some find it necessary to use different names for every type of medium (photovoice, filmvoice, videovoice, comicvoice, paintvoice), but a more generic term like 'visual voice' or 'picture voice' would be an improvement over the proliferation of new terms for similar and related practices.

Streamlining the terminology may help practitioners and newcomers to better comprehend the assumptions and implications of what they are trying to achieve. It would, for instance, be helpful to talk more consistently about 'respondent-generated image production' to indicate the social science studies perspective with a prime focus on analysis and the production of knowledge about a social phenomenon. The term 'participant-generated image production' could be used to refer to more social activist projects geared primarily towards producing change (in attitudes, beliefs, behavior, law, etc.) in the social world.

A similar desire for clarifying the 'current diversity found in professional and non-professional approaches' that are presented as 'participatory visual methods' has been expressed by Chalfen (2011: 186), who proposes distinguishing between participatory 'projects' and 'studies.' The first yields results for the community (community 'projects') and the latter findings for the scientific community (scientific 'studies'; Chalfen, 2011: 190). A process of terminological sanitation is hard to enforce given the broad spread and appeal of these approaches and the many combinations or intermediate positions that projects or studies may take, but attempts to present and claim participatory approaches as novel and innovative by merely introducing new labels for similar approaches seem somewhat pointless and unproductive.

Unfortunately, relatively little systematic research addresses more urgent methodological matters such as documenting, sharing, investigating and integrating specific research experiences with potentially significant differentiators of – respectively – the visual elicitation process, and respondent- or participant-generated image production.

With respect to the 'visual elicitation' method one could for example further investigate the impact of:

- the provenance/origin of the images (different types of found images, researcher-produced, respondent-produced, or images produced for the respondents at their request);
- medium-specific characteristics (comparing the projective potential of photo, film, drawings, paintings, etc.)
- the style elements / formal variation of images (aesthetic choices with regard to use of color, framing, shot types, documentary versus artistic, etc.)
- the type of content (specific/general, explicit/implicit, shocking/ provocative or conventional/reassuring, mimetic/realist or metaphorical/ conceptual)
- using a coherent set of pictures or a mixture of images from different eras, cultures and segments of society (or historic and contemporary

material, color and black-and-white pictures, advertisements and family pictures)
– different interview settings and approaches (one-on-one, focus group viewings, at the respondents' home or elsewhere, interviewer role/personality, types of questions, group dynamics)
– different visual presentational media and formats (paper, electronic, projected)
– different ways to analyze and process the (verbal) outcomes
– particular purposes and aims (goals and objectives) of the study, and setting and approach, and so forth.

Basic aspects in 'respondent- or participant-generated image production' that need further elucidation could include:
– the distinct purposes of various set-ups and their methodological and ethical consequences (knowledge building, educating the participants, empowerment, influencing policy makers)
– the kinds of participation/collaboration (amount, degree, what when where, the real beneficiaries)
– the viability and practicability certain choices of themes or problems have over others, the involvement of different 'agents' in the field, the nature of the briefing and subsequent interventions and constraints (e.g., time, expertise, decision-making)
– different ways to present and process the visual output
– ways to measure the awaited and unexpected short- and long-term effects for the different parties involved.

A more systematic inventory of findings related to aspects such as those listed above, generated through self-reflexivity by researchers, community workers and professionals of different fields (health care, the arts, etc.) could open even more promising vistas for participatory visual approaches. Above all, it would help researchers new to these methods to make more informed decisions about tapping the full potential of participatory techniques and the varied forms of data they can generate.

7   References

Chalfen, R. (1987) *Snapshot Versions of Life*, Bowling Green State University Popular Press.
Chalfen, R. (2011) 'Differentiating Practices of Participatory Visual Media Production.' In: E. Margolis and L. Pauwels (eds.) *SAGE Handbook of Visual Research Methods*, London/New Delhi: Sage, pp. 186–200.
Chalfen, R., L. Sherman and M. Rich (2010) 'VIA's Visual Voices: The Awareness of a Dedicated Audience for Voices in Patient Video Narratives.' *Visual Studies*, 25(3): 201–9.

Chaplin, E. (2011) 'The Photo Diary as an Autoethnographic Method.' In: E. Margolis and L. Pauwels (eds.) *SAGE Handbook of Visual Research Methods*, London/New Delhi: Sage, pp. 241–62.

Collier, J. (1967) *Visual Anthropology: Photography as a Research Method*, New York/London: Holt, Rinehart and Winston. (Later revised with Malcolm Collier (1986), University of New Mexico Press.)

Flaherty, R. (1922) *Nanook of the North*, film, 55 mins., USA: Revillon Frères.

Harper, D. (2002) 'Talking about Pictures: A Case for Photo Elicitation.' *Visual Studies*, 17(1): pp. 13–25.

Hurworth, R. (2003) 'Photo-Interviewing for Research.' *Social Research Update*, 40 [Online]. Available from: http://sru.soc.surrey.ac.uk/SRU40.pdf [accessed October 7, 2012].

Krebs, S. (1975) 'The Film Elicitation Technique.' In: P. Hockings (ed.) *Principles of Visual Anthropology*. The Hague/Paris: Mouton, pp. 283–301.

Lapenta, F. (2011) 'Some Theoretical and Methodological Views on Photo-Elicitation.' In: E. Margolis and L. Pauwels (eds.) *SAGE Handbook of Visual Research Methods*, London/New Delhi: Sage, pp. 201–13.

Lorenz, L. S. (2010) 'Brain Injury Survivors: Narratives of Rehabilitation and Healing.' In: R. J. Berger (ed.) *Disability in Society*. Boulder, CO/London: Lynne Rienner Publishers.

Mitchell, C. and N. de Lange (2011) 'Community-Based Participatory Video and Social Action in Rural South Africa.' In: E. Margolis and L. Pauwels (eds.) *SAGE Handbook of Visual Research Methods*, London/New Delhi: Sage, pp. 171–85.

Pauwels, L. (1996) *De Verbeelde Samenleving, Camera, Kennisverwerving en Communicatie*, Leuven/Apeldoorn: Wetenschappelijke Uitgeverij Garant.

Pauwels, L. (2012) 'Conceptualizing the "Visual Essay" as a Way of Generating and Imparting Sociological Insight: Issues, Formats and Realizations.' *Sociological Research Online*, 17(1): 1–11.

Rouch, J. (1975) 'The Camera and Man.' In: P. Hockings (ed.) *Principles of Visual Anthropology*. The Hague/Paris: Mouton, pp. 83–102.

Segers, J. (1983) *Sociologische Onderzoeksmethoden: Deel 1, Inleiding tot de structuur van het onderzoeksproces en tot de methoden van dataverzameling*, 3rd en. Assen: Van Gorcum.

Wagner, J. (ed.) (1979) *Images of Information: Still Photography in the Social Sciences*, Beverly Hills/London: Sage.

Wagner, J. (1997) 'The Unavoidable Intervention of Educational Research: A Framework for Reconsidering Researcher-Practitioner Cooperation.' *Educational Researcher*, 26 (7), pp. 13–22.

Wang, C. (1999) 'Photovoice: A Participatory Action Research Strategy Applied to Women's Health.' *Journal of Women's Health*, 8(2): 185–92.

Wang, C. and M. A. Burris (1994) 'Empowerment through Photo Novella: Portraits of Participation.' *Health Education & Behavior*, 21(2): 171–86.

Worth, S. and J. Adair (1972) *Through Navajo Eyes: An Exploration in Film Communication and Anthropology*. Bloomington: Indiana University Press. [See also: revised edition: S. Worth, J. Adair, and R. Chalfen, 1997]

7 The 'visual essay' as a scholarly format: art meets (social) science?

1 Visual presentations of knowledge

Most visual research – and even research not based on visual data or phenomena – can benefit at least from some form of visual approach in the presentation of the findings, be it through the considerate selection and combination of visual data (images or other types of collected or produced visual representations) that exemplify or contextualize a visual phenomenon, through graphical representations that summarize or corroborate the findings, or by using visual material to express aspects, experiences and insights that cannot be conveyed in words, or even through visualizing non-visual data from non-visual phenomena for better analysis and communication (Grady, 2006; Pauwels, 2006).

As a related matter, a 'visual' social science worthy of that name should not only try to investigate and 'talk' about the visual, but also try – and this may also apply to social science in a more general sense, as Henny (1986) noted long ago – to become 'more visual' (or even multimodal) in its way of 'communicating' its findings and insights. Fortunately the idea is gradually taking shape that visual (social) science is not just about analyzing and producing visual data but also about visualizing and expressing insights in novel, more experimental and experiential ways (e.g., including arts-based approaches).

In this chapter I draw on these two concerns to examine visual *presentations* of social scientific insight as products and reports not only for visual research but also for more traditional (non-visual) research. At the heart of this examination is the 'visual essay,' a form of representation previously noted by a number of sociologists and other social researchers (Wagner, 1979; Grady, 1991; Pauwels, 1993, 2002, 2010). The visual essay is one of the most visual formats of representation within visual research communities, but its relationship to traditional social scientific practice has been poorly understood and the subject of considerable controversy.

To encourage a more complete understanding of the visual essay's potential value to social scientific research, I will begin by reviewing its cultural roots and evolving features. I will then examine key elements of the visual essay for their potential (in theory) to enrich the social sciences. As illustrations of this potential, I will review several exemplary visual essays. Taken together, these varied accounts and analyses point to a promising future for the visual essay and its intellectual contributions to social scientific enquiry.

2   Roots and features of the visual essay format

The origin of the 'visual essay,' as a broad category of visual representation, can be partially rooted in the one-time successful journalistic and documentary practice of the 'photo essay' in illustrated magazines such as *LIFE* and *Vu* in the 1930s and 1940s. These magazines provided compelling, often socially inspired stories that cleverly combined photographs with captions or longer portions of text. Truly exemplary are W. Eugene Smith's photo essay 'Country Doctor' (*LIFE*, 1948), capturing the drama of everyday life in a small rural town, and 'Spanish Village,' documenting traditional ways of life (*LIFE*, April 1951) which marked a departure of the more strict narrative approach of his earlier work. Noteworthy are also Henri Cartier Bresson's (*LIFE*, March 1963) and Rene Burri's (*LOOK*, April 1963) photo essays of Cuba. The skillful combination of images and text thoughtfully laid out created a synergy between these two modes of expression, a synergy that characterizes the basic or most elementary – but still vigorous – form of the visual essay.

Today the term 'visual essay' is used for a variety of formats which have moved far beyond paper-based pictures and text combinations, varying in length and breadth from concise articles to book-length contributions, from short clips to full-length films on DVD or on the web, from poster-size constructions to room-filling exhibitions and art installations.

In principle a visual essay can consist of any type of images or visual representations: photographic and non-photographic (drawings, paintings, graphics). It can make use of pre-existing images, or images explicitly produced for the purpose. The old practice of photomontage or photo-collage, elevated to great heights by activist artists such as John Heartfield in his fight against nationalism and the devastating effects of Nazi ideology (Willet, 1997) testifies of the power of recombining elements of existing imagery with a sharp critique and observation of society. But the expressive potential of the image and its interaction with other elements of this hybrid communicative form can often be taken even further by producing new images expressly for use in a visual essay.

The static or moving image indeed has a broad range of expressive signifiers (Monaco, 2000; Rose, 2011) that can be activated and combined to support a 'preferred meaning.' Yet 'expression' is not limited to the 'image' part of the visual essay; it may reside in various other elements that constitute the visual essay, some of which are visual as well (e.g., color schemes, typographic parameters, spatial composition of the whole) and some of which are not (e.g., word register and numerous other linguistic traits, narrative strategies and navigational options). Even the choice for a particular subject or theme, or a particular time and place, can be deemed 'expressive,' to the extent that it conveys certain ideas that transcend the immediately manifest content and reveals a particular point of view (Pauwels, 2011).

The relations between visual, auditory and verbal parts and channels can be played out in many different ways. Both tight or more loose relations between these expressive systems may be accommodated. Authors may choose to steer the receiver of the message in a specific direction by furnishing a clear verbal context for the interpretation of the visual parts or, alternatively, pursue a more reciprocal relation between text and image, granting each the possibility to contribute their own part to the overall message; see Barthes's (1999) concepts of 'anchorage' and 'relay.' Textual parts can be very descriptive, evoke certain interpretations, challenge the reader to pursue a personal reading or offer the basic line of narration (Almasy, 1990: 36). They can range from a very factual, informational tone to a more provocative, metaphorical or poetic one. A similar range of options exists for the other modes and sub-modes of expression like sound and graphic design (cheerful, serious, disconcerting, harmonic, …). Different types of hierarchy, interdependency and complementarity can be established between the different modes of expression.

There is a clear danger in defining a visual essay too rigidly, but it is useful to distinguish central tendencies of the ideal type. For example, journal or magazine articles (or other presentational formats) that use images or other visual elements merely as decoration may not warrant consideration as 'visual essays' because the distinctive strength of the visual essay is the complementary interplay between different modes of expression to create a signifying whole that builds on – or even transcends – the expressive capabilities of any one mode on its own.

Like the written essay format, the visual essay may be characterized by an explicit expression of subjectivity or by opportunities to elaborate a personal voice and vision.

Another valued feature of many visual essays is the opportunity that viewers or readers find to independently explore source materials and to probe the intentions of the author – in some cases even to go beyond even these in examining the author's implicit choices of imagery and voice. As a complement to what an author puts into such representations to communicate insights and perspectives, the visual essay can also work as a projection screen or mirror that can reflect ideas and experiences that viewers and readers bring to work of this sort. Indeed, the extent to which a visual essay succeeds in triggering intended audience reactions is typically considered an aspect of its value or worth.

Today the visual essay seems to blossom again in various forms and guises, in art and educational spheres, as well as on social media platforms, and in mass media and activist spheres. Boosted by new media technologies and networking opportunities the visual essay has developed into a contemporary vehicle for voicing and visualizing all sorts of personal reflections, new ideas, arguments, experiences and observations, thereby taking any possible hybrid variation and combination of a manifesto, a critical review, a testimony or just a compelling story.

In conjunction with these recent developments, journalistic media, from which the visual essay originated, also rediscovered the value of visual storytelling. Online versions of newspapers now have the opportunity to take advantage of additional expressive modes like movement and sound. One of the most notable examples in this regard is the *New York Times*, which publishes at a steady rate compelling visual essays using just black-and-white or color photos with concise verbal accounts (written or spoken texts). This basic set-up exemplifies how powerful the combination of two highly complementary expressive systems can be – in this case static or moving images and an off-screen voice – to tell captivating stories of life (see *Lens: Photography, Video and Visual Journalism*: http://lens. blogs.nytimes.com).

More surprising is that even the natural and medical science journals (e.g., *The International Journal of Epidemiology*) invite visual essay contributions and recognize their value in imparting knowledge and experience about their field of research in a different and often more broadly contextualized way (Pauwels, 2005).

New media developments have made any description of the concrete forms a visual essay can take even more specious. It can take almost any form (illustrated articles, exhibition, art installations), and adopt virtually any new feature of any new technology. A more useful approach is to define the visual essay as an approach, a method or set-up that plays out different expressive modalities in a somewhat open-ended/implicit manner rather than by its specific formal qualities. And new technologies indeed keep pushing the boundaries of what is possible in just these terms. Moving images and non-linear features of contemporary technology allow for far more sophisticated combinations of text, images, sound, design and so on evolving towards audiovisual essays rather than purely visual essays. Multimodal or multisensory visual essays that go beyond 'sight and sound' are conceivable, but today the dominant 'senses' addressed in both new and old media (of a non-transient nature) are still vision and hearing.

The expressive potential of visual essays are in part determined by the end medium of presentation and the different media that are combined in that end medium, and subsequently by technological advances and ways that are being invented to take advantage of these. However an increase in expressive signifiers can be both a curse and a blessing. Often the intelligible use of the abundance of possibilities does not succeed in keeping pace with technological innovation. Too often 'means' (features, bells and whistles) are confused with 'ends,' which then in fact results in an expressive deficit. Playing around with too many potential signifiers at once may confuse the audience rather than offering them a novel or innovative experience. The adage 'less is more' most certainly also applies to this line of work.

3   The visual 'social scientific' essay . . .

Considering the visual essay as a valid and viable form of social science research and reporting requires further discussion of specific expectations of this disciplinary activity and its products. These begin with the challenges of social science research and the goal of imparting insights about the social and the cultural world. Further articulation of these expectations is necessary to clarify the theoretical or disciplinary grounding and to contextualize this type of scholarly work and its essential characteristics.

Among the questions we might want to answer are the following: To what extent can the visual essay display or mimic practical expectations of social science disciplines? What kinds of contextualization are required to make visual essays accessible and credible to disciplinary scholars? Can alternatives to narrative modes of organization succeed in reporting social scientific insights? What challenges and opportunities are created for social researchers who include primary source data as multimodal features of their research reports?

The following observations, propositions and arguments provide a partial response to questions such as these and can hopefully clarify what a visual social scientific essay might entail and its potential place within scholarly discourse:

- Though the visual essay as a scholarly format is a 'meeting' of art and science practices it still must address in some way the exigencies (demands, norms and expectations) of its intended disciplinary audience (sociology, anthropology, cultural geography, etc.). This does not imply slavishly emulating the scientific demands posed to data gathering and data representation which anyway are largely based on the types of data the social sciences are used to working with (verbal and numeric), since that would largely kill its unique potential, but it also does not imply a liberation of any empirical reference, or methodological or theoretical standards. For it is far too easy to simply adopt the attitude that 'everything goes.' The visual essay as a form of scholarly communication would not benefit from such a 'garbage bin' definition. Having said this, the visual essay should certainly not try to shed its avant-garde (and thus almost by nature 'contested') skin or character.

- Furthermore, a visual essay will hardly ever be purely visual, in the same manner as visual sociology can never be only visual. I tend to maintain my earlier position (Pauwels, 1993) that a series of images alone probably cannot constitute a visual 'social science' essay. However unique the informative and expressive potential of images and other visual elements can be, I believe that a minimal verbal contextualization is needed, though I am well aware this may be a point of disagreement among visual scholars. This personal stand does not imply that I would object to publishing individual pictures or a simple series of pictures as interesting forms of data in sociology journals, as long as they are not put forward as a (self-contained) visual essay.

- Though having a clear narrative structure has been put forward by the few scholars who tried to theorize this approach – see Harper's (1988) 'visual narrative theory' mode, or Grady's (1991) idea of a documentary film essay – as a typical trait of 'visual essay' type of work in sociology, to me this does not necessarily seem to be constitutive of a visual essay. There is no reason why a visual sociological essay may not also adopt a more experimental, associative, interactive or performative stance or structure (Nichols, 1994). Next to opting for a powerful narrative structure (which often greatly enhances the essay's comprehension) more disconcerting and chaotic approaches that generate experiences and insights should also be envisioned.

- David MacDougall very aptly characterized anthropological film as a mode of research that 'collapses the distance between enquiry and publication. The visual recording – that is, the research data – becomes the fabric of the finished work' (2011: 101). In a similar way the visual essay – and other self-contained visual end products of research – tends to coalesce and partly fixate 'data' and 'vision' at the moment images are produced. These at times stubborn visual materials are not so easily manipulated as words or numbers when constructing the end product. Images do not allow 'rewriting' or editing in the same manner as words do. Though images can be manipulated in post-production and reordered through montage, they still provide the basic input with which to work. Images are by nature very particularistic in what they depict, and the first inclination of many viewers is to decode them on that level only. The challenge of the visual essay, therefore, is to exploit but at the same time try to surpass the purely mimetic qualities of the visual and to give rise to a level of insight that manages to exceed the immediate and particularistic towards a more generalizable type of experience and knowledge.

- As a scholarly product, the default expectation when interpreting a visual essay is that it takes what Plantinga (1997: 17) – based on Wolterstorff's theory of 'Projected Worlds' (1980) – calls an 'assertive stance.' This position implies that the represented 'state of affairs' is asserted to occur in the actual world as portrayed or more precisely to an author's perception of a state of affairs in the actual world (unless explicitly stated as referring to future possibilities, suggested alternatives and unrealized potential). This expectation – which the visual essay also shares with other nonfiction products (like documentary film, news photography) – makes the efforts of others (e.g., other researchers) to investigate the extent to which the proclaimed state of affairs stands – and thus possible attempts to corroborate, challenge or question such a particular scholarly presentation of fact – meaningful (a quest which is clearly specious in the case of the fictional stance, where things may be stated about imaginary worlds as if they were real).

- Finally, the visual essay yields some particular and exigent expectations with respect to a proficient integration of distinct competencies relating to very diverse domains. Whereas some forms of visual research can suffice with a limited knowledge and skill with respect to producing visual records with the required level of detail in a standardized way, the more visual and multimodal expressive modes such as the visual essay format (and the same can be said about the social science film) require a far higher level of visual competency. Such visual expertise involves many aspects (technological, analytical, creative, semantic …) and a multifaceted aptitude to constructively integrate these visual elements with other expressive systems (e.g., sound, music, written or spoken texts) and with the norms and expectations of the discipline. The complexity thus resides both in the production of the visual materials and in the combination of these with other signifiers to generate a scientifically informed whole. Several professionals can be involved in the creation of a visual or multimodal essay but it can also be the work of just one author who has ideally managed to develop and integrate multiple types of expertise. A successive or unrelated production of the different elements of the essay by different specialists – each enforcing their norms and insights – usually does not work very well, as the interplay between the elements – which should be one of the particular strengths of the visual essay – is likely to be jeopardized. While the visual essay is often characterized by a certain degree of (sought) ambiguity and indeterminacy, thoughtless combination of elements that each in their own way (according to their systems of norms, traditions, professional expectations) try to achieve something, but neglecting to focus on how they work together, is likely to fail to transmit a certain intended message, for which its producer should or could be held accountable. This does not imply that the visual essay needs or even can ever tell one story or generate one type of insight, or experience. The most powerful visual essays are often produced by authors or artists (or teams) who manage to integrate the different elements of the whole based on internalized (or shared) proficiencies in different fields of expertise.

These particular traits of the visual social scientific essay suggest that the lines between the visual essay as a social science format and similar practices in non-academic spheres (news media, art, . . .) will remain vague and shifting. In terms of products and representations, the borders between these distinct 'communities of practice' in particular instances be completely blurred and insignificant. Some social documentary work (e.g., Robert Frank's influential *The Americans*, 1959) may indeed impart insight into society in an unmatched manner and some documentary photographers (e.g., Marrie Bot whose work I discussed in an earlier publication (Pauwels, 1993) and will go on to discuss further in the following section) have gone even further by adopting a line of attack – involving crucial aspects such as 'prior ethnography,' extensive rapport building, high ethical standards and a unique combination of expressive skills (photography, writing, layout) that could in all respects serve as a benchmark for social scientists who want to venture into a more multi-modal domain of scholarly expression. Yet it is important not to forget the norms of these 'discursive communities' (journalists, artists, scientists, . . .) to which these distinct practices belong or seek to appeal. Some visual essay applications in social science may closely resemble journalistic, documentary or art practices; it would be unwise, however, to ignore or try to completely blur their somewhat different outlooks, expectations and objectives. It is equally important not to attach an implicit or explicit value judgment or hierarchy to each of those domains (e.g., works of art can produce unique insights in contemporary culture or future/possible versions of it). What is important is that the audiences of those different end products should know what they are looking at, what types of questions can be posed to them and which criteria can be employed to judge their particular contribution.

4   The visual essay in practice: examples and illustrations

Concrete examples and applications of the visual essay may both illustrate the dynamic and hybrid character of the visual essay as a scholarly practice and feed its further conceptualization. It is mainly by carefully looking at its many manifestations that one can start to grasp what exactly it involves as a scholarly conduit and what particular pitfalls and promises it may hold.

However, space limits, copyright issues and medium-specific incompatibilities both limit the choice of visual essays here discussed and the way in which they are represented. So unless URLs to visual essays are provided that reside in full and without access restrictions on the Internet, the examples discussed here will be no more than somewhat 'mutilated' excerpts, representing only snippets of text and a limited number of pictures and often lacking the original layout and context. Yet even these short extracts and some meta-comments may succeed in illustrating some of the characteristics of the visual essay: the irreducible expressive and informational power of images, their ability to almost incessantly generate new questions and views, the synergetic strength of combining images and texts (and sound, when following the hyperlinks) even in their most basic forms.

4.1   Exemplary visual essays in the non-academic sphere

As stated earlier in this chapter, the visual essay is not the exclusive playground of scholars. In fact, some of the most powerful visual essays are produced in a non-academic context, though I should add that those often share traits of solid ethnographic research.

An early example of a limited (e.g., linear, non-interactive) but very effective use of new media is Pedro Meyer's visual essay 'I Photograph to Remember,' consisting of only black-and-white images and an off-screen voice of the narrator on a CD-ROM (Meyer, 1995). In all its simplicity and soberness, this visual essay produces a very impressive account of Meyer's effort to hold on to memories of a cherished past and of the dramatic impact of losing his beloved parents, and transforms insight into grief and grieving as a fact of life. The narration in an exemplary manner complements the images and leaves it to the latter to express what they are uniquely capable of.

Initially distributed as a CD-ROM, this visual essay later migrated to the web, and today can even be downloaded to an MP3 or MP4 player. Meyer was a pioneer of using new media to tell his compelling visual/ verbal stories and yet he did not step into the trap of overusing or ill-using all the features and gimmicks that new technologies were so generously offering. In essence his fairly classic narrative type of photojournalistic storytelling was in terms of expressive means already possible with a slide projector and tape recorder, but he chose the web for its 'accessibility' in a variety of meanings, free of charge and in reach of anybody with an Internet connection (see www.pedromeyer.com/galleries/i-photograph/ index.html for the 35-minute essay). Apart from being a stellar example of a visual essay, this work also clearly demonstrates that very personal types of journalism can bring about themes and insights of a much broader consequence (Figure 7.1).

In terms of non-academic work with a strong scholarly inclination and an unmatched integration of different expressive systems (photography, texts, layout and design) the whole oeuvre of the Dutch photographer Marrie Bot (www.marriebot.com) comes to mind. Bot produced many compelling book-length visual essays about socially relevant subject matter with an important visual dimension to it: penance (*Miserere*; Bot, 1984, 1985), death rituals in ethnic communities in Rotterdam (*A Last Farewell*; Bot, 1998), love and sexuality at older age (*Timeless Love*; Bot,

Figure 7.1 Home page of Pedro Meyer's 'I Photograph to Remember'

2004). My personal favorite is still Bot's study *The Burden of Existence: Photographs and Stories about the Mentally Handicapped* (original title in Dutch: *Bezwaard Bestaan, foto's en verhalen over verstandelijk gehandicapten*; Bot, 1988). This book successfully counters the persistent monolithic views on the mentally retarded and the kind of care they need. It calls for a more differentiated understanding of mentally burdened people and advances a well-balanced argument for a more qualified integration of this differentiated group of people.

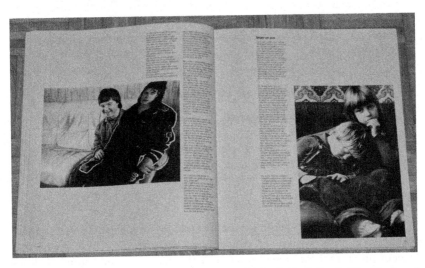

Figure 7.2 One of the inner pages of Marrie Bot's book *The Burden of Existence* (Bot, 1988)

This study truly excels in terms of its theoretical grounding and broad contextualization (based on intensive study of the relevant literature) as well as with respect to the complementary use of verbal and visual means. As exemplary for competent visual ethnographic work are, further, her careful and patient 'rapport building' (the study took eleven years to complete!) with the field (institutional management and personnel, parents and family members, and those with mild intellectual disabilities), and the numerous demonstrations of a reflexive and ethical attitude. Bot's study clearly gives evidence (often visible in the pictures) of a high degree of respect and trust between the photographer/interviewer and the subjects/ respondents. The author went well beyond obtaining prior consent for her photography to ensure that all texts and pictures were discussed with all parties concerned during the whole process. Moreover, very strict arrangements were made regarding future uses of the verbal and visual data.

The photographic language of the author is sober and informative, and not subservient to any formalist canon. The pictures offer a palpable context for the verbal information and testimonials and they also provide specific information about the complex reality of mentally impeded individuals (joy, sorrow, relationships with parents and support personnel, their areas of interest and their aspirations, the arrangement of their physical environment) that cannot be expressed in words (Figure 7.2).

The 'pay-off' or unique contribution of this visual essay is that it offers the audience a broadly contextualized type of (virtual) 'field experience,' which cannot be acquired by disjointedly reading about the subject, or simply looking at a series of pictures and not even spending a limited time in the field.

4.2   Visual essays in a social science context

Turning to visual essay projects that have originated in a scholarly context, I will now briefly discuss the work of a student of mine and a sociology professor turned documentary photographer, then present and provide some meta-comments on a visual essay of my own.

4.2.1   Outgrown rooms

My own practice of teaching visual sociology – which involves graduate students from a variety of disciplinary backgrounds developing and executing a modest, small-scale visual project – very much echoes Grady's idea that the visual essay can revitalize sociology (Grady, 1991: 32), particularly in the classroom setting, but also beyond. Though most of my students opt for more systematic approaches for visual research (playing out the basic mimetic strengths of the camera image), some venture further along the visual expressive path.

One notable example is a visual essay by Nannie Bronshoff entitled 'Outgrown Rooms' (original title in Dutch: 'Ontgroeide Kamers'). It should immediately be conceded that this student already had a professional schooling in photography prior to enrolling for the Master's program in Film Studies and Visual Culture, as the visual essay format usually requires a more advanced form of visual competency.

Nannie Bronshoff's project was inspired by reading the PhD dissertation of sociologist Ineke Lam, about couples' relationships after the children have left home (original title in Dutch: De mythe van het 'lege nest,' Lam, 1994). The thesis contends that parenthood has changed from being an all-consuming and life-long commitment to a distinct period or just one aspect of life. Most parents whose children have left their home no longer suffer from what psychiatrists and sociologists have called 'the empty nest syndrome' (only 5 percent of the parents in Lam's research sample perceived their children moving out of the house as a negative experience). Parents now often have interesting jobs, a large circle of friends, and many plans to move on with their lives. This, of course, does not imply that parents are no longer there for their children when needed, nor that their life-long love for them has diminished in any way. Yet one might observe a form of detachment from the formerly dominant and lasting parent role.

These ideas led Bronshoff to her quest to explore what happened to the children's rooms once they have left home. Are they kept as they were – as a sort of shrine – or are they quickly re-appropriated by other family members and redesigned to serve other functions? What is kept intact and what is changed? How do the children visiting their parents from time to time react to this? (Often they feel that the space is still theirs to some extent.) And how do the parents react to these reactions? Bronshoff's process of depicting the rooms with their former inhabitants spontaneously generated a sort of 'visual interview' process whereby the (changes in the) room began to trigger factual information, memories and projective comments of both parties present (children and parents).

At present this is still a small-scale project, but its basic idea has great potential to trigger a complex problematic that centers around the question of whether and or to what extent the physical removal of the child's belongings and the redesign of the space previously occupied reflects a state of mind of the parents and also influences their relations towards their children. Obviously one should refrain from drawing conclusions too easily: filling the empty space that children have left in a literal sense can have different and even opposing meanings: moving on with one's own life or trying cope with the void that the child's moving out has created.

The project in its present state is not really capable of answering such complex questions, but one of its strengths is certainly that it is capable of generating questions such as these, by re-viewing the pictures and text combinations. This 'inspirational,' hard-to-pin-down quality is exactly what the visual essay format may entail.

Bronshoff's project merits further development into a full-blown research project (and an excellent photo book given the high quality of the pictures), possibly including a detailed analysis of the verbal interactions between parents and children, as well as a meticulous analysis of the type of changes which were introduced after the rooms had been vacated.

Outgrown Rooms / Nannie Bronshoff (2011)

Figure 7.3 Eva's room (N. Bronshoff)

EVA (DAUGHTER, 25): About one day after I had left home, the room was refurbished.

JANNY (MOTHER, 55): Yes, but that is because you took all your stuff, your bed, your desk. It was an empty room.

EVA: I felt bad about it, especially because it happened so fast. The fact that they immediately made something different of it, instead of keeping it for a while as a sort of back-up room. I didn't like it at all; it felt quite awkward.' *(my translation, LP)*

Figure 7.4 Zwier's room (N. Bronshoff)

> JETSKE (MOTHER, 64): Is this room still a bit Zwier's room? Yes,
> I think that some things still feel like when you were here.
> That desk and the fixed layout of the room. The bed up there
> at the top of the ceiling. All my friends love to stay here in
> Zwier's, what's it called ... erm, "sky box."
> ZWIER (SON, 24) AND JETSKE: Zwier's sky box.
> ZWIER: Yeah, I had my walls painted in bright yellow. You didn't
> like that so much. I don't care that she repainted them. But
> because of that it does feel less like my room now.
> JETSKE: Yes and the reason why it is not Zwier's room anymore,
> is that it is very tidy now.
> ZWIER: Hahahahaha. *(my translation, LP)*

4.2.2   Elderly and end-of-life care

An interesting offset to social documentary photographers gradually cultivating a social science perspective (see Marrie Bot) is New York–born sociology professor Cathy Greenblat, who in 2002 chose to retire early from Rutgers University to fully engage in socially inspired photographic projects. Though becoming a full-time photographic artist is a radical career shift, her work on elderly care or end-of-life care remains definitely informed by her scholarly past. This trained sociologist swiftly developed her undeniable photographic talent and this resulted in books and exhibitions that are exemplary of the visual sociological essay approach. Greenblat believes her work of combining photographs and text 'to be the most effective vehicle to open people's eyes, literally and figuratively, providing a better way to help them "face" issues that are generally avoided' (www.cathygreenblat.com).

In her work on dementia (an exhibition and second book on dementia: *Love, Loss and Laughter: Seeing Alzheimer's Differently*, 2012), Greenblat challenges the stereotype that people with Alzheimer's disease have become 'empty shells,' completely lost in their own world.

The photos show what quality health care looks like, and illustrate that such care allows people with Alzheimer's disease to sustain connections to others and to their own past lives at a far higher level than is generally believed to be possible. The photographs reveal that they are capable of experiencing joy as well as sorrow, that loving care can yield loving responses and laughter. (Artist's statement, www.cathygreenblat.com)

Another important long-term photographic project of Cathy Greenblat focuses on end-of-life care. In *Alive at the End of Life*, she intends to provide 'insight into the ways the experience of dying can be enriched, both emotionally and intellectually, for the person who is dying and for those attached to him or her' (www.cathygreenblat.com).

Greenblat sees photography as a powerful tool to fight stereotyping and to show what high-quality care can involve. Her pictures confront us with some of the harshest facts of life, but in a very nuanced, sensitive and

Alive with Alzheimer's / Cathy Greenblat (2004)

The dependent elderly in the USA, especially those who suffer from dementia, are not well provided for through public resources. Many citizens lack basic health insurance and even more lack long-term care insurance. As a result most care for people with Alzheimer's falls to family members, whose financial and emotional capacities are often stretched to the limit. In institutions, people with dementia are often over-medicated to assist the staff, and little is done to maintain the parts of their brains that are still alive. The care at Silverado Senior Living in Escondido, California, a private residential facility for people with Alzheimer's offers a sharp contrast, not only to the usual institutional scene, but to what home caregivers can provide. It is an impressive example of what is possible. These photographs (Figures 7.5 to 7.7) show that people who suffer from the disease can be very much more ALIVE than is generally believed and that we can do much better than we usually do in terms of high quality Alzheimer's care. (Artist's introduction, www.cathygreenblat.com)

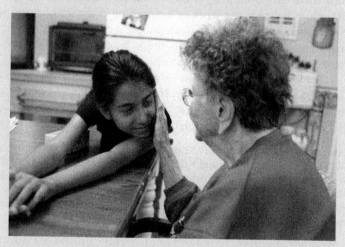

Figure 7.5 Caressing Melissa's cheek (C. Greenblat)

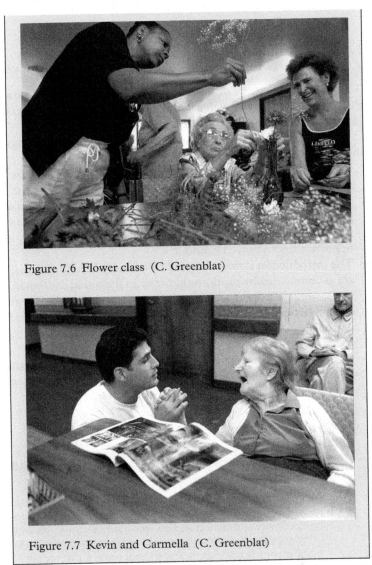

Figure 7.6 Flower class (C. Greenblat)

Figure 7.7 Kevin and Carmella (C. Greenblat)

warm way. Looking at these photographs, a whole array of responses are triggered almost simultaneously: feelings of sadness and maybe fear for our own future or that of our loved ones, next to more optimistic and even activist attitudes, when realizing how loving care and changing attitudes can indeed make a huge difference.

4.2.3   Urban culture exposed

The final example to be discussed is my own attempt to disclose aspects of the city and city life through a combination of texts and unstaged aspects of urban material culture and human behavior.

The words and the black-and-white images of this visual essay interact in three ways:

- First an introductory essay describes and evokes the city as a hybrid semiotic place. Though this text can stand on its own, it contains multiple hints to visual aspects of experiencing the city and as such it helps to read the photographs in a certain way. Similarly the photographs provide a concrete context to the introductory text, as well as opportunities to move beyond it.
- The introduction is then followed by a series of pictures, some of which are accompanied by captions that refer to the visual content in different ways, ranging from more descriptive/contextualizing captions to more evocative ones. The necessity or desirability of using such captions is debatable (with regard to this visual essay they yielded divergent reactions: from them being 'too explicit' to 'illuminating').
- Finally the word-image interplay is also present in the pictures themselves in the form of words from advertisements, traffic signs, graffiti).

**Street discourse: a visual essay on urban signification /
Luc Pauwels**

Cities constitute a constant 'work in progress' of different actors with competing agendas. Cities are the dynamic result of prior necessities and choices and present-day re-articulations and revisions of those. They invariably testify of past dreams and options taken which amalgamate with present projects that reconstitute and reclaim a territory partially occupied by former social, cultural economic, political and religious forces. Some artifacts of the past are simply torn down and replaced but many remain and are re-imbued or re-infused with new meanings, or at the least reframed as a materialized memory of past events and ways of living. In this way the present inscribes itself on the past, layer after layer, and in an asynchronous fashion. In this respects the city can be thought of as a palimpsest which is constantly being rewritten, repainted and re-populated by hurried crowds with a purpose.

The day-to-day metabolism of the city may be observed through its artifacts, which are as much materializations of norms and values and functions as areobjects that are constantly being uploaded with new meanings, or redefined or re-appropriated to fulfill new functions. But the social fabric also becomes apparent through routine behavior, incidents, major events, and the various signs and symptoms of how the city is 'used.'

The city can be looked upon as a huge, out-of-control syntagm, a combination of numerous paradigmatic choices made by many semi-independent actors, with different, often conflicting interests. Some signs have lost their meaning but remain to send their obsolete message (to buy a no longer existing product from a manufacturer no longer in business). These remnants of the past together with the uncontrolled combination of numerous signs that are competing for attention create a visual data overload and 'noise' that may prove highly confusing, while at the same time they may become a source of entertainment for the attentive observer.

Cities are genuine hubs of cultural expression and unusually rich exponents of visual culture. The ongoing process of urbanization goes hand in hand with a growing diversity of functions and people. Urban (visual) cultures emerge from human imagination, ambitions and desires, ample intentional and unintentional choices, and concerted and rival actions. Buildings, streets, squares, parks, monuments, shopping malls and other urban artifacts – the new, the long-established or those that barely survive – eloquently testify to past and present ways of thinking and doing, and together with the multi-formed activities of its inhabitants and visitors constitute the complex human and material fabric of the city.

Cities serve numerous practical, functional, symbolic, ritual and ideological ends, many of which have an undeniable visual dimension. Therefore the city can be literally looked at from different angles that often refer to different orders of signification: the use of space, the types, means and degree of control, mobility, fashion, cultural diversity, entertainment, tourism, commerce, personal, interpersonal and group behavior, the public and the private sphere. Much of this materializes in numerous artifacts and behaviors. Cities are both emanations and reproducers of power and control. They are sites of planning, control and conformism. Yet at the same time the urban context is a token and a breeding ground for resistance, for loss of control, for renewal, for deliverance. These multiple intermeshing discourses – the historic, the political, the social, the multicultural, the commercial, the religious, etc. – provide the city with its unpredictable, multi-layered, never fully graspable character. Therefore cities constitute at once a battlefield for conflicting interests, a playground of ideas and a theatre for our senses, orchestrated by different agents with different temporal referents and audiences in mind.

Sociology and photography represent distinct 'ways of looking' at society. But they are both about 'making the familiar strange,' about questioning the seemingly obvious and 'reframing' it (as social facts or processes or visual statements). Theories tend to work like looking glasses or lenses with their typical distortions and aberrations, and theory-driven observations and recordings may ultimately embody a true merger of the photographic with the sociological. The present visual essay (Figure 7.8 to 7.16) seeks to present metonyms and metaphors for those human interactions that have left their marks deliberately or inadvertently in the urban context (for the full visual essay, see Pauwels, 2009).

Figure 7.8 **The Right Way** / Minneapolis, USA (L. Pauwels)
Religious and traffic control discourses both aimed at showing citizens the 'right way.' The divergent origins of messages and the unpredictable blend of signifiers of all kinds create unanticipated 'third effects' and turn the modern urban area into a surreal spectacle par excellence.

Figure 7.9 Cracked Window / Antwerp, Belgium (L. Pauwels)
Rage against the consumer society and its ideal of youth and affluence? Or simply a token of vandalism? The old couple with the wheelchair reflected to the right as a reference to the real world are in fierce contrast with the dominant ideals of youth and beauty.

Figure 7.10 Framing Race and Class / Southampton, UK (L. Pauwels)
A compartmentalized look through a parked bus can be read as a metaphor of class and urban culture. Oppositions like rich versus poor, white versus black abound. The frames act as separators, prison bars (for the black figure). The white person – through the proximity of the advertisement for luxury apartments – is visually played out against the black man who literally has nothing (except for his Nike shoes . . .).

Figure 7.11 Upward Mobility / New Orleans, USA (L. Pauwels)

Figure 7.12 Urban Panopticon / Los Angeles, USA (L. Pauwels)

Figure 7.13 Hitchcock Meets McDonald's / Los Angeles, USA (L. Pauwels)

Figure 7.14 Uptown-Downtown / San Francisco, USA (L. Pauwels)

Figure 7.15 Heart of the Matter / San Francisco, USA (L. Pauwels)

Figure 7.16 Silent Metropolis / New Orleans, USA (L. Pauwels)

The carefully framed instances work both to contextualize and re-contextualize: bringing aspects together (both instantaneous/fleeting ones and more permanent markers) that would easily go unnoticed, and by cutting out context, and by choosing a particular physical position and a whole array of technical choices to express a particular view.

5   Concluding remarks and outlook

It is in the nature of the 'essay' (derived from the French word 'essayer,' which means 'to try'), to attempt to present things, ideas and events in a more challenging and less orthodox way, thus making it more prone to critique and rebuff. This chapter in itself has taken that form to develop and explicate a cluster of ideas, some of which may be rather subjective or idiosyncratic. Above all it is an effort – in words and images – to make a case for further developing this promising avenue of scholarly enquiry and communication.

Far from being a simple and unchallenged or widely acknowledged scientific practice, the 'visual essay' can be one of the more visual – or even multimodal – and sophisticated forms of visual anthropology/sociology. In exemplars of this form, different constitutive and expressive modes of representation (text and image, above all) are neither excised from the end product, nor reduced to merely illustrative or ornamental function. The major strength of this scholarly form resides in the synergy of the distinct forms of expression that are combined – images, words, layout and design – and that add up to a scientifically informed statement. The visual essay will no doubt develop into an even more hybrid category, thus moving far beyond the original photo essay format, though the latter still has not lost any of its power. As an expressive format, the visual essay is a constant 'work in progress,' a moving target. New media development create new opportunities for the visual essay, but only to the extent that new features are carefully evaluated, selected and combined so that they make a positive contribution to the whole.

Trying to articulate or conceptualize the visual essay as a scholarly form remains a tricky venture, as every effort to elucidate its specific contribution to the understanding of society collapses variation along one or more dimensions, all of which are integral to the essay's effectiveness. However, the dynamic and hybrid nature of a phenomenon does not free us from the need to be as explicit as possible in proposing it as a subject of further constructive debate. An open – bold but critical and self-critical (!) – stance is required to further develop this form in actual practice. Another key factor in discovering its unrealized potential and in identifying its actual strength is a critical review of and subsequent theorizing about these attempts – within and beyond the academic sphere.

The visual essay occupies a particular place in research practice, balancing between art and science, information and expression (viewpoint). Its particular strengths – its broad expressive range; its 'open-ended,' poly-semic, multi-vocal character; its hybrid multimedia or multimodal and cross-platform appearance; its largely uncodified nature – are simultaneously its greatest challenges and a potential source of controversy. Though some mainstream scientists may reject these disconcerting traits as subversions of their trade, this openendedness and multi-interpretable character is not unique to the visual essay. Data do not make sense by themselves. As Grady (1991: 29) rightfully emphasizes, most sociological data, including hard numbers, are prone to 'radical reinterpretation.'

In exploring how the visual essay could acquire a legitimate place in scholarly discourse, without having to renounce its avant-garde character, it could prove useful to grant this type of scholarly representation, at least for a while – a distinct, readily identifiable place in scholarly publications and other outlets (e.g., conferences). This could help minimize unproductive discussion about the 'equivalence' of the visual essay to the canonical scholarly (empirical or theoretical) article or presentation. Most journals that invite visual essay submissions already apply clear indexing of the types of contributions: original articles, review essays, book and multimedia reviews, and visual essays. Integration within established scholarly channels is important to ensuring that scholars with different backgrounds and preferences are acquainted with this novel way of generating and disseminating knowledge and experience. Both scholars and the visual essay would benefit from facilitating that acquaintance.

6   References

Almasy, P. (1990) *Le photojournalisme: informer en écrivant avec des images.* Paris: Centre de Formation et de Perfectionnement des Journalistes.

Barthes, R. (1999) 'Rhetoric of the Image.' In: J. Evans and S. Hall (eds.) *Visual Culture: The Reader*, London: Sage, pp. 33–40.

Bot, M. (1984) *Miserere, de grote boetebedevaarten in Europa*, Dutch edition. Rotterdam: M. Bot.

Bot, M. (1985) *Miserere: The Great Pilgrimages of Penance in Europe*, English edition (also in French and German). Rotterdam: M. Bot.

Bot, M. (1988) *Bezwaard Bestaan, foto's en verhalen over verstandelijk gehandicapten* [The Burden of Existence: Photos and Stories about the Mentally Handicapped]. Rotterdam: M. Bot.

Bot, M. (1998) *Een Laatste Groet, uitvaart- en rouwrituelen in multicultureel Nederland* [A Last Farewell, Death Rituals in the Multicultural Netherlands]. Rotterdam: M. Bot.

Bot, M. (2004) *Geliefden / Timeless Love.* Rotterdam: M. Bot.

Frank, R. (1959) *The Americans.* New York: Grove Press.

Grady, J. (1991) 'The Visual Essay and Sociology.' *Visual Sociology* 6(2): 23–38.

Grady, J. (2006) 'Edward Tufte and the Promise of a Visual Social Science.' In: L. Pauwels (ed.) *Visual Cultures of Science.* Hanover, NH: University Press of New England, pp. 222–65.

Greenblat, C. (2004) *Alive with Alzheimer's.* University of Chicago Press.

Greenblat, C. (2012) *Love, Loss, and Laughter: Seeing Alzheimer's Differently,* Lyons Press.

Harper, D. (1988) 'Visual Sociology: Expanding Sociological Vision.' *The American Sociologist* 19(1): 54–70.

Henny, Leonard (1986) 'A Short History of Visual Sociology.' *Current Sociology* 34(3): 1–4.

Lam, I. (1994) *De mythe van het 'lege nest': over echtpaarrelaties als de kinderen het huis uit zijn.* Utrecht: ISOR.

MacDougall, D. (2011) 'Anthropological Filmmaking: An Empirical Art.' In: E. Margolis and L. Pauwels (eds.) *SAGE Handbook of Visual Research Methods,* London/New Delhi: Sage.

Meyer, P. (1995) *I Photograph to Remember.* Interactive CD-ROM for PC Windows (Voyager CityRom).

Monaco, J. (2000) *How to Read a Film. The World of Movies, Media, and Multimedia: Language, History, Theory,* 3rd edn. Oxford University Press.

Nichols, B. (1994) *Blurred Boundaries: Questions of Meaning in Contemporary Culture,* Bloomington: Indiana University Press.

Pauwels, L. (1993) 'The Visual Essay: Affinities and Divergences between the Social Scientific and the Social Documentary Modes.' *Visual Anthropology* 6(2): 199–210.

Pauwels, L. (2002) 'The Video- and Multimedia-Article as a Mode of Scholarly Communication: Toward Scientifically Informed Expression and Aesthetics.' *Visual Studies* 17(2): 150–9.

Pauwels, L. (2005) 'Culture, Community and Disease Control: Photo Essay.' *International Journal of Epidemiology* 34(3): 534–6.

Pauwels, L. (2006) 'A Theoretical Framework for Assessing Visual Representational Practices in Knowledge Building and Science Communications.' In: L. Pauwels (ed.) *Visual Cultures of Science: Rethinking Representational Practices in Knowledge Building and Science Communication,* Lebanon, NH: Dartmouth College Press.

Pauwels, L. (2009) 'Street Discourse: A Visual Essay on Urban Signification'. *Culture Unbound: Journal of Current Cultural Research* 1: 263–72. Available from: www.cultureunbound.ep.liu.se [accessed April 22, 2015].

Pauwels, L. (2010) 'Visual Sociology Reframed: An Analytical Synthesis and Discussion of Visual Methods in Social and Cultural Research.' *Sociological Methods & Research* 38(4): 545–81.

Pauwels, L. (2011) 'Researching Websites as Social and Cultural Expressions: Methodological Predicaments and a Multimodal Model for Analysis.' In: E. Margolis and L. Pauwels (eds.) *SAGE Handbook of Visual Research Methods*, London/New Delhi: Sage.

Plantinga, C. (1997) *Rhetoric and Representation in Nonfiction Film*. Cambridge University Press.

Rose, G. (2011) *Visual Methodologies: An Introduction to Researching with Visual Materials*, 3rd edn., London/Thousand Oaks, CA/New Delhi: Sage.

Wagner, J. (ed.) (1979) *Images of Information: Still Photography in the Social Sciences*. Beverly Hills, CA/London: Sage.

Willett, J. (1997) *Heartfield versus Hitler*. Paris: Éditions Hazan.

8 Social scientific filmmaking and multimedia production: key features and debates

1 The multifaceted nature of social scientific filmmaking

The initial appeal of the camera to anthropological and ethnographic research was that it made traditional fieldwork lighter and more interesting for researchers, who previously had to try to capture the complexity of the cultures under study using pencil and paper. Whatever escaped their attention or was hard to put into words was therefore inevitably lost to the research (Mead, 1963, 1975). As a consequence of technological innovations, shooting pictures in the field soon became less cumbersome. Fewer technical obstacles meant that researchers could engage more actively and more variedly in a dialogue with their field of research, and to an extent this is what happened. Yet technological progress alone could never have brought about social and scientific innovation. After all, the integration of this important visual approach into scientific practice implies the development of a theoretical framework and an adapted methodology, issues that only took shape very slowly and indeed continue to be debated today. The emphasis that anthropologists have put on the documentation of often disappearing societies has, quite often, been at the expense of the striving to theoretically underpin the visual productions and to put these new means of research at the service of new insights. The implicit schemes that were adopted were often indicative of a naïve-realistic and ethnocentric outlook on the multicultural meeting that anthropological fieldwork essentially is.

Besides providing a description or (an inevitably imperfect) reflection of certain aspects of the reality studied, social scientific filmmaking represents a specific form of scientific communication that is directed towards specialized practitioners of the trade, aspiring social and cultural scientists or, as the case may be, a broader public (although in the latter case it may concern very diverse kinds of film). The usefulness of film for data collection – both in observation and in experimentation – is now beyond question, but the possibilities it offers in terms of the integration of images into a scientific discourse and the precise rules that should be followed in this respect are still very much up for debate.

Several authors have tried to distinguish between films that are little more than raw footage and films as stand-alone expressive scientific constructions. According to some, a social scientific film can only consist of 'pure data' that has been collected under meticulously controlled circumstances, while others argue that such products cannot possibly be scientific because, being primary sets of data or pure descriptions, they cannot offer a 'processed' and scientifically sound perspective of the phenomenon under study. Some visual researchers have tried to label this polarity (i.e., between emphasizing 'mimesis' or scientifically motivated 'expression'). Lajoux (1975), for example, refers to a dichotomy between 'scientific film' on the one hand and 'expressive film' on the other. De Heusch (1988) calls the pure-data form 'research film' as opposed to the more processed 'sociological film.' Leroi-Gourhan makes a distinction between 'filmic notes' and 'documentary' (quoted in Chiozzo, 1989: 11), and Collier (1967) uses the term 'cultural documentation' for the more mimetic variant, which he distinguishes from respectively the 'anthropological film' and 'cultural drama for a broader public.' Wolf (1967) feels that one should differentiate between 'research film' ('Forschungsfilm') and 'documentation film' ('Dokumentationsfilm'), arguing that these two genres are fundamentally divergent in terms of their truth claims, scientific significance and use of specific filmic means of expression. Prost introduced a similar division between 'representational film' and 'illustrative film,' in which the former term refers to cinematographic material that can be used as a scientific data source, while the latter can merely fulfill an illustrative purpose, much like documentaries and educational films do. However, Prost does concede that it is much harder to make this distinction in practice and that, at best, there is a gradual difference in the manner in which an effort is made to guard the scientific integrity of whatever is depicted. Moreover, a piece of film (sequence) may be 'representative' for one research purpose and merely 'illustrative' for another (Prost, 1975: 325–7).

If the divergent *purposes* of film in a scientific or educational context are taken into account, as well as their different target *audiences*, it soon transpires that this crude dichotomy (mimesis-expression, or raw data versus elaborated view) only reflects part of the existing diversity.

Decades ago Crawford (1992) attempted to grasp the hybrid nature of film as used or produced in an ethnographic context. His typology still provides useful elements for further debate on the distinctive characteristics of social scientific film and its many subgenres:

1) Ethnographic *footage* is unedited film material, which may be used in its unedited form for research purposes or eventually be edited into a film.

2) *Research* films are edited films made specifically for research purposes and hence not intended for public screening or an audience other than a highly specialized academic audience.

3) The ethnographic *documentary* is a film which has a specific relevance to anthropology but which is in one way or another part of documentary filmmaking in general. . . .

4) The ethnographic *television* documentary is a film made for, and very often by, a television company, with the intention of reaching a wide non-specialized audience. . . .

5) *Education* and *information* films are made for educational purposes and meant for classroom audiences or the general audiences. . . .

6) Other *non-fiction* films include journalistic reports, newsreels, travelogues and so on. . . .

7) *Fiction* films and drama documentaries may be labeled ethnographic because of their subject matter. . . .

(Crawford, 1992: 74)

This attempt exemplifies that there is still need for a more qualified approach and specification with regard to the notion of film (or any other time-based visual creation) as a component or an end product of scientific endeavor in either the broad or the narrow sense. The implicit or explicit claims made in such films and their scientific usefulness cannot be separated from specific goals and target groups, and indeed a mode of production that is adapted to this purpose. Ultimately, one needs to address the delicate question what 'scholarship' is or should be, and to ascertain what may be regarded as legitimate scientific objectives and how they are best attained.

2   Filmic codes and controversies: expressiveness up for debate

The structure of a social scientific film may tie in closely with the inherent structure of the events recorded or it may provide a very manifest and scientifically founded and processed perspective on these events, using filmic means to construct an argument. According to Wright (1992: 276) controversies over this issue are also related to the fact that there are diverging opinions on the so-called 'natural state' of the medium – subjective constructed meaning versus an objective 'transparent' recording.

The strongly dramatized exoticism of a number of early films that were labeled as ethnographic, even though they were not necessarily made by ethnographically schooled filmmakers, soon made way for a striving towards a more 'scientifically sound' camera use. This resulted in a very sober, minimalist style of shooting, aimed at collecting data as accurately as possible in their broader context.

Many researchers in this somewhat naïve realist tradition used to have (and indeed still have) almost blind faith in the automatic objectivity of the camera, in which they saw the long-hoped-for elimination of subjectivity and selectivity of field notes.

Especially, the creative or constructive editing of images into a film was considered to be incompatible with scientific praxis – or at least it was felt that it should be kept to a minimum – because it entailed a moment of subjective selectivity that would destroy the 'truth value' of the image. This is a somewhat short-sighted view that was nevertheless shared by influential theoreticians of the fictional genre (e.g., Bazin, 1975). Young asserts about this stalwart view that 'it was looking at only a very small part of the problem that led to anthropologists in the early days to ask filmmakers to preserve all the footage exposed and not "edit" it into a "film"' (1975: 66). The choice of what is filmed, at what moment in time and in which manner is an equally selective process; it is already a form of 'editing' (selection and rearrangement) of reality. The decision not to edit recorded material merely has an influence on the preservation of the integrity of the recorded film – the original chronology and context – but in itself it offers insufficient guarantees that the visual document is complete and objective (which is an unattainable goal anyway). Nevertheless, it remains useful to save all recordings in their original sequence, even after the material has been edited into a film. In the course of time, or after repeated viewing, certain details can lead to new insights or questions that necessitate a close review of the original material.

Editing is still a crucial and controversial aspect of scientific filmmaking, probably because this aspect, more than anything else, highlights the constructed nature of film. It is indisputable that editing according to non-scientific standards can seriously compromise the research value of the recorded material (e.g., the application of cinematographic principles for purely aesthetic or dramatic purposes: rapid succession of shots, alternating frame size in order to create variation or artificial tension and dynamism). On the other hand, a careful selection and ordering of shots according to the principles of scientific research and in accordance with the purpose of the research (accurate description or communication of insights) need not result in a less scientifically sound product. Similar 'interventions' (selection of moments and ordering of time and space) also occur *during* the recording, at shot level, whereby one needs to respond swiftly to unexpected circumstances, mostly unaware of the precise unfolding of events. The possibility of ordering the recorded material in a considered manner and according to an empirically and theoretically motivated structure largely constitutes the strength of the film as a form of scientific communication.

Besides the ordering of the images, the relation between the visual representation of an event and the synchronically recorded sound is usually of great significance. Synchronic sound – be it vocal or non-vocal – presents an important complementary dimension. Sound film in varying genres will rarely contain soundless moments. In addition to synchronic sound, most film productions also make extensive use of sounds that are recorded later and that tie in with the images (so-called wild sound), off-screen commentary and background music. These kinds of additions should be handled with great care and circumspection from a social scientific perspective. Music, except if it is actually performed during the recording and is thus an integral part of the reality conveyed (i.e., synchronic sound), can indeed easily have a disrupting effect on the process of knowledge transfer. Sound that is added afterwards can set a particular mood and thus impose a certain interpretation upon the viewer, for which there may be no scientific grounds whatsoever. Or it will at least distract some of the viewer's attention, which would otherwise be focused on the actual material. Likewise, the use of commentary, be it 'guiding' or not, remains a hotly debated aspect of audiovisual productions by social scientists. The viewer needs to receive the required information in order to be able to put whatever is shown in its proper context. This, for that matter, need not necessarily happen (entirely) in the film itself, but may also be achieved through a verbal introduction, written information and so on.

The application of motivated punctuation, a scientifically functional rearrangement and selection of raw material need not imply a loss of research value, but may in fact be enriching from a scientific point of view. To claim that the use of filmic means is simply incompatible with scientific goals holds a danger that a number of specific possibilities of the image as a means of knowledge transfer or communication will remain unused. Moreover, this conviction is based on the faulty premise that there is such a thing as unprocessed data. Even in the most sober verbal or numeric representation of facts lies hidden a particular way of seeing things, a perspective or belief – in other words, a theoretical stance. To try to banish this from scientific endeavor is simply an illusion. Wright, too, subscribes to this view when he asserts quite resolutely that 'even in the act of pointing we cannot escape some degree of construction. . . . So, if narrative is unavoidable, this gives an important emphasis to the need to understand the terms in which narrative has been established. It cannot simply be regarded as the unfolding of events before the camera'

(1992: 276). It is therefore clearly unrealistic to demand that the producer of images should merely be an intermediary and must never express a point of view. For that matter, the unconscious conveyance of a view can be much more dangerous than expressing it consciously and explicitly. It is therefore paramount for the scientific filmmaker to make assessments on the basis of scientific insights and to use the appropriate expressive devices without succumbing to the temptation to apply much more attractive means of expression in an uncontrolled and unmotivated way.

It is clear that scientific criteria should always come first, not the striving towards a smooth production according to the standards of the entertainment industry. Rollwagen stresses quite emphatically the role of scientific theory in the film production process. He sharply criticizes filmic approaches that do not put scientific theory central and that rely instead on other frames of reference (e.g., purely cinematographic ones), among other reasons because the filmmakers involved are not or insufficiently trained in the research discipline (1988: 290–293). At the same time, however, opportunities are missed because researchers are unable to integrate rather than just cumulate the two areas of expertise and the different mental frameworks. Integration implies that one is capable of translating scientific views and insights into visual information and, conversely, that one can distil scientific information appropriately from visual manifestations.

On the other hand, lack of fluency and visual aplomb is not synonymous with 'being scientific.' Science, too, stands to benefit from effective communication. The point is, however, that another set of rules needs to be obeyed; rules, for that matter, that are often yet to be formulated and implemented. More concretely, this boils down to a well-considered selection and acceptance of existing, possibly adapted, (visual) codes and the development of specific conventions for a visual scientific discourse. It is clear that the audience of sociological films (and by extension 'scientific films' in general) will need to get used to the audible and visible absence of familiar filmic devices and slowly come to accept other norms and conventions with regard to the application of such devices. Also, the intended target audience (experts, prospective scientists, non-experts) should be made aware of what precisely they are watching, what are the constitutive rules of whatever has been visually represented.

In some circles, an understandable but exaggerated response to the naïve realism of many filmmakers and consumers resulted in the view that visual observation as such is contaminated while the verbalized views of the subjects in the field are considered the source of salvation.

Example 1 The mimetic approach in ethnographic filmmaking

The mimetic tradition in ethno-cinematography is well exemplified by *Tobelo Marriage* (1985), a film made by anthropologist Dirk Nijland from Leiden University (Figure 8.1). It describes a marriage ceremony in the village of Paca (Northern Moluccas, Indonesia) and the somewhat difficult negotiations between the two groups of relatives. The gradual progress in the process of negotiation and exchange is explained: situations and problems are introduced; sometimes they are depicted or summarized in diagrams; the key figures and entourage are clearly identified for the benefit of the viewer; conversations in Tobelo and Indonesian have been subtitled. Still, few of the expectations that Western viewers typically have, both formally and in terms of content, are being met. On the whole, the framing is kept fairly broad to provide as much possible image-internal context. The long shots relate to the rhythm of events as they slowly unfold. The subject, which contains hardly any dramatic moments (e.g., disputes), is dealt with in a detached and didactic manner. Much care is given to the provision of ethnographic context and the establishment of a good 'rapport' with the community studied.

Film is seen here not as a substitute for a written anthropological report, but as an addition of those aspects of cultural activity that are easier to depict with images and harder to put into words, and seen in their meaningful context. Besides the use of the camera to support observations, attention is paid to the possibilities for acquiring additional data through visual feedback to participants and local experts, in order to be able to determine the accuracy of the execution of rituals and their filmic representation as well as the appreciation of the specific actions by participants that are shown (Nijland 1989: 148–151). *Tobelo Marriage* is a very meticulous study in which the mimesis of a cultural activity or artifact is central. Thus it is a typical example of the ethnographic tradition of retaining as much as possible the integrity of the pro-filmic. What appears before the camera is important, not the camera as a mediating agent with its own lingual/expressive possibilities. The filmmaker explicitly aims to make representative and descriptive recordings that follow the 'natural unfolding of events' and that preserve as much as possible their 'source value.' These meticulously recorded sequences of images may to some extent be considered more 'open representations' (Folmer 1992: 4) than, for example, purely textual constructions or exuberantly edited film, but every visual representational act inevitably involves selectivity and rearrangement (both at the level of the recording, and at the level of editing). Moreover, reducing film to a mimetic tool denies its potential to become a vehicle of scholarly insight. *Tobelo Marriage* has been challenged as a clear example of 'naïve realism,' yet it does have its merits, if only because it rightly contests the growing degradation of the visual aspect and methodological rigor in some more recent approaches that appear, moreover, to propagate uncontrolled subjectivity and an emphasis on the verbal ('talking heads').

Figure 8.1 Still from *Tobelo Marriage* (Asinoellah/Rioly)

Consequently, more contemporary, post-modern films often tend to embody less visual approaches. Such films then consist primarily in verbal exchanges with and within the research field, and the verbal accounts of the persons under study are promoted to a new kind of anthropological or sociological truth. Yet the utterances by participants remain views of individuals, rather than of entire communities or cultures, which are subsequently edited in accordance with the insights of the researcher or the dramatic instinct of the editor. In essence, one naïve perspective is replaced with a set of equally naïve or one-sided views, more in particular the idea that research subjects are truthful, that groups under study always have full and accurate insight into their own situation, and that a pure representation of dialogues highlights the underlying reality and makes it understandable. Such approaches contribute very little to the further development of a theoretically and methodologically sound form of visual data collection and communication whereby the complementary nature of word and image should be exploited to the full. Of course, the views and the perceptions of those involved do remain important sources of information for the acquisition of a qualified scientific understanding of a situation.

In a much-debated publication, the anthropologist/filmmaker Jack Rollwagen sharply criticized ethnographic filmmakers who claim that the structure of reality can be uncovered through pure observation (as in 'observational cinema') and that the viewer can thus acquire full insight into events merely by watching the film. At the same time, however, he challenges the previously mentioned post-modern, altogether language-oriented, approach that purposely foregrounds the (often entirely verbalized) view of the informants of the culture and the author of the audiovisual text, but that offers very little in the way of theoretical underpinning or guidance:

[A]nthropological filmmaking is not simply the recording of what human beings say or do but the interpretation of those recordings within the disciplinary framework of anthropology throughout the total filmmaking process from conception to execution. ... The incorporation of anthropology into anthropological filmmaking as a conscious process is a statement by the anthropological filmmaker that he/she is willing to have his/her ideas and conclusions subjected to the same rigorous evaluations by colleagues as a written work receives. There is no room in such framework for evasion of responsibility as there is in an approach which suggests that 'what is recorded speaks for itself.' (Rollwagen, 1988: 295)

3   The meeting of researcher and researched: towards multi-vocality and mutual promotion of interests

In the past, many ethnographic filmmakers tended to minimize the impact of the camera on exhibited behavior as well as the specific styling possibilities and choices in the various phases of the production process. They often believed that their productions were extremely objective and systematic observations. Quite characteristically for this view is, for example, Goldschmidt's definition of ethnographic film: 'Ethnographic film is film which endeavors to interpret the behavior of people of one culture to persons of another culture by using shots of people doing precisely what they would have been doing if the camera were not there' (Goldschmidt, quoted in MacDougall, 1975: 114). MacDougall rightly notes that conceptions (or misconceptions) such as those expressed by Goldschmidt often go hand in hand with another illusion, namely that the camera can grasp the totality of events. The invisibility of the camera is a fiction (with the exception of truly hidden cameras). To pretend that the presence of the camera (or the camera crew) has no influence whatsoever on exhibited behavior actually entails a denial of an existing situation. As MacDougall asserts, 'no ethnographic film is merely a record of another society: it is always a record of the meeting between a filmmaker and that society' (1975: 119). The striving towards objectivity, and a befittingly sober and meticulous filmic style, is nevertheless very legitimate, except that an almost exclusive attention for these aspects can easily result in other important methodological questions being ignored. Furthermore, by restricting oneself to trying to make the most accurate representation of perceivable reality leaves unused a number of new possibilities for scientific communication.

The ethnographic ideal of invisibility still persists in certain circles. Consequently, we can distinguish between at least two camps among researchers/cinematographers: on the one hand, those who feel that the impact of the camera on events is negligible or at least controllable and, on the other, those who clearly recognize the reactivity of those observed to the presence of the camera and who try to apply this insight (with varying degrees of success), so that scientifically valuable data could still be collected and made into a film. The underlying idea among the latter is that the explicit entry by the camera crew into the world of the research subjects and the ensuing possibilities for the acquisition and verification of information through the participation of the subjects examined in the research project enhance the authenticity of the acquired material rather than create an unreal, disrupted and therefore scientifically invalid situation. Rouch (1975: 100) typifies this important shift in thought: 'The anthropologist is no longer an entomologist observing his subject as if it were an insect ("putting it down") but rather as if it were a stimulant for mutual understanding.' The camera's presence should be recognized as being an integral part of the real situation, an element that may have a great or a small impact on other elements in this unusual setting.

Besides the fact that one needs to realize that the contribution and cooperation by the group studied are necessary to acquire more in-depth knowledge, there is also an important human driving force involved in participative or interactive forms of visual research, namely the desire to reshape the traditional research situation into a more egalitarian relationship. Those who are being researched should not be kept under tutelage or subjected to arbitrariness on the part of the researcher. Moreover, they should, if at all possible, take something away from the cooperation with the research team, for example in the shape of knowledge or means to address an undesirable situation (such as economic deprivation or political oppression). Although they are essentially commendable, certain conceptions (e.g., the notion of 'shared' production) need to be approached with some circumspection. Sometimes, they appear to be rationalizations that hardly tie in with research practice. The participatory idea is rooted in an unarticulated feeling of guilt among anthropologists occasioned by a colonial past and the often dubious role that their discipline played in it. The camera in particular proved to be a very useful instrument for creating and sustaining a particular image of the homeland that supported a certain political doctrine or scientific experimentation with an outspokenly Western perspective.

Despite this understandable and legitimate response to a colonizing use of the camera and the ensuing rearrangement of the relation between the researcher and the researched, it makes little sense to conceal that researchers ultimately play a steering role, and must continue to do so in order to adequately fulfill their scientific mission. But clearly there can be various degrees of imbalance between researcher and researched and there are, moreover, real alternatives for the relationship between the two. This relationship used to be a matter of the researcher needing something from the researched and subsequently disappearing with the loot.

The necessary reformulation of the meeting between researcher and the researched may be facilitated through the skillful use of visual participatory techniques (see Chapter 6). These approaches may under certain conditions help to give a voice to the field (both visually and verbally),

---

Example 2 A post-modern provocative anthropological film

A stimulating and provocative example of anthropological filmmaking is *Polka, Roots of Conjunto Accordion Playing in South Texas* (1986) by Robert Boonzajer and Maarten Rens. The film explores the connections between the emergence and the development of the 'Chicano Polka' in the border region between Mexico and Texas (in which the diatonic accordion played a central role) and the central European (German, Austrian) traditions of polka and accordion music. The researchers brought the Chicano musicians into contact with the direct descendants of their musical ancestors through video recordings they had made in Salzburg just a few weeks earlier. Afterwards, the recordings of the polka-performing Chicanos were shown to the Austrian musicians. The reactions of the two groups to their counterparts' performances were recorded visually and incorporated into the film. While the Chicanos reacted very enthusiastically to the music and the playing styles of the Austrians and immediately felt an urge to imitate them, the Austrians were rather critical of the 'corrupt' polka of the Chicanos and they liked to show before the cameras 'how it should be done.' The comments by the Austrians mainly concerned the (low) social position of the Chicanos ('this is gypsy music and it has nothing in common with the Austrian style'). The film also deals with the social and political functions of Chicano music. Originating in a mixture of styles, Chicano music appears to play an important role in the retention of cultural identity by a population group that is still severely discriminated by the white community.

This production, which from a traditional perspective is somewhat provocative, visualizes a number of typical problems and points of debate with regard to field research and the role of the researcher. Unlike in many other anthropological films, no attempt is made to conceal the role of and the actual interferences by the researcher in the situation. Especially striking in this production is the 'rapport' that the anthropologist, himself a accomplished accordionist, succeeds in establishing with the research subjects and the overt interventions by the anthropologist who is almost constantly in the picture and interacts very directly with the field. While there is evidence of an unconcealed recognition and exploration of the influence of the filmmaker on the pre-filmic aspect, this is much less the case at the filmic level (camera handling), where the approach is expressive but not always motivated, well-considered and explicit. The authors honour the hyperbolic statement that 'every documentary is a feature film,' which often results in an abandonment of any reflexive action in the cinematographic field rather than a striving for deliberate and explicit scientific expressiveness. In their films, Boonzajer and Rens try to emphasize the 'showing' rather than the 'telling' and, for this reason, they resolutely reject the use of explicative commentary or off-screen narration. The researchers believe that the subjects should 'tell their own story.' One of the consequences of this approach is that their 'visual' study depends largely on 'verbal' sources (albeit in their nonverbal context). Therefore, it largely remains a 'telling' of events, albeit from the perspective of the field rather than that of an off-screen commentator (though the hand of the filmmaker is clearly visible in the editing of the interviews). As no attempt is made to provide an informed scientific view from the exterior as a complement, the film is for a large part restricted to the (scientifically valuable, yet incomplete) view of the Chicanos and the Austrians or, to be more precise, of a number of individuals from these two distinct cultures. The rather loose and unmotivated use of such cinematographic means as editing and framing, the prominent presence and influence of the anthropologist, the very strong verbal impact and the idea that the respondents have complete insight into their own situation, but also the remarkable rapport with and participation of the field make this a 'post-modern' anthropological film that provides extremely interesting food for thought regarding the further development of scientific film as a mimetic and expressive genre (Figures 8.2 and 8.3).

Figure 8.2 and 8.3 *Polka*: the Austrian's choice of framing. *Polka*: the Chicano's preferred way of framing.

At one point, the researcher found that the Austrian accordionists were not happy with the manner in which they were being filmed: they wanted the camera to be placed further back, so that 'everything would be visible.' Then the Austrian father purposely positioned himself very centrally, together with his son, who was however in slightly less favorable position than himself, surrounded by numerous signs of Austrian affluence and culture (Figure 8.2). The Chicanos, too, seemed to feel nothing for the' medium' shot. However, rather than moving the camera back, they preferred to bring it closer to the performance, so that only the most important parts of the instrument and the hands that were playing it were in the shot (Figure 8.3). Heads and limbs were regarded as interferences: all attention had to be focused on the music. This spontaneous form of feedback illustrates quite clearly how music is closely interwoven with broader cultural conceptions. In the initial version (or raw cut) of the film, which was shown at the 1986 IVSA (International Visual Sociology Association) conference in Bielefeld, this process of 'reframing' was incorporated in full (focusing and zooming in and out until the desired frame size was found), but this spontaneous and very meaningful form of visual intervention by the field was unfortunately not retained in subsequent versions. This was probably due to the fact that the more 'professional' editor of the definitive version did not understand this 'bungling' with the camera or did not want to come across as incompetent. As the authors stubbornly refuse to provide 'commentary,' this event is not even mentioned verbally in the later cuts.

certainly if the viewpoint of the subjects or the community also receives a prominent place in the visual end product and in subsequent activities that may be initiated to the benefit of the researched.

4   Reflexivity, or the meta-discourse of filming the meeting of cultures

Increasingly, the (visual) representation of cultures is seen as an extremely complex meeting of cultures: first and foremost, between those of the researchers and those of the researched, but subsequently also with the culture of the viewers or users of the resulting visual product. A scientist is not an objective and emancipated subject who observes, but a 'positioned' and 'repositioned' subject (Rosaldo, 1989), with personal beliefs, preferences, experiences, characteristics, cultural backgrounds and so forth. From this position, the scientist approaches a field of study, influences it and is influenced by it. The audience of scientific products is also inevitably positioned and actively introduces its own world into the interpretation of whatever it is presented with.

Moreover, it has become quite clear that each medium, even one that looks as realistic as film, inevitably has mimetic limitations and cannot but reduce or reshape (be it in a consciously or an unconsciously expressive manner). And finally, awareness is growing that the primary research object itself (an aspect of the culture studied) is extraordinarily multifaceted and dynamic and can therefore never be grasped in a single or even a whole series of representations.

Reflection upon the generative process of science and the role of the scientist as an individual is not new in this respect. However, by gradually abandoning the persistent mental image of the objective scientist, contemporary scientific writings and visual productions have come to focus more on the notion of *reflexivity*. Yet it often remains unclear what this notion means precisely.

Some authors restrict themselves to attaching new labels to existing methodological principles and praxis. Moreover, they tend to claim that past research projects and visual productions never considered that perhaps their approach contained a degree of subjectivity. In addition, however, reflexivity does concern broadened insights, principles and focal points that should be appropriately incorporated into scientific praxis.

Ruby provides a clear and qualified description of what the term 'reflexivity' may signify in an anthropological context: 'To be reflexive, in terms of a work of anthropology, is to insist that anthropologists systematically and rigorously reveal their methods and themselves as the instruments of data generation and reflect upon how the medium through which they transmit their work predisposes readers/viewers to construct meaning of the work in certain ways' (2000: 152). How the various aspects should be dealt with more concretely, however, is not so easily resolved. Indeed, this leads to new misunderstandings. Closer attention for one's own influence need not gain the upper hand over the actual topic of a visual production. While reflexivity should result more in a better qualification of the results and viewpoints, some researchers and film-makers do sometimes use it as a means to put themselves in the picture in an almost self-glorifying manner. Such strongly autobiographically oriented explorations can, paradoxically enough, be at the expense of insight into the broader cultural meeting that they believe they should strive for. The same holds for exaggerated reflexive approaches that in turn may quickly degenerate into a repetitive meta-discourse on filmmaking and scientific work, against an alternating background of given cultural contexts. There are no quick or simple procedures for a reflexive approach: occasionally filming oneself or the crew (to say 'hey, this is only film not reality!'), or a merely verbal acknowledgment of reflexivity, provides little insight into the driving forces behind a scientist and the scientific usability of the product. A fierce advocate of a thoughtful and well-balanced reflexivity, Ruby (2000: 155) does admit that it is extremely difficult to determine exactly how much knowledge and precisely which aspects of the producer and the production process are needed and, conversely, what should be considered an excess or superfluous and thus detrimental to the end result.

In any case, the conclusion that there is inevitably much subjectivity involved in the creation and the further use of visual representations in a scientific context does not mean that all approaches are equally (in)valuable for developing an insight into the phenomena that surround us and for the conceptual constructions that scientists weave around them. To a scientist, reflexivity or reflexive action does not mean liberation from a rigid and explicit methodology, but for each scientific activity, a necessary and demanding expansion of it. After all, non-recognized subjectivity or the denial of subjective influences and the unmistakable epistemological consequences of all choices made inevitably lead to much less scientifically useful insights, although this might not always appear to be the case at first sight. Ruby does draw attention to the paradox that, as scientists become better at this demanding assignment, their scientific status appears to be increasingly undermined: 'their methodological statements then begin to appear to be more and more personal, subjective, biased, involved, and culture bound – in other words, *the more scientific anthropologists try to be by revealing their methods, the less scientific they appear to be*' (2000: 163).

Reflexivity encompasses a clear recognition that all scientific knowledge is provisional, positioned and incomplete, but it should go beyond that recognition. A justification of the procedures followed in research – including the subjective influences and influencing – must assume the concrete shape of a carefully considered meta-discourse that is partly continued in the film (internal contextualization) but usually also outside it (external contextualization – e.g., through verbal elucidation, study guide, book). The audience of a visual end product must be allowed to become as conscious as possible of the 'status' of what is shown: Why were certain choices made? Is one looking at natural occurring phenomena, elicited behavior or (re)staged events? Are the materials resulting from covert observation or from cooperation with the field? What difficulties have been experienced during the shooting and editing? To what extent can what is shown be generalized?

Example 3 A visual expressive and reflexive anthropological film

A truly exemplary visually expressive and reflexive anthropological film is *A Country Auction: The Paul V. Leitzel Estate Sale* (1983). This film, produced by Robert Aibel, Ben Levin, Chris Musello and Jay Ruby, is about the social, personal and economic aspects of an auction of the last 'general store' in a rural community in Pennsylvania (Figure 8.4). The film follows the relatives of the deceased manager on the eve of the public auction, as they go through all the objects and comment on them. Then the day of the auction is shown: members of the community turn up in large numbers to look for bargains, to purchase a memento, or to swap memories and take a final look at the store. After the big auction, the camera follows a number of sold items to their new owners. At the basis for the production lies the belief that this kind of public auction serves various social purposes: a household is physically dismantled, so that the next of kin of the deceased person experience the disappearance of their relative very intensely; the members of a community are given an opportunity to acquire certain objects (with a primarily symbolic/emotional value); antique dealers can make a living and they distribute a considerable share of the goods over large areas. The film uses filmic techniques and conventions very thoughtfully in order to construct a scientific argumentation. Both the intentions of the makers and the various methods employed are dealt with explicitly in this production. The actual production process of the film and the filmmakers are also a topic of this visual study, so that the role of the researchers and the research process are not concealed.

Figure 8.4 Still from *A Country Auction*

Having designed their production as social science, the authors subjected their film and its accompanying materials to similar (though not necessarily the same) and equally rigorous standards as those that are imposed on written forms of science. The 'study guide' that accompanied the film provided the necessary context. It also elucidated the theoretical framework surrounding the production and revealed and substantiated each of the cinematographic choices made. An extract of the study guide illustrates the very thoughtful approach which typifies this important anthropological film:

The 'look' of this film is not the result of a belief in any one particular aesthetic of documentary realism, but due to a set of pragmatic decisions about how best to convey social science knowledge in film. Narration and a brief methodology statement were included near the beginning of the film in order to establish the guiding analysis and to make the filmmakers' purposes clear. The interviewer was often left in the frame so that viewers were reminded of the interactive quality of the scene. Dissolves were used reflexively to avoid 'artificial' continuity in editing. Fades to black were used to distance viewers from the narrative surface of the film and to divide theoretically distinct segments of the event. An editing structure was developed which periodically diverged from the chronology of the auction in order to develop particular concepts. ('Study Guide' in Aibel et al., 1983).

Interestingly, twenty-five years after the film's release, the team decided to go back to the town where the auction took place to

> pick up the story with the people who had been at the sale. The team also used this return to the field to further reflect on and discuss the limitations and opportunities of their initial ethnographic record, which explicitly included the assumptions and viewpoints of the makers. This resulted in *Reflexive Musings: A Country Auction Study Film*, a film that perfectly complements the original film (Machuca and Ruby, 2012).

5   Concluding thoughts: multimedia and scholarly expression

The debate on scientific filmmaking remains very complex, because it is at the same time a debate about the status and the potential of a particularly diverse and culturally embedded medium (formal aspects, visual and verbal codes of expression, impact of technology, truth claims) and a debate about the essence and the possibilities of social science as a culturally specific and evolving practice.

Film as a medium of representation is exceptionally rich. Compared to types of non-camera-based visual representations films have a particularly strong mimetic and expressive potential because of their time-based (enabling development over time) and powerful multimodal character (sound, image, text).

A complex visual medium in its own right, film can also include non-camera-based visual representations (charts, drawings, computer simulations, etc.). Thus film is not limited to merely reflecting a pro-filmic reality – or in other words not confined to dealing with depicting naturally occurring, elicited or re-enacted phenomena or aspects of material culture – but is also able to reproduce or construct more conceptual or symbolic representations. Many recent anthropological films tend to take advantage of this capability to mix representations and discursive strategies of a very different kind.

Current digital media technology facilitates the further expansion of the discursive potential of film and make it into an even more hybrid product with more possibilities and challenges. Digitized images, texts and sounds on a non-linear digital base offer numerous possibilities to bypass the sometimes too rigid linearity of the moving image and may accommodate their content for various audiences (according to their level of knowledge and specific interests). New media, rather than merely supplanting the older media, are both emulating and extending many of their features as well as producing completely new ones. If well thought

Examples 4 and 5   A social scientific video article and a multimedia production

An early but still illuminating attempt to produce a stand-alone scientific audiovisual product that can match and indeed surpass the traditional scholarly article is the video article entitled *Mise en images d'un rituel: La messe catholique à la télévision française, un approche sociologique* (1991) (The Visual Representation of a Ritual: The Catholic Mass on French Television, a sociological approach), produced by the French sociologist Jean-Paul Terrenoire. Of particular interest is the visual article's multi-layered structure: it is basically about a ritual (a first 'representational' practice) as captured by a television crew (and thus made into a second-level representation: the television program). Moreover, the relationship between the two types of representation is discussed within a third: that of the 'video article' (which is itself a media product).

Terrenoire's video article provides an interesting illustration of the typical tension that exists between the real-life flow of events (which may or may not be staged or prescribed) and their 'representation,' which necessarily embodies some sort of – intended or unintended, functional or dysfunctional – reinterpretation. Moreover, it points quite clearly at the 'alterable' status of the implied spectator as imposed by the camera (through position, distance, movement, framing; Figures 8.5 and 8.6). Or, put in more general terms, it illustrates the powerful impact that the 'point of view' (POV) can also have in non-fictional productions. Though this is not claimed explicitly by the author, Terrenoire's production may be considered to be a powerful statement in favor of the thoughtful development of more appropriate ways of integrating visual media and visual information into scientific practice. In other words, it strongly rejects the notion that there should or could be such a thing as a standard visual culture or grammar that is suitable for visualizing any event or phenomenon, irrespective of its purpose.

Figures 8.5 and 8.6 The camera's point of view as marked by infographics 'constructs' a spectator role.

The video article's introduction and conclusion consist of considerable portions of text scrolling from the bottom to the top of the screen. While this may seem a very 'non-visual' approach (and the pace of the scrolling can hardly be set to suit all readers/ spectators), one should never foster the illusion that an audiovisual, supposedly self-contained article will ever be able to get round the need for some sort of verbalization (be it in the shape of on-screen text, an off-screen voice, an on-screen speaker or an accompanying study guide).

Though there is certainly room for improvement with regard to several aspects (e.g., the balance between text, sound and images, the choice of fonts and of background colors) the product still succeeds in transmitting scientific insight in a way that a written article could not, or at least not as well. With today's technology one could surely overcome a number of limitations (e.g., by offering ways of bypassing the strictly linear construction and the imposed pace of the images and of the texts, which still make up a considerable part of the product, and by offering opportunities for revisiting portions of the analysis or to consider selected bits of images and text at one's own pace and level of interest). These enhancements are connected with increasing the level of proficiency of the producers, who are forced to integrate several different types of expertise, as well as with deploying the characteristics of the ever-evolving visual media.

Today's digital media provide much easier and more intelligible ways of combining text, sound and images compared to the rather unwieldy analogue video formats. Films also can also become part of a larger multimedia structure.

A pioneering example in this regard is the CD-ROM titled *Yanomamö Interactive* (1997), made by Peter Biella, Napoleon Chagnon and Gary Seaman. This multimedia product is built around a complete digitized version of Timothy Asch and Napoleon Chagnon's complex and multi-layered anthropological film *The Ax Fight* (1975). Users of this cleverly designed multimedia product can at their own pace explore this rich anthropological event in a non-linear fashion and have access to illuminating genealogical charts, maps, biographies, analytical texts, annotations, diagrams and audio narration (Figure 8.7). They can also replay scenes, freeze frames or use slow motion for added convenience. Additional contextual information is provided on a web site, which, in contrast to the CD-ROM format, permits easy updating.

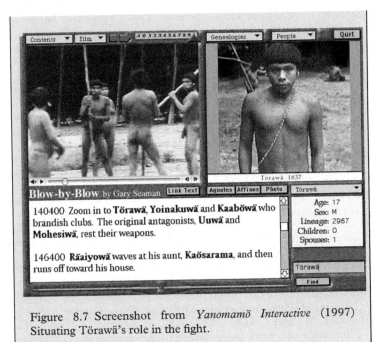

Figure 8.7 Screenshot from *Yanomamö Interactive* (1997) Situating Törawä's role in the fight.

through and skillfully applied these new opportunities may enrich the science discourse dramatically.

However tempting and promising it may seem in its own right, technology should in any case remain the servant of ideas and insights, not the driver of a scientific project. This is not an unqualified plea for a very sparse use of the growing – and largely unexplored – capabilities of visual media, but a certain degree of sobriety will often remain essential to create valuable scientific products. New opportunities should always be measured against their affordances.

6   References

Aibel, R., B. Levin, C. Musello and J. Ruby (1983) *A Country Auction: The Paul V. Leitzel Estate Sale.* Film, 56 mins, Pennsylvania State University, Audiovisual Services.

Asch, T. and N. Chagnon (1975) *The Ax Fight.* Film, 30 mins, University Park, PA / Watertown, MA: Center for Documentary Anthropology, Pennsylvania State University / Documentary Educational Resources.

Bazin, A. (1975) *Qu'est-ce que le cinema?* Paris: Cerf.

Biella, P., N. Chagnon and G. Seaman (1997) *Yanomamö Interactive: The Ax Fight*. CD-ROM, Fort Worth, TX: Harcourt Brace and Company.

Boonzajer Flaes R. and M. Rens (1986) *Polka: Roots of Conjunto Accordion Playing in South Texas*. Video, color, 50 mins, University of Amsterdam, Center for Visual Anthropology.

Chiozzi, P. (1989) 'Reflections on Ethnographic Film with a General Bibliography.' *Visual Anthropology*, 2(1): 1–84.

Collier, J. (1967) *Visual Anthropology: Photography as a Research Method*, New York/London, Holt, Rinehart and Winston. (Later revised with Malcolm Collier (1986), University of New Mexico Press.)

Crawford, P. I. (1992) 'Film as Discourse: The Invention of Anthropological Realities.' In: P. I. Crawford and D. Turton (eds.) *Film as Ethnography*. Manchester/New York: Manchester University Press.

De Heusch, L. (1988) 'Ethnographic and Sociological Films.' *Visual Anthropology*, 1(2): 99–156 (reprint of a 1962 UNESCO paper).

Folmer, P. (1992) 'Het postmodernisme en de etnografische film,' paper methodologie, (http://ruls01.fsw.leidenuniv.nl/-etno/pomo.html) [accessed March 25, 2003].

Lajoux, J. D. (1975) 'Ethnographic Film and History.' In: P. Hockings (ed.) *Principles of Visual Anthropology*. The Hague/Paris: Mouton, pp. 167–84.

MacDougall, D. (1975) 'Beyond Observational Cinema.' In: P. Hockings (ed.) *Principles of Visual Anthropology*. The Hague/Paris: Mouton, 109–24.

Machuca, M., and J. Ruby (2012) *Reflexive Musings: A Country AuctionStudy Film*. Film, 47 mins (www.der.org/films/a-country-auction.html) [accessed April 20, 2015].

Mead, M. (1963) 'Anthropology and the Camera.' In: W. Morgan (ed.) *The Encyclopedia of Photography*, New York: Greystone Press, Vol. 1, pp.166–84.

Mead, M. (1975) 'Visual Anthropology in a Discipline of Words.' In: P. Hockings (ed.) *Principles of Visual Anthropology*. The Hague/Paris, Mouton, pp. 3–10.

Nijland, D., in cooperation with J. Platenkamp (1985) *Tobelo Marriage*. Film 16mm, color, 108 mins, ICA.

Nijland, D. (1989) Schaduwen en Werkelijkheid: Cultureel bepaald kennen, waarnemen, nonverbaal communiceren en onderzoek daarvan via de terugvertoning van de etnografische film 'Tobelo Marriage', PhD dissertation, Rijksuniversiteit Leiden.

Prost, J. (1975) 'Filming Body Behavior,' In: P. Hockings (ed.) *Principles of Visual Anthropology*. The Hague/Paris, Mouton: 325–63.

Rollwagen, J. (ed.) (1988) *Anthropological Filmmaking: Anthropological Perspectives on the Production of Film and Video for General Public Audiences*. Chur/London: Harwood Academic Publishers.

Rosaldo, R. (1989) 'Grief and the Headhunter's Rage.' In: R. Rosaldo *Culture and Truth*. Boston, MA: Beacon, pp. 1–21.

Rouch, J. (1975) 'The Camera and Man.' In P. Hockings (ed.) *Principles of Visual Anthropology*. The Hague/Paris: Mouton, pp. 83–102.

Ruby, J. (2000) *Picturing Culture: Explorations of Film and Anthropology*. University of Chicago Press.

Terrenoire, J.-P. (1991) *Mise en images d'un rituel: La messe catholique à la télévision française, un approche sociologique.* Video article, Paris: CNRS.

Wolf, G. (1967) *Der wissenschaftliche Dokumentationsfilm und die Encyclopaedia Cinematographica.* Munich: Johann Ambrosius Barth; Göttingen: Institut für den Wissenschaftlichen Film.

Wright, T. (1992) 'Television narrative and ethnographic film.' In: P. I. Crawford & D. Turton (eds.) *Film as Ethnography.* Manchester and New York, Manchester University Press: 274–282.

Young, C. (1975) 'Observational cinema.' In: P. Hockings (ed.) *Principles of Visual Anthropology.* Den Haag/Paris: Mouton, 65–79.

Part IV

Applications / case studies

9 Family photography as a social practice: from the analogue to the digital networked world

1 Something old, something new: the social functions of private photography

1.1 Culture and technology in the post-modern era

The blending of fact and fiction and the blurring of the boundaries between the private and public spheres would appear to be two characteristic traits of post-modern society. In the post-modern world, couples fight their marital battles in front of greedy audiences, on TV shows such as *Jerry Springer*, *Ricky Lane*, *Oprah Winfrey* and 'reality-TV' programs such as *Supernanny* and *Wife Swap*. Private emotions, convictions and events are commodified to serve a variety of individual and institutional needs.

These trends have not bypassed what used to be called 'private' photography, the snapshots or more formal witnesses of lives lived. After a long and successful 'analogue' period, family photography – one of the original pillars of the photographic industry – has also entered the digital age. Opportunities to construct and disseminate desired pasts and presents, and to tailor them for growing audiences and for various purposes, have since increased significantly.

Digital and network technology would appear to embody – or at the very least to facilitate – many typical aspects of post-modernity: the loss of clear authorship and ownership, the deconstruction of traditional norms and institutions, the drifting and multiplication of meanings, the hybridization of forms and functions, and the blurring of boundaries – most notably those between the private and the public spheres.

Technological changes are impacting the nature of images and the contexts of production and consumption alike. Consequently, the social and cultural uses and meanings of photography are affected. But the reverse is equally true: societal needs steer technological developments, even to the extent that technological products may be considered 'materialized' aspects of particular cultures and ideologies. The

193

complex – and at times unpredictable – exchanges between society and technology may yield quite different outcomes: sometimes existing uses and practices are merely facilitated or reinforced by technological innovations, on other occasions practices become obsolete and gradually disappear, and at other times still more profound evolutionary processes unfold, for example changes in purposes and target audiences.

Mitchell (1992), a well-known observer and theorist of the digital turn in visual communication, in an otherwise very commendable book, somewhat overstates the inherent post-modern nature and inevitable consequences of digital technology. While the shift to digital technologies may very well suit the needs of a more fragmented, heterogeneous and indeterminate approach, it may equally serve the needs of more traditional approaches and functions. Speaking of a 'post-photographic era,' as Mitchell does, is somewhat misleading, since new technology does not necessarily radically and inevitably change the role of the camera-based image in society. New technologies often seem to trigger hasty assessments of supposed or expected changes and the real, only gradually unfolding impact remains largely unnoticed and barely studied. An example is the shift to new audiences and functions on the one hand, and the simultaneous rejuvenation and reinforcement of older functions on the other.

Credibility, one of the most discussed issues in this field, may very well have come under additional strain by the ease with which digital imagery can be changed. But this belief in the truth value of the camera image has certainly not disappeared completely, nor was it ever unchallenged in bygone (analogue) days, when tampering with images was not necessarily any less common than it is today. Brugioni illustrates an example of manipulation as early as the 1850s, in which multiple negatives were used to create non-existent scenes (Brugioni, cited in Reis 2004). Reis, an expert in imaging technology for forensic applications, points out that digital technology did not introduce image manipulation; it simply provides additional technology for it (Reis 2004).

So, generally speaking, one should be wary of technological determinist views, irrespective of whether they predict benevolent or malevolent futures and consequences, through radical shifts or revolutions. Usually technological changes do not simply wipe away existing cultures, in this case photographic and social rituals and uses. Older visual media are not simply supplanted by newer media and contemporary social practices. Yet the interplay between technology and social and cultural factors does merit ongoing scrutiny.

1.2   *Family photography from the early days to the recent past*

The French sociologist Pierre Bourdieu (1978: 38–54) was one of the first scholars to underscore the very important 'integrative' function of family photography. According to Bourdieu, family snapshots help to establish and maintain a bond between family members, while the photographic practice or ritual itself also serves as an index for the degree to which families are 'integrated.' This fundamental social function of private photography also to an important degree explains the stereotypical, even boring aspect of most family snaps. Social and cultural norms tend to determine to a considerable degree what or whom (moments, events, actors) will be remembered, marketed or used by posterity, as well as how (aesthetic, style, directions).

While the traditional 'great moments in family life' that constitute the core of Bourdieu's theory have lost much of their significance in contemporary society, and photographs are now taken much more commonly and in (seemingly) much more informal ways (Musello, 1979), this practice has still not lost its social function and its highly normative character. Family pictures were and still are cherished for what they represent (i.e., beloved ones and memorable times) yet they are still as normative as before in the ways they strive to construct and present idealized images of the family, both through careful selection of occasions and rigorous staging of events (Figures 9.1 and 9.2).

From the beginning, photography as a social practice has steered (and been steered by) technological advancements. Most recently, the all-important and now well under way transition from analogue to digital imaging has stirred the world of photography and most of the sectors in society that make use of it for a variety of purposes.

Digital technology has indeed altered some of the basic features of the photographic image. As a result, it also has an impact on photography's various social uses and how it is generally 'perceived' in society, most notably with regard to its credibility, its status as evidence of 'real events.' The transformation of a previously synchronous and continuous tonal space (the analogue image) into separately accessible 'bits' of information (the pixelated picture) – while not necessarily altering an image's indexical relation with what it depicts – seems to encourage, and facilitate as it were, a 'creative treatment of reality,' as altering the picture's content is made increasingly simple. But also during the shooting of digital images, we can make as many 'versions of reality' as we want, check and negotiate the results with others, and delete images that we think should not be kept. Digital image-making, especially in the domestic sphere, has often

Figure 9.1 (left) Soldiers photographed in front of a carefully chosen pious background (first quarter of twentieth century) for paper-based distribution to family and friends (collection: L. Pauwels).

Figure 9.2 (right) Digitally revisiting the past: If Auntie is no longer in favor, the cherished moment can still be saved (Action Photo catalog)

become more of a group negotiation process, whereby the photographer loses some of his/her control.

While many players in the world of visual information and communication (particularly journalists, documentary makers and scientists) have always expressed concern about the possible impact of the digital turn, particularly on the issue of trustworthiness of the picture (Mitchell, 1992), these discussions and concerns have largely bypassed private practice (Pauwels, 2002a).

Family photography has always maintained a rather loose connection with 'Truth' and has at all times provided a very selective – or highly normative – view of family life. Family pictures were never objective records of lives lived in all of their aspects. Selectivity, manipulation and construction have been the norm right from the inception of photography in the nineteenth century. And this holds true with respect to the pre-photographic level, such as the mise-en-scène (studio backgrounds, props) and the selection of moments and subject matter, as well as with regard to the post-photographic level, for example through framing, cropping, soft focusing, retouching, photomontage (de Haas, 1975;

Boerdam and Oosterbaan Martinius, 1978; Pauwels, 1979, 1994, 2002a; Freund, 1980).

In a previous publication, I contended that the rapid shift from the analogue to the digital image may very well further challenge the representative character of family photography in an unprecedented way, since opportunities to construct and disseminate highly tampered pasts have increased dramatically. Yet, I immediately added that this does not necessarily involve a dramatic shift in the basic social functions and practices of private photography, nor does it imply a loss of scientific value of these visual products as cultural documentation (Pauwels, 2002a). The value of these unique family accounts for the social researcher resides not in their being 'truthful depictions of family life' (which they clearly are not), but precisely in their having been selectively 'pieced together,' and in their unique ability to visualize values and norms, aspirations and so on. Furthermore, it should be noted that 'image alterations' and narrative twists are not necessarily deliberate acts of deception. And even when they are, in a sense they are often 'self-deceptions,' things one likes or wants to believe, tokens of dreams, aspirations, and wishes. Yet again, these may be more revealing to the social researcher than so-called objective records of life events.

Family snappers embraced the digital (r)evolution as soon as its tools and products became affordable. In a computer-immersed society, the ease of use and increased functionality of the digital process was greeted with a certain enthusiasm. For family photographers the digital image offers a number of interesting – primarily post-production – opportunities to further construct and share a 'desired' past. Quality has now risen dramatically to a level where both private and professional image producers embrace digital imaging as a practical tool for many purposes. Both groups welcome the considerably increased levels of control during production and the highly facilitated means of dissemination.

So looking purely at the shift from the analogue to the digital process of image registration, it would appear that the digitized image complies very well with the basic functions of family photography as a social institution. It does not by its mere nature significantly alter the essence of private photography. Observations of family websites show that digital family photography still focuses primarily on celebrating the family bond and on reproducing the core values of family life to its members, relatives, friends, acquaintances and potential members (e.g., candidates for marriage) (Pauwels, 2002a). Family photography, so it seems, has effectively and effortlessly made the transition to the digital age.

1.3   Into the semi-public realm: family snapshots in cyberspace

However, the digital (r)evolution described above goes beyond a new way of making and storing images, as a collection of discrete – separately addressable – elements. Therefore, we should not confine our attention to the nature of the image and the increased possibilities for altering the contents of the picture, but ought also to examine the very significant technological developments with respect to text and image communication through electronic networks and devices.

One fairly recent phenomenon in private photography and family communications is the 'electronic family album' (see an example in Figure 9.3), constructed and accessed through the web. The World

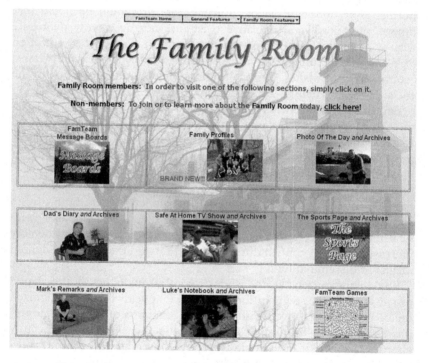

Figure 9.3 The enhanced opportunities for reorganizing the past into a desired narrative are attractive to both the producers and the very varied group of 'users' (family members and friends, anonymous visitors). This evolution may also benefit those social and cultural scholars who are willing to make the effort to meticulously decode these extremely rich sources of cultural information.

Wide Web is gradually being discovered as a vehicle for displaying and disseminating these hitherto 'private' stories. A growing number of families have created websites dedicated to advertising their successes and activities, and to sharing their domestic highlights and personal fields of interest with what, in theory at least, is a global audience. A reliable estimate of the spread of this relatively new practice is not available – a common problem when studying web phenomena (Weare and Lin 2000: 278) – though popular portal sites such as Yahoo and Google have already indexed many thousands and their number is literally growing by the day.

2   Studying family websites: methodology and ethics

The following observations and my subsequent theorizing in this paper, are premised from a long-standing research interest in (paper-based) family photography (Pauwels, 1979, 1994), and subsequently in studying and hypothesizing the social and cultural impact of the move from the analogue to the digital image and to cyberspace (Pauwels, 2002a, 2002b, 2005a, 2005b). Figure 9.4 shows the first web family album which

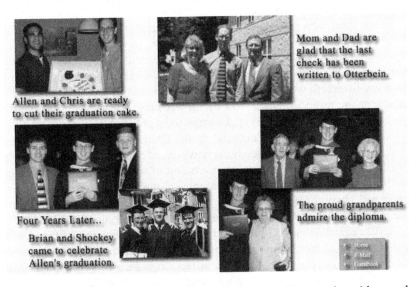

Figure 9.4 Private websites are often extremely expressive with regard to prevailing values in a particular culture. Pictures and stories about love and caring for kin (grandparents, parents, children and pets), material possessions (cars and houses), educational and sporting achievements, the military 'tour of duty,' are typical expressions of values that are often celebrated on American family websites.

I encountered (by chance) several years ago, and which demonstrated immediately the great potential impact that moving family albums from paper to the web could have in terms of both societal significance (shifts in audience, functions and expressiveness) and sociological research potential (access, data richness). Subsequent searches using numerous search engines and key words such as 'family albums,' 'family web' and so on unearthed few further examples; in fact, most family websites are not retrievable using these key words. More successful, however, were searches through thematically organized web portals such as Google and Yahoo; here many thousands of family albums are neatly listed as family websites with many sub-categories (e.g., baby sites, pet sites or genealogical sites).

Using a grounded theory approach, I studied a random sample (n=approximately 400) of websites from the many thousands listed in Yahoo and Google. For a more limited number (n=6), I contacted the owners to discuss their websites in depth. This preliminary exploration led to a series of observations, relating to the very profound social and cultural impact of digital technology on new ways in which family pictures, and increasingly wide-ranging grassroots narratives, are presented, disseminated and consumed.

From these observations, I developed a series of hypotheses as to the 'why' and the 'what for' of family websites (its 'uses and gratifications' in communications studies). To answer these questions, I developed an online survey for a random sample of family website owners. The survey was sent to every twentieth website listed on the Google 'family websites' directory, which at the time contained over 8,000 websites. For the websites whose owners responded to the survey, I completed a preliminary website analysis using the 'Hybrid Media Analysis' model (Pauwels, 2005a). Full survey results are to be reported elsewhere; however, of relevance to this chapter is the finding that a preliminary interpretation of survey responses, together with analysis of the form and contents of the corresponding websites, validated hypotheses formulated from the preliminary explorations described above, and I discuss these further with examples below.

With regard to ethics, it should be made clear that the web is not a no-man's land from which content may be copied and used by anyone for any purpose. As Lee has noted, 'research in cyberspace falls within the scope of existing guidelines on ethical research practice in respect of informed consent, privacy and confidentiality and the need to protect research participants from harm' (Lee, 2000: 135). Websites are semi-public spaces that need ethical consideration and are not a free place or public domain content for anyone to use in any way they like.

But the challenge often remains how exactly to apply existing ethics standards to the hybrid and heterogeneous nature of the Internet. In the same way that public and private spheres are uneasily distinguishable in the real world, the Internet reflects equally ambiguous private and public spheres of cyberspace. It is only basic ethical practice to obtain permission from website owners to use their websites as screenshots in publications or as online examples during a conference, and to stipulate exactly what you intend to do with the information. Obtaining this consent is not always so simple; my research revealed that many family websites are rather short lived (interpreted from lack of recent website updates or failure of a web owner to respond when contacted). On the other hand, once owners of active websites are convinced that a researcher's aims are truly academic, without commercial or other undisclosed motivation, they are often very willing to permit researchers to use parts of their website, and eager to comment on their motivations and choices.

3   Looking at changes in online family albums

3.1   *A more flexible and expressive medium*

The multimedia context of the web provides private image makers and storytellers with an increasingly flexible medium for the construction and dissemination of fact and fiction about their lives. The family website creator has acquired new features and means to construct a desired past: not just easy-to-manipulate individual pictures, but series of pictures that, in various ways, can be combined into a story with the aid of text, sound, design elements and so forth. These expanded means offer better ways of transferring factual information (texts and pictures) about what are regarded as highlights of family life and its context. They also allow one to add emphasis, to express values and norms, and to construct fictions and fantasies. Digitized (and possibly digitally 'adjusted') family snapshots, further 'dramatized' in a web format with text, layout and design features, may be considered even less faithful reflections of reality than their analogue paper-based predecessor (the classic family album), but by the same token they may reveal more about the immaterial side of family culture: the values, beliefs and aspirations of a group of people.

3.2   *Power dynamics and the multiplicity of voices*

Families, like any other type of social group, are not necessarily entities where all views and values are shared among all of its members. To some extent these different views surface just by studying the different 'voices' that are heard and how much space each member is allotted, and the hierarchy of place (prominent in home page or buried deep down in the structural hierarchy of the website). But most often a rather uniform view will be presented of the family which may reflect one dominant sender (or more unlikely, a group of people who really see eye to eye). In this respect websites prove to be strong indicators of the power dynamics within the family. Some websites reveal a very democratic approach, with all family member 'sub-sites' accessible on equal terms from the home page and showing clearly distinct voices (styles, content, views), while others display a strong hierarchy (e.g., in terms of age, gender, role) and often speak from one point of view (an impersonal voice or an 'I' who introduces and positions the other members: in both cases this is most often the father, and in the second position the mother; see an example of this in Figure 9.12 later).

These power dynamics should be investigated further via interviews or surveys with the website owners (and preferably with other 'unheard' members, although this may prove problematic), asking them about who decides on content for the websites, whether all family members have a say in website creation, and whether there are ways to amend, negotiate or prevent a particular representation or definition of the family.

3.3   Connecting with a virtual audience

Browsing a paper family album usually allows for real-time interaction between the family members and their immediate audience. Pictures are commented upon from both sides with those showing the album being able to provide customized background information, and those browsing the album providing direct feedback. With the electronic family album, producers have lost this direct (face-to-face) type of exchange. In this disembodied environment, therefore, they have to find ways to 'reconnect' with the audience. In the absence of face-to-face contact between the website owner and the visitors, the many visual and verbal communication features help to channel the possible interpretations (or 'readings') by visitors into the 'preferred' reading as implicitly constructed by the website owner. Web-based photographs are most often captioned (Garner et al. 2003), and observations of web-based versions of family albums suggest that text often takes precedence over the image. More than ever before, family history has become an 'unfinished business,' temporarily materialized in 'episodes' and 'remakes', a multimedia narrative that is easy to update and change, which proves to be very dynamic over time.

Though the producers and consumers of electronic 'family albums' remain physically separated, efforts are made to encourage interaction. Often, websites invite visitors to sign a guestbook and to give feedback: some phrases of appreciation, suggestions or comments. Furthermore, they often allow the visitor to contact the webmaster by email.

3.4   Ways of coping with an extended audience

Similar to how family website owners are aware of and seek to address the extended audience, the issues they choose to cover seem to expand far beyond domestic activities and values. Some private websites also contain – explicitly or more implicitly – verbal and visual statements about gender relations and role patterns, politics, religion, sexual orientation, leisure and sports preferences (see Figure 9.5). They provide access to particular stories in people's lives and, in a more general sense, testify to

David Bayless and Family | Somebody Special | Photos | Pets | What Really is Important! | Pass This On | IT
IS NO SECRET WHAT GOD CAN DO | DREAMS | My Wife Marilyn | My Favorite Stories | MORE ABOUT ME |
Home   Odds and Ends | Family | Our Church | Faith, Hope and Love | Favorite Links | Contact Me | COWBOY PRAYER

DAVID'S LITTLE PLACE ON THE NET

David Bayless and Family

click here to play sound

I am Married to a wonderful and exceptional woman who is "The Love of My Life." I live in Southern Missouri, in a place that is called "The Ozarks." Marilyn and I have 2 sons and a wonderful daughter-in-law who is like a daughter to us. Anthony our youngest, attends college in Oklahoma. Lon and Julie presently live in Alabama. We also have a Pekignese called "Snickers." Just say the words: "Truck" or "Ice Cream" and he is right there, ready to go.

I work in the Agriculture/Farm Industry and I have a B.A in Business & Farm Management. I grew up on a farm here in Missouri and have raised Cattle, Sheep and Horses. I love Animals, and needless to say I live in the country. One of my greatest joys has been working with FFA.

Have You Prayed Today?

Figure 9.5 Many private websites contain – explicitly or more implicitly – verbal and visual statements about gender relations and role patterns, politics, religion, sexual orientation, leisure and sports preferences. They provide access to particular stories in people's lives as well as testifying more generally to cultural norms and values of broader groups of people in a certain temporal and spatial setting.

Figure 9.6 Private image collections and narratives on the web can be looked upon as displays of ideologies that have gained, and sometimes deliberately targeted, a broader and largely unknown audience. The home page on this website, and several others in the sample researched, was adapted soon after the tragic events of 9/11.

cultural norms and values of broader groups of people in a certain temporal and spatial setting (see Figure 9.6). Website technology has thus further expanded the opportunities for families' 'public relations' activities. Whereas the emphasis of the paper family album was on internal public relations (uniquely directed towards friends, family members and potential family members, like a kind of 'reputation management' to internal groups), the quest for displaying a favorable self-image now potentially expands to an uncontrollable number of external visitors.

However, not all family website owners consciously embrace or hail this opportunity. Some use the web merely or primarily to maintain contact with distant friends and relatives, or because it is cheap, fashionable and easy to update. They tend to take the 'public' implications of being on line as an unsought consequence rather than a sought opportunity for communicating their family values and broader views to a much larger audience. Some are actually quite aware that their website may well be boring to strangers. For example, a disclaimer in the sample researched reads:

'this is a very personal webpage I made for our family so please don't put it on any "worst-of-the-Web" sites!' So outsiders are welcomed or tolerated as an unsought consequence of using the public domain. Although today many options exist to restrict access to websites (see, e.g., http://radar.net, 'Show and Tell. Instant Picture Conversations with your favorite people and no-one else') these restrictions do have a price in that they obstruct the open communication with an unknown but possibly interested audience, a bonus that many family web owners still seem to value. Availability of new options to protect web space from uninvited visitors does not imply that all website owners are aware of them, or that people who are uneasy about the public character of their website will succumb to this fear, and forfeit the benefits of being connected to the world at large. Every web format seems to develop its own combination of functions, purposes and potential audiences, so publishing a website under an open access list of 'family websites' may for some groups still be the best means to connect to a broader audience interested in this particular format and usage.

The extended audiences are dealt with and referred to in various ways: they may simply be ignored, they may be warned and offered apologies for the website's trivial content, they may be directly addressed with communications related to personal values or stories, or they may be greeted as highly appreciated publics that need to be entertained (for example, see Figure 9.7) and invited to provide feedback. The functions of family websites are thus more diverse than those of the more traditional family album, a topic which I now move on to discuss.

4   Sought and unsought functions and effects of 'grassroots' web communication

4.1   Commercializing and prefabricating private stories

Many families are rapidly acquiring the skills to publish and promote their memories and testimonies on the web. However, those who lack the skills or time to create their own website from scratch are now also offered help by an increasing number of commercially operated family website operators (e.g., Photofun.com, Fam.com; see Figure 9.8). The evolution of the Internet in general is marked by a rapid move from media organizations alone providing online content, to a web infrastructure that allows non-media professionals (individuals and groups) to upload their own content in often highly visible places. This is particularly obvious in 'social software' or Web 2.0 offers, such as Flickr, YouTube, Wikipedia and Facebook.

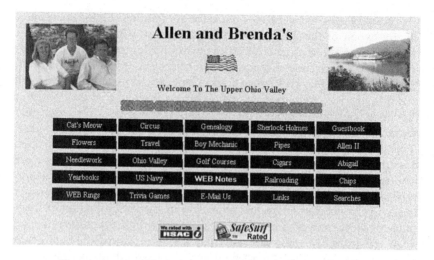

Figure 9.7 Quite a number of website owners invest much effort in trying to entertain visitors with all sorts of games and topics of general interest. These add-ons are supplementary means of getting in touch with, or raising and maintaining the interest of an extended audience. By increasing the degree of interactivity and offering a wide choice of topics, the website creator draws visitors into a happy and successful virtual site, and the visitors thus expose themselves to the creator's agenda.

The family-oriented web spaces allow anyone to publish (digitized) family snapshots and to create a personal (prefabricated) website for 'free' and in very little time. Not surprisingly, using such 'free' websites implies exposure to a sophisticated 'web' of commercial offerings, such as spam with 'good gift ideas' at Christmas, New Year or other topical purchasing times during the year, and invitations to spend money on self-disclosed occasions, such as a birth(day), marriage or other rites of transition dates, to make these highlights of family life even more memorable.

These family website templates tend to predefine and categorize events and occasions that are 'worth showing.' Implicitly they also embody a view about what should *not* be shown. Thus the structured effort to memorize and celebrate the past and share it with others at the same time fosters a kind of collective amnesia. Categorizing experiences through a predetermined structure ('given for free') potentially constitutes a very powerful tool for cultural reproduction, thus serving a societal status quo (provided that people really choose to surf one another's memories and that family websites gain prominence on the web). So, in

Figure 9.8 Prefabricated family websites. The market logic rules. 'There's never been an easier way to share your memories and showcase your life and personal pictures for all the world to see – snapshots of the new baby, special occasions like birthdays, parties, graduations and weddings, your new house or latest car. Your friends and family can view your websites anywhere and at any time' (promotional text from the Photofun.com website).

a way, these prefabricated websites potentially fulfill ideological as well as commercial purposes.

4.2 Spaces of self-expression, self-empowerment and consolation

However, by emphasizing possible propagandistic and commercial uses of family websites, I may create too bleak a picture of this interesting and complex phenomenon. Family websites are, to an extent, unique spaces of expression: places to voice opinions and views on a growing number of issues, and to bond with like-minded individuals and groups or people with similar characteristics (ethical, political, sexual or hobby-related). Or they can be used to exercise and display one's creative skills. Gaining

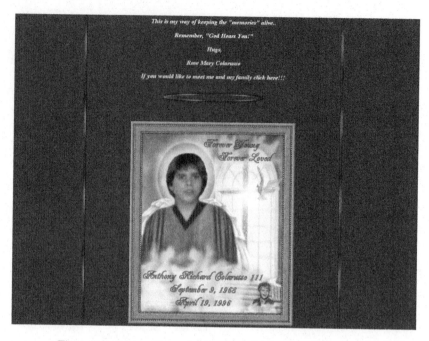

Figure 9.9 'You will not be forgotten.' The web may also become an electronic site of remembrance, a place to cope with one's personal grief and to communicate with an unknown audience, as an outcry of despair or as a way to contact individuals who have suffered similar tragic events.

access to media that target broader audiences used to be a very costly affair. Getting coverage in the classic media or producing folders or books was far beyond the reach of ordinary folk. However, a growing number of people now have access to the web, where they can share and promote their achievements, views and products at virtually no cost.

To some people, family websites may also become a means of dealing with a traumatic past, or of coping with mixed emotions. Communicating to an unknown audience in such a manner can help to bring some order to a chaotic life, or can help someone 'make sense' of a traumatic event (e.g., the loss of a child or partner: see Figure 9.9). This 'grave-dressing function' of private websites clearly shows that choosing the semi-public space of the web can in fact serve an inner as well as an outer purpose. Some people may not be seeking contact with others, but may merely want to create a shrine, a spot in cyberspace as a commemorative sign, as a means of literally giving a dramatic event a meaningful place in one's further life.

4.3   Motives and functions

Thus, family websites can indeed be looked at from very different angles. On occasion, we may be stunned by the amount of self-disclosure (e.g., love letters, intimate pictures, very personal testimonies) people are willing to present to the greedy eyes of an unknown audience of web surfers; or we may be truly amazed by the self-glorifying accounts people sometimes give of themselves; at other times we may be genuinely shocked by the expression of blatantly extremist viewpoints. However, we should never overlook the emancipatory, democratic, self-expressive and even therapeutic potential of such websites.

Further research is needed to provide a more thorough insight into this phenomenon. But apparently the perceived benefits of maintaining a private website seem to outweigh the possible harm or undesired consequences (forms of harassment and stalking, unsolicited use of private data, unwanted attention from suspicious individuals). It has become clear from this study that many family website owners, in addition to pursuing the more traditional purposes, actively seek to bond and connect with the outside world, albeit for a wide variety of reasons. Figure 9.10 groups some of the more common functions a family website may fulfill for its initiators. Most of the websites studied combined several functions, and these functions themselves tend to blend in with one another.

Inherited and emerging functions of web-based family communications

Functions shared with traditional family albums
- Preserve fond memories
- Celebrate family values and tighten family bonds
- Socialize newcomers
- Share experiences and views with remote family

New and emerging functions of web-based family albums
- Make new friends via mutual interests / hobbies / views on life
- Voice and propagate strongly kept (class- and culture-specific) values and views (regarding family, marriage, religious conviction, politics, etc.) to the outside world
- Exercise and show-off creativity and/or technical skills
- Advertise personal capabilities, sell products and services, seek new job opportunities
- Display pride in ancestry, get in contact with bearers of the same name to further family research
- Try to cope with traumatic events, to give the misfortune a 'place' in one's life and make way for new, more happy, experiences

---

Figure 9.10 Web-based family albums continue to foster and promote family-related values and functions, but also tend to entertain a growing set of new functions directed towards a broader audience. (L. Pauwels)

5   Scientific disclosure: issues of access and decoding

In the previous sections, I have discussed how even commercial restrictions imposed through templates for constructing family albums can reflect values through the topics included and omitted. I have illustrated the extraordinarily expressive nature of family websites, and the expanding social functions effected through these websites, over and above the functions common to traditional family albums. I have thus shown how family websites can both shape and communicate the cultural and social practices. I now turn to consider various methodological aspects relevant to researching family websites.

5.1   *Value, verity and authenticity of web constructs*

The web, in addition to its ability to bridge time and space, would appear to offer certain advantages over face-to-face contact. One can, for example, easily avoid particular threats associated with real-life encounters, like the danger of being assessed on the basis of first impressions and such 'irrelevancies' as looks, age, gender, class, and social skills. By presenting oneself in pictures on the web, one does not, of course, conceal one's 'looks' altogether, but one can at least control which pictures and poses are displayed. A number of relational or physical characteristics that may have a determining influence in face-to-face relations (e.g., shyness, stuttering) will have no or a lesser impact. Website owners have much greater control over how they present themselves. They can carefully construct a desired identity and leave out aspects they consider unwanted or possibly damaging.

Cheung (who in fact studied personal home pages rather than family websites) speaks of the 'emancipatory potential' of the private website in the sense that it 'insulates the author from direct embarrassment, rebuff and harassment' (Cheung, 2000: 48), forms of intimidation that are more likely to occur in face-to-face interaction, where humiliation, embarrassment or rejection may be experienced directly. So in this sense, the web may be considered a 'safer place' for some people; a place where they feel more 'at home' (Chandler and Roberts-Young, cited in Cheung, 2000: 48). This may also imply that the representational account of family life of those people, while more 'constructed,' may nevertheless be even more truthful and revealing than directly observable manifestations of family life presented to observers.

However, the fact of the matter is that we have no way of telling who is revealing more on a website than they would in a real-life encounter (which usually involves a smaller potential audience, but tends to be more directly confrontational), and who is painting a totally different, 'sanitized' picture of their family life. Self-censorship and impression management is in play both in real-life contacts and in representational accounts such as a website or a family picture, though the means employed differ greatly. If asked whether their website or family album presents a fairly accurate image of their family life, most respondents (at least those who are in control of the contents, so not necessarily all family members), would probably respond affirmatively, though we know from family album and website research that most present a very selective and 'brushed-up' account. Yet 'accurate' should not be understood here as 'complete,' but rather as 'not containing pertinent lies.' Omission is not practiced as a form of lying or deception. The fact that people want to present and remember only the good things they have experienced is not so strange: there is, after all, no reason why we should expect them to be objective and act as detached documentarians or chroniclers of their own lives. This issue remains important for researchers, however, in the interpretation of website representations and communications.

5.2   *Increased access*

Browsing and sharing private photo collections used to be an activity that was often confined to a rather narrow circle of close relatives or friends. Consequently, family researchers had very restricted access to other people's imagined memories and had to ground their research on a very limited number of painstakingly negotiated uses of private collections. Alternatively, they could rely on anonymous collections that often lacked essential references and offered no clues regarding contextual data. The booming phenomenon of online family narratives has dramatically changed this situation for the better. Vast numbers of websites from many different cultures (though admittedly the number of American sites by far exceeds that of any other nation) are just a mouse click away from researchers' hungry eyes.

Researchers seeking additional data can also benefit from invitations to get in touch with the webmaster via an email address or feedback area. Most family website owners whom I contacted in this way responded favorably to this more intrusive type of approach.

Still, we need to be aware of an inherent bias here: only the more extrovert (exhibitionist and 'escribist') families and individuals will choose to disclose their lives or better 'versions' of their lives to the web community. Thus the study of family photography per se, and private photography in a more literal sense, cannot shift its focus completely to these web-presented worlds.

5.3   *Increased expressiveness*

The fact that 'wired/networked' families and individuals have acquired better ways of transferring factual information (texts and pictures), of providing context, of adding emphasis and of giving shape to their values, aspirations and fantasies, has proven equally beneficial to the researcher. These qualities significantly contribute to a more adequate deciphering of cultural meanings, both factually and metaphorically/ expressively. The traditional paper-based family album could also have a 'multimedia' nature through the use of captions and the inclusion of various 'alien' materials, such as bills, entrance tickets, natural objects and written reports. But websites in general are much more complex constructions than the traditional photo album, and their more elaborate multimedia qualities provide a better context for interpretation and are at the same time culturally richer. The cultural decoder thus obtains a much clearer image of the values that the website producers are seeking to transfer and of the broader context in which all the data need to be interpreted. Online albums thus differ enormously from traditional paper-based family snapshots, which often lack context and, as a result, prove to be deceptively polysemous or even downright cryptic. But despite these advantages of family websites, decoding will always be a very demanding task, not least because analytical and theoretical approaches (content analysis, semiotics, iconography, rhetoric) have not been successfully integrated into a multifaceted tool. Moreover, methods used continuously fail to account for the significance of the new features of hybrid media such as the Internet.

5.4   *Decoding the hybrid form and content*

Many research questions with respect to the social and cultural significance of family communications through websites require detailed quantitative and qualitative analysis of the form, content and organization of text and imagery: the selection of moments and subjects, their posture, the interconnectedness with verbal elements and so on. The researcher should also develop a skill for interpreting the many different aspects of the design: choice of colors, typography, tunes, shapes – insofar as they may carry a symbolic (national, ethic, religious, political . . .) or metaphorical meaning – as well as the overall structure, including the navigational strategies, as these may ultimately also reveal a social hierarchy (e.g., power structures within the family: see Figure 9.11).

More difficult than identifying and categorizing visual and verbal content is identifying the point of view expressed throughout the website

Deb, Jason and Gabby, 1999.

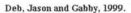

Jim, Jay and Brian, 1999

All of us, 1999

This is Deb, Gabby and me, 1995.

This is Deb and me at Ruston Police Department annual Awards Banquet in 1997

Figure 9.11 Making an inventory and classification of topics and issues that are covered (and to some extent of aspects and events that are not) in a selected set of websites is a good starting point for disclosing their rich cultural content. Also, the manner in which the information is structured may be highly relevant: What comes first? What stands out most prominently? Does this particular hierarchy of elements reflect, either explicitly or more implicitly, another, perhaps more fundamental, order of a social or cultural nature (e.g., gender roles, parent-child relations)?

(see Figure 9.12). Culturally decoding a website also implies scrutinizing what is systematically *not* shown or talked about, for these things may offer just as much evidence of certain value orientations as topics and events that feature prominently in family narratives. It also requires particular attention to the many different features (choices) and their particular combinations (i.e., both paradigmatic and syntagmatic analysis, the meaning of the choice of elements and the effects of their particular combination) (see further Pauwels, 2005a). Being complex cultural constructs, family websites also inevitably convey information that may not have been intended by the producer, and yet may prove extremely valuable to the attentive decoder (e.g., the implicit hierarchy between family members).

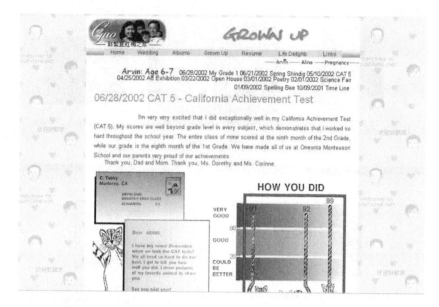

Figure 9.12 Whose 'voice' is (really) heard and for what purpose? And who is the intended or implied audience? The above web page exemplifies through a false point of view how an 'ideal child' is being 'constructed': the child is polite, thankful for his parents, grandparents and educators, and good school results are presented. While taking the point of view of the child, it is clearly one of the parents who is 'speaking' here.

Websites are in part intentionally constructed to communicate a certain 'image' of the family, which may or may not be far from their real 'identity.' Again, this will not necessarily undermine their value as a cultural data source, as long as the researcher is duly aware and continues to regard the information as 'expressions' of a varied nature rather than as facts.

5.5   Delineating 'family photography' and 'family websites' as fields of research: a term and a phenomenon under pressure

In a sense, 'family' photography, as a term describing a particular genre of images and practices, is increasingly a misnomer, since the visual online accounts of private life go far beyond the confines of the family, and the issues covered extend far beyond the domestic sphere, both spatially and in terms of values. Still, our research suggests that it is legitimate to say that the majority of websites that list themselves under the family category websites in Google and Yahoo still celebrate the family bond to an important degree.

One could opt to use the more general term 'private' photography, but this label may also be challenged in the light of the present trend to place private pictures in the public arena of the web. So there would seem to be an inherent paradox in the fact that 'private' photography should choose to employ such a public forum as the Internet. In a way, this paradox is resolved by the expanding and shifting social practice of this grassroots form of communication; people are becoming increasingly aware of the potentials of the new medium and of ways to take advantage of it. Notwithstanding their growing diversification, family websites or private websites are still a powerful format on the web, fulfilling distinct functions. But private websites are obviously not confined to groups of people such as families. Web spaces created by individuals ('personal home pages') or simply uploaded with their content (e.g., 'Profiles' in MySpace: see Figure 9.13) are much more widespread. Web logs (or 'blogs'), another type of 'user-generated website content' which began as personal online diaries, have, in a similar fashion to family websites, expanded in scope, even to the extent that they have sometimes developed into alternative media, commenting upon information that mainstream media provide and on occasions even becoming the leading source of a story, which the mainstream mass media subsequently try to pick up. As blogs come in many shapes and for many purposes, (under names such as photoblogs, videoblogs or vlogs, warblogs, travel blogs, fashion blogs, corporate blogs), some forms blend with family websites both in form and goals. Today, recognizing the growing importance of these popular expressions, mainstream media, corporations and politicians try to connect to the culture of blogging for outreach and opinion forming.

These constantly evolving 'user-generated content' formats typically combine text, images, elaborate design features and sometimes complex connections and links to other data sources on the web. Some types partially emulate the functions of family websites, of which they sometimes become a part (so-called 'Slog' or 'website log').

There is some expectation that the novelty value of blogging and other very time-consuming online practices will wear off. This was illustrated by family websites we surveyed, whose owners did not respond to the survey. Many of these sites had not been updated for several years, and so appeared to be abandoned by their creators, possibly because the task was too time-consuming, or the owners had lost interest, or taken on an alternative challenge.

However, web spaces fuelled and entertained by private persons, whatever form they take in future, will remain particularly rich and

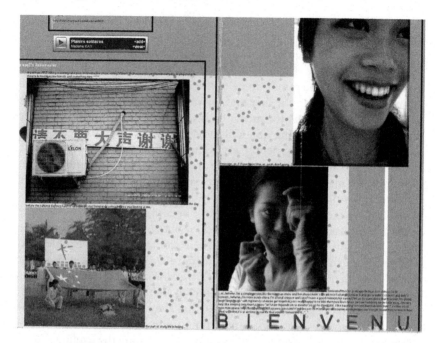

Figure 9.13. A sophisticated personal 'profile' (hosted by Blog. myspace) containing numerous references to the physical and the mental world of the private content provider: her life history, hobbies, favorite music, films and books, an elaborate description of her circle of friends, her idols, dreams, anxieties . . .

interesting phenomena on the Internet, a platform which continues to evolve rapidly both in a technological and a socio-cultural sense. Such websites will continue to offer elaborate and culturally expressive accounts of individuals and small groups in their root setting and beyond.

The rapid development and adoption of technology is bringing 'moving images,' including those from the domestic sphere, to the fore. Video accounts of the private life and of private views on the broader world have become a new hype through hosted video blogging applications such as the immensely popular YouTube. Both the visual products that are being posted to such web spaces and the discourse that develops around them provide fascinating material on how individuals choose to disclose themselves to the web community, and argue their points on a variety of subjects in vivid interactions. All these applications and options further amalgamate into increasingly hybrid web spaces that try to do many things for many purposes involving many types of audiences, posing unrivalled challenges to social scientists.

6 Conclusion

This chapter examined the impact of digital technology on the way in which family pictures are presented and consumed today. Rooting private photography in its analogue and digital past, where it mainly served a 'socialization' and 'integration' function confined to next of kin and propagating mainly domestic values to a fairly secluded audience, I have addressed the issue of family ('home-mode') photography on the web, with respect to the consequences of this shift at a social, cultural and social scientific level. Whereas the social functions and practices of private photography hardly seem to have changed as a result of the shift from the analogue (silver-based) to the digital image, from the form and content of many hundreds of family websites, there seems to be a very significant effect of going on line, approximating to a genuine sociocultural swing. The expressive means have increased dramatically and the practice has moved into the public or semi-public realm, catering for an anonymous mass of web surfers. Stories and functions seem to have expanded and changed and include functions such as making new friendships beyond the family sphere, often by exploring mutual interests, acquiring a voice to relay political and social views, and promoting skills and achievements to potential customers or employers. Industry has also rapidly and successfully moved to appropriate or colonize this 'private' aspect of the web.

Private image collections and narratives on the web can thus be looked upon as displays of ideologies that have gained, and sometimes deliberately targeted, a broader audience. These ideological discourses have broadened in scope as a result of the new social setting. They often contain implicit or explicit statements regarding politics and social issues, religion and so forth to an – in principle at least – boundless and largely anonymous audience. To the extent that these public displays of private ideologies are indeed visited by an increasing number of people (which remains to be seen), this phenomenon may develop into a significant tool for cultural propaganda (be it to serve cultural reproduction or to advocate change). However, I have also touched upon the democratic, emancipatory, self-expressive and healing potential of this very hybrid online phenomenon.

Family websites, as one of the recent evolutions in family media communications, are among the more 'normative' sites on the web. They present a fascinating area of research into cultural change and reproduction, and the complex role of technology in those processes at the 'grassroots' level. This, of course, implies new challenges (e.g., an adequate decoding of all aspects of these hybrid constructions to the cultural meaning) and new research opportunities (expanded access and increased 'expressive' means) for the researcher that merit further exploration. Technology continues to interact with the social practice of photography and its social scientific study.

7   References

Boerdam, J. and W. Oosterbaan Martinius (1978) 'Het Fotogenieke van het Samenleven (part 1 and 2).' *Amsterdams Sociologisch Tijdschrift* 5(1), June: 3–36, and (5) 2, October: 301–25.

Bourdieu, P. (ed.) (1978) *Un art moyen: essai sur les usages sociaux de la photographie*, 2nd edn. Paris, Les Éditions de Minuit (first edition 1965).

Cheung, C. (2000) 'A Home on the Web: Presentations of Self on Personal Homepages.' In: D. Gauntlett (ed.) *Web.Studies: Rewiring Media Studies for the Digital Age*. London: Arnold, pp. 43–51.

De Haas, W. (1975) *De Fotografie in Sociologisch Perspectief, bijdrage tot een sociologie der techniek*, PhD dissertation, Rijksuniversiteit Leiden.

Freund, G. (1980) *Photography & Society*. London: Gordon Fraser. (Original: *Photographie et Société*, 1974, France.)

Garner, R., M. Gillingham and Y. Zhao (2003) 'Writing photo captions for the Web.' *First Monday* 8(9). Available from: www.firstmonday.org/issues/issue8_9/garner/index.html [accessed May 14, 2007].

Lee, R. M. (2000) *Unobtrusive Methods in Social Research*. Buckingham/Philadelphia, PA: Open University Press.

Mitchell, W. J. (1992) *The Reconfigured Eye: Visual Truth in the Post-Photographic Era*. Cambridge, MA: The MIT Press.

Musello, C. (1979) 'Family Photography.' In: J. Wagner (ed.) *Images of Information: Still Photography in the Social Sciences*. Beverly Hills, CA/London: Sage, pp. 101–18.

Pauwels, L. (1979) *De Fotografie Sociologisch Belicht: 1. De geschiedenis van de fotografie als een samenspel van sociale en technologische ontwikkelingen en 2. Aanzetten tot een sociologie van het foto-amateurisme* (unpublished Master's thesis), University of Antwerp.

Pauwels, L. (1994) 'De Betekenis van het Banale, familiefotografie als sociale praktijk en sociologische databron.' *Tijdschrift voor Sociologie* 15(1): 5–24.

Pauwels, L. (2002a) 'Communicating Desired Pasts: On the Digital Construction of Private Histories: What Is Really at Stake?' *Journal of Visual Literacy* 22, Autumn: 166–44.

Pauwels, L. (2002b) 'Families on the Web.' In: D. Newman *Sociology: Exploring the Architecture of Everyday Life*, 4th edn. Thousand Oaks, CA: Pine Forge, pp. 231–35.

Pauwels, L. (2005a) 'Websites as Visual and Multimodal Cultural Expressions: Opportunities and Issues of Online Hybrid Media Research,' *Media, Culture & Society* 27(4): 604–13.

Pauwels, L. (2005b) 'De Private Fotografie als Sociaal-cultureel Fenomeen en Wetenschappelijke Databron: van familiealbum tot webstek.' In: L. Pauwels and J.-M. Peters *Denken over Beelden: Theorie en Analyse van het Beeld en de Beeldcultuur.* Leuven/Voorburg: Acco, pp. 105–61.

Reis, G. (2004) *Digital image integrity.* Available from: www.adobe.com/digitali-mag/pdfs/digital_image_integrity.pdf [accessed May 14, 2007]

Wakeford, N. (2000) 'New Methodologies: Studying the Web.' In: D. Gauntlett (ed.) *Web Studies: Rewiring Media Studies for the Digital Age.* London: Arnold, pp. 31–41.

Weare, C., and W. Y. Lin (2000) 'Content Analysis of the World Wide Web: Opportunities and Challenges.' *Social Science Computer Review* 18(3): 272–92.

10 A visual study of corporate culture: the workplace as metaphor

---

1 Visual aspects of corporate culture

1.1 Corporations as (sub-)cultures

Corporate culture has become a trendy word that is often used and misused in management literature to explain the success or failure of a company. Indeed, the concept of culture is a very relative one that is certainly not confined to national borders or ethnic groups. In fact, wherever one can distinguish an arrangement of material and immaterial achievements resulting from and in turn influencing the ways of thinking and doings of a group of people, the term 'culture' can be applied (Pepper, 1994).

In this way organizations, too, may be thought of as (sub-)cultures. For, while to a great extent the basic values and norms, beliefs and so on of society at large remain active, individuals entering an organization to work there for eight or more hours a day are being brought into a particular setting, of which they literally are becoming a 'part.' 'Dressed for the occasion,' the employees or members of the organization immediately, without giving it much thought, emulate the specific expectations, norms, values and beliefs (towards personnel, customers, suppliers and the outside world), formal and informal codes of conduct, ways of sanctioning and rewarding, as enacted by other members. To individuals who are well 'socialized,' culture seems not just a learned, and thus a conventional and arbitrary, way of thinking and doing, but a 'natural' way of thinking and acting, which also creates expectations towards other people's ways of behaving, whether or not they are members of the same (sub-)culture. Other ways of living are judged only from one's own perspective, and if others significantly deviate from it, they are considered weird, unprofessional, unreliable, ill-adjusted, inefficient or in some other way inadequate.

Newcomers are either socialized (acculturated) to an acceptable degree, or if they do not manage to comply with the existing ways of thinking and behaving, are soon bound to leave the company. Some corporate cultures prove to be very strong in spreading their influence

220

over almost everything that members do – even in their free time – while other organizations demand from their members little more than to carry out their job or role as they see fit or according to very limited task-oriented instructions. Culture within an organization is more and more being recognized as an important factor in its survival and success.

Corporate cultures in part explicitly communicate their norms and values (via vision and marketing statements, induction programs, advertisements, annual reports, safety or quality campaigns, all sorts of written procedures), but also they exercise their influence through a variety of less explicit, but equally important, (visible) channels and practices.

1.2   Visual metaphors

A corporation's culture to a significant degree discloses itself in visually observable behavior and in the construction and use of the material environment. The building as a whole and space within private offices, communal workplaces, corridors, elevators, cafeterias and lobbies, are imbued with specific kinds of meaning.

Through studying these cultural products and other material traces we can acquire significant information about aspects of a corporation's culture which otherwise often remain intangible or inaccessible.

A particular floor in a building may consist of a series of private offices (with transparent glass walls or completely hidden from an outside view), or large communal rooms with rows of desks neatly aligned or reworked as a 'landscaped' area. These spaces may display a very uniform and standardized look or present considerable diversity. Variations in the corporate environment may be read as visual indicators offering relevant information regarding such issues as social relations and control, status, the organization's identity and desired image. The visual environment may reveal some interesting information about the organizational culture, such as the respect for the individual, the personal space (literally and metaphorically) one is entitled to, the opportunities for social contacts and exchange of information, the nature of the work (confidentiality, required concentration), the overall work atmosphere and organization (work flow, ways of cooperation), the trust or distrust the organization has in its employees, the degree and nature of exercised control, the role of hierarchy and status, and its focus on efficiency, productivity, confidentiality or safety.

While the 'look of things' may seem to offer some apparent clues about the organizational culture, the interpretation of these factual pieces of information requires extreme caution. Though the idea that 'form follows function' may prove fruitful to analyze the environment, modern corporations increasingly recognize the value of the physical environment as visual metaphor. So hired professionals (e.g., interior designers) and laypeople alike are encouraged to create through the visual environment a 'desired image,' which may or may not coincide with the corporation's identity (its real-life strengths, weaknesses and particularities). Service companies, in particular, strongly feel the need to express in one way or another the qualities of their intangible 'products.' In advertisements, and also through the visual corporate environment, they try to communicate their efficiency, reliability, innovativeness, creativity, superior technical ability, client centeredness, or some other invisible qualities, to build or maintain their desired image. Within the visual landscape of the corporation, design, office decoration and in general the look of things are particularly well-suited channels to convey ideas both to members of the organization and to the outside world. The environment is often deliberately constructed to convey the same message concerning the intangible services which the organization provides, whether in line with reality or not.

So while the look of things may often be revealing, by the same token it may prove deceptive, or at least may send many at first sight contradictory messages.

A very bureaucratic, hierarchic culture, for example, will certainly not lose its strongly hierarchic approach in favor of a more progressively managed organization just by moving to a newly designed building or by changing the dress code. On the other hand, the visual environment allows the testing of a number of proclaimed cultural norms and values against their lived reality. Strict formal rules and principles (safety rules, dress codes, confidentiality measures) may in reality be hardly observed or even completely contradicted by what can be seen (no adequate use of safety equipment, casual wear, unlocked drawers and heaped-up desktops, etc.) and thus point at the degrees of freedom of the 'verbalized' culture. As such, a visual approach to culture helps to correct the very biased tendency of mainstream sociology to focus predominantly on verbalized behavior instead of looking at what is really happening. A culture, for example, may have changed quite significantly before its written rules and regulations have.

1.3   The role of design and different management views

Looking carefully presupposes some kind of theory. Reading the corporate environment may benefit considerably from organizational theory, which will help to open our eyes to certain visual appearances and allow those appearances to be placed in a broader vision of management and organizations. But again, these theoretical frameworks should not be handled as fixed schemata for which participant observers collect clues that confirm this or that vision; rather, such frameworks should help them to stimulate critical interaction between new data and data collected so far.

If an organization at first sight seems characterized by efficiency or a bureaucratic approach, one is easily tempted to read all signs to comply with that impression. However, most of the time reality is far more complex. Different visions on management and human nature may exist simultaneously within an organization and even within the same person. The past is never fully eradicated by the present, so tokens of different conflicting visions may continue to exist next to each other.

The expression of 'self' in general conflicts with the principles of scientific management in a strict sense, which advocates standardization to the highest degree for the purpose of productivity. It also seems to conflict with the aim to display a consistent corporate image. Nevertheless, more recent visions on management acknowledge the importance of social relations and personal well-being with regard to increasing or maintaining productivity or ensuring the continuity of operations. However, the tension between allowing individuality and sociability to leave its traces in the environment, and maintaining a consistent corporate image cannot be fully resolved.

Design plays a crucial role in creating an overall friendly atmosphere, thus reducing the urge to 'humanize,' or customize (personalize) the environment. Apart from nice-looking office furniture, providing standardized decorations with a limited range of variation is another way of creating a relaxed, un-factory-like atmosphere while at the same time ensuring a consistent professional look. Some companies provide a middle-of-the-road kind of artwork – which is carefully selected not to offend anyone, but by the same token is often not particularly pleasing to anybody either – to humanize the environment.

Designers seem to have done a good job in trying to turn the harsh industrial-looking office space into a colorful, well-lit and ventilated environment, thus placing the needs of the individual at the center; however, such readily made deductions may prove deceptive and even somewhat naïve. I tend to agree with Forty when he says that 'management aims remained at the root of all design for the office' (Forty, 1986: 155). Nevertheless, we should not overlook among other things the creative designers' own aspirations, which, as is often the case with advertising artists, may not fully serve the predetermined purpose of the commissioning company or target audience. The urge to be an artist may at times seriously conflict with the demand to think in a business-like way or with an explicit purpose in mind. Again, a qualified view is needed here. Also, one should keep in mind that rules that govern the semi-public space of the internal and external corporate environment constitute codes that may differ significantly from those governing the private sphere. Therefore, one needs to be careful not to simply read the signs in a predetermined sense and remain blind to differences and inconsistencies, which should urge the researcher to continue the complex task of decoding corporate culture through its sometimes ambiguous visual manifestations.

1.4   Display of status and hierarchy

Status and rank are often particularly well-defined aspects within corporations. Also, these aspects tend to be very visual; status and hierarchy typically need to be 'shown.' Many companies have strict procedures and rules for granting status attributes. Office space may be defined by a number of square meters per job level. Written procedures often clearly state who is entitled to have a private office, carpet, curtains, personalized stationery, a secretary (or two), a company car (and what type exactly), a private parking place and so on.

Apart from those standard items and issues, a great number of items are employed to underline certain achievements or valued memberships: certificates, plates and other artifacts with appropriate inscriptions that can be put on the desk or hung on the walls of the office. Such status symbols and other tokens of 'being special' are used to impress external visitors and members of the organization alike. They regulate social relations in as much as they externalize a person's responsibility, value and success within the corporate culture. They serve as indicators of the 'distance' that needs to be observed and of the amount of respect to which an individual is entitled.

Personal customizing of the environment has often clashed with the need for efficiency, which has been a particularly strong drive in corporate cultures since Taylor (1911) laid down his principles of 'scientific management,' and has also come into conflict with the need to demonstrate hierarchy and status. 'Exceptional reasons were found to justify executives having different tools and material from clerks,' Forty points out, 'although their basic activity in time and motion study terms – sitting reading or writing at a desk – was exactly the same' (Forty, 1986: 128). So higher-level employees often have larger desks, more comfortable chairs, more luxurious desktop finishing (solid wood rather than metal or synthetic materials), more square meters of space, more storage capacity, and more sophisticated office equipment, while strictly speaking they often have less need for it to execute their job efficiently.

Some corporations today, responding to modern management ideas and values within society at large, try hard to reduce the material and symbolic gap between roles at the top and bottom of the hierarchy and pursue a certain amount of egalitarianism in look. The more uniform look of things may serve distinct purposes: it may indeed point to a genuine striving within that culture to reduce differences among ranks, but it equally can be used to cover up the real inequalities in power, privilege and remuneration. Also, uniformity of look is often primarily used to display a consistent professional image to the outside world. Dress codes, as well as standardized design furniture and office environments, may fulfill a crucial role in this effort.

Even within corporate cultures that explicitly propagate or strive for a more egalitarian approach, new items tend to emerge that serve to express differences between people inside the organization. Status and hierarchy constantly seem to demand their tokens to maintain some kind of order in the corporate society.

2   Case study: visual symbolism in the Brussels head office of a Norwegian multinational chemical company

Each of the issues touched upon above will be further elaborated on and exemplified through a series of pictures that were taken during an exploratory study about the visual dimensions of the corporate culture of the Brussels office of a Norwegian chemical multinational. The researcher-produced visual data were made during a couple of weekends in the presence of a manager of that company, who also provided useful background information, which helped to interpret the images. If such visual data gathering is done after office hours or during the weekend – as was the case here – one should take into account that only 'overnight' items remain: some personal, sensitive and/or expensive things may be locked away at the end of a working day.

The observations and assumptions that will follow are based on a careful analysis of the images, but they are also inspired by and grounded in a long-standing research interest and many years of first-hand experiences (participant observation) with several multinational companies (Pauwels, 1996).

2.1   Entering a corporate culture: front stage and backstage

The lobby and reception area may immediately offer significant information to observant visitors about the culture they just stepped into

Figure 10.1 Lobby and reception area: the visitor's outlook (L. Pauwels)
The design and decoration of the corridor, hall and reception desk seem directed towards displaying a professional image through a sober application of good-quality materials, greenery and art (a statue of a sower, which subtly refers to the company's main line of business: fertilizers for the agricultural industry).

Figure 10.2 Lobby and reception area: the receptionist's outlook (L. Pauwels)
Shown here is the very limited personal space of the receptionist from an angle visitors do not normally see. All personal items as well as the security and communication equipment are kept out of view of visitors. The imbalance between tokens of corporate professionalism and the very limited opportunities for expression of self can be clearly felt.

(Figures 10.1 and 10.2). Does this space emanate hospitality, indifference or distrust? Does the emphasis lie on physical safety or on service to the customer? In what ways does one seek to make a positive impression on the visitor: is this accomplished by exhibiting products, art or technological gadgets?

2.2 Personal preferences and departmental sub-cultures

Companies in varying degrees have to negotiate between permitting their personnel to express their individuality (through personal items, appearance) and maintaining a consistent corporate image, which implies more uniformity and standardization. If there is some leeway, as is often the case, considerable differences may be found with regard to the personal customization of the environment within the same company (Figures 10.3 to 10.6). These differences can be attributed to the

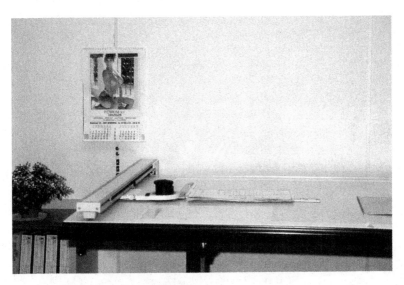

Figure 10.3 Technical / drawing office (L. Pauwels)
Significant differences were found regarding what was deemed appropriate to display in different departments within the same company: erotic calendars and posters (displaying both female and male nudity) were only to be found in this part of the office building.

Figures 10.4 and 10.5 Chartering department (L. Pauwels)

A typical feature of both the chartering and the commercial depart-ment was the presence of flags and world maps. Apart from being instrumental in some way, these items could also be interpreted meta-phorically as the striving or ambition to conquer the world with the products of the company.

Figure 10.6 Purchasing Manager's office (L. Pauwels)
Some people eschew mixing private spheres of interest with professional ones, while others feel the urge to overtly or in more subtle way express their personal preferences and interests in their work environment. The Purchasing Manager of this company clearly conveys his passion for Ferrari cars (but clearly shows a lack of trust in mankind, since all his Ferrari replicas were tightly fixed to the cupboards and shelves with bolts). His management rank entitles him to a separate office and to the liberty of personalizing it to a certain extent.

personal preferences of an employee but also depend, as became clear in the receptionist environment, on the amount of freedom that is granted to individuals, based on their role and position, on the culture of a department and on the public character of the space in question (more 'public' usually means more controlled).

2.3   *Managing impressions*

Tokens of physical activities and work-related items (calendars, office equipment, work schedules, piles of paper files) so abundantly present in the rank-and-file employees' and lower management office spaces, tend to disappear as individuals climb to the upper end of the hierarchy. A certain detachment from concrete work seems to be created through an environment where expensive materials and artifacts (paintings, sculptures, posh gadgets) are used to construct a

Figure 10.7 Chartering department (L. Pauwels)
Apart from the more explicit status symbols, a host of other items are used in an ongoing process of 'impression management': white boards in private offices are often used as personal billboards showing, for instance, complex schemes, lists of names of international contacts, snapshots with important people, an impressive list of things to do and so forth. Thus ultimately these boards function as more than an instrumental aid, in as much as they serve to emphasize the importance and skills of the owner.

privileged – often semi-domestic – environment that signifies the superiority and power of the occupant (Figures 10.7 to 10.13).

The display of family pictures is fairly common in all ranks of the organization, varying from hastily pinned-up snapshots to neatly framed studio-posed pictures on cupboards, walls or as computer wallpapers. These displays of the private world may to some extent be considered as another way to impress visitors and colleagues, by testifying that also in private life one is respected, responsible and successful.

2.4   Conclusion: looking for the bigger picture through data and method triangulation

This very modest project epitomizes the 'mimetic mode' (Chapter 5) in visual research. The visual data were produced using a standardized

Figure 10.8 Desk of the Executive Secretary to the President and the
Vice-President Finance (L. Pauwels)
    The desk of this high-ranked secretarial position displays many job-
related items in an orderly manner. An overloaded desk may signify a
number of contrasting things: importance of the job, energy, work
overload, inability to cope with work pressure or lack of organizational
skills.

shooting script and the camera was handled in such a way that it refrained
as much as possible from creating any 'additional meaning' (expression).
However, as noted before, every position taken by the camera/researcher
implies a 'point of view' – in a literal and metaphysical sense – which
highlights certain aspects at the expense of others. Alternative
approaches – such as using these pictures in an interview with different
members of the organization, or asking members of different job levels
and departments to produce their own visual accounts of their work
environment and experience – could complement this mainly 'etic' (or
'well-informed outsider') perspective with a more 'emic' ('insider perception and experience') inspired view.
    In conclusion, looking at the visual manifestations of organizations
may offer a unique path to interpreting essential aspects of the culture of
a company. Many written and unwritten, spoken and unspoken norms
and values indeed will in very subtle ways 'materialize' in visually

Figures 10.9 and 10.10 Office of the Vice-President, Technology and Production (L. Pauwels)

In this office, the good-quality furniture and wall decorations clearly indicate the inhabitant's hierarchical position. The 'sub-top' positions still need to express their commitment to the company and emphasize their particular role in it, so often references to the trade are made through large color plates depicting an aerial view of the manufacturing plant, a process scheme or work flow or an elegant display of product samples, as is the case here.

Figure 10.11 President's office, view from behind the desk (L. Pauwels)
Here we have definitely entered the realm of the symbolic, which today is to be felt even in the most functional-looking office environment. The spaciousness and the physical layout of the president's office emphasize the inhabitant's top position. At the same time some clues to the consultative structure are offered (the table in front of the president's desk could suggest frequently held staff meetings, whereas early twentieth-century pictures of managing directors' offices (e.g., Forty, 1986: 144) often contained, apart from the inhabitant's desk and chair, only one extra chair for the (un)lucky person summoned). The extensive well-designed environment needs to stimulate a broad vision and at the same time serve as a metaphor of this 'breadth of vision.'

observable phenomena (practices, artifacts, erosion measures, behavior). Also, many formal rules and regulations or loudly acclaimed principles may be checked for their compliance in the day-to-day reality of the organization.

Nevertheless, we should not promote the environment or other visual manifestations to the most important shaping or reflecting constituent of corporate culture: first of all, because the visual environment and its depictions are by nature ambiguous and thus difficult to decode, and secondly, because visual appearances may be deliberately used

Figure 10.12 President's office, rear wall and cupboard (L. Pauwels)

Reading the titles of this carefully positioned row of books (eighteen in total) reveals remarkably well the top manager's professional role model, national identity and pride: an English book on Norway, two books in Norwegian language (business subjects), three books on the company's business sector (agricultural chemicals), one on environmental concerns, an alumni directory, one book with a blank spine, two books on (EU) legislation and of course an obligatory selection (seven books) of bestseller management literature and reports.

to communicate a desired 'image' rather than truly reflect an organization's identity. So, a myriad of reasons may account for 'the way things look'; it would be reductionist and naïve to cling to one set of observations or to a limited number of theoretical frameworks. Finally, it should be clear that not all significant cultural aspects have identifiable visual referents; quite some aspects remain literally out of sight. It is therefore essential to validate, confront and supplement visual information with as many other visual and non-visual data sources as possible (interviews, statistical information, personnel newsletters, office memos), for 'culture,' even in the more confined setting of an organization, is never a simple and straightforward phenomenon.

Figure 10.13 Executive boardroom (L. Pauwels)
The executive boardroom is often considered the 'sanctum' of the corporation, the 'official' decision center (even if in reality decisions are made elsewhere: e.g., on a golf course). Meeting in this room significantly adds to the importance of the event. This particular boardroom imitates, in a rather awkward and somewhat superficial way, a high-class living room: the ceiling lights, for instance, have not been replaced by a more classic-looking type of lighting. The lampshades, wooden chairs, table, paintings, and antique clock abruptly and purposefully mark the difference from the other very modernly designed rooms of the office building.

3   References

Forty, A. (1986) *Objects of Desire: Design & Society from Wedgwood to IBM*. New York: Pantheon Books.

Pauwels, L. (1996) *De Verbeelde Samenleving: Camera, Kennisverwerving en Communicatie*. Leuven/Apeldoorn: Garant.

Pepper, G. (1994) *Communicating in Organizations: A Cultural Approach*. New York: McGraw-Hill.

Taylor, F. W. (1911) *The Principles of Scientific Management*. New York/London: Harper & Brothers.

11 Health communication in South Africa: a visual study of posters, billboards and grassroots media

1 Message design codes: the cultural challenge

Health promotion materials should, both visually and verbally, 'talk the language of the receivers.' This implies more than simply using a language they can understand (e.g., in a South African context, English or Afrikaans or any of the indigenous tongues – Ndebele, Northern Sotho, Sotho, Swazi, Tswana, Tsonga, Venda, Xhosa and Zulu – and culturally specific pictorial languages); it must also be a language with which the receivers feel comfortable, and which has few or no negative connotations for them. After all, both a language as a whole and specific phrasing or usage may detract from the message for the target group. All visual and verbal elements of media messages must meet certain criteria of readability and legibility. The criterion of 'legibility' demands that both the visual and the verbal elements should be easy to discern given certain viewing conditions (i.e., elements should be large enough, the right color combinations should be used to increase visibility, an easy-to-read type font and size should be chosen and the layout should 'steer the eye'). The issue of 'readability' is much more complex than legibility (or visibility) since it pertains to what extent a text can be understood in all of its aspects (syntax, meaning of words, style).

Pictures and other visual representations, in particular the more 'realistic' ones, are often considered to constitute a universal language and are therefore widely regarded as ideal forms of communication in multicultural and less-literate environments. However, while pictorial information may indeed serve a crucial role in intercultural and development communication and education, it would be unwise to think that pictorial information is easily comprehensible and invariably effective. Pictorial materials are, often in unacknowledged ways, very much culturally coded, and their uses, too, can be highly culturally specific. Pictures and visual aspects of communication also constitute a cultural language that to a large extent needs to be learned (for an overview and extensive bibliography on this subject see: de Lange, 2000).

236

The problem with (visual) codes is that they are often taken for granted. The anthropological and development communications literature is replete with famous intercultural misunderstandings (Zimmer and Zimmer, 1978; Fuglesang, 1982) occasioned by this neglect. The use of perspective, scale, color, shape, level of detail, the suggestion of motion in a static medium, the depiction of processes and of cause-and-effect relations may all lead to potentially serious misinterpretations (Brouwer, 1995).

Generally speaking, the use of color may, for instance, be more attractive and informative than black-and-white images, yet color is particularly culturally specific and may invoke powerful and sometimes unanticipated associations. Epskamp (1992: 88) found that, in some cultures, dark colors are associated with ill-health. He also refers to an unsuccessful anti-conception campaign in India: its failure was due in part to a wrong choice of color (light blue) for the packaging of contraceptive pills, as this was associated with constipation (Brouwer, 1995: 19). Color can distract, and using it sparingly may confuse people: a black-and-white drawing of hands being washed under a tap, with the water colored bright blue to signify it being fresh and healthy (conventional sign), may be quite confusing to people who decode the message in an iconic way and expect water to be blue (Brouwer, 1995: 20).

Even relatively simple media, such as those dealt with hereafter, namely posters and billboards, involve many pertinent considerations and choices with regard to how to properly address the audience. All of the media and message design parameters need to be carefully considered in the light of their cultural implications and effectiveness in conveying what needs to be communicated. Involving culturally knowledgeable people is therefore of the utmost importance. Many errors can be avoided by involving local artists, designers, and the like, who will almost automatically, unwittingly even, apply the appropriate codes. Nevertheless, explicit and thorough research is still needed to complement and further explore this expertise, since such local collaborators, too, will inevitably have a limited cultural and disciplinary scope and practice.

2   Health promotion posters: the medium and the message

In regions where large portions of the population cannot – or cannot sufficiently – be reached through the classic mass media (newspaper, TV and radio, the Internet), or where different cultures and languages are living together, well-designed and properly displayed posters can prove to be a vital medium for health communications. Because of their relative inexpensiveness, they can be produced in small quantities for different purposes in different versions. Well-designed health promotion posters must meet a multitude of criteria: they must provide clear information; address personal, social and cultural concerns; attract and hold attention; enhance message retention; convey an appropriate level of realism; avoid offending the target audience and other viewers; and trigger the intended kind of response (see research by Rhodes and Wolitski on instructional videotapes on AIDS knowledge and attitudes, cited by Markova and Power, 1992: 123). However, an important additional challenge in the case of poster campaigns is that they should be displayed in the right places – in other words, in places where the target groups can be reached and where they have enough time to take in the message (e.g., public spaces, waiting rooms, clinics).

2.1   Examining three health-related posters

Below, three posters will be analyzed in more detail to illustrate the complexity of meeting the challenge of communicating health-related matters in a culturally effective way. These posters were collected during visits (2001–03) to several hospitals and clinics in the Free State in South Africa. I am grateful to Professor H. Van Rensburg and his staff from the Health Research and Development Centre of the University of the Free State for facilitating the collection and production of the data for this chapter.

2.1.1   Analysis of the 'Tekens en Simptome' poster

The 'Tekens en Simptome' ('Signs and Symptoms') poster (Figure 11.1) is clearly intended for wide distribution and is meant to attract the attention of large groups of people, since anyone may be infected by TB. Two different messages are skillfully combined here without creating confusion: the first relates to the early recognition of the various symptoms of TB, while the second propagates the DOTS-philosophy ('directly observed treatment short-course') and the importance of compliance if one is diagnosed with the illness.

The use of drawings rather than photographs may, in this particular case, foster better understanding, because it allows a graphic simplification of persons and situations. Photographs can sometimes be too detailed, providing unnecessary and therefore possibly distracting information. However, it also enables the use of codes that are confined to drawing (e.g., short dashes to indicate spit particles that are expelled during coughing or when producing sputum for diagnostic purposes). However, extreme caution should be observed when applying such drawing codes. Research in Rwanda (Albrecht et al., 1990: 151) has identified some serious problems in relation to such a poster image of a coughing boy, as the abundantly

Figure 11.1 'Tekens en Simptome' poster (Department of Health, South Africa)

depicted spit particles were decoded as solid objects (i.e., they were seen as a bundle of hay coming from the boy's mouth).

In the case of this poster, the target group is also assumed to be able to recognize that each of the depicted symptoms is a possible and sufficient indication in its own right, rather than part of a process or just one of several symptoms that need to occur concurrently for the patient to seek medical help. The targeted individuals are also assumed to be able to correctly interpret the spatial and temporal divide (marked by the darker frame) between the visualized symptoms at the top of the poster and the image of a person receiving medicine from a health worker below.

In this instance, the use of visual images may on the one hand make the poster more widely applicable, yet on the other make it appeal to a more specific audience – by depicting a person of a certain age, wearing specific clothing, belonging to a particular class or gender and so on. In other words, while specific images may arouse the interest of certain groups, they may – for entirely comparable reasons – cause others to feel the message does not concern them.

The visual specificity of visuals – and this applies even more so to photographic images – may be both a strength and a weakness. Visuals can provide a more detailed description and convey a sense of verity. However, if they are ill considered, they may also foster a sense of exclusion, merely distract or even cause offense. Representing a diachronic process, such as an evolution over time or a cause-and-effect relation, is always difficult to achieve with a static medium like a poster and in a cultural context, where the conveyor of the message is uncertain about the exact level of visual literacy of the audience. Using a sequence of pictures to convey the message that 'if you are ill and you take these pills you will get better' may, for example, be read in reverse order or it may be interpreted as a synchronic event, so that taking the medicine is actually associated with becoming ill rather than being cured.

2.1.2   Analysis of the 'Patient-centered care' poster

Health communication campaigns may target a variety of actors, not just people at risk. In the case of the 'Patient-centered care' poster depicted in Figure 11.2, health workers are reminded of the importance of nurturing a good relationship with the patient and what precisely this entails. The poster format is a useful medium, given its low cost and its flexibility of display. Obviously, this poster is intended for display in the workplaces of health workers only.

The purpose of using color photography rather than drawings or no pictures at all may have been to add some realism and to literally put a

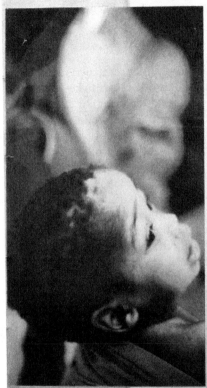

Figure 11.2 'Patient-centered care' poster (Department of Health, CTP Book Printers, Cape)

face on those needing help. However, in this instance the photographs are not self-explanatory and they serve a subordinate role to the written advice. This is most obviously the case for the larger picture, which tries to underscore – be it not very convincingly – the notion that one should 'be sensitive to the patient's situation.' Again, it is clear that pictorial language has limitations, as certain aspects cannot be expressed adequately by means of (static) visuals. In addition to the abovementioned issues regarding depictions of diachronic events and processes, problems also arise in the visualization of both abstract concepts and generalizations.

2.1.3   Analysis of the 'Prevent HIV/AIDS' poster

Research by Witte et al. (1998) has indicated that campaign materials to combat serious diseases such as AIDS and TB must make individuals 'feel *at risk*' (perceived susceptibility) if they are not yet convinced of the severity of the problem (perceived severity). In addition, they must make people believe they are '*able to effectively perform* a recommended response' (perceived self-efficacy) and that 'the recommended response *works* in averting the threat' (perceived response efficacy) (1998: 360).

The 'Prevent HIV/AIDS' poster in Figure 11.3 does not use a *fear appeal.* Nor does it explicitly address the *severity* of the matter and the aspect of *susceptibility* – though visually it implies that every couple engaging in sexual intercourse should be cautious. This is not necessarily a problem if there is already a high level of *perceived susceptibility* and if the audience is already convinced of the *irreversible consequences* of infection with HIV. Thus, an implied threat may work well if there is already a high level of threat perception within the target audience. This poster is particularly well suited – and probably purposefully designed – to enhance the *perceived self-efficacy*, the idea that *they can do it and that it really works.*

Research has shown that 'role modelling and detailed pictures showing condoms being used, for example, are ideal for increasing perceptions of self- and response efficacy' (Witte et al., 1998: 361). Unlike in many other posters, the visual part is not just subordinate to or a repetition/illustration of the verbal statements, but it in fact carries much of the information and arguments (some of which are echoed in the small print). Apart from providing clear instructions on *how to use* a condom by means of a sequential set of pictures, the larger illustration also shows *where to get them* (clinics) and conveys the message that they can be obtained for free. In this manner, two additional barriers are addressed: availability and cost. In a more implicit way, a further 'barrier' or prejudice is also dealt with: the happy faces imply that using condoms does not spoil the enjoyment of sexual intimacy. The poster as a whole thus promotes the idea

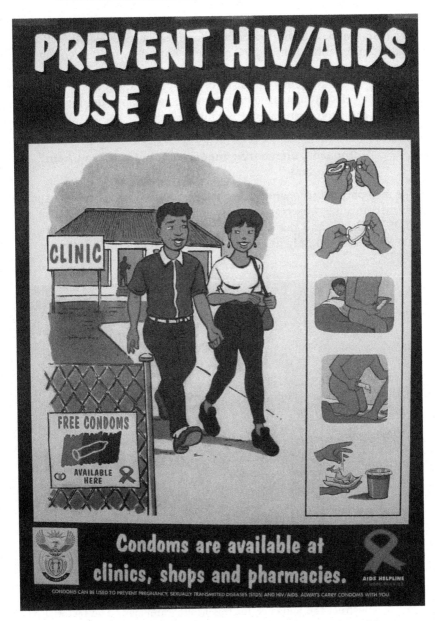

Figure 11.3 'Prevent HIV/AIDS' poster (issued by the Beyond Awareness Campaign, HIV/AIDS and STD Directorate, Department of Health)

that using condoms is an integral part of sexual intercourse. The choice for a fairly simple drawing rather than, for instance, detailed photographic images is probably inspired by a concern, not only with clarity, but also with achieving an acceptable degree of sexual explicitness. To the westerner's eye, this may seem a simplistic or unsophisticated poster, but it is in fact a very cleverly constructed health message that puts many of the proven health communication rules into practice.

3   Billboards, alternative media and their environment: a visual essay

The final part of this chapter consists of a 'visual essay' (Pauwels, 1993), which comprises observations regarding the devastating effects of the AIDS epidemic and the social and cultural factors and circumstances that alleviate or amplify its impact (Figures 11.4 to 11.13).

Figure 11.4 'AIDS Helpline' billboard, Bloemfontein (L. Pauwels)
   The medium (a huge billboard), the message (get on the phone to seek help) and the location (a busy crossroads in Bloemfontein) construct the audience for this health campaign. The pictorial part contains several visual metaphors: the shape and position of the phone unmistakably have sexual connotations, and the curl in the red phone cord mirrors the shape of a well-established symbol of the fight against AIDS. However cleverly constructed, this concept will probably not work for the high-risk population living in the vast townships nearby (Figure 11.5). The painted advertisement for 'Sunrise Tombstones, now and forever' on the wall behind the billboard inadvertently underscores the severity of the threat.

Figure 11.5 Bloemfontein's black township (L. Pauwels)

Figure 11.6 'Love Life' billboard, Bloemfontein (L. Pauwels)

This billboard, located in an impoverished part of Bloemfontein, seems to testify to the gap that often exists between the culture of the campaign builders (often large international groups are awarded such major projects) and the culture of (at least important parts of) the target audience. Even more seasoned and well-educated mass-culture consumers will have a hard time trying to work out what exactly ought to be 'talked about' or what precisely the question 'Love yourself enough?' refers to. This campaign's effectiveness seems highly jeopardized by its excessively sophisticated or almost completely incomprehensible approach.

Figure 11.7 'ABC of AIDS' billboard, Kingdom of Lesotho (L. Pauwels)
The ABC of combating AIDS according to a Lesotho health campaign is: 'Abstain, Be faithful or Condomise.' This is a straightforward approach – executed in several languages along the road – offering clear advice on how to avert the threat, though the viability of each of the options proposed depends very much on the social and cultural norms that prevail within the targeted community. The publisher's message at the bottom of the billboard, apart from being an example of plain advertising, is also a token of endorsement of the health message and thus recognition of the health threat by the community. These small-sized billboards, using unsophisticated but clear messages and drawing on cultural representational codes that are understood well by the target audience, will most probably do a better job in getting the message across than huge billboards with generic messages (which are often produced by multinational advertising agencies) or overly sophisticated appeals that are above people's heads.

To a large extent, it addresses matters of effectiveness of roadside health communications in their physical and cultural context. For, indeed, billboards and other forms of roadside media can, in addition to posters, be effective for health promotion purposes, especially when used in support of more in-depth methods such as personal counselling and flyers. However, as they can convey only a limited amount of information (much less than posters or flyers), their use should be

Figure 11.8 Christian place of devotion, Kingdom of Lesotho (left) and Figure 11.9 'AIDS does not forgive' billboard, Kingdom of Lesotho (right) (L. Pauwels)

Efforts to promote healthier behavior should not go against existing belief systems (though they should not refrain from combating harmful misconceptions). Instead, they should adopt a cooperative approach. This billboard along the main road to Maseru (Lesotho) and close to a church is a simple, but effective example of how this can be accomplished.

Figure 11.10 Traditional healer's shack, Bloemfontein (L. Pauwels)

Caption for Figure 11.10   (cont.)

This image portrays the wall of a traditional healer's shack advertising its 'health offerings.' The shabby outside contrasts sharply with the huge billboards displaying their slick health messages. However, this visual discrepancy may prove deceptive to the outsider, since traditional belief systems still exert a profound influence on large parts of the population of contemporary African society. To simply ignore or fight them is inevitably counterproductive. A culture-sensitive approach also implies that one should try to reconcile traditional culture with more contemporary ways of acting and thinking.

Figure 11.11 AIDS-related 'grassroots' mural, Bloemfontein (L. Pauwels)

'Hug Me I Have AIDS, I can't make you sick!' This school mural fights the stigmatization of and misconceptions about AIDS patients, and the exclusion they may suffer as a result. Grassroots responses are among the best indicators that a community is taking ownership of a problem. Both the location and the execution of these types of messages may serve as a powerful complement to more formal communication channels. They work particularly well on issues of acceptance and solidarity. Other grassroots or community media that are often used to express views on social and political problems include quilts, cloths, handbags and clothing.

Figure 11.12 South African funeral home, 'Now Open' (L. Pauwels)
A morbid aspect of many cities and villages in South Africa is the omnipresence of funeral parlors. Often they are also among the most thriving businesses in many of these highly burdened communities. Undertakers' businesses have a large customer base, advertising as supermarkets tend to do and sometimes even resembling them.

Figure 11.13 Graveyard Bloemfontein (L. Pauwels)

Caption for Figure 11.13   (cont.)

Fairly deserted during the week, this huge graveyard is a busy place during the weekend. Long rows of open ditches are waiting for new arrivals. Reading the names and the dates on the graves tells the story of how whole families and generations of young people in their twenties and thirties have been wiped out, mainly by AIDS. Although they have very little, the families of the deceased tend to invest heavily into a proper farewell.

restricted to displaying a single and very clear message, and possibly contain a reference to other sources of health information. Particular strengths of billboard messages and roadside signs include their fairly broad reach, a potential twenty-four-hour exposure to the messages, and – if well researched – the possibility to optimize the location of the message to reach particular groups (in terms of geography or demographics).

4   Concluding remarks

While numerous cultural factors permeate almost every aspect of health promotion and health intervention activities, their defining role in the effectiveness of a health activity is often not fully understood. Therefore this chapter combined a marketing communications perspective with an applied visual social science approach to focus more on the cultural aspects of health message design elements and on the intricacies of using different media in rolling out those messages. It tried to emphasize that effective health promotion and disease control activities in a multi-cultural context should try to:

1) choose the right kind of appeal and 'feed' the target audience with well thought-out message elements that promote the desired kinds of perceptions, attitudes or behavioral responses;
2) affirm participants' cultural identities and self-concepts;
3) speak the language of participants in a literal and metaphorical sense;
4) acknowledge and accommodate cultural diversity; and
5) be sensitive to the contextual nature of meaning.

These crucial issues of health message design and dissemination have been covered through analyzing and presenting individual health posters and photographs of health messages (billboards and murals) in their context of use. The materials have been selected from a fairly extensive set of materials that were collected or produced during several visits to South Africa and Lesotho as part of a joint Flemish–South African research project on TB control in the Free State.

As a mainly exploratory study, this contribution does not seek to provide any conclusive answers or an overall assessment of the effectiveness of particular campaigns' materials in the visited region. The materials that have been discussed were primarily chosen for their ability to bring about several crucial points related to designing effective health messages and to illustrate possible cultural misunderstandings. However, one does frequently encounter the selected posters and billboards in the abovementioned regions. So they may be considered to some extent as 'typical' materials in the struggle to control TB and AIDS. Moreover, these materials addressed different audiences for different reasons; they thus illustrate some of the wide variety of messages and approaches that are needed to cope with complex health issues.

A more representative and systematic study, aimed at assessing – and if needed, remedying – the current health promotion approach, would require a more in-depth knowledge of the specific cultural context (including language issues, role patterns, health beliefs, cultural codes and connotations, and possible 'barriers' of a varied nature: economic, religious, social), of the predispositions of the target audience (their knowledge, attitudes, current behaviors, level of visual literacy) and of particulars of the health organization and infrastructure.

Obviously this can only be acquired through extensive multidisciplinary research, which would require the active involvement of the target audiences as well as different types of cultural experts and professionals (such as outreach workers, local artists, and political and spiritual/religious 'opinion leaders') in the various stages of the design, implementation and evaluation of a health promotion campaign or process.

Health communication entails much more than just producing relevant information and simply exposing audiences to it. Changing attitudes and health-related behavior is a very complex process that requires a long-term perspective and the mobilization of an interdisciplinary body of knowledge and practices. It encompasses a wide variety of disciplines such as psychology, sociology, public health, marketing, anthropology and graphic design. The goals of health communication are equally varied, including minimizing health risks and improving health in general through information, providing psychological or other types of support and comfort, countering recidivism or non-compliance, and fighting stigmatization associated with certain illnesses and so forth.

Health communications may develop into a very powerful instrument, but only if applied with great care and through mustering various types of expertise and stakeholders, and when developed in concert with other instruments such as medical treatment, infrastructure, financial support, training, legislation and so on. A truly integrated approach is needed that goes far beyond what is routinely understood by the craft of communication. It is not a separate body of expertise that comes at the end (designing materials) or at the beginning (the immediate and standard solution to a problematic situation), nor the exclusive domain of art directors, copywriters or other communication professionals. After all, health communication is not an omnipotent instrument. A communication campaign cannot solve problems that the medical world, the community or the government is incapable of solving (McGrath, 1995: 208).

References

Albrecht, H., H. Bergman, G. Diederich, E. Grober, V. Hofman and P. Keller (1990) *Agricultural Extension, Vol. 2: Examples and Background Materials.* Eschborn: BMZ/GTZ.

Brouwer, H. (1995) 'Communicating with Pictures: The Role of Pictures in Health Education in Outpatient Clinics of Rural African Hospitals.' *Visual Sociology* 10(1–2): 15–27.

De Lange, R. (2000) 'The Effect of Culture on the Efficacy of Pictures in Developing Communities: A Review of Certain Research and Some Guiding Principles.' *Journal of Visual Literacy* 20(1): 59–72.

Epskamp, K. (1992) *Cross-Cultural Interpretations of Cartoons and Drawings. The Empowerment of Culture: Development Communication and Popular Media.* CESO paperback No. 17. The Hague: Centre for the Study of Education in Developing Countries (CESO).

Fuglesang, A. (1982), *About Understanding: Ideas and Observations on Cross-Cultural Communication.* Uppsala: Dag Hammarskjöld Foundation.

Markova, I. and K. Power (1992) 'Audience Response to Health Messages about Aids.' In: T. Edgar, M. A. Fitzpatrick and V. S. Freimuth (eds.) *AIDS: A Communication Perspective.* Hillsdale, NJ: Lawrence Erlbaum Associates, pp. 111–30.

McGrath, J. (1995) 'The Gatekeeping Process: The Right Combinations to Unlock the Gates.' In: E. Maibach and R. L. Parrott (eds.) *Designing Health Messages: Approaches from Communication Theory and Public Health Practice.* Thousand Oaks, CA: Sage, pp. 199–217,

Pauwels, L. (1993) 'The Visual Essay: Affinities and Divergences between the Social Scientific and the Social Documentary Modes.' *Visual Anthropology* 6: 199–210.

Witte, K., K. A. Cameron, M. K. Lapinski and S. Nzyuko (1998) 'A Theoretically Based Evaluation of HIV/AIDS Prevention Campaigns along the Trans-Africa Highway in Kenya.' *Journal of Health Communication* 3: 345–63.

Zimmer, A. and F. Zimmer (1978) *Visual Literacy in Communication: Designing for Development*. Teheran/London: International Institute for Adult Literacy Methods/Hulton Educational Publishers.

Part V

Visual research in a wider perspective

12 Ethics of visual research in the offline and online world

1 Key ethical questions in visual social research

In a society that is increasingly characterized as a 'visual culture,' images play a prominent role in very diverse domains of social life. Despite their wide distribution and considerable functionality, the specific nature of visual representations, in particular their remarkable iconic and indexical properties and consequent relative 'irrefutability,' raises ethical questions – in scholarly as well as other contexts – which are often difficult to answer. Although the value of images and visual representations in the sciences is now beyond doubt, here too an array of general and more discipline-related issues come to the fore. All scientific research requires careful consideration of ethical issues, and such issues may vary according to the nature and design of the research and the data collected. With audiovisual recordings of human behavior for research, ethical issues become particularly salient, because visual data differ so fundamentally from verbal or numerical data. Using visuals in research therefore requires a specific approach to ethical issues. The discussion in this chapter focuses specifically on the use of recorded images of human behavior for scientific research. The central question is: How can social and behavioral scientists use visual media to collect data or communicate insights, while at the same time guaranteeing that such research and its dissemination will not harm their subjects? This at once raises questions such as: What precisely do we mean by 'harm' subjects? What are acceptable limits and how can we encourage or enforce researchers to comply with such principles? Finally, what is or should be the role of ethical committees in this respect, and connected with that, how feasible is using and producing visual records of people in the current research climate?

Although global standards[1] are evolving to address new research issues, many questions pertaining to visual research remain unanswered in the

[1] Ethical standards and guidelines for research in the social sciences are documented elsewhere: for example, see the American Sociological Association *Code of Ethics* (ASA, 1999), the British Sociological Association *Statement of Ethical Practice* (BSA, 2002), the American Anthropological Association *Principles of Professional Responsibility* (AAA,

257

Figure 12.1 Efforts to preserve anonymity and avoid possible harm for research subjects pose a conundrum for visual research. (L. Pauwels)

ongoing debate. The discussion will mainly provide a 'status quaestionis' to help further visual researchers find the ethical approaches appropriate for their specific research designs, contexts and participants and it will also try to make members of ethical committees more aware of the specifics of visual research. In no way is this chapter suggesting that currently visual research is routinely performed in unethical ways or that academic institutions would be mainly concerned with securing their liability at the expense of the rights of research subjects or of innovative types of research that involve visual recordings of people. However, it is contended that this complex issue does require separate attention since current procedures and standards for assessing and enforcing ethical behavior do not sufficiently account for the many aspects and actors that are involved.

2   Preserving anonymity as the core problem

Researchers have an ethical responsibility towards the scientific community (the discipline, peers and students involved in research), the subjects

2012), the International Visual Sociology Association *Code of Research Ethics and Guidelines* (IVSA, 2009) and the Economic and Social Research Council (ESRC, no date) and European Science Foundation (ESF, 2000) guidelines.

they study (irrespective of culture and capabilities), and the society as a whole (citizens and sponsors). Personal commitment and enthusiasm for a topic or a viewpoint are positive qualities in researchers, unless they undermine the scientific nature of a study.

Ethically responsible behavior in visual research is not limited to honesty and integrity in the scientific community. Scientists also need to consider any negative consequences of their research for all those involved, irrespective of whether subjects appear in an image. Researchers must take precautions to prevent any such consequences or to reduce them to acceptable levels. An important means of preventing undesired consequences for those involved is protection of identity – that is, preserving the anonymity of individuals in visual information.

Realistically, an absolute guarantee of anonymity cannot be achieved in any kind of research. In written surveys commonly used in scientific research, however, anonymity is often regarded as a non-issue (see Swanborn, 1981: 153) and there is seldom motivation for a respondent to be traced in any case. However, with camera observation, the protection of the subject's identity is a concern of the first order.

Typical merits of images appear to turn into distinct drawbacks in protecting subjects' identities. Images have a unique iconic and indexical relationship with reality. The 'irreducible nature' of the camera image means that it forfeits much of its communicative strength when converted to an alternative medium, such as words or numbers, or if parts, such as a subject's face, are made 'illegible' to protect anonymity. With visual research, we are not concerned with opinions of individuals who are not immediately identifiable, as in the case of textual survey data, but with instances where, in most cases, private persons remain very 'visible.' If visual data are incorporated into the final research report, or in extreme cases, included in a film for broad release, the persons portrayed remain identifiable to the audiences.

This iconic and indexical relationship of images with the reality they represent underpins the concerns which test subjects may have when their images are captured by a camera. Grimshaw (1982) specifies a number of (partly overlapping) reasons why people may prefer not to be photographed or filmed:

- a feeling, . . . that some part of the self is being stolen
- a sense of loss of anonymity
- the nondeniability of presence on a scene when records are made
- a sense of concern that the features of permanence and reproducibility may make one vulnerable to ridicule or some other, unknown, risk.

(Grimshaw, 1982: 235)

These concerns may well be justified under certain circumstances. Researchers may also overlook subjects' objections, or not be able to understand them, particularly if they have little insight into the social context in which their research activities are unfolding. Conversely, experienced researchers may be aware of potential risks of which subjects are oblivious. It is then the researcher's duty to inform and protect subjects as far as possible. Some risks may also be overlooked by both subjects and researchers, which is unfortunately unavoidable.

Sometimes protecting anonymity of subjects and objects is less crucial or relevant, for example:

- in situations where the images are only used within a restricted circle;
- if the images are merely an intermediate step towards further coding or quantification;
- if the spatial (or cultural) distance between data collection and presentation is sufficient that individuals are unlikely to be recognized, such as footage of an indigenous community in Papua New Guinea for use in a British university;
- if the individuals filmed are unrecognizable for technical reasons, for example if subjects are part of a large crowd or far away so that their images are too small for identification.

Even in such cases, however, anonymity is virtually impossible to guarantee.

Transformation of images to protect anonymity is one solution to the dilemma of visual research and protection of anonymity. Developments in the field of digital image processing have significantly increased the possibilities for making elements in an image, such as faces or company logos, unrecognizable or illegible, through blurring and so on. However, this is not simple to achieve or always possible. Such interventions may also cause significant data to be lost. We can also apply techniques during the recording process, to try to safeguard the anonymity of individuals and locations, for example protecting anonymity by filming subjects with their backs to the camera, in the dark, or in disguise. Once again, however, this usually implies loss of (sometimes essential) contextual information. Additionally, nonverbal information particularly significant to this type of research, such as facial expressions, may also be lost.

3   Overt and covert recordings in the private and public spheres

Further issues relevant to individuals' rights to privacy are their expectations in private and public domains, and the issue of overt versus covert recording of behavior.

Distinguishing between private and public spheres is a particularly challenging task. For example, anyone visiting tourist attractions must accept that their image may occasionally appear by chance in the photo album of complete strangers. Random capturing of images in this way is unavoidable and is accepted as an inevitable consequence of the democratization of private image production. An entirely different situation presents itself when more intimate aspects or behaviors are deliberately recorded for research or other purposes, implying a certain degree of public disclosure.

In practice, the right to privacy is interpreted differently for public figures and private individuals. It also seems to make a difference whether we are recording large masses of individuals in a public space or more intimate behavior by potentially identifiable persons (Grimshaw, 1982: 234). However, there is by no means a general consensus on such matters, in part because the concepts and terminology applied in the debate are often particularly vague and ambiguous.

Researchers such as Becker suggest that presence in a public space and performing acts that may affect public well-being may compromise an individual's right to privacy (Becker, 1986: 258–9). This viewpoint is aligned with prevailing forms of journalistic reporting. Individuals attending a music festival, for example, are more likely to appear on television than if they had stayed at home, particularly if their behavior is socially unacceptable. Politicians and film stars, on the other hand, are usually expected to tolerate more routine and much greater infringements on their privacy than other citizens. There are also considerable differences between professional ethics practiced even within the same discipline, as illustrated by the differences between broadsheet and tabloid newspaper publishers. Gold also defends a differentiated approach arguing that socially marginalized and vulnerable groups, such as children or prisoners, should receive better protection against infringements of privacy than individuals of social standing and power. In reality, only the latter group is usually able to press charges against a researcher who has crossed the line (Gold, 1989: 108). Schaeffer adopts an entirely different position, arguing that camera registration should only be allowed under very restrictive conditions and without distinction between individuals. Schaeffer is also opposed to public disclosure, though it is not entirely clear what this term entails (Schaeffer, 1975: 255). Such ambiguity pervades the entire debate on privacy and recording of visual information. Even if we reach scientific agreement on the need to distinguish between the public and private spheres, questions remain such as how these spheres should be defined, who are public figures and which actions by public figures should nevertheless belong to the private realm.

Further, a clear distinction needs to be made between a highly controllable and artificial laboratory setting and observations in real-life public spaces. When recording images on a public square or in a public building, it is usually very difficult or even impossible to inform research subjects beforehand. It is unreasonable and unrealistic to expect researchers or camera people to be able to predict who will cross their scope of vision. It is equally difficult to determine the identities of such chance subjects after they have been filmed.

With advances in visual technology, covert registration became increasingly simple, for example with telephoto lenses, miniaturization, greater photo-sensitivity and one-way screens. Consequently, the permissibility of covert registrations of individuals and/or the conditions for such practices are important issues in the debate on ethics of visual research.

Covert or non-consensual registration is tolerated less as we trespass deeper into the private realm. It has been argued from a psychological perspective (Bosch, 1984: 17) that social scientists attach greater importance to the interest of the general public than to the interest of the individual, so that they are less concerned with choices of covert, or non-consensual, observation. However, the vast majority of sociologists practicing visual research feel this reproach is unwarranted and object to covert forms of observation. They rationalize, albeit in an unqualified manner, that such observations have far less scientific value than overt observations. Grimshaw (1982), for example, argues that covert registration tends to overlook the ethnographic context and is therefore less valuable. Additionally he points out that conscious change of, or control over, behavior due to the presence of external observers is generally not a major problem with camera observation (Grimshaw, 1982: 232–47), thus removing the main justification for covert observation in ethnographic research contexts. He therefore recommends avoiding covert recording as much as possible. Schaeffer, too, asserts that the possible benefits of covert observation rarely, if ever, outweigh the potential problems caused to the researcher and the person observed (Schaeffer, 1975: 255). The concern with safeguarding the rights of the research subject is, of course, legitimate. However, the suggestion, also on scientific grounds, that overt observation is invariably the best choice is untenable.

There are often situations where it is impossible to obtain prior permission, because this would fundamentally change the behavior of subjects. Some data collection is only meaningful if the individuals concerned are not (or only superficially) informed beforehand. Otherwise, subjects may change their behavior due to knowledge that they are being monitored. If possible, such subjects should be consulted after the recording and any objections considered seriously.

Even when subjects are aware that they are being observed – as in so-called overt observation – they are rarely aware of precisely what is being observed, so that they are ignorant of possible implications or risks. In both covert and overt observation, researchers are trying to register representative behavior, and lack of knowledge over the exact focus of the observations may render subjects unaware of the risks in both scenarios.

An interesting interaction of technological advances and research practices is the merging or lack of distinction between subjects' expectations in overt and covert research scenarios. Even the most outspoken proponents of overt observation are rarely opposed to the use of technical devices such as telephoto lenses and remote-controlled cameras. Such devices are used in overt observation to encourage subjects to forget their behavior is being recorded and thus avoid any influence of the research context on the subject. Using these devices raises exactly the same kind of ethical questions as covert observation. The scenario in which a subject is ignorant of being recorded or ignorant of the research goals varies little from the scenario in which the subject has forgotten that he or she is being recorded. Indeed, the differences between concealing the precise research goal, applying technological aids to disguise the research situation, and covert registration of human behavior are not necessarily discrete in nature.

4   Defining 'harm' and acceptable limits

Whatever observation approach is adopted, all research scenarios demand equal attention to prevention of potentially negative consequences for subjects. Statements of ethical principles by anthropologists, sociologists and psychologists often specify that the researcher should avoid any form of harm or damage to subjects.

Where research involves the acquisition of material and information transferred on the assumption of trust between persons, it is axiomatic that the rights, interests, and sensitivities of those studied must be safeguarded (Council of the American Anthropological Association, cited in Heider, 1976: 118–20).

This ethical charter also stipulates without further explanation that anonymity should be safeguarded, including the case of camera registration. The subjects under study should be fully informed prior to the event, and the research should only go ahead if the persons involved have consented explicitly. Although these are healthy principles, their rather vague and general formulation means that they are not so readily applicable in practice.

The questions of the extent to which one can and must take action to prevent negative consequences and whether or not it is possible in practice to obtain consent on the basis of full information deserve further elucidation.

Adhering strictly to a guideline to avoid any harm or negative consequences for subjects would make research impossible. Any statement about reality inevitably relates to someone or something. In particular, with new or divergent information, there is always the possibility that subjects may incur damage of one kind or another. For each concrete situation, we therefore need to assess whether the risks involved are acceptable.

It is not easy, however, to draw a clear line between discomfort or a degree of embarrassment caused by the data collected on the one hand, and genuine harm through that data or the ensuing conclusions on the other (Becker, 1986: 258–59). For example, if you have ever been filmed on a training course, your self-perception may have been damaged when confronted with images showing that your behavior did not quite match the ideal. Usually, this discomfort remains within acceptable limits (unless the images are later abused for other purposes). Even if research is conducted in a fair, non-manipulative manner, individuals vary in how well they handle such confrontational information. Researchers cannot predict levels of personal sensitivity among subjects, so that the safest approach is to assume that they are extremely sensitive.

The issue of preventing possible negative consequences is relevant mainly in the recording of behavior (e.g., in interaction research). However, we cannot exclude the possibility that undesired or damaging effects may result even from the registration of purely material subject matter, which is often affected by behavior, for example an individual's working area. In most cases, the harm or damage is limited to the personal, immaterial sphere; financial or physical harm, although less likely, is still possible, however. Damage to an individual's reputation, for example, is first and foremost a moral issue (e.g., rejection by significant others), but may ultimately cause persons or organizations to suffer material losses: declining sales figures, fewer promotion options, reduced chance of re-election and so on. Such consequential harm from scientific research means that safeguarding subjects requires anticipation of potential long-term consequences. Additionally, the ethical responsibility of the researcher does not end with the completion of the scientific product, but extends to the restrictions applying to the accessibility and disclosure of that product – in other words, the dissemination of the research findings.

Thus, while there is cross-disciplinary agreement that subjects should be protected from harm, achieving this in practice is challenging, and a rule-based approach would inhibit visual research entirely. All research focusing on reality may lead to negative personal or material consequences, in both the short and long term. Not only the research approach, but also the accessibility and disclosure of research findings must be taken into account when assessing potential harm. In particular with visual research, subjects may even suffer from viewing their own images, and as subjects vary in their sensitivity to such risks, an overcautious approach is recommended. The challenge to ethical decision-making for visual research, therefore, is assessing whether the potential risks are acceptable, for each research context and the subjects involved.

5   Consent as an ongoing process or the inadequacy of a purely 'contractual' approach

In addition to safeguarding subjects against harm, the ethical charter quoted above stipulates fully informed and explicit, prior consent of subjects. Indeed, it is often argued that test subjects must be allowed to choose freely whether to participate in a study, in full knowledge of the possible implications. This is known as the informed consent or voluntary consent principle: Schaeffer formulates this as follows:

Voluntary consent implies, first, that ultimate control for involvement in research lies with the participant. Such control cannot be exercised intelligently, however, without the participant's full and clear understanding of research goals, procedures, and implications. It is the researcher's responsibility to provide an explanation of the research which permits this understanding. Second, voluntary consent implies mutual respect, confidence, and trust between participant and researcher. That is, upon consent a researcher-participant relationship is established that persists throughout the research. It must be founded in a mutual regard that the researcher may not betray. (Schaeffer, 1975:254).

Schaeffer's principle of voluntary consent requires that the participant should be fully aware of the research goals, the procedures and the implications. This ideal is impossible to achieve in practice. Many test subjects have very little idea of what social or behavioral scientific research entails, how one proceeds and to what use the data may be put. Furthermore, they generally underestimate the possibilities of the visual media applied. It is therefore the researcher's important duty to inform the participant as honestly as possible. However, research is often a long-term process, the course of which can be entirely unpredictable, even to the most experienced and bona fide researcher. Consequently, from an ethical perspective, even prior consent that is supposedly based on accurate and complete information does not suffice. Undesired consequences can also manifest themselves suddenly and late on in the research process, sometimes even upon publication or dissemination of the images, or years after (Grimshaw, 1982: 242).

Researchers can only try to inform test subjects as honestly and as comprehensively as possible in a manner that is understandable to them. This may entail providing information regarding the method of data collection, how this data will subsequently be processed, how and to whom the results will be shown, the risks which are involved and the precautions taken to limit them, and so forth.

Marshall (2003) summarizes a number of issues regarding informed consent that need addressing, including whether written or verbal consent suffices. Some research institutes explicitly demand a written statement of consent from participants. However, this is not always feasible in practice; for example, observation of unknown people in public places often precludes informed consent. When working with diverse cultures in international settings, obtaining written consent may be particularly problematic because of the nature of the study, illiteracy, or the social vulnerability of the participants (Fluehr-Lobban, cited in Marshall 2003: 271–2).

The mandatory requirement for written consent by some research institutes is usually not so much out of concern with the well-being of the research subjects, but rather to avoid personal or institutional accountability. Gold quite justifiably voices serious ethical concerns about such a contract-based approach, especially as, in visual and/or interaction research, it does not provide adequate protection for the subject (Gold, 1989: 104). Becker also notes that, certainly from an ethical viewpoint, prior consent provides insufficient guarantees. He argues that even from a legal perspective such agreements may be invalid, because test subjects are rarely fully aware of what they are giving permission for (Becker, 1986: 259). The dominant focus on obtaining (written) informed consent is a 'legalistic' approach that largely ensures that researchers and their institutions are protected from possible harm, but is inadequate to ensure privacy, confidentiality and minimal levels of harm for subjects throughout and after the research project. Marshall advises that 'Judgments about whether or not to seek written or verbal consent should be based on the nature of the research, the context of the study, and the seriousness of the risks involved for participants in signing an informed consent document' (Marshall 2003: 275).

During image registration, subjects can execute a degree of control and are able to object immediately to certain unexpected or undesired events, such as an emotional utterance, or situations in which they feel cornered, or from which they wish to distance themselves. However, the recording phase is only one aspect of visual media production. Usually, the material is subsequently edited. Through this process of reordering and selection, new meanings can be created with the raw material: aspects that are physically unrelated can be brought together for reasons of comparison or contrast. Likewise, the commentary that is added can give a twist to the initial event that is entirely undesired by the persons involved. This creates a dilemma: on the one hand, it is unfair that the subject should only have a say during registration and not during the subsequent editing process, but on the other, few films would ever be finished (and remain analytically useful) if the subjects had an unlimited say (Heider, 1976: 121).

While it is obvious that full information and consultation throughout the research process are impossible to achieve, researchers should not simply proceed alone after an initial approval from subjects, but should continue to consult with subjects as the research progresses. They should adopt an open attitude towards queries and grievances from participants and, if possible, explicitly ask for feedback during previews organized especially for this purpose. Researchers should always be able to guarantee that the data are being used in precisely the (confidential) manner previously outlined. Any imprudence or nonchalance on the part of the researcher in this respect counts as a serious professional error.

A further question to be raised is who should be asked to provide consent for group observations. In this case, it is necessary to involve all the stakeholders, rather than to rely solely on approval of those in positions of authority. For example, permission from management to film in a school or a company does not automatically entitle filming of anyone within the school or business premises without the consent of the individuals concerned. Clearly, this has the disadvantage that it increases the likelihood of delays or opposition.

Particularly in the participatory approaches to visual research, some radical ethical principles are being explored: it is claimed, for example, that researchers and test subjects should determine the research goals and progress together (see, among others, Kjølseth, 1983). While such cooperation models may hold real potential, which is partly realized, a critical attitude is still required. Usually, researchers are largely in control of the research activities and decide on the tools applied and on the reporting of results. Such an essentially unequal balance of power should not be concealed by purely methodological or theoretical statements of principle. One needs to ascertain to what extent mutual respect and trust – two fundamental components of ethical behavior – find expression during the course of the research process.

6   New media, new ethics?

Social and cultural researchers recognize the value of the Internet as a field of study, as a tool to support study and also for communication. The Internet's hybrid and unrestrained character as both a field of study and medium for communication poses a particularly complex set of ethical questions and considerations for research.

A vast supply of information is publicly available over the Internet, unprotected by passwords or firewalls and therefore accessible to anyone. Researchers can therefore access discussions between other Internet users, and browse websites to read personal information such as photographs, personal biographies or letters. Researchers can easily join in online discussions without other discussants being aware that their behavior is being researched. A major advantage of unobtrusive research techniques is the absence of effects of monitoring and other types of unwanted reactivity provoked by the knowledge that subjects are being researched. However, once again, covert observation raises ethical concerns.

Some scholars and many members of the public recognize the Internet as a public domain, from which data can be appropriated. On the whole, however, a more pervasively accepted notion is that 'research in cyberspace falls within the scope of existing guidelines on ethical research practice in respect of informed consent, privacy and confidentiality and the need to protect research participants from harm' (Lee, 2000: 135). The challenge is therefore how to apply existing ethics standards to the hybrid and heterogeneous nature of the Internet. In the same way that public and private spheres are uneasily distinguishable in the real world, the Internet reflects equally ambiguous private and public spheres of cyberspace, with a continuum of private to public users.

Mirroring practice in the real world, researchers are expected to obtain the explicit consent of subjects participating in research projects. Research goals, uses of the results or supporting materials and any potential risks must be fully explained. The Association of Internet Researchers (AoIR) published recommendations from their ethics working committee (Ess and AoIR 2002), guiding researchers to contemplate the questions likely to help ethical decision-making for a particular Internet research design and context. Considerations for researching computer mediated communications over the Internet include:

- What are the in-context ethical expectations?
- What ethically significant risks does the research entail for the subject(s)? For example, if the content of a subject's communication were to become known beyond the confines of the venue being studied – would harm likely result? . . .

By contrast, if the form of communication is under study not what is being communicated – this shift of focus away from content may reduce the risk to the subject. In either case (i.e., whether it is the form or content that is most important for the researcher), if the content is relatively trivial, doesn't address sensitive topics, etc., then clearly the risk to the subject is low.

• Are participants in this environment best understood as 'subjects' (in the senses common in human subjects research in medicine and the social sciences) – or as authors whose texts/artefacts are intended as public.

(Ess and AoIR, 2002: 7–8)

Thus, again similar to the ethics of researching real-world contexts, we return to identifying three key issues in the cyberspace context: subject expectations, whether information is public or private, and potential risks to subjects. Additionally, the very nature of the Internet introduces another variable relevant to the researcher's dilemma, its fluid state. For example, acquiring informed consent from online populations of discussion groups can be extremely difficult because of the transient nature of the membership (e.g., Lee, 2000: 136; Hine, 2000). However, the focus of this paper is visual research, for which reason I limit my discussion here to the ethics of researching websites as visual-verbal constructions of a more permanent and 'pre-meditated' character. Websites are made available or 'published' publicly, so using website content as research data should prompt fewer ethical concerns. However, are pictures and texts in websites truly public performances, freely available for any academic or other use without prior permission? Can we infer from a web owner's choice of a publicly accessible medium that permissions are implied? What are the website owners' expectations?

Earlier, under 'Overt and covert recordings in the private and public spheres', the differences between expectations of privacy for private and public individuals have been discussed. Can one map the same ethical rules for private and more public persons and organizations (politicians, government sites, corporations) from the physical world onto cyberspace? In publishing their websites, haven't these website owners forfeited their rights to privacy considerations normally applied to private individuals? Does socially unacceptable behavior on websites forfeit web owners' rights? These questions need careful analysis and contextual considerations.

Relating to the second question cited above from AoIR guidelines, and central to discussion of all research ethics, is what exactly one intends to do with the acquired information. The original purpose of a website may simply be to connect with like-minded folk (fellow hobbyists or 'soul mates'); other uses may never have been anticipated. Is such use, which lies outside the website owner's expectations, ethical? For example, can anyone include a link to someone else's website without contacting the website owner? While some of the answers to such questions are covered by simple 'netiquette' (or rules of courtesy in an electronic environment), others require more careful thought, because the consequences could be harmful to the website owner concerned. We need to distinguish between 'the ethics of access to information and the ethics of its use' (Reid, quoted in Lee, 2000: 13). Having access to some kinds of information does not automatically entitle viewers to its use or at least not any type of use. For example, citing a website or including a link to a website is a very different use from drawing comparisons which result, for example, in a website being nominated as the worst in its genre (see 'Worst of the Web'). Pointing to a particular website in this way could also trigger web stalking, such as the website owner being targeted with unwanted emails, or the website being vandalized and so on. In some cases, even just providing additional exposure to a website (by referring to it in an article or a book) may result in unwanted consequences for the web owner or other individuals. Such consequences are not limited to cyberspace activity: where personal information is available on websites, this may be collected and misused to contact or stalk website owners or their families in the physical world.

Visual research of images presented in websites introduces yet more questions of ethics. Such images are effectively 'self-published' imagery, as opposed to pictures taken and selected by the researcher or drawn from some very private source. However, once again the irreducible iconic nature means that coding into textual or numerical form diminishes their value. In the same way that researcher-produced imagery may need to be transformed to protect anonymity, images analyzed from websites may need the same treatment in the reporting of research. However, this visual reduction or transformation again encumbers the assessment or replication of existing studies (Lee, 2000: 136). The richness of the image's communication is lost.

The last question cited above from the AoIR guidelines raises a new issue in the use of images from websites, the issue of copyright. While web owners may be considered as human subjects themselves for certain research, they are also the authors of their artifacts, the texts and images they publish. To complicate the issue even further, website owners often use pictures and text that they do not 'own' themselves, so that use of such content requires the consent of a third, often unknown party. While creators should naturally be entitled to the credit and ownership of their work, it would be useful for researchers to be allowed to 'quote' a visual resource for non-commercial purposes (such as teaching and research) without cost, as practiced with texts from books or articles. Visual researchers would welcome an international consensus on 'fair use' practices for scholarly purposes.

The Internet and subsequent technologies with a prominent visual dimension will continue to impact what we study, the ways in which we study and how we communicate and share knowledge. The research opportunities and ethical questions emerging from this technological and cultural evolution deserve focused attention. Some researchers believe traditional ethical guidelines apply equally to cyberspace and others have designed specific guidelines for Internet-based research. Questions from both schools of thought apply to ethical decision-making for visual research. Issues regarding covert research in the physical world apply equally to visual research in cyberspace. However, there are new questions emerging from Internet research; we need to differentiate between accessibility and use of publicly available data on the Internet; access rights do not equate to usage rights. Researchers need to query the in-context expectations of website owners regarding use and any potential harmful consequences. Further, we need to treat images collected from websites with the same discretion regarding anonymity as those we register directly in the physical world; finally, we need to recognize research subjects as authors and owners of their images and respect the copyright regulations, while at the same time striving for less stringent control over use of images for scholarly purposes. To benefit from the Internet as a rich cultural resource and agent, we need constructive interplay between technological advancement, ethical consideration, theoretical reflection and methodological innovation.

7   Society and the sciences: emergence of double moral standards

An unusual emerging phenomenon is the polarization of ethical expectations in science and society, which creates a 'double moral standard.'

The presence of cameras in many sectors of society is ever increasing, together with people's astonishing indulgence towards privacy-invading practices (e.g., hidden cameras and reality-show formats) that by far exceed what even the most unscrupulous researcher would ever imagine doing. Yet, quite paradoxically, within certain domains of scientific practice, the opposite trend predominates. Indeed, an ever wider gap is appearing between strict scientific standards for the visual recording of human behavior and the increasing and astonishing permissibility with regard to intrusions into, and disclosure of, the most intimate aspects of the personal sphere. Examples are abundant in reality-TV formats and other 'pioneering' forms of visual reporting, and also within the semi-public space of the

Internet (Pauwels, 2006). Clearly we need to resist further dilution of ethical conscience. From another perspective, however, an excessively rigid, inconsistent or undifferentiated ethical position can also induce inertia.

Even more unusual is the polarization between acceptable research ethics in different academic disciplines. Social scientists in the US, for example, are today confronted with almost impracticable ethical standards within their academic institutions when it comes to using or producing visual materials registering human activity. Institutional review boards (IRBs) have been set up in the US to protect the rights of human subjects in any kind of research. The main goals of these boards are to minimize risk and harm, to ensure documentation of informed consent and to impose stringent rules with respect to privacy and confidentiality. In many other countries ethics committees are similarly trying to regulate and control approval of research proposals with the same aims in mind. While it is a commendable and necessary initiative, the members of these IRBs are not always familiar with social science methods, particularly the more innovative and qualitative methods. Visual methods face the double burden of being perceived as qualitative and not canonical. In particular their special needs with respect to implementing workable solutions for informed and voluntary consent are largely ignored.

Ethics commissions generally adopt a very hesitant, sometimes extremely restrictive, attitude towards the sanctioning of projects involving visual recordings of persons, especially if material needs to be produced by the researchers themselves. The most remarkable thing is that comparable projects, likewise involving representations of individuals, but presented as arts projects, are not subjected to as many restrictions and are thus approved more easily.

As evidence from discussion groups and visual conferences shows, this odd state of affairs is resulting in exasperated and desperate (social) scientists recommending to their colleagues that they should try to get their research (e.g., visual analyses of people in their living and working environment) approved as an 'arts project' and to subsequently pursue the research as a regular social science project. In a special issue of *Visual Studies* on ethics in visual research, sociologist Diana Papademas asserts that the redefinition of social scientific research as 'art' or 'journalism' to avoid problems in obtaining approval is not to be recommended (Papademas, 2004: 124). However, it would often appear to be the only way for researchers to make use of the extensive and innovative possibilities of a visual approach to scientific data collection and communication.

The emergence of such ethical 'shortcuts' is indicative not only of the growing gap between ethical sensitivities in science and society – a new kind of 'double moral standard' – but also of the problematic differences in terms of ethical sensitivities between the various academic disciplines. This once again demonstrates the continuous necessity for the contextualization of ethics in its broader societal setting. On the basis of a sound information round and debate, appropriate solutions need to be found that ensure a broad societal legitimacy.

Marshall (2003) contends that IRBs are often overzealous in the interpretation of federal rules because the Office for Human Research Protections has terminated a number of research projects at US institutions which it considered to violate human subjects' rights. She stresses that the powerful position of IRBs encourages uneasiness: 'In the current environment of regulatory controversy, reports of research ethics abuses, and revisions of existing guidelines, IRBs may be inclined to interpret rules and make decisions based on fear – that their institution might be sued, that their institution might have all research activities shut down by the "feds" for a lack of oversight' (Marshall, 2003: 273).

The more restrictive and unqualified the demands of IRBs or similar ethical committees become, the more researchers will be drawn to develop less overt (and/or less ethical) methods. Alternatively, they may simply be discouraged from undertaking research projects at all because of the restrictive procedures involved in obtaining approval. Thus, research which may be important for science or the subjects involved may never be completed. As Marshall (2003: 281) observes, neither of these consequences is acceptable and she provides a number of recommendations to improve the IRBs' procedures.

Fluehr-Lobban (2000: 37) argues that, in our era of globalization, research ethics can no longer be confined or dominated by Western national or domestic discourses. New actors, new methods and new environments have changed and continue to change in the post-colonial world and thus require new standards of conduct. She also insists that social scientists (and anthropologists in particular) should take a more proactive and leading role in the international debate over the nature and condition of research that involves human subjects.

Although society's views on ethics seem to have become increasingly elastic, ethical conduct remains a prime responsibility of researchers, and ethical considerations should be an integral part of any type of research. Overzealous restrictions do not appear to be the solution, but will only encourage improper 'shortcuts' to approval, and may inhibit or even prevent certain types of research. Researchers need to develop norms by themselves, especially in these rapidly evolving and unpredictable technological environments. Technological advances and globalization demand a broader approach to the ethics of researching human behavior than one based on Western or national values alone. This is not just a matter of staying within the boundaries set by law, but of acting sensibly and ethically in the many instances where legal stipulations fail, are lagging behind or remain too vague.

8   Contextual ethical decision-making

Ethical behavior cannot be prescribed in strict rules; it is rather the result of an attitude whereby a particular conduct is suggested in concrete cases. What this requires first and foremost is knowledge and experience in relation to expected or possible consequences of a research decision on the lives of the persons involved. Further, it requires insight into the specific sensitivities of the research field and the participants in the study, which in turn necessitates a considerable degree of involvement with whatever is being studied. Researchers must ultimately also rely on their own perception of a specific situation as members of society. In this phase, it becomes clear that social scientists in particular not only study social norms and values from a distance, but are also confronted with them more directly in their scientific endeavors, where they must be integrated appropriately.

Scientists' efforts to work in an ethically sound manner may be expected to constantly place them before dilemmas, both in visual and in other forms of research. Although this issue deserves closer attention, the vagueness cannot be resolved entirely. There are, after all, different interests and strivings at stake here, which will never coincide fully and between which a compromise needs to be sought. These are:

- Safeguarding the privacy and the dignity of the research subjects.
- The scientific striving for representative data.
- The requirement of public disclosure of scientific material.
- The ethical conscience of the researcher and changing ethical norms in society.
- The striving for personal success (fame, promotion) on the part of the researcher.

If data may inflict real harm or damage for participants or third parties, it is possible that although the data are valuable, they cannot be used. This may be the case even if the data concern behavior that is not reprehensible or that has hardly any public consequences, but may disrupt the self-image of the respondents, or their relationship with others. However, visual data can be used in different ways; researchers need to ask whether visual data should always be accessible to everyone. For example, with direct researcher observation, where textual notes are recorded rather than images being registered, visual data cannot be accessible to others; we are already dealing with coded information. However, visual media providing access to the primary data, albeit in an intermediary form, is a distinct advantage that needs to be exploited whenever possible.

At first glance, there is a certain resemblance between the practices of visually oriented science on the one hand and those of photojournalism and documentary filmmaking on the other, as the latter activities are generally also restricted by an implicit or explicit ethical code. However, scientific visual praxis needs to be subjected to more and stricter criteria of both a scholarly (scientific principles, methodology) and an ethical nature (responsibility vis-à-vis the research field and society at large). The use of images in scientific research into human behavior should never be regarded as a simple alternative to more laborious procedures. A hit-and-run mentality, as sometimes encountered among the occasionally less ethically conscientious image collectors who work for commercial newspapers, magazines or television stations, is incompatible with responsible scientific practice.

The ethical questions surrounding the use of visual recordings in research into human behavior remain very complex. In spite of this, visual researchers tend to encounter very few problems in obtaining cooperation from the field under study. Although unpleasant consequences can never be excluded altogether, we know from practical experience that many people are willing to cooperate in such projects, be it for diverse reasons. Grimshaw refers to, among others, altruistic motives, such as a willingness to contribute to science, and more personal reasons, such as relative fame and attention through participation (Grimshaw, 1982: 244). Most finished products (scientific or educational films, illustrated articles or multimedia products on websites, CD-ROM or DVD) will give rise to certain objections among some of the subjects involved. It is up to the image maker to anticipate such objections as effectively as possible through preliminary research and consultation, and to stay alert to possible problems and risks. Careful consideration of the questions that were raised in this chapter may help researchers to assess and apply the appropriate ethical guidelines to their research design, participants and context.

9   Summary and conclusion: developing best ethical practices in visual research

Working out a solution for any complex problem requires first of all asking the right questions. With respect to the problem of promoting ethical behavior in visual research, these questions are manifold, as there are many actors involved, as well as many goals and contexts. This chapter tried to shed some light on this intricate topic and in doing so probably posed many more questions than it answered. The intention was not to point a finger at individual visual researchers or at people who shoulder responsibility in committees trying to ensure that no harm is done to research subjects or researching organizations. Indeed, the need to raise ethical conscience of researchers involved in visual data-recording is far less than the need to gather and spread insight into the specifics of visual research, and to develop best practices, so that an ethical decision-making process can be put into practice productively.

The chapter began by stressing that protecting subjects' anonymity in visual research is crucial to limiting concerns of subjects and potential harm. The relatively irrefutable nature of (camera) images contributes communicative strength to research reporting, but also facilitates communication of identity, thus requiring careful attention. Sometimes researchers and subjects are unable to anticipate all possible risks, and in other scenarios the risks may be less important. In either scenario, it is impossible to guarantee anonymity entirely. Image-editing techniques may offer solutions to reduce the feasibility of identification of subjects, but also reduce the communicative strength of visual representations. As the scientific requirement of intersubjectivity entails access to collected data, the visual data must be distributable. The question then arises how this may be achieved by the visual researcher, while protecting subjects' anonymity. This dilemma requires complex consideration of contextual issues relevant to the particular research, including aspects such as how recognizable subjects are in images, the acceptability of possible negative consequences, the conditions for access to the data, and the extent of participation on the part of those involved. Due attention must be paid to a deontological analysis of the particular research project, resulting in general principles of conduct regarding protection of anonymity, rather than in universally applicable standards.

Further, the chapter discussed how public and private individuals have different expectations of privacy and that some researchers are differentiating between privacy rights according to presence in a public space, socially acceptable behavior, or the power status of groups. With respect to the issue of overt versus covert research, some visual researchers argue that the influence of research on behavior is insignificant, so that overt observation, which also captures richer contextual information, should always suffice. However, in real-life research, there are scenarios which prevent overt or consensual capture of visual images, either because it would change the behavior of subjects and thereby the value of the research, or because it is not practicable. In conclusion, each research context requires assessment of the privacy expectations of the individuals concerned. Only from such context-specific assessments will the appropriateness of overt or covert observation emerge.

So there are a number of issues relevant to protecting subjects' control over their involvement in visual research. The inevitably dynamic nature of research means that fully informed consent is rarely possible at the beginning of a project; researchers can only advise subjects of honest expectations of how data will be collected, for what purposes and with what consequences, and to which audiences the data will be disseminated. The appropriateness of written or verbal consent depends on the nature of the research, the context of the study, and the seriousness of the risks involved for participants in signing consents (Marshall, 2003: 275). Consent should be at an individual not an organizational level, and contractual consents alone do not suffice, because at the beginning of projects, very little is known of the ultimate direction and design of research. Subjects need to be informed and updated regularly as research progresses, as honestly as possible. Feedback on progress and findings should be invited and may even move researchers towards a more radical participatory research model, in which the power of control is more evenly distributed between subjects and researchers. To achieve meaningful research with such a model accentuates the need for mutual trust and respect between researchers and subjects.

A separate section in this chapter briefly addressed ethical aspects of researching online phenomena, an area that is becoming increasingly important, but that still generates a lot of confusion and problematic behavior.

Finally the chapter touched on the emergence of a remarkable moral divide between the very strict norms that are being observed in the (social) sciences and the overly indulgent attitude towards privacy-invading practices in the broader society. Linked to this latter problem and crucial to the further development of ethical practice, the role of ethics committees has been discussed. While the aim was not to question the necessity for ethical charters and committees, concerns have been raised with respect to the appropriateness of their applicability and visual expertise respectively. A recent conference session on ethics in visual research and in particular on the role of ethics review committees (IVSA Annual Conference, New York, August 2007) revealed the urgent need to address these issues and also the willingness of most parties involved to improve the situation. Many participants testified about IRBs which worked strictly by the book and were ignorant of the specific demands of visual research, and thus in good faith provided obstacles to innovative and well thought-through research. But there were also examples of review boards which did include people experienced in visual research, and which succeeded in making headway. Research review committees should preferably include a member who is experienced in visual research when such projects are being assessed, at least until knowledge of best practices in this field have become 'common' knowledge that is aptly translated into ethical decision-making procedures or criteria for assessing such research.

10   References

AAA (2012) *Principles of Professional Responsibility*, American Anthropological Association. Available from: http://ethics.aaanet.org/category/statement [accessed April 19, 2015].

ASA (1999) *Code of Ethics*. American Sociological Association.

Becker, H. S. (1986) *Doing Things Together: Selected Papers*. Evanston, IL: Northwestern University Press.

Bosch, J. (1984) *Leren Observeren: een introduktie in het gebruik van systematische gedragsobservaties*, 3rd edn. Muiderberg: Coutinho.

BSA (2002) *Statement of Ethical Practice for the British Sociological Association*, March 2002 (Appendix updated May 2004).

ESRC (Economic and Social Research Council) (no date) *Research Ethics Framework*. Available from: www.esrcsocietytoday.ac.uk/ESRCInfoCentre/ Images/ESRC_Re_Ethics_Frame_tcm6–11291.pdf [accessed February 7, 2007].

Ess, C. and the Association of Internet Researchers (AoIR) (2002) *Ethical Decision-Making and Internet Research: Recommendations from the AoIR Ethics Working Committee*, approved by AoIR, November 27, 2002. Available from: www.aoir.org/reports/ethics.pdf [accessed August 23, 2006].

European Science Foundation (2000) *Good Scientific Practice in Research and Scholarship*. Available from: www.esf.org/sciencepolicy/170/ESPB10.pdf [accessed August 24, 2006].

Fluehr-Lobban, C. (2000) 'Globalization of Research and International Standards of Ethics in Anthropology.' *Annals of the New York Academy of Sciences* 925: 37–44.

Gold, S. (1989) 'Ethical Issues in Visual Field Work.' In: G. Blank, J. McCarthy and E. Brent (eds.) *New Technology in Sociology: Practical Applications in Research and Work*. New Brunswick, NJ: Transaction Publishers, pp. 99–109.

Grimshaw, A. (1982) 'Whose Privacy? What Harm?' *Sociological Methods & Research* 11(2): 233–47.

Heider, K. (1976) *Ethnographic Film*. Austin/London: University of Texas Press.

Hine, C. (2000) *Virtual Ethnography*. London/Thousand Oaks, CA/New Delhi: Sage Publications.

IVSA (International Visual Sociology Association) (2009) *Code of Research Ethics and Guidelines*. Available from: http://visualsociology.org/about/item/introduction.html [accessed April 20, 2015].

Kjølseth, R. (1983) 'Evidence and Imagination: Photography in Enquiry.' *International Journal of Visual Sociology* 1: 20–4.

Lee, R. M. (2000) *Unobtrusive Methods in Social Research*. Buckingham/ Philadelphia, PA: Open University Press.

Marshall, P. (2003) 'Human Subjects Protections, Institutional Review Boards, and Cultural Anthropological Research.' *Anthropological Quarterly* 76(2): 269–85.

Papademas, D. (2004) 'Editor's Introduction: Ethics in Visual Research.' *Visual Studies* 19(2): 122–5.

Pauwels, L. (2006) 'Ethical Issues of Online (Visual) Research.' *Visual Anthropology* 19(3–4): 365–9.

Schaeffer, J. (1975) 'Videotape: New Techniques of Observation and Analysis in Anthropology.' In: P. Hockings (ed.) *Principles of Visual Anthropology*, Chicago, IL: Aldine, pp. 253–82.

Swanborn, P. (1981) *Methoden van Sociaal-Wetenschappelijk Onderzoek: Inleiding in ontwerpstrategieën*. Meppel: Boom.

13 A meta-disciplinary framework for producing and assessing visual representations

Though visual social science for a long time predominantly equaled using cameras and camera images to study a fairly limited set of aspects of society – and occasionally was challenged for it – gradually it broadened its focus to include other visual media and techniques, other disciplinary fields, and a more extensive array of topics and research interests. Today, one could rightfully contend that the mission of visual social science is to further disclose society and culture in all of its visually related aspects and to help develop and provide the tools and skills to foster a more visually adequate communication and dissemination of the thus acquired insights.

More concretely, this implies that a visual social science could, for example, also engage in matters of visual representation of aspects that are not visual or visible in nature – like concepts or quantitative data – but that have a sizeable impact on how we think about nature and culture and life in the broadest sense. It also implies that visual social science not only broadens its scope to include all the visual representational practices within its own discipline (e.g., charting, mapping, conceptual representations), but includes the study of practices and uses of visual representations in, for example, the life sciences or different professional contexts.

To that aim, this chapter presents a final integrated framework or model which charts the very differentiated and complex problematic of visualizing nature, culture and knowledge. The ambition is to provide an analytical tool which is serviceable for virtually all disciplines and social endeavors (research, policy development, education) and can be applied to most sectors of society, to make better informed decisions about the production and/or use of visual representations for specific purposes.

1 The visual production of 'scientific reality'

The issue of 'representation' touches upon the very essence of all scientific activities. What is known and passed on as 'science' is the result of a series of representational practices. Visual, verbal, numeric and other types of representations are used in all sciences and in various types of scientific discourses: by and between specialists (intra-specialist and inter-specialist stages), with students (the 'textbook' stage) and the general public (the popularization stage). Lemke characterizes the science discourse fundamentally as a 'multimedia genre' and sees concepts of science as 'semiotic hybrids' (1998: 87) consisting of modalities that are 'incommensurable,' since 'no verbal text can construct the same meaning as a picture, no mathematical graph carries the same meaning as an equation, no verbal description makes the same meaning as an equation, no verbal description makes the same sense as an action performed' (1998: 110). Visual representations are not to be considered mere 'add-ons' or ways to popularize a complex reasoning; they are an essential part of scientific discourse.

Science is not just about truthfully describing or trying to replicate reality, but about making it more understandable and accessible in myriad ways. Likewise, when seeking to better understand and use visual representations in science, one should not see the process of visualization primarily as an effort to reproduce reality as it presents itself to the observer, since science is not about copying nature and culture, but about revealing it. Visual representations in science need to serve a number of distinct purposes that go far beyond the act of reproducing the natural world. Their value is judged by their functionality for resolving a problem, filling gaps in our knowledge or facilitating knowledge building or transfer. Lynch astutely remarks that the study of visualization really is about 'the production of *scientific* reality' (Lynch and Woolgar, 1998: 223).

Image practices, and practices of visualization in social and natural sciences, involve the complex processes through which scientists develop or produce (and communicate with) imagery, schemes and graphical representations, computer renderings or the like, using various means (ranging from a simple pencil on paper to advanced computers or optical devices). Therefore, not just the result, but also how it was attained (i.e., the implicit or explicit methodology) and the subsequent uses to which the result is put should all be scrutinized as to their impact on the nature of what is visually represented and the ways in which this representation can be employed.

Scholars from very diverse disciplinary backgrounds (e.g., sociology of science, medical imaging, philosophy of science, history of science, geographical information systems, geology, biology, physics, visual anthropology, business sciences, information design, mathematics, communication studies, anthropological linguistics) have gradually taken an interest in the complex issue of visualization in science. They have studied a broad range of types, aspects and uses of visual representations in the sciences, and each of those research traditions has contributed a lot to clarifying the huge potential as well as the many tribulations visual representational practices may implicate. Many aspects of the technical and social development of visual representations and the ways in which they are being employed have been approached from distinct theoretical paradigms and a variety of research methodologies (including, e.g., ethnomethodology, phenomenology, semiotics, social constructivism, conversation analysis, interaction studies, ethnography, semiotic analysis, experiments, surveys, interviews, video recordings, field notes). Researchers have scrutinized processes of perception as well as knowledge acquisition and negotiation with representations through detailed studies of practices and discourses of groups of people in different social and professional settings such as those of fieldworkers (Lynch, 1985a; Roth and Bowen, 1999), laboratory scientists (Latour and Woolgar, 1979; Knor-Cetina, 1981; Lynch, 1985b), teachers, engineers, students, publishers, navigators and lawyers (Goodwin, 1994, 1995, 1996; Pea, 1994) to name just a few. A variety of products and media of visualization have been studied in great detail, such as diagrams, photographs, drawings and various scanning techniques. In particular, graphs and the social and technical processes that accompany their creation and their use received much attention (Roth et al., 1999, 2002; Roth and McGinn (1997). Particularly influential are Tufte's books (1983; 1990; 1997) on the analysis and visual display of data and information and thus on the representation and use of knowledge in diverse sectors of society (see Grady, 2006).

Scientific visualization – in a broad sense – has been studied in view of its practicability in fostering educational processes and in bridging theory and practice (Gordin and Pea, 1995), pointing at both unique opportunities and issues/obstacles. It may be seen as an enculturation device in a community of practitioners or scientists-in-process (Roth and Bowen, 2001), but also as an evolving means of scientific and other areas of expression (Pauwels, 2000, 2002) and a prime tool in the development of scientific literacy (Gordin and Pea, 1995) among a diversity of audiences.

The many and highly divergent studies of scientific visualization add up to an impressive body of knowledge that occasionally comes together in themed journal issues, readers and conferences, next to occupying a niche in the different disciplines and specialized journals. Synthesizing the many contributions could be, as Cambrosio et al. (1993: 663) called it many years ago, a 'hopeless task.' Yet working towards integrating at least part of this knowledge and translating it into generic and more customized modules for use in many, if not most, academic curricula would be a significant step forward.

The generic model that I will introduce in this chapter essentially tries to integrate and clarify the impact of the social, cultural and technological aspects involved in the production and handling of visual representations, as well as the different normative contexts that may be at work and thus exert a determining influence on the eventual appearance and the usability of visual representations for scholarly (and other) purposes. Visual representations in science differ significantly in terms of how they relate to what they purport to represent (i.e., their representational and 'ontological' status), the means, processes and methods by which they are produced, the normative contexts involved, the purposes served and the many ways in which they are used and combined, to name but some of the more crucial aspects.

2   The varied nature of the referents

The array of objects or referents of visual representations in science is very broad and of a highly heterogeneous nature. Visual representations in science may 'refer' to objects that are believed to have some kind of material or physical existence, but may equally refer to purely mental, conceptual, abstract constructs and/or immaterial 'entities.'

Material or physical referents may have visual characteristics that are *directly observable* to the human eye (e.g., various types of human interaction, animals, trees; Figure 13.1). On the other hand, there are objects and phenomena with aspects that *only become visible with special representational means and devices* (e.g., they can only be observed using special techniques or instruments such as high-speed photography, satellite image transmission, a telescope, a microscope, or an endoscope). The reason is that either these aspects are too fast (e.g., an explosion, eye movements), too slow (e.g., transformations in a living organism), too big (e.g., stellar configurations), too small (e.g., microscopic organisms; Figure 13.2), too similar (e.g., color of vegetation) or too far away (e.g., planets) for the human eye to discern, or they are hidden (e.g., inside a living body; Figure 13.3) or inaccessible unless destructive course of action is taken (e.g., the dissection of an organism, the creation of a cross-section of an object, the excavation of remains).

Furthermore, physical objects or phenomena may not have visual characteristics as such and still be *translated from a non-visible state* (e.g., sound waves, thermal radiation) *into visual representations* using special devices (Figure 13.4).

Figure 13.1 Directly visually observable phenomena. Aspects of human behavior and material culture (photo: L. Pauwels)

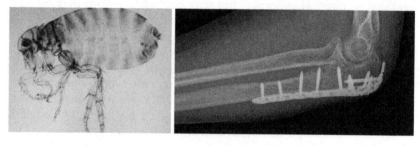

Figures 13.2 and 13.3 Material referents visually observable via technical aids.
Left: microscopic image of dog parasite. Right: X-ray photograph of fractured human elbow with osteosynthesis materials.

Representational practices in science often do not seek merely to 'reproduce' visual or non-visual phenomena, but also to provide *visual data representations* (e.g., charts) of aspects of these phenomena based on measurements of some kind (length, weight, thickness, resistance, quantity, temperature, verbal responses, etc.). In the latter cases, 'data' are derived from or constructed on the basis of an observed reality and

Figure 13.4 Visualization of non-visual phenomena.
 The visual representation of Chopin's Mazurka in F♯ Minor illustrates its complex, nested structure. (Source: Martin Wattenberg 'The Shape of Song,' www.turbulence.org/Works/song/index.html)

subsequently represented in a visual form that allows one to discern changes or see relationships more clearly. While the resulting representations are based upon empirical observations or interrogations in the field, they are not 'reflections' of visual natural phenomena. They are rather visual representations of observations in the physical world that are not necessarily visual in nature. In other words, what is represented are not physical objects or phenomena, but 'data' that are constructed by observing aspects of the physical world. The relationships among the data and their representation is much more abstract/arbitrary and conventional, though some aspects may be also be 'motivated' or iconic (i.e., they may bear some resemblance to the referent). For example, graphical representations of the evolution of the birth rate within a particular population over a certain period of time, temperature fluctuations during one month in summer, or the number of murders per state do not necessarily entertain a visual iconic or indexical relationship with a physical or material referent, as often there is none. Instead, these data representations may have a 'mental' referent as far as the source is concerned, since the representations are not so much 'depictions' of phenomena in the real world as conceptual translations of aspects of it (Figure 13.5). Yet, they are based at least in part on quantifiable or qualifiable aspects of an observed 'reality' of some kind and thus are not purely invented or products of the imagination.

The referent of a representation may be even more *immaterial and abstract* in nature. Representations that primarily seek to visualize relations between observed phenomena visualize hypothetical relationships,

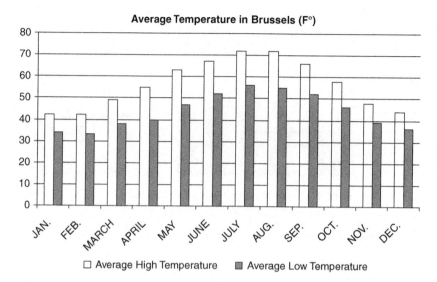

Figure 13.5 Visual representation of non-visual empirical data.
A histogram of average monthly temperatures in a city.

postulated phenomena (Figure 13.6) or effects, and even purely abstract concepts (Figures 13.7 and 13.8). The referent of such representations may become an almost purely mental construct that has no 'pre-existence' in the physical, historical world whatsoever. Nonetheless, representations of these kinds of referents may play an important role in understanding or influencing that world.

Finally, it should be noted that many representations in science combine several of the abovementioned aspects and thus have *multiple referents*. Certain aspects of the representation may, for example, refer to an observed visual reality in an iconic way (e.g., it might mimic its shape or color) and include conceptual structures (such as metaphors) or symbolic elements (arrows, markers, colors, shapes). An edited film will refer iconically to the depicted subject matter (i.e., it will 'reproduce' to a certain extent), but at the same time it might allow scientists to express their vision or theory by means of the manner of recording and subsequent editing processes. In fact, mimesis without expression is virtually impossible. At the root of every presentation of fact is an implicit or explicit theory, a particular way of looking. In fact, visual representations may not only refer to the material world or to an abstract or imaginary world but may also refer to a 'possible world,' which may be the case when performing simulations to get an idea of

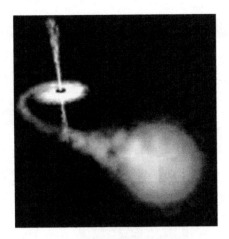

Figure 13.6 A postulated phenomenon.
Artist's impression of a 'black hole' Source: Wikipedia, GNU Free
Documentation License

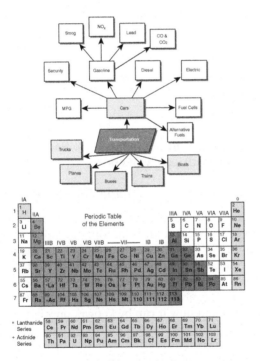

Figures 13.7 and 13.8 Visualizing Concepts, Ideas and Relations.
Top: Mind map of transportation aspects; bottom: Mendeljev's periodic
table of the elements

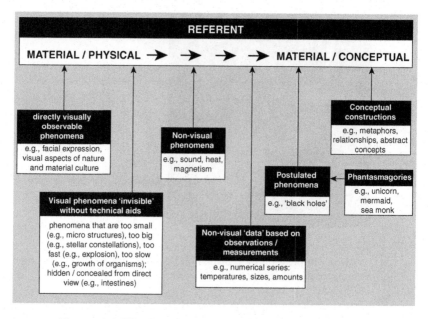

Figure 13.9 The divergent nature of the referent: from material existence to mental construction.

what might happen when combining such and such parameters or phenomena (Figure 13.9).

3   Representational production processes: Social, technological and cultural aspects

3.1   Inscription, transcription, invention and fabrication

Every 'representational' process involves a translation or conversion of some kind; a process of inscription, transcription and/or fabrication whereby the initial source (phenomenon, concept) is captured, transformed, or even (re-)created through a chain of decisions that involves several actors (scientists, artists, technicians), technological devices and normative settings. This complex process of meaning-making has an important impact on what and how it can be known, on what is revealed or obscured, and on what is included or excluded.

As I have argued in the previous section, the divergent nature of the referent in science prefigures the crucial importance of the equally divergent processes of producing a visual representation. These processes not only involve technical issues but also encompass important social and cultural aspects. Obviously, technology and each of its products are part and parcel of culture (i.e., they are both a cultural product or 'result' and a cultural actor or 'force'), both in a broad cultural and a more restricted sub-cultural sense, and thus they embody specific norms and values. Apart from the characteristics of the instrumentation, which are to some degree a result of cultural processes as well, a host of other social and cultural influences at the moment of choosing and selecting the objects, samples, etc., also have an important impact on how the representation will appear as well as on the purposes it may subsequently serve.

3.2 Analyzing the social and cultural setting: scientific labor division and normative contexts

Rosenblum's (1978) sociological study of photographic styles demonstrates how the 'look of things,' particularly the appearance of press, art and advertising photographs, is to a significant degree a function of various social, technological and cultural factors and constraints that are connected with their creation. The division and standardization of labor, technological constraints, professional ethics and time pressures, as well as economic factors, all play a significant role in their creation, look and value. Sociologists of science, on the other hand, have studied the complex interactions in a laboratory setting where science is being 'produced' (Latour and Woolgar, 1979; Lynch, 1985b), an approach that yields insight into how an object of enquiry is selected, delineated and 'prepared' to fulfill its role. Lynch has looked at the laboratory setting and the processes by which natural objects are visualized and analyzed. Preparatory procedures that tend to turn the object of investigation into what Lynch calls a 'docile object' fit to be studied according to the established methods and mores of science, as well as various aspects of the instrumentation and the laboratory set-up, challenge the idea that scientific visualization provides an unproblematic or uncompromising 'window' onto the natural world (Lynch, 1985b: 43–4). Similar processes are at work when scientists make observations in the 'field', as objects are here too selected and prepared to be subjected to scientific practices or made to participate in data-generating procedures.

Not only natural scientists, but also social scientists try to produce 'docile objects' through sampling techniques, pre-structured questionnaires and statistical operations. What cannot be measured, or only very inconclusively, is often overlooked and assumed to be non-existent. The 'picture' that is obtained by the established procedures is often presented as a reliable and valid reflection of a broader phenomenon or population.

Furthermore, the issues of research funding, academic recognition, peer relations and societal trends must all be taken into account if one endeavors to reveal and explain the processes that lie at the heart of particular visual representations of facts or ideas. They likewise may influence what is selected and how it is selected, and the way in which it is processed.

3.3   The varied nature of visual and non-visual transcription

There is a fairly significant, though not exclusive or unconditional, relation between the nature of the referent and the processes through which a representation is or ought to be produced.

Obviously, *conceptual constructions* that have no material, let alone visual, substance cannot be recorded automatically or according to standardized and repeatable processes (e.g., mental images cannot be photographed or scanned electronically), as they are the result of multiple intentional acts that, first and foremost, require a suitable production technique for such highly intentional activity (e.g., pencil and paper or a computer drawing package). The involvement of the originator of the idea is paramount, and a demanding process of translating a mental image into an inter-subjective visible image is required. Aspects or dimensions that cannot in any way be visualized or verbally described are in fact lost to science.

Objects or phenomena that are *visible to the human eye* through direct observation, on the other hand, can be captured by representational devices such as a photographic camera that will produce detailed representations characterized by uniform time and continuous space. This may result in a kind of 'indifference' (some might say 'objectivity,' though this may be too burdened a term to use), since all elements and details are treated equally (even though photographers have ways of foregrounding or emphasizing certain aspects at the expense of others, such as through the choice of lens, film, filters, lighting, framing, viewpoint, etc.). However, directly observable phenomena also can be represented through more manual techniques, using simpler media, such as pencils and brushes, which require a more *intentional* series of acts by humans (draftsmen, illustrators). These techniques produce imagery that do not have a uniform time (in fact, quite some time may pass during the creation of the different parts of the representation) and that are not bound by continuous space or a uniform use of scale.

Every representation requires some kind of device or medium. Yet it is useful to make a distinction between mediation processes that are highly automated, or *algorithmic* processes (e.g., photography), and more manually and intentionally performed activities (e.g., hand-drawn or driven representations). However, these are not absolute categories and it is better to think about this useful distinction as two extremes of a continuum. Moreover, current digital technologies have blurred the dichotomy between 'machine-generated' and 'hand-made' imagery, and increasingly have allowed for more complex combinations of the two (for instance, digital photographs that can be manipulated at will with the aid of sophisticated software).

The process whereby one works from a *directly visible referent to a visual representation of it* would appear to be the most straightforward, but even then a great variety of techniques are available. Moreover, even the more commonly applied techniques have their intricacies, which are easily overlooked. This is true of relatively simple and ubiquitous techniques, including photography of directly observable phenomena, where one often has the advantage of being able to compare the referent (the object or phenomenon with a material existence) and the depiction (a drawing or photograph). However, as much such devices may differ in terms of the manner in which they 'translate' an object or phenomenon into a record of it, it is important to note that both the source or the referent (the natural object or phenomenon) and its representation are 'visual' in nature and are respectively captured and constructed by methods or processes that are essentially visual as well. In such instances, there is at least the theoretical option of comparing the source and its representation in order to assess to what degree and in which respects they resemble one another. Thus, a 'check of correspondence' can be performed, albeit only to a certain degree.

A much more complex translation process occurs when the referent is visual and physical in nature (though often hidden from direct observation), while the *intermediate steps are not based on reflected visible light waves*. This is the case, for example, when ultrasound scans or X-rays are used. In these instances it is not light reflected by the object that is recorded, but a reaction of other types of 'invisible' waves to some characteristic or aspect (e.g., density) of the structure of the referent. These translations, while equally 'indexical' in nature, typically require a more cumbersome process of decoding and calibration (Pasveer, 1992); they do not allow a simple check of 'visual correspondence.' Radiologists, for instance, need to learn how to 'read' these images, and even then they may differ on how a particular one should be interpreted.

If the translation process is not visual or if the referent is inaccessible or invisible to the unaided human eye, one has to rely on – and thus transfer authority to – the 'machine' (Snijder, 1989) in order to chart often unknown territory. In such cases, one has to be particularly aware of the possibility that one is looking at *artifacts of the instrumentation* – that is, the 'objects' and effects that are generated by the representational processes themselves and that do not refer to anything in the 'outside world' or at least not to the phenomenon that is under scrutiny. In many data-generating processes, it is not always easy to differentiate 'noise' from 'data'. Artifacts or effects thus may be attributed erroneously to the outside world, while in fact they are produced standardly by the instruments or as a result of technical failure. Moreover, an atypical representation also may result from an unexpected and unaccounted event or coincidence in the physical world.

So, especially if the referent is of an uncertain nature, the problem of artifacts of instrumentation may arise. This may be the case when the existence of the referent is postulated rather than confirmed by fact and the process of representation serves the purpose of providing such evidence; or when complex instruments are being used; or when aspects of reality can only be seen through the instruments (that is to say, as a 'representation'). But even with very realistic renderings of directly visible objects (e.g., simple camera images of directly observable phenomena), one should be wary of the possibility of 'effects' induced by the instrumentation. Such effects can present themselves to the uninitiated eye as qualities or traits of depicted objects (color, shape, spatiality) while in fact they are merely properties of the instrumentation (e.g., the extremely foreshortened perspective when using telephoto lenses makes objects appear much closer to one another than they are in reality; internal reflections may produce flare and ghosting). In a similar way, scientists should be aware of the possibility that important aspects of the referent might not be captured by the instrumentation (e.g., because of an inadequate resolution or insensitivity caused by a limited spectral range) or might mistakenly be weeded out as noise. Instruments, in addition to capturing or recording data, invariably both reduce (or lose) data and tend to mold (and add) data in a particular way. These two phenomena in themselves should already warn against a naïvely realistic view of the merely technical aspect of representation (Figures 13.10 and 13.11).

3.4   Algorithmic versus non-algorithmic processes

Technically sophisticated instruments that produce representations or images in a highly automated and standardized way (such as cameras and scanning devices) are generally thought of as the most suitable for scientific purposes, as they produce coherent, reliable and repeatable representations with a predetermined level of detail. Moreover, they tend not to rely too much on personal judgment or skills in the process of image generation, unlike manual techniques such as drawing. (Though the interpretation of such representations may still require a lot of personal judgment and experience!)

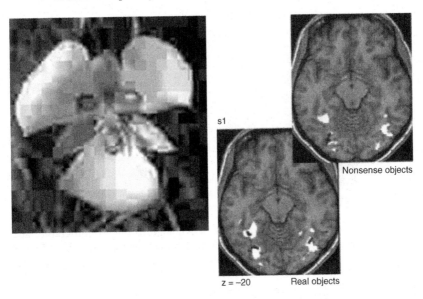

s1

Nonsense objects

z = −20   Real objects

Figures 13.10 and 13.11 'Artifacts of instrumentation' generated by inadequate resolution
Left: a flower displaying a 'pattern' that does not refer to the anything in the physical world due to low resolution; right: a brain scan displaying objects that are 'produced' by the scanning device and thus may lead to an incorrect diagnosis.

However, in some cases more intentional processes and products may be far more convenient. This is true, for instance, if the depiction is *too detailed* for the intended purpose. This may be the case when using a highly automated and 'indifferent' process such as a camera recording. Such a recording can be indifferent in the sense that all visible elements in front of the lens receive the same treatment, irrespective of whether they are relevant to the researcher. Thus, the essence of the recording may be obscured by unneeded, distracting or irrelevant detail that can impede comprehension. Furthermore, intentional processes allow a much swifter combination of *different types of signs (iconic, indexical, and symbolic) and levels of signification*. Consequently, they may yield a more functional expressive presentation of fact and vision. A third important consideration is that intentional processes may provide a much-needed *synthesis of features* rather than a simple transcript of a particular (snapshot-like) instance of a phenomenon.

Figures 13.12, 13.13 and 13.14 An algorithmic (photograph) and two non-algorithmic (hand-drawn) representations of a blue heron. The context and purpose of use should steer the choice of representational technique as well as the stylistic options within that technique.

For instance, ornithologists who use imagery to determine the species of a particular bird encountered in the field may be better off with well-crafted illustrations of a number of similar-looking species – such as a colored drawing that contrasts a heron (*Ardea cinerea L.*) and a purple heron (*Ardea purpurea L.*). After all, they can derive from such a drawing how the two birds differ 'in general.' Color photographs, on the other hand, unavoidably show a particular specimen of each type of heron in a particular stage of its development and photographed against a particular background, in particular light conditions, from a particular angle and so on. This photographic 'particularity' may be less helpful in determining the species of an individual bird in the wild. On the other hand, purposefully simplified representations and abstractions may instill some misconceptions in people's minds if they are not duly communicated or if they are used for other than the initially intended purpose (Figures 13.12 to 13.14).

For example, medical students may be baffled by the visual differences between stylized and simplified anatomical drawings of heart, lungs and vascular system in their introductory courses and the 'real thing.' Similarly, engineering students may be surprised by the differences between a highly stylized drawing of engine wiring and the three-dimensional reality of a dismantled engine that needs reassembling.

Scientific illustration as a sub-discipline of science is an interesting example of a specialism that has evolved in recognition of the fact that both scientists and artists generally lack the skills to produce renderings of birds, human anatomy or complex technical artifacts with the required level of detail and generic faculties. Using artists who are very skilled in drawing, but largely unaware of the exact purpose of the illustration, inadvertently will produce imagery that may thwart that purpose. Scientific illustrators, on the other hand, need to be well versed both in the art of illustration and in specialized fields of science. They are trained to have a thorough and fully integrated knowledge of the subject matter or concepts that they are asked to draw and of the exact scientific and didactic purposes their products need to serve.

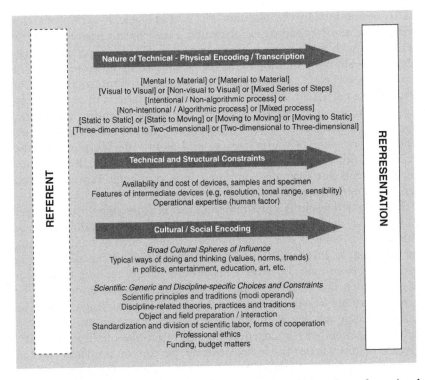

Figure 13.15 Determining aspects of the production and transformational processes on the appearance of the visual representation.

4   The visual product: the impact of medium and execution/style

4.1   Cultural impact on style and use of media

Visualization obviously results in a product that can be 'seen': a graphic representation, a photograph, a computer rendering. The products of a visualization process emanate the characteristics of the (final) medium or successive operations as well as the features of the particular application or instance: the selections and choices of what and how to depict.

The end medium or the medium of presentation has an important impact on the final appearance of a visual representation. Although each medium has a number of preset characteristics, within each medium there is almost always a great variety in the manner in which a particular referent may be represented (mimetically and expressively). This choice and combination of specific formal options henceforth will be referred to as the 'style of execution.' The style of execution is only partly determined by the medium. The notion of a wide variety of styles within the same medium is illustrated easily by divergent painterly traditions such as Cubism and Hyperrealism. Similarly, scientists may choose a variety of methods and techniques (ranging from realist to extremely stylized, to metaphorical, or even phantasmagoric) for depicting a particular subject or idea. These variations in style have to do with genre conventions, cultural schemata, scientific traditions, specific circumstances of the production process, skill, preferences, and idiosyncrasies of the maker, as well as the specific purposes the representations need to serve. To complicate matters further, various media and styles may be combined in a particular representation, lending it a highly hybrid character.

Even if the referent is a phenomenon that is accessible through direct observation, this is still not a guarantee for a 'faithful' or reliable reproduction, especially if a non-mechanical process, such as hand-drawing or painting, is involved. This is particularly true if the phenomena are drawn from memory after a brief and perhaps exciting encounter (for instance the early drawings of newly discovered animals). For representations based on first encounters or limited study, even the scientists may not know to what extent their representations have a rule-like (general) as opposed to an exception-like quality (deviant). Even if memory is not the major obstacle, perception is always colored by prior knowledge of other phenomena: drawing conventions, cultural representational schemata, matters of skill, and mental processes. The human mind, as Gestalt psychologists have revealed, seems very eager to fill in the gaps and to make us see what we want to see. Art historian E. H. Gombrich (1994) provided a textbook example of this when he commented on Dürer's famous woodcut of a rhinoceros (1515): 'he had to rely on second-hand evidence which he filled in from his own imagination, colored, no doubt, by what he had learned of the most famous of exotic beasts, the dragon with its armoured body' (Gombrich, 1994: 70–1). But even drawings that are claimed to have been made 'from life' ('sur vif'), such as Villard de Honnecourt's *Lion and Porcupine* (about 1235), may not provide us with depictions that are as faithful as the medium allows but highly idiosyncratic or artistic renderings, which, in de Honnecourt's case, included a quirky stylized lion that would better serve heraldic purposes than (naturalistic) representational ones. Gombrich concluded that the claim that something was made 'from life' clearly must have had a different meaning at that time: 'He can have meant only that he had drawn his schema in the presence of a real lion' (Gombrich, 1994: 68). In this same classic of art criticism, Gombrich provides another remarkable example of the impact of cultural schemata on the style of a representation when he comments on a strangely oriental-looking illustration of Derwentwater in the English Lake District by Chiang Yee:

We see how the relatively rigid vocabulary of the Chinese tradition acts as a selective screen which admits only the features for which schemata exist. The artist will be attracted by motifs which can be rendered in his idiom. As he scans the landscape, the sights which can be matched successfully with the schemata he has learned to handle will leap forward as centres of attention. The style, like the medium, creates a mental set which makes the artist look for certain aspects in the scene around him that he can render. Painting is an activity, and the artist will therefore tend to see what he paints rather than to paint what he sees. (Gombrich, 1994: 73)

4.2 'Visual representational latitude': coping with variation in the depicted and the depiction

Though visual media and techniques provide many unique advantages in representing the physical world and in expressing scientific ways of thinking, as soon as a certain level of abstraction or generalization is needed – an essential facet and phase of many scientific undertakings – some distinctive problems may arise. Verbally, for instance, one can state that a certain bird species may have three to seven spots on its wings. However, when producing a visual representation, one inevitably must draw a definite number of spots. Visuals, unlike oral descriptions, do not offer the option of indicating a range, say 'from three to seven.' Instead, a choice needs to be made out of the five possibilities when representing in a single drawing a species that exhibits that amount of variation. Moreover, if a photograph is used, one is even forced to show a particular specimen of the species (or a series of photographs of different specimen), of a particular age and sex, in specific circumstances (habitat, weather, time of day, season, etc.). Neither intentional nor more automated (algorithmic) visual images can in themselves express in a simple way the variation (in shape, color, amount, etc.) one may expect to encounter in the real world. Nor can visual depictions fully explain the connections among the particularities of the representation (the variation in the depiction) and what they seek to refer to (the phenomenon and the different forms it can assume in reality).

This multifaceted problem of different types of justified or unjustified variation in scientific representations, combined with both the variation that exists within the species or phenomenon that is depicted and the variation in the depiction of certain phenomena or ideas, is what I would propose to call 'visual representational latitude.' This latitude will be determined partly by the capacities of the medium applied (e.g., intentional versus algorithmic media) in coping with the variation observed within the depicted phenomenon or process, but more

Figures 13.16 and 13.17 The issue of 'visual representational latitude' exemplified.
      Do these non-algorithmic representations of a porcupine each refer to different (sub-)species or to observed variation within a particular (sub-)species, or do they merely embody different artistic interpretations of the same (sub-)species?

importantly by the *manner* in which that medium is used, including the stylistic options it offers, the scientifically motivated choices and the various 'liberties' that producers allow themselves. The 'room for man-euver' or representational margins may or may not be purposeful, functional and understood.

Visual representational latitude, therefore, is not just a producer's (or sender's) problem; that is, it is not just a matter of deciding how to express variation, of choosing the right level of iconicity or abstraction for a specific purpose. It is also a user's (or receiver's) problem: what kind of variation is to be expected in the real world, and which elements in this particular representation are 'motivated' by a perceived reality, and which others are due to specific, intentional, or unintentional choices of the producer, limitations of the medium or larger production context? To what extent is every choice to be interpreted as 'necessarily so' or as just

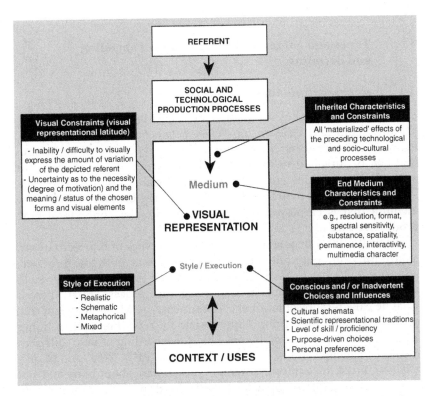

Figure 13.18 Inherited, medium-related and execution-specific characteristics and constraints of visual representations.

'one way of putting it'? If, for instance, a physical phenomenon is depicted as consisting of a core with, say, twenty-three particles revolving around it, one is still uncertain whether this exact number of particles is a unique and thus determining trait of the phenomenon, or whether the person who produced the diagram merely meant to indicate that 'many' particles are revolving around the core. Similar questions could be raised with respect to the relative distance of the constituting parts of the drawing, their scale, color, shape and so on.

Verbal comments (e.g., in the form of an extended 'legend') are one way of making sure that users know what they are looking at, what codes are being used, what semiotic variation is being employed, and what representational claims are put in effect by the representation. Another way is to develop further a visual language of scientific representation, which in a sense restricts the ways in which visual elements may be employed, but at the same time enables a more visual and less ambiguous form of information transfer and expression.

5   Types and contexts of use: matters of encoding and decoding

5.1   Representational constraints

Representations cannot serve adequately just any purpose or intent. Various significant relationships exist between the type of referent, the production process, the medium, and the types of uses and claims that can be attached to them. Visual representations must have the necessary 'properties' to comply with certain functions or uses. Properties, for that matter, refer not only to the characteristics of the medium that is employed but also to the broader contexts of both production and use.

Mitchell (1992) distinguished between two types of representational 'constraints' or, put differently, two factors that both the producer and user will have to take into account when trying to apply visuals successfully in a communication and cognitive process. First, there is what he called 'representational commitment,' by which he meant that certain techniques are (more) appropriate for recording certain things and less suited or even totally unsuited for recording others: 'different medical-imaging techniques – CT, ultrasound, PET, MRI, and so on – are committed to acquiring different types of data about bony and soft tissue diseases and physiological activities, and so are used for different diagnostic purposes' (Mitchell, 1992: 221). Similarly, black-and-white photography may offer the right kind of detail to study naturally occurring phenomena in a social context and thus may be an ideal tool for anthropologists and sociologists, but in some instances this representational choice will be less than adequate. This could be the case when documenting trends in fashion, home decoration and the like, where the use of color embodies essential information; or when a detailed account of processes is required, which can only be achieved by means of a continuous record of moving images. A second requirement that Mitchell puts forward is that a visual representation 'must have the correct type of *intentional relationship to its subject matter*' (Mitchell, 1992: 221). Some examples may help to illustrate the importance of this requirement: the picture of an escaped convict may help police track down that particular individual, but his facial characteristics cannot be used to identify other individuals with criminal tendencies before they can actually commit a crime. Likewise, a scan of a pathogenic heart may serve as a diagnostic tool to help one particular patient, but that is not to say that it is the most appropriate representation for use in a general biology textbook.

However, the same medium types of representation may serve many purposes and entertain widely divergent relations with the depicted matter. Furthermore, a particular visual representation that was made for a specific purpose may be suitable for other purposes, even for some that were not envisioned at the time of production. However, in most cases one needs to know exactly how the images or visual representations came about and what their broader context of production was before one can assess their validity for those other purposes. The use one can make of a representation is determined, to a considerable extent, by its generative process (choice of visual medium and broader production aspects: choices regarding style, selection and preparation of subject, normative systems) vis-à-vis its intended use. So, insofar as this is possible, a predetermined purpose should guide the production process. Some purposes, such as the exploration of a naturally occurring phenomenon, may require an indifferent, detailed account of particularistic data in their specific context, whereas others, such as educational aims, may better be served by highly stylized and synthetic representations highlighting only the essence of a more general phenomenon. So the medium and the techniques in part will determine the uses that can be made of a representation, but even representations produced with the same medium or technique may have widely divergent intents and representational positions.

5.2 *Kinds of intents and purposes*

The intents and purposes of visual representations in scientific discourses are manifold. For one thing, natural phenomena might be visualized for the purpose of *further analysis*: to make a diagnosis, to compare, to describe, to preserve for future study, to verify, to explore new territory, to generate new data and so on. Representations that serve these primary purposes often will be algorithmic in nature and they may have an only 'intermediate' function, since they are primary 'data.' Visual representations that have no material referent may serve primarily to *facilitate concept development* or to uncover relationships, evolutions (e.g., through charts of all kinds) and, in general, to make the *abstract more concrete* and thus more accessible for further enquiry. Forms of externalized thinking (conceptual graphs) may be useful both on an intra-personal level (for example to guide researchers in a dialogue with themselves) and an interpersonal/inter-specialist level (e.g., to exchange ideas in an early stage, to invite feedback or to prompt cooperation from peers). Visual representations not only serve analytical and intermediate purposes, but they are also often used to *summarize or synthesize* empirical findings or a theoretical line of thought. Thus, they may provide an overview, display results in their spatial organization or conceptual relations, or clarify the textual or numerical part. In science, more synthesized or purposefully assembled visual representations generally serve to facilitate knowledge transfer in a variety of ways and seek to communicate with diverse audiences. They can illustrate, demonstrate or exemplify features, relations and processes, or provide mediated experiences, in ways that are adapted to the audience (which may vary from highly specialized to lay audiences).

Many visual representations intentionally or inadvertently will embody an implicit or more explicit view on or argument about what is being presented visually, through the many elements and choices that make up the representation. This expressive function of scientific visualizations need not be a problem as long as it is duly acknowledged and, if required, explained. As intentional forms of communication and through the selection and formal execution of the representations as well as by their thoughtful arrangement in the broader context of an article, a presentation or a multimedia product, visual representations will attempt to exert a certain amount of persuasion. Often, receivers or users of the representation will, in subtle ways, be invited, seduced or even compelled to adopt the views of the sender and to perform the preferred actions (to believe, give approval, appreciate, change opinions, donate money or support morally). For those reasons, but also for the more acclaimed function of cognitive transfer and education, a visual representation may perform the function of an eye catcher, a means to arouse and maintain attention and interest, or even to entertain the reader/spectator (and thus bring them into the right mood for acceptance). Some aspects of a visual representation in science may even perform no other function than to appeal to the aesthetic feelings of the receivers or just be an expression of the personal aesthetic preferences of the maker. These latter functions, though not readily associated with a scientific discourse, are not necessarily detrimental to the mission of a scientific undertaking, as long as these traits do not interfere with the more fundamental functions of data or cognitive transfer, and on condition that transparency is provided.

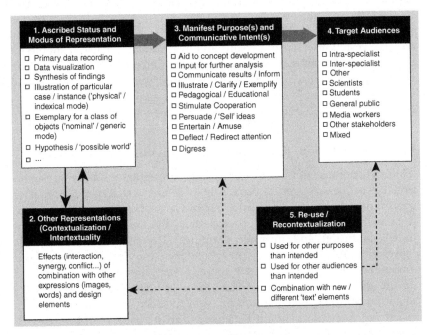

Figure 13.19 Representational status, context and use: connections between representations, purposes and audiences. Visual representations with a particular ontological status (1), in interaction with other representational and presentational elements (2) may be used for different purposes and intents (3) with specific target audiences (4) in mind. Subsequent uses (5) may involve new goals (3) and new 'textual' combinations (2) for different audiences (4) and may challenge the ontological status and the representational 'fit' of the original representation (1).

While we can never be complete in the listing of possible functions and intents of a scientific visual representation, this brief discussion of functions demonstrates that the idea that scientific visualizations and representations are solely meant to generate and present 'objective' data or to facilitate pure cognition should be abandoned. It should be clear that most functions and intents that are found in human communication also will be found in scientific representation, though some functions and intents obviously will serve a more central role, whereas others will not feature prominently or may be intended to perform an auxiliary function. Moreover, it should be clear that any visual representation used as part of a scientific discourse will serve and combine different functions at the same time, whether intentionally or unintentionally. These purposes may be scientific in a narrow sense, but they may also have to do with intents that lie outside the realm of the acknowledged scientific purposes, such as to serve vested interests of persons and institutions. Finally, it should be stressed that the different functions that are embodied by aspects of the visual representation may be read or 'decoded' in many different ways by different receivers (based on their intents, experience, formal background, etc.) in different contexts and over time (Figure 13.19).

6   Conclusion: developing visual scientific competencies

The basic premise of this chapter is that representations and representational practices may be extremely helpful in developing, clarifying or transmitting scientific knowledge. However, when not produced and used with extreme care and competence, they may create at least as much confusion and misunderstandings. If one considers scientific representations and the ways in which they can foster or thwart our understanding, it is clear that a mere 'object approach,' which would devote all attention to the 'representation' as a free-standing product of scientific labor, is inadequate. What is needed is a *process approach*: each visual representation should be linked with its context of production. Moreover, it cannot be understood sensibly outside a particular and dynamic context of use, re-use and reception. However, given the great many types of referents, representational techniques, purposes and uses, it seems fair to assume that the vast consequences of this requirement are hardly grasped by the growing number of people who produce and use visual representations on a daily basis.

Scientists should more actively develop a sensitivity for the wide variety of visual representational practices and products and the many ways in which they can be deployed in scientific discourse. Furthermore, a real set of skills is needed in order to be able to *assess* the usability of given representations based on a thorough knowledge of their generic processes, and to be able to *produce* visual representations with the required representational and expressive properties in relation to their purpose(s).

Visual representations invariably have a strong communicative function, certainly with regard to the originator (e.g., to guide his/her thinking, or to serve as data for further analysis), but often also towards a variety of specialized and non-specialized audiences. Unconsciously applied and/ or unmotivated use of aesthetics and unexplained use of certain conventions are a potential hazard, whereas well thought-out and reflexive use of aesthetics and formal choices, and well-explicated representational codes and conventions may create hitherto not fully exploited opportunities to further scientific knowledge building and communication. Modern technology offers many complex ways of generating images, but few users have a clear understanding of all the steps involved. To counter this emerging 'black box syndrome,' it is clear that scientists need to keep track of new media technologies to the extent that they offer new ways of looking and (not) knowing.

This complex set of requirements involving specific knowledge attitudes and skills may be understood as a specific kind of visual literacy or competence for scientists. Visual competence for scientists can therefore be defined as a reflexive attitude (throughout the production process), a specific body of knowledge, and even a certain level of proficiency or skill in assessing and applying specific characteristics (strengths and limitations) of a particular medium, and awareness of cultural practices (codified uses, expectations) and the actual context of use (including the 'cultural repertoire' of the intended audience). In other words, a visually competent scholar should be aware of the impact of the social, cultural and technological aspects involved in the production and handling of representations, as well as the different normative systems that may be at work and how he/she exerts a determining influence on the eventual appearance and the usefulness of representations.

Visual scientific competency should not just imply establishing a clear division of labor (every person keeping to his/her trade) and then linking together those various types of expertise, as in fact they need to be merged rather than developed and applied according to a separate logic for each specialized aspect. The different normative systems (e.g., scientific, technical, creative, cultural ...) that are consciously or unconsciously employed need to be skillfully combined with a view to the ultimate purpose of the representation. While expertise obviously cannot be accumulated endlessly in one and the same person, a serious effort should at least be made at providing a unifying framework whereby each contributor should develop a knowledge about and sensitivity for the bigger whole. What they should not do is lock themselves up in their own area of expertise, as hardly any choice that is made along the way is without epistemological consequence.

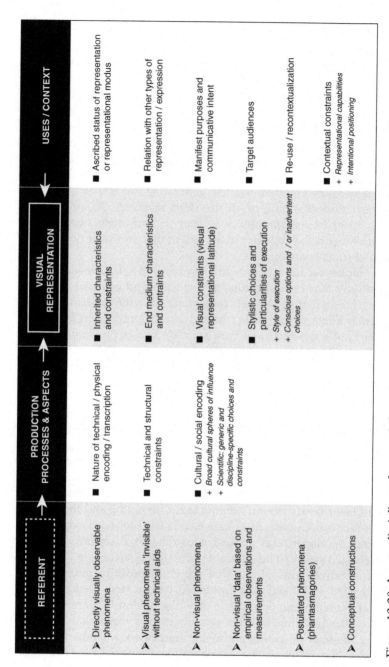

Figure 13.20 A meta-disciplinary framework for producing and assessing visual representations.

The aspects and issues that have been discussed in this chapter may serve as a theoretical framework for the thoughtful production of visual representations in science or they may be used as a tool to critically assess the appropriateness of different aspects of particular representations. Such a framework may prove useful in examining the complex interdependencies that exist between the nature of the referent, the social, technological and cultural context of production, the choices with respect to medium and the style of representation, and the purposes and uses that need to be achieved. Figure 13.20 attempts to summarize and visualize the elements and arguments of this framework as gradually developed from section to section. Visual representations will always be used to enlighten and broaden our understanding, but at the same time, they will continue to obscure it. Concerted and integrated efforts in delineating and developing visual competencies will considerably help scholars to optimize the production and uses of visual representations in various types of research and communication.

7 References

Cambrosio, A., D. Jacobi and P. Keating (1993) 'Ehrlich's "Beautiful Pictures" and the Controversial Beginnings of Immunological Imagery.' *ISIS* 84: 662–99.

Gombrich, E. H. (1994) *Art & Illusion: A Study in the Psychology of Pictorial Representation*. London: Phaidon (first published 1960).

Goodwin, C. (1994) 'Professional Vision.' *American Anthropologist* 96: 606–33.

Goodwin, C. (1995) 'Seeing in Depth.' *Social Studies of Science* 25: 237–74.

Goodwin, C. (1996) 'Transparent Vision.' In: E. Ochs, E. A. Schegloff and S. A. Thompson (eds.) *Interaction and Grammar*. Cambridge University Press, pp. 370–404.

Gordin, D. N. and R. D. Pea (1995) 'Prospects for Scientific Visualization as an Educational Technology.' *The Journal of the Learning Sciences* 4: 249–79.

Grady, J. (2006) 'Edward Tufte and the Promise of a Visual Social Science.' In: Luc Pauwels (ed.) *Visual Cultures of Science: Rethinking Representational Practices in Knowledge Building and Science Communication*, Hanover, NH/London: Dartmouth College Press / University Press of New England, pp. 222–65.

Knor-Cetina, K. (1981) *The Manufacture of Knowledge: An Essay on the Constructivist and Contextual Nature of Science*. New York: Pergamon.

Latour, B. and S. Woolgar (1979) *Laboratory Life: The Social Construction of Scientific Facts*. London: Sage.

Lemke, J. L. (1998) 'Multiplying Meaning: Visual and Verbal Semiotics in Scientific Text.' In: J. R. Martin and R. Veel (eds.) *Reading Science*. London: Routledge, pp. 87–113.

Lynch, M. (1985a) 'Discipline and the Material Form of Images: An Analysis of Scientific Visibility.' *Social Studies of Science* 15: 37–66.

Lynch, M. (1985b) *Art and Artifact in Laboratory Science: A Study of Shop Work and Shop Talk in a Research Laboratory*. London: Routledge & Kegan Paul.

Lynch, M. and S. Woolgar (eds.) (1998) *Representation in Scientific Practice.* Cambridge, MA: The MIT Press

Mitchell, W. J. (1992) *The Reconfigured Eye.* Cambridge, MA: The MIT Press.

Pasveer. B. (1992) *Shadows of Knowledge: Making a Representing Practice in Medicine: X-Ray Pictures and Pulmonary Tuberculosis, 1895–1930.* University of Amsterdam: dissertation.

Pauwels, L. (2000) 'Taking the Visual Turn in Research and Scholarly Communication: Key Issues in Developing a More Visually Literate (Social) Science.' *Visual Sociology* 15: 7–14.

Pauwels, L. (2002) 'The Video- and Multimedia-Article as a Mode of Scholarly Communication: Toward Scientifically Informed Expression and Aesthetics.' *Visual Studies* 17(2): 150–9.

Pea, R. D. (1994) 'Seeing What We Build Together: Distributed Multimedia Learning Environments for Transformative Communications.' *Journal of the Learning Sciences* 3: 285–99.

Rosenblum, B. (1978) *Photographers at Work: A Sociology of Photographic Styles,* York/London: Holmes & Meier Publishers.

Roth, W.-M. and G. M. Bowen (1999) 'Digitizing Lizards: The Topology of "Vision" in Ecological Fieldwork.' *Social Studies of Science* 29: 719–64.

Roth, W.-M. and G. M. Bowen (2001) '"Creative Solutions" and "Fibbing Results": Enculturation in Field Ecology.' *Social Studies of Science* 31: 533–56.

Roth, W.-M. and M. K. McGinn (1997) 'Graphing: Cognitive Ability or Practice.' *Science Education* 81: 91–106.

Roth, W-M., G. M. Bowen and M. K. McGinn (1999) 'Differences in Graph-Related Practices between High School Biology Textbooks and Scientific Ecology Journals.' *Journal of Research in Science Teaching* 36: 977–1019.

Roth, W-M., G. M. Bowen and D. Masciotra (2002) 'From Thing to Sign and "Natural Object": Toward a Genetic Phenomenology of Graph Interpretation.' *Science, Technology & Human Values* 27: 327–56.

Snijder, J. (1989) 'Benjamin on the Reproducibility and Aura: A Reading of "The Work of Art in the Age of its Technical Reproducibility."' In: G. Smith (ed.) *Benjamin: Philosophy, Aesthetics, History.* University of Chicago Press, pp. 158–74.

Tufte, E. (1983) *The Visual Display of Quantitative Information.* Cheshire, CN: Graphics Press.

Tufte, E. (1990) *Envisioning Information.* Cheshire, CN: Graphics Press.

Tufte, E. (1997) *Visual Explanations.* Cheshire, CN: Graphics Press.

14   Advancing visual research: pending issues and future directions

Visual social research in various shapes and guises continues to gain a wider acceptance and develop into a feasible option for scholars. Evidence of this can be found in the ever increasing number of visual science journals, monographs, edited volumes, conferences and specialized organizations. This pull towards the visual – to forms of research using visual means to gather data and to communicate findings more visually – is definitely a positive evolution. However, while visual practices and approaches are being invented and reinvented from a myriad of disciplinary and theoretical positions, there is also a growing need to better *integrate knowledge and expertise* in these fields of enquiry and to develop a *critical-constructive stance* to past, present and future efforts, to truly take advantage of the rich visual dimension of society.

The final chapter of this book, therefore, seeks to summarize, mark out and discuss some crucial issues in the effort to advance the increasingly popular and diversified field of visual research. Some of these issues are old dilemmas (e.g., the collaboration between researchers and professional image makers); some are lingering problems (e.g., required visual competencies) that could have been better handled had they been better defined and brought to the surface. Other aspects are challenges of a more recent nature, triggered by current developments in society (e.g., globalization issues, new technologies). However, many of these issues can be turned into opportunities for advancement when dealt with appropriately (Pauwels, 2010).

This chapter will take a slightly provocative, but constructive, stance to highlight essential aspects of visual research, which need constant and heightened attention. The observations and comments made here inevitably tend to generalize and may sound somewhat prescriptive. Both these characteristics (generalization and prescriptiveness) may cause offense or put off readers, who are (or think they are) really much further down the road towards a more visual social science. The effort to characterize and to some extent criticize this vast field of visual research in general terms may indeed at times not do justice to a growing and highly diversified group of visual scholars, who operate at the forefront of this exciting endeavor.

1   Utilizing the full potential of the visual

Advancing the field of visual research will first and foremost require a better understanding of the visual and of ways to deal with it in a more proficient, encompassing and explicit way. Understanding the complex nature of the visual, of visualization processes and practices, and of visual technologies is key in this respect. Clearly this knowledge base is already largely available, but it is first of all scattered between different fields of enquiry and secondly not always brought into practice by scholars, from a variety of backgrounds, who have at some point become attracted to this field or who have preset ideas about the visual (such as: 'images should speak for themselves'). As a result, many discussions on the research value of the visual are of a repetitive and shallow nature.

A considerable number of issues and misunderstandings regarding visual research can ultimately be related to limited views and existing confusion with regard to the iconic, indexical and symbolic properties of visual products and visual media, as they reside with commissioners, producers, users and sponsors of visual projects.

Quite some discussion about the nature of the visual and its research potential originates in confounding 'indexicality' and 'iconicity' and in failing to consider the expressive and conceptual powers of visuals that transcend these traits. Naïve realists tend to overlook the constitutive character of the medium and the impact of its use: the fact that every act of representation obliterates many aspects of the depicted and at the same time adds new elements through the specifics of the instrumentation and the way the representational process is executed (i.e., including stylistic choices). As a result, they tend to have an almost unmitigated belief in the veracity of the visual representation. The other side of the spectrum is populated by (visual) researchers, who in an unqualified manner rage against any iconic and indexical potential of images and visual representations and contend that visual representations are almost purely arbitrary constructions (oddly enough they tend to use visuals in much the same way as their opponents). More importantly, however, many researchers – from both ends of the spectrum – often overlook the vast expressive potential of visual representations that opens up the way to scholarly argumentation and new avenues of expressing the unspeakable and unquantifiable. Visual representations not only give way to the depicted subject or object, but also tend to embody very revealing aspects about the producer and culture of production. There is no benefit in simply denying or oversimplifying the complex 'referentiality' of most images (in both iconic and indexical ways); the task ahead is to further clarify the exact nature of this referentiality and to explore its functionality for social scientific research and communication. Also, since referentiality is but one of the functions of visual communication, it is of paramount importance that the creative or constructive potential of visual representational practices is further explored and developed. Scholarly work, be it written, visual or numeric is not (just) about describing or reflecting aspects of the outer world, but about making it more revealing, accessible, insightful, and possibly more predictable or controllable.

Thus visual scholars should no longer disregard or neglect the vital importance of style and form (the 'how') in conveying any content (the 'what'). Both are inseparable in any process of meaning-making, which in turn is more and more intertwined with technology (e.g., the increasing impact of digital, multimedia, networking technologies, locative media such as GPS and Google Earth, eye-tracking and virtual reality (VR) photography). While commenting on this persistent tendency to under-utilize the expressive potential of style in scientific communication, it would be unfair not to mention that there are a number of visual and media scholars who in a myriad of ways are gradually and productively building on this.

Aesthetic properties of media and representational practices in general should no longer be considered aspects that need to be 'controlled' in the sense of: reduced to an absolute minimum or left to 'specialists' who are trained to put things 'in proper shape.' Rather, such a functional aesthetic sensitivity should be stimulated in a more thoughtful and considerate way, to result in better, richer forms of scholarly communication that will help data transfer and argumentation, and possibly even generate new types of knowledge. What constitutes an appropriate approach when producing and using imagery and media in a scholarly context depends heavily on the goals of the production: is the primary goal to educate (who? about what precisely?), to shape, reinforce or change attitudes or behavior, to distract or entertain, to offer 'a real-life experience,' to stimulate scientific or critical thought? Clearly there is no single 'right' approach, but a visually oriented scholar may benefit from trying to very consciously select and combine as many as possible of the visual and non-visual elements ('signifiers') that make up the end product.

The matter of 'functional' aesthetics and 'appropriate' expressiveness will most likely continue to trigger divergent views or fuel controversies. There should definitely be room for more experimentation and for example for more metaphorical types of expression. This may require some more audacious and creative impetus from scholars. The main restriction that needs to be imposed on such experiments is that the audience should know what it is looking at, and/or reading or hearing. A visual product that claims the same status as a scholarly journal article should at all times be clear about its highly codified nature, even or precisely when highly iconic data (e.g., camera images) are presented, since they by their very nature tend to foster the illusion of offering an unmediated experience to the spectators.

Visual research and visual communication of research have always entertained a strong link with technology and will continue to take stock of new opportunities they may offer to data collection, production and dissemination. Digital visual technologies ranging from regular digital cameras to action cams and cam-phones, geo-locative devices, satellite image applications and Internet-based technologies (like Google Street View: Odgers et al., 2012), which today are used in society and by innovative researchers, are able to generate ever more interesting types of data as well as novel ways to present and disseminate knowledge. New media technologies as reporting tools can, to a certain extent, help to accommodate different audiences and purposes (e.g., users can browse menus and various options, go for further information, go back or skip information and choose their own path). However, technology does not automatically solve all problems (e.g., of an epistemological, ethical, expressive or educational nature). Therefore, (new) technologies should not be the driver of a research project, as they may introduce (new) problems as much as they may help to solve existing ones. Nor should they merely be used as vehicles for old messages and approaches. While it is legitimate to turn to technology solely to make current ways of thinking and doing cheaper, the emphasis should be on what one can do with it in terms of growing research opportunities (new forms of data, disclosing new aspects of human behavior) and of communicating visual statements more fluently and clearly. While a modest and thoughtful approach to applying technologies is preferable, it would be inadvisable to confine scholars to a very sparse use of the many (largely unexplored) capabilities of visual media. Researchers should feel stimulated to explore new capabilities of visual media (Coover, 2011), but they should not be tempted to introduce or adopt features that do not add any meaning or that are more likely to generate confusion. Nor should they adopt practices from other fields (e.g., social media templates and practices, music video editing techniques) without rethinking them to best fit their specific scholarly aims. Given these requirements, it does not suffice for visual scholars to have a superficial knowledge of visual technologies and of the specific formal and meaning-related aspects of the visual media, as almost every technical or formal choice is bound to have epistemological (and various other) consequences. After all, these choices determine 'what' one is able to see, 'how' it presents itself to researchers and their audiences, and what remains hidden; they partly determine, reveal and steer the mode of thought of a given culture.

Solid social and cultural research that seeks to be more 'visual' in every respect should be characterized by precise decisions about when (and when not!) to use which kinds of visuals and for which purposes, and by an unambiguous communication of these choices and their limitations. Visual sociologists and anthropologists need to be very critical with respect to using visuals in their end products, whichever form they take (articles, slide shows, exhibitions, installations, DVDs). They should constantly ask themselves: are the selected or created visual representations and all other visual elements (e.g., layout and design features) the most appropriate options, do they add essential information or insights that cannot be – or would be less effectively – communicated in numbers or a verbal description and argumentation, and do they interact in the most effective way with other expressive systems and modes?

2   Towards a more integrated and inclusive approach

Visual research in general could benefit from a better theoretical and methodological grounding and a more sophisticated analytical set of tools. Visual researchers seem to have a broad range of theories and analytical frameworks to choose from when trying to make sense of images and visual artifacts: e.g., content analysis, social semiotics, iconology, ethnomethodology, rhetoric (Peters, 1977; see Berger, 1986; Van Leeuwen and Jewitt, 2000; Smith et al., 2005; Rose, 2006). Unfortunately, they hardly offer a well-integrated and clear methodology to systematically interrogate visuals with respect to their social and cultural significance, and most methods and frameworks are ill-equipped to handle larger sets of visual data. Semiotic analysis, for instance, is arduous to apply to larger sets of visual data as it requires much time and interpretation; content analysis, on the other hand, may be better suited to handle larger data sets, but is hitherto not very well adapted to explore the full richness and the holistic potential of the visual, as it is often restricted to counting elements of the pro-filmic or to collecting data on just a few easy-to-code (e.g., camera distance or angle) – although not necessarily the most important – parameters of an image. In short, they are often not fully adapted to deal with the complex nature of visual images, or for that matter with the increasingly hybrid multimodal constructions (e.g., websites; see Chapter 4). Whereas the analysis of existing ('found') visual products can rely on a fairly broad literature and tradition, methodologies for producing and processing (selecting and reordering, analyzing, presenting) visual data are far less explicitly developed and documented. As these issues embody the core aspects and the specific contribution of a more visual social science, scholars in the field should address this matter more vigorously than they have so far.

The in-depth study of the visual typically requires a more integrated and consequently a truly interdisciplinary approach. This demand provides a good point of departure for returning to a more integrated science. Still, one cannot but observe that, hitherto, a systematic and integrated study of the increasingly important visual aspects of society is lacking, despite the growing need for a more critical approach to visual expressions – either intermediated or not – of today's high-tech cultures. Knowledge of the visual remains fragmented between various disciplines, where it is often further scattered over sub-disciplines. One could say that the visual is so much part of so many disciplines that it becomes almost invisible or taken for granted. Efforts to expand the domain in turn are too often inspired by re-appropriating, extending or narrowing it to the discipline or interest of the writer/speaker.

Clearly there is no single discipline that can claim the central position in the study of visual culture (not art history, not visual communication, not cultural studies, not (even) visual sociology or anthropology, etc.). Scholars need to further clarify the distinct and at times joint or overlapping contributions each of their disciplines can make and put more effort into trying to build on each other's insights and achievements. Visual research should not be narrowed down to researching 'image culture,' nor to producing photographic records of society. The 'visual' aspect of our world does not manifest itself uniquely in the visual media, but it actually pervades our daily lives in most of its facets: in looking, being looked at, visualizing, depicting (reproducing) and so on. So apart from becoming more integrated, the study of the visual and the study through and by the visual should become more 'inclusive' as well.

Looking at recent research applications, visual social and cultural science is fortunately becoming more inclusive in terms of visual and visualized 'referents' (including now also concepts, abstract processes, visualizations of the invisible), media (not just photography and film, but also drawings, maps, artifacts, new media) and fields of interest. Consequently, camera-based representations and techniques (both static and moving images), and directly observable culture have lost the almost exclusive position they have held for years.

Moreover, the insight is growing that visual (social) science is not just about analyzing and producing visual data, but also about visualizing and expressing insights in novel, more experimental and experiential ways (e.g., arts-based approaches). It is important to note that this mission to become more integrated and inclusive should not be confined to the humanities and the social sciences. The fragmentation that characterizes many fields and sub-fields of the social sciences and the humanities is nowhere as dramatic as the proverbial divide that still exists between these fields and the so-called 'sciences' (exact sciences, life sciences . . .), where the visual and visualization play a crucial role in knowledge building and dissemination. However, it should be clear that several fields and sub-fields of these 'science' disciplines (neurology, neurobiology, physics, scientific imaging and analysis) could enrich the social and behavioral sciences and the humanities a great deal with regard to disclosing the nature of vision and visualization. However, the reverse is also true (as exemplified by the better work in sociology of science: e.g., Latour and Woolgar, 1979; Knor-Cetina, 1981; Lynch, 1985; Lemke, 1998), although convincing the 'other side' of this may prove even more cumbersome. While the study of images and visualization in terms of their impact on society, knowledge construction and dissemination (including discussions about visual manipulations and alterations) tends to be recognized as an 'issue' more in the social sciences and humanities than in the 'sciences,' where visualization practices are considered the site of distinct specialists and where particular visualizations are often considered uncontested state-of-the-art products, scientists could learn from social sciences about the social construction of their 'truths' and facts. For visualization – whatever its field of application – is a very complex process that not only relies on more or less transparent technologies, but also embodies numerous interventions of scientists and support personnel, not all of which are duly documented or discussed with respect to their effects. Every resulting visualization is the combined result of a long trajectory of decisions of a very varied nature. The opacity of this process may hamper the knowledge that can be derived from particular images and in more general terms foster less than adequate conceptions of the real-world aspects to which the images seek to refer. To a certain extent every specialism tends to be locked up in its current ways of thinking and doing, often focusing on only parts of the problem and taking for granted existing practices and traditions. However, what is also true is that every specialism potentially holds unique insights into what at first sight might seem to be unrelated aspects or fields of enquiry. As discussed in Chapter 13, a more integrated and inclusive study of the visual, therefore, will be better able to address fundamental questions with respect to the intricate relations between a visual representation and its referent (a physical phenomenon, a concept and anything in between . . .), the determining role of technology and of different scientific and representational traditions, and the hybrid set of competencies that this presupposes for both producers and users of scientific visualizations. The truly interdisciplinary nature of visual research could prove the ideal showcase in the effort to bridge the persistent and often unproductive gap between the 'Two Cultures' (the 'Sciences' versus the 'Humanities'; see Snow, 1960) and to overcome the stereotypical conceptions about 'the other' fostered on both sides.

Ultimately, the call for more integrated and inclusive types of visual research should also question the primacy of the visual and its relation to other senses and modes of expression. Notwithstanding its central and under-examined role, it is clear that the visual should not be studied in isolation and simply exclude the other senses and the many expressive modes that may address these other senses (see Pink, 2011). Yet with respect to 'mediated' experiences, even the most hybrid and advanced (multi)media technologies still only succeed in addressing two out of our five senses (sight and hearing), and usually fail to transmit tactile, olfactory or gustatory experiences. Likewise, so-called 'multimodal research' (Kress and Van Leeuwen, 2001; Bateman, 2008; Van Leeuwen, 2011) has focused on examining the interplay of different expressive systems in the production of meaning and effect, as applied to mediated representations (and as opposed to direct encounters: e.g., a walk in the city or interactions between people), and is, in fact, limited to two (super) modes: the 'visual' and the 'auditory,' ruling out all modes that address the tactile, olfactory and taste senses. However, the visual mode in its wider meaning already includes a variety of expressive systems that are often not readily considered as 'visual': the textual parts (which have to be 'viewed' most of the time), typography, layout and design features. Likewise the auditory mode (spoken or sung texts, music, noises) exhibits a growing diversity of aspects and applications and a corresponding importance in today's converging media. It is important to note that multimodal analysis not only takes different modes into account as generators of meaning, but also has a strong focus on the effects of their interplay. The older concept 'multimedia' has a far more restricted meaning, as it refers mainly to the capabilities of a technical device or to a technology (not to a communicative act or to the perceptual processing of data by people). Multimodal research is an ambitious venture given the fact that even most forms of mono-modal or single mode analysis (for example, the analysis of static photographs) are still underdeveloped – in other words, not able to tap into the full expressive potential of media and visual artifacts/performances. Moreover, to some extent multimodal research seems a mere relabeling of long-existing research traditions (e.g., nonverbal communication, sound-image studies). The basic idea of multimodal research with its emphasis on the effects of specific interactions between different expressive systems is definitely a path that visual research should try to follow to some extent, without losing its focus on the specific complexities of visual perception, visual analysis, visual production and visual applications.

Whereas multimodal research today already manages to attract scholars from very varied fields, visual research in the social and cultural sciences too has benefited in recent years from interdisciplinary enrichment from fields like geography (McKinnon, 2011), design (Boradkar, 2011), arts, history, education, science and technology, and so on. Thus it seems legitimate and may be more correct to say, in fact, that opposing processes of interdisciplinary enrichment and integration on the one hand, and disciplinary appropriation and fragmentation on the other, are simultaneously influencing the future of visual research.

3   Developing visual competencies and productive collaboration

The above elaborated recommendations for visual research to become 'more visual,' integrated, inclusive and more technologically astute will also have a profound effect on the 'level and breadth of expertise' that is needed for doing such forms of visual research, and implicate the question of how exactly the multitude of hybrid competencies can or should be 'developed' and 'combined.'

It is clear that different types of visual research may put very different demands on the researcher depending on the method, the medium and the subject chosen. Some types of research require rather limited skills (or skills that can easily be left to technicians) and hardly tap into the expressive potential of different visual media. Others, however, are much more exigent. For example, producing cultural inventories of home settings could be left to a well-briefed (professional) photographer, who should be able to make pictures with fine detail according to a meticulous shooting script. More expressive means of visual research, such as the visual essay or anthropological film (Rollwagen, 1988), demand more integrated skills from researchers, who need to be able to combine and amalgamate their scientific and visual abilities in a kind of 'visual scientific literacy' (see Chapter 13).

Whether or not 'assisted' by visual professionals or technicians, sociologists and anthropologists should actively seek to develop their visual research and communication skills in order to gradually appreciate the difficulties and problems of the different media and their sheer limitless expressive capabilities. Producing photographic materials with the right levels of mimesis and expression is quite different from creating conceptual representations as an aid to knowledge building and communication. When studying or applying any representational medium or technique, researchers should be aware of their specific transformational qualities, and of the fact that no representational technique can produce 'complete' and 'objective' records, let alone undeniable statements. This should not imply, however, that such records cannot be used as 'reliable' data of some sort. Constant researcher attention is required, to avoid stepping into a naïve realist trap of implicitly equating 'representations' with full and objective records of reality. A broad and thorough knowledge of the visual media and of the many interconnected transformational – technical, social and cultural – processes in which they are rooted is needed to employ the visual in the varied processes of scientific data gathering, processing and communication. Currently this requirement is not always met, nor recognized to its fullest extent (see Pauwels, 2006; Grady, 2011).

The issue of how to develop and combine or integrate different types of expertise in fact goes back to the heated discussions in the field of ethnographic and anthropological filmmaking: whether the anthropologist should be the filmmaker or if it is better to work together with a professional filmmaker to produce 'visual ethnography or anthropology' (Mead, 1963; Rouch, 1975; Ruby, 1986, 2000; Rollwagen, 1988). However, this old question becomes ever more pertinent as media opportunities continue to grow and a commensurate development of visual competencies remains to be desired. In fact, there are currently so many types of expertise involved in performing and presenting visual research that these can hardly be mastered by the same person at the best possible level of proficiency, so that forms of collaboration seem unavoidable to some extent. As mentioned earlier, simply delegating the different types of expertise to separate specialists may also fail to produce an optimal result. It is not just a matter of adding up distinct skills, but of normative systems and traditions that may work together or against each other. Growing pressure falls on the users of visual technology who really want to use it in the most meaningful manner to assimilate and integrate a multitude of skills. These skills will not be acquired automatically and go far beyond reading the operations manual of a device or knowing how a software package 'works.' Video editing or website authoring, for example, is not just about learning software packages, but about acquiring a multitude of insights and skills in highly specialized fields, such as typography, graphic design, narratology, camera work and so on. Applying 'technologies' also presuppose a thorough understanding of the human learning process and of social and cultural characteristics of the target audience. Thus, in conclusion, the further development of visual scientific competencies should be put high on the agenda of visual researchers and in fact on that of virtually all scholars of most disciplines.

4   Fostering critical-constructive and reflexive attitudes

Looking further at how visual research could make significant progress in the years to come, it might benefit from becoming somewhat more (self-) critical, modest and reflexive.

When discussing or advocating different options in visual research, visual scholars should try to avoid taking too rigid a position – for example, by believing that there is only 'one right way.' It is not very productive to overemphasize or celebrate one kind of visual research at the expense of other kinds. For instance, one should not dismiss more mimetic-oriented research as naïvely realist, or conversely reject the more aesthetically inspired, experimental or expressive approaches as unscientific. So, for instance, meticulous re-photography projects aimed at reading social change (Rieger, 2011) through the reproductive capacities of the camera, or micro-analytical studies of interaction using video recordings (Heath et al., 2010; Knoblauch and Tuma, 2011) in very standardized ways should be able to blossom next to more implicit and ambiguous artistic approaches (O'Donoghue, 2011). The latter perhaps lack the rigor and control of the more basic and accepted approaches, but in return excel either in expressing what cannot be put in words or numbers or in transmitting holistic capacities of the visual as intricate amalgamations of content and form.

The field needs to remain open to approaches that try to go further than using visual media as mere transmitters of characteristics of the depicted, but which instead creatively use their features as vehicles of expression of scientifically informed insight, and at the same time continue to recognize the research potential that resides in the reproductive capacities of visual media.

A genuinely (self-)critical stance implies that one constantly questions both one's own and borrowed mental frameworks. Insight into the structure (the building blocks, expressive means, codes) as well as the culture of the image and the visual material world in the broadest sense (production, reception and practices) remains a precondition for being able to formulate both well-founded criticism and sound scientific statements. Such an attitude requires consciously taking the transformational properties (the technical and cultural mediation processes) and the stylistic choices (the 'aesthetics' or formal properties) of the visual representations and the wider (visual and other) context of their use into account.

Some visual scholars would benefit from abandoning an 'author cele-bratory mode' (often leading to very predictable and repetitious findings) to a truly more critical mode that seeks to confront established ideas with one's own viewpoints and visual experiences. First and foremost, visual scholars should try to 'look more closely' at what is offered visually, and not simply adopt the interpretations of authors with a guru-like stature. While theories ideally serve as 'eye-openers,' they should not stimulate prejudice or inhibit a fresh and original look. Also, scholars should drop the urge to invent a new term for a field, a method or technique each time they are dissatisfied with the current version, and in particular when they have only a very limited view of the current offer (and history) of the discipline, method or technique. Paradigms or ideological positions should not be promoted to whole disciplines, and a critique on a parti-cular paradigm of a discipline should not lead to the dismissal of the whole disciplinary tradition. Often too much effort is put into delineating and appropriating the visual field, at best out of ignorance and at worst for self-gratifying purposes. A rather innocent example of this urge to rein-vent and relabel practices and techniques can be found in the variety of idiosyncratic and overlapping descriptions of very similar, or the same, forms of respondent-generated image-making: participatory video, photovoice, shooting back and so forth. One could also refer here to unproductive discussions or struggles around terms like 'visual cul-ture,' 'visual studies,' 'visual cultural studies,' 'image-based research,' 'visual communication,' 'media studies' and 'visual rhetoric,' which are frequently too focused on the presumed unique character of one's approach (or discipline), but often result in vain efforts to reinvent the wheel and while doing so just add confusion rather than insight.

Constructive self-criticism should go hand in hand with more appro-priate types of 'reflexivity' as discussed in Chapter 8. MacDougal (2011: 111) sees reflexivity, essentially, as contextualizing the content of a visual production (anthropological film in his case) by revealing aspects of its production in both explicit (interactions between filmmakers and the field, voice-over commentary, etc.) and implicit (e.g., editing choices as signs of the presence of the filmmaker) ways. However, it remains a difficult task to determine what kind and how much reflexivity is needed, what form it should take and how it should relate to the actual topic(s) of the visual study.

5   Attending to external impediments

While visual research, as discussed above, faces many challenges that can largely be addressed by researchers themselves, there are also some obstacles from outside their immediate sphere of influence that continue to encumber its progress. Most of these hurdles have to do with persistent misconceptions or ignorance with respect to dealing with the implications of the visual in different segments of society. Issues covered here include: the need to prepare the diverse audiences of visual research in a society that is not as visually literate as one would rightfully expect; the impact of the legal void (Rowe, 2011) and the ethical confusion with regard to the production and use of imagery, and the various institutional practices that are still ill-prepared for the visual.

Developing more visually astute forms of visual research, including as mentioned above a more sophisticated and explicit 'aesthetics of scholarly communication,' may imply the gradual construction of a specific set of codes and practices or even a culture (or cultures) of visual science, which may divert in many important – though not necessarily always very apparent – ways from the established visual representational cultures (TV shows, feature film, documentary, entertainment, news formats, etc.). Therefore, while trying to produce a 'more visual' science, one should make sure that the audience does not 'get lost' in the process (Pauwels, 2000). The road towards more visual or media-literate forms of science clearly should involve both producers and consumers. It is very important that the intended (specialized or lay) audiences should be able not only to 'follow' the scholar's discursive intentions, but also to retain their right to interrogate the form and vision that is put into the end product by its makers. This preference for active and knowledgeable receivers performing oppositional or at least 'negotiated' readings (Hall, 1973), is also best served by a more explicit (and 'honest') use of stylistic means and codes. At all times it should be clear what the 'representational status' of what they are looking at is. The involvement of the user, the audience and (not forgetting) the well-informed and respectfully treated subjects may even lead to more participatory and ethical forms of visual research (see Chapters 6 and 12).

However, 'educating' citizens in visual proficiency is also a task for society at large. Despite the unmistakable importance of developing distinct visual competencies in virtually all domains, visual competency is hardly regarded as a societal (educational, political, scientific . . .) priority. Consequently, there is still a significant degree of 'visual incompetency' in present-day 'high-tech' societies, which are inundated with images, visual representations and visual experiences of all sorts. Moreover, the rare concerted efforts devoted to this aspect are primarily focused on trying to 'inoculate' or 'arm' citizens and in particular the most vulnerable groups among them (youngsters, elderly, the less educated) against the presumed deceitful effects of visual media. Instead of fostering this negative

attitude of shielding people from the harmful aspects of visual communication, the development of a more active knowledge and skill with
respect to the expressive means of the visual and visual media should be
pursued through a well-structured and thought-through program to
enhance visual competency in its many aspects (perception, analysis/
decoding, creative production, cultural and technological encoding,
active use). Developing visual competencies should go far beyond the
typical media education courses, which are often based on the belief that
learning how to produce an actual media product automatically implies
the acquisition of knowledge of the complex meaning-making structures
and elements. Mere technical proficiency does not equal knowing the
complex expressive structures and their potential impact.

Another paradox in present-day societies has already been reported in
Chapter 12: the striking imbalance between the very rigid standards to
which visual research is being subjected versus the astonishing tolerance
with regard to the disclosure of the most intimate aspects of the personal
sphere as witnessed in the mass media. While getting permission to
undertake research projects with a visual aspect often proves quite a
challenge, even if researchers are willing to attend to sometimes impractical ethical requirements, seeing that visual work actually gets published
in a proper way adds a fresh set of problems grounded in the traditions of
scholarly review processes and science publishing practices. There are, in
other words, also several 'institutional' aspects involved with trying to
establish a more visual science. Appropriate channels and formats need to
be found both for publication and dissemination of visual end products as
well as for their funding. Acceptance by the academic world is a prere-
quisite, and a peer-review process is a necessary though not sufficient
requirement. It may help new formats that play out the visual to be
accepted as 'real' scientific output, consequently making their production
more eligible for funding, but it will only prove beneficial if reviewers
themselves are well versed in assessing the expressive capabilities of the
media that are being used in the context of scientific practices. If, for
example, reviewers maintain a bias towards allowing predominantly
realist and mimetic approaches and systematically weed out more experimental and expressive productions, or, on the other hand, do not develop
a critical eye for the many ways in which inconsiderate use of the medium's parameters may obscure visual statements on culture, then there is
little hope for this type of work to blossom.

Also, there are the intricacies of the publishing side to consider. The
earlier mentioned question of the 'ideal' division (and combination/inte-
gration) of labor and expertise is not confined to visual data production or
to the more innovative forms of presentation, but also comes into view

when results are presented in a more traditional scholarly format. Today, even the more basic multimedia features (typographic, graphic and design elements, the interplay of visuals and captions or text) are not capitalized in science communications to their fullest potential, despite the fact that they are an intricate part of communicating scientific ideas and results, and can help to embody or express the unspeakable or unquantifiable. A further complication is that even if researchers have the many skills and types of expertise required, they often have little control over the final 'look of things,' especially when publishing in scholarly journals. Few scholarly journals (the paper-based, but also the electronic) venture to go beyond a rather conservative use of visual media. In most cases, they hold on to the classic article structure and often force authors to stick to rigid templates to publish their visual work. Fortunately, some specialized visual journals do provide exceptions to this state of affairs, for instance, by allowing authors to provide fully composed PDF contributions, so that they remain in full control of all the purposeful, multimodal aspects of their work, or by creating dedicated web-based environments that allow much more creative freedom (e.g., through the use of sound, color and moving images, and interactive schemes and set-ups).

In addition to the intricacies of page design, many academic publishers remain very hesitant to adopt a more workable application of the fair use principle and far too easily lean towards a legalistic approach, placing all the burden on the authors to acquire permissions and refusing to publish any work that is not completely cleared in writing (even in those cases where the presumed copyright holders themselves are not sure about who holds the copyright, or when copyright information is simply lacking after serious efforts). This restrictive attitude often results in a less than adequate use of visuals both in quantitative (using as few as possible) and qualitative (using those visuals that are easy to get permission for, rather than those that make most sense) terms. To help resolve this issue, scholars could decide to become more audacious and demanding to get things done, and work only with publishers offering more support and understanding with these particular burdens of visual research. However, in truth, young scholars often cannot afford to be too demanding and need to submit to well-established journals and publishers in their discipline to advance their careers.

6   Conclusion

This final chapter addressed different but often interrelated challenges and opportunities for visual social science, as summarized in Figure 14.1. It started with a call for a more explicit methodology and a more truly

Key Challenges and Opportunities of Visual Social Science	
Exploring and Using the Full Potential of the Visual	– Improve knowledge and understanding of the visual (visual artifacts and visual representations) and of visual technologies (their reproductive, transformational and expressive capabilities; 'technology as culture'). – Develop proficiency in using 'style' (the 'form' or the 'how') both as a *source* of information (visual 'data' in addition to the 'content' or the 'what') and as a *tool* to better communicate visually as social scientists.
Working Towards a More Integrated and Inclusive Approach	– Work towards a better integration of existing theories and frameworks for visual analysis. – Work towards more solid and explicit visual production methodologies. – Work towards a more truly and productive interdisciplinary approach of the visual. – Expand the scope of the study of the visual in terms of referents, types of media and technologies, and fields of interest. – Explore the visual in relation to other forms of expressions and sensory experiences (multimodal and multisensory research).
Developing Visual Competencies and Productive Forms of Collaboration	– Further define and develop both generic and specific (re: media, technologies, formats, fields of applications, research foci) visual competencies. – Determine and cope with the required level and breadth of expertise. – Develop more productive ('meaningful') forms of collaboration with other involved specialists (e.g., designers, technicians) based on mutual understanding and shared knowledge.
Fostering Critical-constructive and Reflexive Attitudes	– Open up to a broad range of mimetic and expressive approaches. – Engage in critical self-evaluation of selected theories and authors, and develop more refined and better-documented methods and techniques. – Opt for a constructive-cumulative approach rather than a further division and re-appropriation (relabeling) of the field. – Adopt a more reflexive and explicit attitude when reporting research findings.
Attending to External Impediments	– Manage the expectations, standards and understanding of research audiences and approving bodies (review boards, peer-reviewers, consumers/users). – Address the legal and ethical voids (re: production and use of images). – Address the fragile position of the visual researcher in publication matters (e.g., reluctance towards the 'fair use' principle, and lack of control over final design).

Figure 14.1 Key challenges and opportunities of visual social science

'visual' practice, for which the development of a more explicit 'aesthetics of scholarly communication' in close conjunction with rapidly evolving technological opportunities is deemed necessary. Next, reflecting on how visual research could make progress in years to come, this contribution also emphasized that visual scholarly activities should become more 'integrated' and 'inclusive' in terms of subject areas, disciplinary angles, media, modes and sensory experiences. Closely related to the first two proposals, it was argued that there is an urgent need to further define and specify the diverse visual competencies that are needed to perform innovative visual research from start to finish; such competencies must be actively developed and productive forms of cooperation stimulated between the highly divergent types of expertise and their sometimes somewhat conflicting professional norms and expectations.

Contemplating some unproductive paradigmatic quarrels of the past and present, this chapter then argued that at least a portion of the growing groups of enthusiastic visual researchers could profit from a more self-critical and reflexive attitude towards their visual work and from fostering a more open and constructive attitude towards those of others. Both novice and seasoned scholars may benefit from regularly revisiting their work and asking 'self-critically' questions like: What is the status of the visuals that we are employing, and to serve what ends, and to what extent do these images or visualizations really contribute? What types of unique data do they contain or what kinds of insights are expressed through these visuals that are largely inexpressible in words and of value for the particular points to be made? And how exactly do the different expressive systems interact: do the images work together with the words, does the layout add any meaning? These are questions one could productively pose time and again, regardless of one's level of skill or experience.

The final section of this chapter then discussed a series of challenges that involve the broader world of science and society and of which visual researchers are consequently not in full control. These concerns basically all relate to the huge task of informing, educating and even persuading very diverse audiences and institutions with regard to the specific opportunities – and demands of an ethical, legal and expressive nature – of visual work.

How the future of visual research is finally going to play out, whether progressing as a more highly integrated trans-disciplinary venture, or simply continuing its course as specialized pockets of interest and expertise dispersed over different disciplinary areas of enquiry, is hard to predict. Again, however, the idea should be nurtured that visual research and visual studies offer a domain 'par excellence' for revisiting the way the sciences, social sciences and humanities are currently organized and for creating new opportunities for captivating ways of knowledge building and dissemination.

7   References

Bateman, J. A. (2008) *Multimodality and Genre: A Foundation for the Systematic Analysis of Multimodal Documents*. Basingstoke: Palgrave Macmillan.

Berger, A. A. (1986) *Media Analysis Techniques*. Beverly Hills, CA/London: Sage.

Boradkar, P. (2011) 'Visual Research Methods in the Design Process.' In: E. Margolis and L. Pauwels (eds.) *SAGE Handbook of Visual Research Methods*. Los Angeles, CA/London/New Delhi/Singapore/Washington, DC: Sage, pp. 150–68.

Coover, R. (2011) 'Interactive Media Representation.' In: E. Margolis and L. Pauwels (eds.) *SAGE Handbook of Visual Research Methods*. Los Angeles, CA/London/New Delhi/Singapore/Washington, DC: Sage, pp. 619–38.

Grady, J. (2011) 'Numbers into Pictures: Visualization in Social Analysis.' In: E. Margolis and L. Pauwels (eds.) *SAGE Handbook of Visual Research Methods*. Los Angeles, CA/London/New Delhi/Singapore/Washington, DC: Sage, pp. 688–709.

Hall, S. (1973) *Encoding and Decoding in the Television Discourse*. Birmingham: CCS.

Heath, C., J. Hindmarsh and P. Luff (2010) *Video in Qualitative Research: Analysing Social Interaction in Everyday Life*. London: Sage.

Knoblauch, H. and R. Tuma (2011) 'Videography: An Interpretative Approach to Video-recorded Micro-Social Interaction.' In: E. Margolis and L. Pauwels (eds.) *SAGE Handbook of Visual Research Methods*. Los Angeles, CA/London/New Delhi/Singapore/Washington, DC: Sage, pp. 414–30.

Knor-Cetina, K. (1981) *The Manufacture of Knowledge: An Essay on the Constructivist and Contextual Nature of Science*. New York: Pergamon.

Kress, G. and T. Van Leeuwen (2001) *Multimodal Discourse: The Modes and Media of Contemporary Communication*. London: Hodder Arnold.

Latour, B. and S. Woolgar (1979) *Laboratory Life: The Construction of Scientific Facts*, 2nd edn. Princeton University Press.

Lemke, J. (1998) 'Multiplying Meaning: Visual and Verbal Semiotics in Scientific Text.' In: J. R. Martin and R. Veel (eds.) *Reading Science*. London: Routledge, pp. 87–113.

Lynch, M. (1985) *Art and Artefact in Laboratory Science: A Study of Shop Work and Shop Talk in a Research Laboratory*. London: Routledge & Kegan Paul.

MacDougall, D. (2011) 'Anthropological Filmmaking: An Empirical Art.' In: E. Margolis and L. Pauwels (eds.) *SAGE Handbook of Visual Research Methods*. Los Angeles, CA/London/New Delhi/Singapore/Washington, DC: Sage, pp. 99–113.

McKinnon, Innisfree (2011) 'Expanding Cartographic Practices in the Social Sciences.' In: E. Margolis and L. Pauwels (eds.) *SAGE Handbook of Visual Research Methods*. Los Angeles, CA/London/New Delhi/Singapore/Washington, DC: Sage, pp. 452–73.

Mead, Margaret (1963) 'Anthropology and the Camera.' In: W. Morgan (ed.) *The Encyclopedia of Photography*. New York: Greystone Press, pp. 166–84.

Odgers, C. L., A. Caspi, C. J. Bates, R. J. Sampson and T. E. Moffitt (2012) 'Systematic Social Observation of Children's Neighborhoods using Google Street View: A Reliable and Cost Effective Method.' *Journal of Child Psychology and Psychiatry* 53: 1009–17.

O'Donoghue, D. (2011) 'Doing and Disseminating Visual Research: Visual Arts-Based Approaches.' In: E. Margolis and L. Pauwels (eds.) *SAGE Handbook of Visual Research Methods*. Los Angeles, CA/London/New Delhi/Singapore/Washington, DC: Sage, pp. 639–52.

Pauwels, L. (2000) 'Taking the Visual Turn in Research and Scholarly Communication: Key Issues in Developing a More Visually Literate (Social) Science.' *Visual Sociology* 15: 7–14.

Pauwels, L. (2006) 'A Theoretical Framework for Assessing Visual Representational Practices in Knowledge Building and Science Communications.' In: L. Pauwels (ed.) *Visual Cultures of Science: Rethinking Representational Practices in Knowledge Building and Science Communication.* Hanover, NH/London: Dartmouth Colled Press, pp. 1–25.

Pauwels, L. (2010) 'Visual Sociology Reframed: An Analytical Synthesis and Discussion of Visual Methods in Social and Cultural Research.' *Sociological Methods & Research* 38(4): 545–81.

Peters, J.-M. (1977) *Pictorial Communication.* Claremont, CA: David Philip.

Pink, S. (2011) 'A Multi-Sensory Approach to Visual Methods.' In: E. Margolis and L. Pauwels (eds.) *SAGE Handbook of Visual Research Methods.* Los Angeles, CA/London/New Delhi/Singapore/Washington, DC: Sage, pp. 602–15.

Rieger, J. (2011) 'Rephotography for Documenting Social Change.' In: E. Margolis and L. Pauwels (eds.) *SAGE Handbook of Visual Research Methods.* Los Angeles, CA/London/New Delhi/Singapore/Washington, DC: Sage, pp. 132–49.

Rollwagen, J. (ed.) (1988) *Anthropological Filmmaking: Anthropological Perspectives on the Production of Film and Video for General Public Audiences.* Chur/London: Harwood Academic Publishers.

Rose, G. (2006) *Visual Methodologies: An Introduction to the Interpretation of Visual Methods,* 2nd edn. London: Sage.

Rouch, J. (1975) 'The Camera and Man.' In: P. Hockings (ed.) *Principles in Visual Anthropology.* Chicago, IL: Aldine, pp. 83–102.

Rowe, J. (2011) 'Legal Issues of Using Images in Research.' In: E. Margolis and L. Pauwels (eds.) *SAGE Handbook of Visual Research Methods.* Los Angeles, CA/London/New Delhi/Singapore/Washington, DC: Sage, pp. 710–25.

Ruby, J. (1986) 'The Future of Anthropological Cinema: A Modest Polemic.' *Visual Sociology Review* 1: 9–13.

Ruby, J. (2000) *Picturing Culture: Explorations of Film and Anthropology.* The University of Chicago Press.

Smith, K., S. Moriarty, G. Barbatsis and K. Kenney (eds.) (2005) *Handbook of Visual Communication: Theory, Methods, and Media.* Mahwah, NJ: Lawrence Erlbaum Associates.

Snow, C. P. (1960) *The Two Cultures.* Cambridge University Press.

Van Leeuwen, T. (2011) 'Multimodality and Multimodal Research.' In: E. Margolis and L. Pauwels (eds.) *SAGE Handbook of Visual Research Methods.* Los Angeles, CA/London/New Delhi/Singapore/Washington, DC: Sage, pp. 549–70.

Van Leeuwen, T. and C. Jewitt (eds.) (2000) *The Handbook of Visual Analysis.* London: Sage.

Index

accidents, 100
action cams, 312
advertisements, 17, 35, 47, 49, 57–60, 118, 156, 222
advertising, 17, 48, 55, 71
  photographs, 289
algorithmic, 34, 78, 290, 298, 302
  vs. non-algorithmic, 292–295
American Anthropological Association (AAA), 4
analysis, 24, 27, 200–201
  advertisements, 57–60
  cross-modal, 80–81
  feedback, 26
  hegemonic, 55
  iconographical, 56
  iconological, 56
  image, 7, 9, 50–52, 56, 62, 70
  intra-modal, 77–80
  legibility, 236
  meta-disciplinary framework, 280–306
  multimodality, 65–90, 316
  negative, 76
  object approach, 304
  paradigmatic, 213
  posters, 238–244
  process approach, 304
  readability, 236
  reflexive attitudes, 319–320
  repeat/re-photography, 108–109
  rhetorical, 54
  syntagmatic, 213
  visual, 60
analytical framework, 9, 59–60, 62, 85, see also framework
angle of view, 30, 121
animation, 36, 77
annotations, 186
anonymity, 13, 35, 60, 66, 67, 257–260, 270, 276,
anthropological film, 38, 98, 144, 177–187, 317, 320

anthropological filmmaking, 175, 177, 318
anthropological pictures, 19
anthropology, 3, 7, 22, 71, 175, 314
architecture, 23, 25
archives, 20, 33, 49, 82, 106, 118
art, 35, 48, 49, 56, 142, 146, 164, 289
articles, 3, 140, 270, 313
  illustrated, 36, 142, 275
  journal, 141
  magazine, 141
  video, 185
artifacts, 6, 17–18, 47, 156, 291, 313, 314
art installations, 140, 142
artwork, 17, 223
Association of Internet Researchers (AoIR), 268
audio narration, 186
auditory mode, 316
author celebratory mode, 320
auto-ethnographic, 133

behavior, 6, 20–32, 66, 251, 257, 262
  elicited, 21
  expected, 83, 220
  impact of camera on, 175
  intimate, 261
  monitored, 31
  naturally occurring, 21
  observable, 6
  reactive, 99
  recalled, 6
  staged or re-enacted, 22
  verbalized, 222
behavioral reconstructions, 22
behavioral sciences, 4, 38, 315
bias, 89, 100, 124, 211, 222, 322
billboards, 237, 244–250
biographies, 186, 268
blogs, 84, 215,
browsers, 80, 85
bulletin boards, 84

camera angle, 25, 53, 313
camera distance, 25, 30, 53, 185, 313
camera images, 35, 111, 113, 119, 280, 292
camera movement, 185
camera position, 25, 60, 82, 108, 185
camera technique, 26, 50
camera work, 318
cam-phones, 312
cartoons, 17
CCTV, 17, 48
CD-ROM, 36, 147, 148, 186, 275
censorship, 18, 31, 84, 211
charts, 6, 23, 49, 78, 112, 184, 186, 280,
    302
chat rooms, 84
clothing, 52, 60, 240
codes, 24, 52, 55, 62, 78, 172, 184, 222,
    236–252, 300, 321,
coding, 76, 124, 260, 270
collected visuals, 37
colonial gaze, 25
color, 24, 36, 77, 80, 88, 121, 212, 223,
    236, 237, 301
comic books, 49
comicvoice, 135
community video, 11, 126
composition, 50, 53, 141
compositional interpretation, 53
computer rendering, 281, 296
computer simulations, 184
conceptual constructions, 181, 290
conceptual representations, 23, 78, 280,
    318
confidentiality, 200
connotation, 52, 54, 80, 236, 251
content analysis, 28, 52–53, 59, 65, 76, 212,
    313,
context of production, 19, 29, 301, 304,
    307
contextual information, 18, 34, 48, 106,
    109, 114, 186, 276
conversation analysis, 282
cookies (web), 84
copyright, 14, 18, 35, 48, 84, 147, 270, 271,
    323
corporate culture, 12
    decoding difficulty, 230–234
    definition of, 220–221
    display of status/hierarchy, 224–225
    impression management, 229–235
    mimetic mode, 230
    personal/departmental subcultures,
        227–229
    role of design and management,
        222–224

visual indicators/metaphors, 221–225
visual symbolism, 225–226
corporate websites, 68
cross-modal analysis, 76, 80–81
cubism, 296
cultural codes, 26, 56, 251
cultural expressions, 10, 20, 26, 65, 74, 85,
    104, 157
cultural markers, 86
cultural self-portrayal, 20
cultural studies, 28, 56, 61, 314
cultural usability, 74

data production methods, 7
database, 17, 85, 101
decoding, 12, 25, 52, 58, 68, 73–74, 145,
    212–214, 224, 233, 304
denotation, 54
depiction process, 50, 53
dérive (drifting), 100
design, 12, 68, 81, 86, 89, 112, 148, 163,
    225, 237, 250
    elements, 36, 323
    features, 36, 72, 201, 313, 316
    graphic, 141, 251, 318, 323
    information, 6, 281
    layout, 72, 79–80, 146, 148, 163, 201,
        313, 316, 325
    page, 74, 323
    signifiers, 79–80
    typography, 72, 212, 316, 318, 323
diagrams, 17, 173, 186, 282
digital cameras, 104, 312
digital imagery, 194
digital images, 51, 195
digital media, 184, 186
digital photographs, 291
digital technology, 111, 193, 194, 195, 200,
    217
direct observation, 37, 97, 275, 290, 291,
    296
discourse analysis, 55–56, 60
discursive communities, 146
documentary, 49, 54, 73, 140, 321
documentary film, 35, 49, 110, 145, 178
documentary realism, 183
drawings, 3, 17, 21, 23, 27, 62, 78, 118,
    140, 184, 238, 282, 292, 297, 314
    children's, 23, 48
DVD, 36, 140, 275, 313

editing, 25, 110, 170, 178, 267, 276, 286,
    312, 320
educational films, 168, 275

educational technology, 23
electronic family album, 198
email, 84, 203, 211, 270
emic, 6, 88, 117, 127, 132, 231
entertainment, 321
ethics, 13, 21, 35, 200
    bias, 123–124, *see also* bias
    contextual decision-making, 274–275
    double moral standard, 271–274
    harm, 263–265
    informed consent, 48, 200, 265–267
    Institutional Review Boards (IRBs), 272
    legal aspects, 35
    new media/online, 268–271
    online environment, 13
    photovoice, 129–130
    privacy, 260–263
ethnographic film, 175
ethnographic filmmaking, 175, 318
ethnographic pictures, 19
ethnography, 282
ethnomethodology, 57, 282, 313
etic, 88, 117, 127, 132, 231
exhibitions, 36, 128, 140, 142,
    153, 313
existing imagery, 140
existing images, 47, 97, 109
expressions, 8, 57, 84, 128, 141, 164, 184,
    207, 214, 314
    cultural, 10, 20, 26, 65, 74, 85,
        104, 157
    facial, 260
    modes, 7, 141, 316
eye-tracking, 311

fabrication, 288
facial expressions, 260
family
    albums, 106, 198
    communications, 12
    elicitation, 123
    home video, 123
    images, 123, 195
    photography, 17, 25, 69, 123, 193, 195,
        211
    pictures, 17, 18, 47, 49
    researchers, 26
    snapshots, 55, 195, 201, 212
    websites, 12, 83, 123, 199–206,
        214–217
fashion, 25
feature film, 49, 60, 178, 321
feminist theory, 28
fiction film, 17, 50
figures of speech, 54

film, 3, 11, 62, 110, 167–187
    anthropological, 38, 98, 144,
        177–187, 317, 320
    audiences, 168
    documentary, 49, 110, 145, 178
    educational, 275
    elicitation, 21
    ethnographic, 175
    feature, 49, 60, 178, 321
    fiction, 17, 48, 50
    full length, 140
    in websites, 78
    non-fiction, 17, 48
    post-modern, 174
    scientific, 275
    self-contained, 3, 36
    social scientific subgenres, 168
film elicitation, 21, 118, 119
filmmaking, 124, 167–187
    anthropological, 11, 175, 177, 318
    documentary, 275
    editing and subjectivity, 170–171
    ethnographic, 175, 318
    expressive, 182–184
    expressive vs. mimetic, 168–172
    expressiveness/subjectivity,
        169–172
    mimetic, 173–174
    naïve realism, 174
    objectivity, 175–176
    observational cinema, 175
    participatory, 176–180
    postmodern (anthropological),
        177–179
    reflexive, 182–184
    social scientific, 167
    synchronic sound, 171
    typologies, 168–169
filmvoice, 135
first impressions, 75, 83, 210
Flickr, 205
focal length, 54, 108, 109
focus groups, 65, 118, 119, 121
formal analysis, 52–53
formal portraits, 20
found. *see also* pre-existing
    imagery, 12, 47
    images, 37, 48, 50, 106
    materials, 3, 17–18, 19, 48
    texts, 12
framework, 69, 71, 74, 81, 86, 89,
    305
    cultural, 86
    integrated, 16–40, 280
    meta-disciplinary, 13, 280–306

multimodal, 74
  theoretical, 28, 111, 167
framing, 25, 30, 50, 60, 108, 121, 173, 178,
  185

gadgets, 229
games, 48, 49
gender roles, 59, 60, 83, 86
gentrification, 29
geo-locative devices, 312, *see also* GPS
gestures, 52, 72
Google Earth, 311
Google Street View, 312
GPS, 34, 311
graffiti, 23, 156
graphic design, 251, 318, 323
graphics, 140
graphic representation, 37, 281, 296
graphic tools, 85
graphs, 36, 76
grassroots, 12, 131, 200, 215
grounded theory, 30, 88, 200

hand-made imagery, 291
health communication, 244–252
hegemonic analysis, 55
high-speed photography, 283
home video, 123
humanities, 4, 5, 38, 315, 316, 325
hybrid media, 73–74, 200, 212
hyperlinks, 84, 147
hyperrealism, 296

iconic, 4, 23, 24, 59, 77, 79, 88, 111, 113,
  257, 259, 283–288, 293, 310, 312
iconographic/iconological, 60
iconographical analysis, 56
iconography, 56, 212
iconological analysis, 56
iconology, 28, 56–57, 313
icons, 54, 78
identity construction, 66, 67
illustrated articles, 36, 142, 275
illustrated books, 106
illustrative film, 168
image analysis, 7, 9, 50–52, 56, 62, 70
image collectors, 18, 275
image-elicitation, 118, 120
imagery, 26, 54, 57, 61, 62, 117, 121, 127,
  141, 212, 281, 294, 295, 311, 321
  camera-based, 23
  digital, 194
  existing, 18, 62, 140
  found, 12, 47

hand-made, 291
iconic, 23
indexical qualities, 23
machine-generated, 291
mimetic, 98
pre-existing, 29
researcher-generated, 29
researcher-produced, 18, 270
respondent generated, 20, 21, 123, 124,
  125–126
self-published, 270
societal, 20, 29, 47, 49, 118
images, 9, 17, 25, 47, 61, 72, 163, 184
  camera, 111, 113, 119, 280, 292
  digital, 51, 195
  documentary, 55
  elicitation, 118–123
  existing, 47
  existing vs. mimetic, 97
  family, 123, 195
  family in elicitation, 123
  fictional, 50
  formal qualities, 8
  found, 12, 37, 48, 50, 106
  iconic/indexical relationship with
    reality, 259
  interval, 105
  material characteristics, 78
  mental, 290
  mimetic, 111
  moving, 34, 142, 216, 301, 314, 323
  photographic, 73, 240, 244
  pre-existing, 49, 140
  propaganda, 55
  reality, 61–62
  referentiality, 311
  researcher-produced, 12
  series of, 106, 144
  signifiers and codes, 78
  static, 105, 142, 314
  visual, 55, 60, 240
  visual essay, 140
  webcam, 79
impression management, 66, 211, 229–235
indexes, 54, 59
indexical, 4, 79, 88, 111, 113, 257, 259,
  285, 291, 293, 310,
information design, 6, 281
information visualization, 7
informed consent, 48, 200, 265–267
inscription, 224, 288
installations, 140, 142, 313
Institutional Review Boards (IRBs), 272
institutions, 7, 28, 48, 55, 154, 193, 272,
  304, 325

integrated framework, 9, 16–40, 280
intentional techniques, 24
interaction studies, 282
interactive, 144, 176, 323
International Communication Association
    (ICA), 4
International Journal of Visual Sociology, 5
International Sociological Association
    (ISA), 4
International Visual Literacy Association
    (IVLA), 4
International Visual Sociology Association
    (IVSA), 4, 5
internet, 10, 12, 35, 65–90, 205,
    268–271
intersubjectivity, 276
interval images, 105
interval photography, 10, 104–105, *see also*
    time lapse
interviews, 6, 51, 105, 119, 178, 202, 231,
    234, 282
    elicitation, 3, 118–123
    one-to-one, 121
    online mode, 65
    verbal, 119,
    visual, 26, 119, 120, 133, 151
invisibility, 175, 176
iPod, 148
IVSA. *See* International Visual Sociology
    Association

journal articles, 141

key words, 200

layout, 72, 79–80, 146, 148, 163, 201, 236,
    313, 316, 325
legibility, 77, 236

machine-generated imagery, 291
magazine articles, 141
map-making, 57
maps, 6, 17, 23, 24, 49, 101, 186, 269, 280,
    314
master narratives, 82
material culture, 6, 20, 22, 26, 35, 56, 66,
    71, 97, 99, 103, 156, 184
material reconstructions, 22
material translation, 85
medical-imaging techniques, 300
mental images, 290
meta-disciplinary framework,
    280–306
mimesis, 8, 168, 173, 286

mimetic, 4, 10, 13, 25, 37, 105, 150, 184
    analysis, 111–112
    ethnographic filmmaking, 173
    genre, 179
    imagery, 98
    mode/approach, 12, 97–99, 108,
        113–115, 230, 322
    recording techniques, 10
    sampling, 99–103
mimicry, 52
modalities, 65, 72, 142, 281
modality, 72
mode, 72
mode of depiction, 78
models, 6
modes of expression, 141
moving images, 34, 142, 216, 301, 314,
    323
multi-disciplinary research, 251
multimedia, 73, 185–187, 212, 311,
    316
    features, 65, 323
    genre, 89, 281
    messages, 89
    production, 11
    products, 3, 275, 302
    programs, 36
    reviews, 164
    technologies, 316
    web context, 201
multimodality, 13, 54, 57, 65–90, 323
    analysis, 10, 316
    character, 184
    constructions, 57
    framework, 10
    hybrid constructions, 313
    research, 7, 316, 317
    visual essays, 143, 145, 146, 163
    websites, 65–90
multisensory, 5, 115
    research, 7
    visual essay, 143
multi-vocal, 82, 164
murals, 23, 250
MySpace, 205, 215

naïve realism, 61, 113, 172, 174, 310,
    318
narratology, 318
native image production, 16, 20, 123, 128,
    135
negative analysis, 76, 81
netbooks, 123
netiquette, 270
network technologies, 17, 193, 311

new media, 47, 184–187, 314
    ethics, 268–271
    technologies, 142, 305, 312
    visual essay, 142, 147–148
new technologies, 6, 7, 142, 148, 309
news formats, 321
news photography, 100, 145
news reels, 17, 49
non-algorithmic, 23, 24, 78,
    292–295
nonfiction film, 17, 48
nonfiction genres, 49
nonfiction products, 145
nonfictional productions, 185
non-photographic, 118, 140
    representations, 23
non-visual, 13, 40, 100, 139
    data, 22, 23, 234
    elements, 311
    form, 111
    research, 139
numbers, 8, 111, 259

object approach, 304
observational cinema, 175
one-to-one interviews, 121
online. *See* websites
online culture, 8
online environment, 13, 65–90
online ethics, 268–271
online family websites, 12
online image collections, 106
online interviewing mode, 65
operationalization, 25, 70, 85, 88
opportunistic approach, 31, 103
opportunistic sampling, 30, 102
orientation phase, 100

page design, 74, 323
paintings, 23, 49, 60, 62, 78, 118,
    140, 229
paintvoice, 135
paradigmatic analysis, 213
paradigmatic choices, 74, 86, 157
paradigms, 28, 54, 282, 320, 325
participant-generated image production,
    136
participant observation, 225
participatory filmmaking, 176–180
participatory research, 11, 118, 132, 277
participatory video, 127, 320,
participatory visual methods, 136
participatory visual research, 132, 135
participatory visual techniques, 133

participatory/collaborative, 117–137
participatory/joint forms, 33
passwords, 84, 268
phenomenology, 282
photo-collage, 140
photo elicitation, 3, 11, 16, 26, 118–137
photo essay, 140, 163
photogrammetric techniques, 111
photographic, 118, 130, 140, 158, 318
    choices, 59
    images, 73, 195, 240, 244
    practice, 47, 195
    record, 23, 98, 105, 314
    survey, 102
photographs, 3, 37, 78, 104, 195, 238, 268,
    282, 296
    advertising, 289
    digital, 291
    family, 48
    in websites, 78
    press, 55
    series, 298
    static, 73, 316
photography, 24, 62, 146, 148, 291
    contesting stereotypes, 154
    continuity/longitudinal aspect, 107–108
    data source, 6
    elicitation, 21
    family, 12, 17, 25, 47, 69, 193, 195–198,
        211
    formal portraits, 20
    high-speed, 283
    in anthropology, 98
    indexical quality, 195
    interval, 10, 104–105
    news, 100, 145
    police, 20
    press, 49
    private, 193, 195, 211, 217
    repeat, 30, 105–110
    research tool, 6
    school, 48
    time lapse, 10, *see also* interval
    virtual reality (VR), 311
photojournalism, 275
photomontage, 140, 196
photo novella, 11, 126, 130–132, 135
photovoice, 3, 11, 126, 127, 135, 320
    community video, 127–129
    ethics, 129–130
pictorial language, 236, 242
pictures, 70, 98, 99, 106, 129, 130, 150,
    202, 236,
    anthropological, 19
    archive, 49, 82, *see also* archives

pictures (cont.)
  ethnographic, 19
  family, 17, 18, 49
  ID card, 48
picture voice, 135
point of view (POV), 50, 57, 81–83, 172,
    185, 212, 231
police photography, 20
politics of representation, 62
poly-semic, 120, 164
post cards, 49
post-colonial theory, 28
posters, 36, 140, 237, 238–244
post-modern, 175, 193
  film, 174, 179
  filmmaking, 177–179
post-production, 8, 25
POV. See point of view
poverty, 29
power dynamics, 202
power relations, 26, 55, 60
pre-existing, 9, 19, 25, 29, 33, 35, 47–50,
    118, 140
presentational formats, 16, 36, 130, 141
press photography, 49, 55
privacy, 13, 200, 260–263, 277
private photography, 193, 195, 211, 217
private websites, 203, 210, 215
process approach, 304
pro-filmic, 25, 53, 98, 173, 184
programmed sampling, 103
programming languages, 85
prospective studies, 106–107
provenance, 18, 19, 51, 84
psychoanalysis, 28
psychotherapists, 26

rapport, 173, 178
rapport building, 100, 146, 149
readability, 236
reality TV, 193, 271
re-enactments, 32, 107
reflexive attitudes, 75, 129, 319–320
reflexivity, 34–35, 76, 180–182
repeat/re-photography, 30, 105–110,
    112–113, 319
representational, 61, 210
  codes, 24
  commitment, 300
  constraints, 300–301
  film, 168
  practices, 26, 281
  processes, 288–289
  status, 321
  techniques, 6, 23

traditions, 316
representative sample, 68, 102
representativity, 6, 67–68, 101
reproductive capabilities. See mimesis,
    mimetic
researcher-generated, 18, 23, 25, 121–122
researcher-initiated, 20
researcher-produced, 3, 12, 18–19, 37, 270
respondent-generated, 3, 11, 19–20, 21, 27,
    123–126, 131, 132
retrospective/prospective studies, 106–107
rhetoric, 28, 55, 77, 83, 212, 313
rhetorical analysis, 54–55, 59
riots, 100
rules of conduct, 84

sampling, 30, 99–103
  digressive/semi-randomized search, 103
  opportunistic, 30, 102
  photographic survey, 102
  programmed, 103
  random, 30
  stratified, 30
  ten-step approach, 102
  websites, 67–68
satellite image applications, 312
satellite image transmission, 283
scientific films, 168, 179, 275
scientific illustration, 294–295
scientific image-making, 57
scientific reality, 280–283
sculptures, 229
secondary audience, 82
secondary meaning, 56
secondary research material, 19
secondary visual reality, 18
self-published imagery, 270
semiotic analysis, 313
semiotic approach, 59
semiotic hybrids, 281
semiotics, 28, 54, 212, 282, 313
series of images, 104, 106, 144
shooting scripts, 30, 101, 231, 317
signage, 23
signifiers, 54, 59, 78–79, 143, 311
  cultural, 72, 74, 85
  expressive, 140
signs, 54, 59, 118, 157
simulations, 6
Situationists, 100
slide shows, 313
smartphones, 123
snapshots, 26, 99, 104, 193, 230
  family, 55, 195, 201, 212
SNSs. See social networking sites

social change, 104, 106, 109, 135, 319
social constructivism, 282
social networking sites, 84, 85
societal imagery, 17, 29, 47, 49, 118
Society for Visual Anthropology (SVA), 4
sociology, 3, 5, 6, 71, 158, 222, 281
socio-semiotics, 28, 54
sound, 141, 142, 147, 184, 323
spatial set-up, 52
spot news, 100
static images, 54, 105, 110, 142, 314
static photographs, 73, 316
statistical materials, 52, 234
statistics, 6
stereotyping, 154
street art, 25
study guide, 182, 183, 186
style, 25, 27, 52, 121, 236, 297, 311
style of execution, 296–297
stylistic choices, 28, 310, 319
Surrealists, 100
surveys, 6, 65, 69, 132, 200, 282
SVA. *See* Society for Visual Anthropology
symbolic, 54, 77, 79, 88, 157, 286, 293, 310
    information, 24
    meaning, 56, 212
    representations, 184
symbols, 54, 59, 78, 118
syntagmatic analysis, 213
syntagmatic structure, 53
syntax, 89, 236
systematic recording, 16, 30, 38

tables, 36, 76, 78
tablets, 123
taboos, 51, 76, 81
tagging, 51
technologies, 8, 12, 62, 85, 108, 109, 121,
    195–196, 316
    cultural implications, 193–194
    database, 17
    digital, 111, 193, 194, 200, 291, 312
    educational, 23
    internet-based, 312
    multimedia, 316
    network, 17, 193, 311
    new, 6, 7, 142, 148, 309
    new media, 142, 305, 312
    visual, 5, 312
    web, 8
technology studies, 6, 23
templates, 80, 82, 85, 206, 312, 323
ten-step approach, 102
texts, 24, 73, 82, 85, 147, 148, 184, 201,
    270

analytical, 186
found, 12
journalistic, 82
power relations and ideology, 55
spoken or sung, 316
verbal, 55
visual, 54
written, 52, 72, 77
thinking, 31, 65, 220, 312
    dichotomous, 71
    externalized, 302
    visual, 5, 29
time-lapse movie, 105
time-lapse photography, 104–105, 114,
    see also interval, mimetic
traffic signs, 156
transcription, 97, 288, 290
transformational processes, 13, 62, 113
transformational properties, 319
TV shows, 193, 321
typographic signifiers, 77
typography, 72, 141, 212, 316, 318, 323

validity, 6, 301
verbal, 65, 67, 72, 141, 149, 150, 242
    accounts, 142
    clarification, 127
    codes, 184
    comments, 300
    communication, 36, 202
    consent, 266, 277
    cues, 120
    data, 257
    descriptions, 111, 313
    design, 12
    documentation, 34
    elements, 212, 236
    elucidation, 182
    exchanges, 174
    feedback, 24
    interactions, 151
    interviews, 119,
    reactions, 26, 126
    responses, 5, 284
    texts, 55
video, 3, 61, 62, 104, 177
    article, 185
    blogging, 216
    community, 11, 126, 128
    editing, 318
    home, 123
    links, 84
    participatory, 127, 320
    program, 128
videovoice, 135

virtual audience. *See* websites:audience
visual aesthetics, 8
visual analysis, 28, 53, 56, 60–62, 111, 317
visual anthropology, 3, 5, 6, 49, 102, 163, 281
visual approaches, 7, 137, 174
visual competencies, 8, 13, 29, 317–319,
    321, 322, 325
visual cultural studies, 56, 320
visual culture, 14, 23, 30, 47, 157, 257, 314,
    320
visual data production, 10, 99–103, 322
visual data representations, 284
visual data sources, 17, 48, 49
visual diaries, 133
visual elicitation, 3, 21, 27, 118–123,
    136–137
visual essay, 11, 12, 16, 36, 98, 132,
    139–164, 317
  as book, 148–149
  assertive stance, 145
  decoding, 145
  expressive modalities, 142
  material culture and human behavior,
    156–162
  mimetic qualities, 145
  multimodal, 143, 145, 146, 163
  multisensory, 143
  new media, 142, 147–148
  of billboards, 244–250
  social science context, 150–162
visual feedback, 123–125, 173
visual images, 60, 240, 276, 313
visual interviews, 26, 119, 120, 133, 151
visual language, 50, 300
visual mode, 72, 124, 316
visual narrative theory, 144
visual practices, 6, 309
visual presentations, 139–140
visual production methods, 3, 30, 115
visual representational latitude, 297–299
visual representations, 21, 26, 29, 37, 47,
    78, 111, 140, 310
  intents and purposes, 301–303
  scientific labor division, 289
  type and signifiers, 78–79
  varied nature of referents, 283–288
visual research, 16–40, 61, 139
  ethics, 35, 257–278
  expressive modes or formats, 98
  focus of analysis, 27
  key modes, 18
  legal aspects, 35
  mimetic mode, 12
  participatory, 117–137
  representational practices, 26

sampling, 101
(sub)fields, 6
theoretical framework, 28
visual rhetoric, 54, 78, 320
visual sampling strategies, 102
visual scientific competence, 29,
    305, 319
visual scientific discourse, 29, 172
visual scientific language, 14
visual scientific literacy, 29, 317
visual sociology, 3, 5, 6, 163, 314
visual specificity, 240
visual storytelling, 142
visual study, 98, 320
visual technologies, 5, 14, 18, 109, 262,
    310, 312, 318
visual thinking, 5, 29
visual voice, 135
visualization, 281, 282, 296, 315
  elements, 36
  information, 7
  scientific, 282
visualizations, 3, 19, 47, 325

web, 65, 66, 140, 148, 199, 215,
    269, *see* websites
Web 2.0, 205
webcams, 66, 76, 79, 84
websites, 36, 48, 186
  analysis, 10, 200–201
  as sites of remembrance, 207–208
  audience, 202–206
  authoring, 84, 318
  content, 17
  copyright, 270
  corporate, 68
  cross-modal analysis, 80–81
  cultural aspects, 68–71
  cultural markers, 86
  decoding, 68, 212–214
  expected behaviors, 83
  family, 12, 83, 123, 199–206,
    214–217
  films, 78
  first impressions, 75–76
  image analysis, 70
  intra-modal analysis, 77–80
  layout and design signifiers,
    79–80
  master narratives, 82
  mode of depiction, 78
  multimedia products, 275
  multimodality, 10, 65–90
  netiquette, 270
  photographs, 78

power dynamics, 202
private, 210
problematic reductionism,
   71–72
sampling/representativity, 67–68
sonic types and signifiers, 79
structure and navigation, 83–84
typographic signifiers, 77
verbal/written signifiers, 77

visual representational types and
   signifiers, 78–79
voice/point of view (POV), 81–83
Wikipedia, 205
wikis, 84
words, 8, 36, 55, 76, 111, 130, 150, 163,
   236, 259, 325

YouTube, 84, 205, 216

CPSIA information can be obtained at www.ICGtesting.com
Printed in the USA
BVOW06*1433231015

423577BV00006B/68/P

9 781107 008076